CW00816336

BRITISH ROCK GUITAR

BRITISH ROCK GUITAR

THE FIRST 50 YEARS, THE MUSICIANS AND THEIR STORIES

MO FOSTER

northumbria | press

Published by Northumbria Press
Trinity Building, Newcastle upon Tyne NE1 8ST

First published 2011

A catalogue record for this work is available from the British Library.

ISBN: 978-0-85716-000-3

Designed by Northumbria Graphics, Northumbria University
Printed in Slovenia on behalf of Latitude Press Ltd.

DEDICATION

For Billie and Charles, my mum and late dad, who made sandwiches for the band in spite of the baffling racket in their living room.

And for Kay, my wife, who must have heard every story at least ten times.

And lastly for my oldest friend, the late Peter Watkins, without whose inspiration I may never have become a musician.

ABOUT THE AUTHOR

Mo Foster is an unlikely hero but there are few bassists in the world who are not in awe of his playing. Had he continued in his chosen academic subject of physics, he would doubtless have excelled as Mo is nothing if not meticulous. However, he discovered a talent for the bass guitar that he has been sharing with the world for over forty years. From the London Symphony Orchestra to Jeff Beck, from Gil Evans to Phil Collins, Mo's effortlessly beautiful basslines have graced literally hundreds of albums and thousands of concerts. A quick Google search will give you the list, but needless to say it is impressive and unmatched. His own albums and productions of other artists' recordings take him far beyond the realm of session-man. For sheer musical artistry, he is recognised and revered globally.

Mo is also a man whose attention to detail has made him the archivist of just about every sad, silly and scurrilous occurrence the musical community has experienced. The residual vestiges of his scientific mind have engendered a fascination with what makes musicians tick. Few dinner guests can match his anecdotes and quips, and his storage capacity for musical tales seems inexhaustible. Being one of the finest bassists in the world opens doors, but it is Mo Foster's charm and humour that has unlocked the memory banks of the great musicians quoted herein. Mo has spent almost half a century playing with and befriending musical legends and they have given him free rein to tell you their stories.

As you flick through the pages of this book it will soon become apparent how many people are happy to call Mo Foster their friend. I am extremely proud to be one of them.

Neville Farmer

ACKNOWLEDGEMENTS

Extra special thanks go to:

Mark Cunningham who helped me enormously with the editing of the original book.

Kurt Adkins for re-scanning and copy-editing the original text, and restoring all of the images.

The late Ronnie Scott for showing me that it was possible to combine beautiful music with wonderful humour.

Ray Russell for guidance and enthusiasm.

Andrew Peden Smith of Northumbria Press for having the vision to make this edition possible.

Finally, I would like to extend my thanks to the following people, each of whom has made an important contribution to the stories in this book, and I apologise to anyone that I've missed out:

Keith Altham, John Altman, Mark Anders, Dave Arch, Rod Argent, Joan Armatrading, Tony Ashton, Ronnie Asprey, Malcolm Atkin, Roy Babbington, Tony Bacon, Ralph Baker, Paul Balmer, Terry Bateman, Bruce Baxter, Paul Beavis, Jeff Beck, Martin Benge, Brian Bennett, Ed Bicknall, Steve Blacknell, Brian Blaine, Debbie Bonham, Jason Bonham, Stuart Booth, Dougie Boyle, Rob Bradford, Andy Brentnall, Martin Briggs, Terry Britten, Joe Brown, Pete Brown, Richard Brunton, David Bryce, Peter Bullick, Peter Button, Hugh Burns, Laurence Canty, Clem Cattini, Simon Chamberlain, Paul Charles, Chris Charlesworth, Phil Chen, Roger Clarke, B.J. Cole, Ray Cooper, Peter Copeland, Jeff Crampton, Bob Cullen, Joan Cunningham, Paula Cunningham, Mike d'Abo, Mitch Dalton, Bryan Daly, Sherry Daly, Patrick Davies, Ray Davies, Paul Day, Dick Denney, Ralph Denyer, Emlyn Dodd, Shirley Douglas, Gus Dudgeon, Anne Dudley, Judy Dyble, Duane Eddy, Bobby Elliot, John Etheridge, Stuart Epps, Tommy Eyre, Andy Fairweather-Low, Neville Falmer, Ray Fenwick, Philip Fejer, John Fiddy, Guy Fletcher, Vic Flick, Graham Forbes, Alan Foster, Pete Frame, Pam Francis, Colin Frechter, Brian Gascoigne, Gordon Giltrap, Roger Glover, Julie Glover, Brian Goode, Kim Goody, Graham Gouldman, Mick Grabham, Keith Grant, Steve Gray, Colin Green, Mick Green, Brian Gregg, Isobel Griffths, Cliff Hall, Richard Hallchurch, Pat Halling, David Hamilton-Smith, Dave Harries, Jet Harris, George Harrison, Paul Hart, Mike Hawker, Alan Hawkshaw, Tony Hicks, Christian Henson, John Hill, Colin Hodgkinson, Bernie Holland, Hugh Hopper, Ian Hovenden, Jason How, Linda Hoyle, Jeffrey Hudson, Les Hurdle, Mike Hurst, Gary Husband, Neil Innes, Neil Jackson, Christina Jansen, Graham Jarvis, Alan Jones, John Paul Jones, Mike Jopp, Stewart Kay, Carol Kaye, Gibson Keddie, Adrian Kerridge, Martin Kershaw, Mark Knopfler, David Kossoff, Chris Laurence, Jim Lawless, Jim Lea, Paul Leader, Adrian Lee, David Left, Adrian Legg, Geoff Leonard, Jon Lewin, Mark Lewisohn, Julian Littman, Brian 'Licorice' Locking, Claudine Lordan, Wes Maebe, Ivor Mairants, Phil Manzanera, Bernie Marsden, Jim Marshall, Neville Marten, Sir George Martin, Hank Marvin, Dave Mattacks, Brian May, Brendan McCormack, Chas McDevitt, Tom McGuinness, Tony Meehan, Mark Meggido, Mickey Moody, Gary Moore, Mike Moran, Joe Moretti, Charlie Morgan, Sarah Morgan, Maurice Murphy, Jeremy Neech, Roger Newell, John Morton Nicholas, Kay O'Dwyer, Pino Palladino, Phil Palmer, Rick Parfitt, Alan Parker, Dave Pegg, Richard Pett, Guy Pratt, Simon Phillips, Phil Pickett, Willis Pitts, David Porter, Duffy Power, Bill Price, Judd Procter, Andy Pyle, Paul Quinn, Chris Rae, Jim Rafferty, Noel Redding, Tim Renwick, Sir Cliff Richard, Dave Richmond, Maggi Ronson, Francis Rossi, Allan Rouse, Ray Russell, Martin Sage, Ralph Salmins, Grant Serpell, Noel Sidebottom, Lester Smith, Marcel Stellman, Jim Sullivan, Andy Summers, Roger Swaab, Alan Taylor, Martin Taylor, Phil Taylor, Danny Thompson, Richard Thompson, Kevin Townend, Ken Townsend, Rob Townsend, Tim Tucker, Peter Van Hooke, Dave Vary, Peter Vince, Derek Wadsworth, Bernard Watkins, Charlie Watkins, June Watkins, Peter Watkins, Michael Walling, Greg Walsh, Terry Walsh, Bert Weedon, Dennis Weinrich, Bruce Welch, Chris Welch, John Wetton, Geoff Whitehorn, Ian Whitwham, Diana Wilkinson, Neal Wilkinson, John Williams, Carol Willis, Pete Willsher, Pete Wingfield, Ron Wood and Bill Worrall.

CONTENTS

INTRODUCTION

Out of the blue, I got a call to dep for bass guitarist Paul Westwood on *Sky Star Search*, a legendary TV talent show that was so appalling it was actually worth watching (they held auditions for the show, and everybody passed). The musicians in the band assembled at 8 a.m. on Sunday 12 February 1989 in London Weekend Television's Studio Two at the South Bank Centre, and during this gruelling but hysterical twelve-hour session we supported 35 mostly abysmal acts. (Later that evening my face muscles actually hurt from laughing!)

I sat next to guitarist Vic Flick – the man who, in 1962, had played the main guitar riff on the famous James Bond movie theme. During the breaks we chatted and, having recently found some ridiculous old photographs of my school band, I was curious to know how Vic had started out as a musician. His stories, involving throat microphones and home radios, were such a revelation to me that I no longer felt quite so embarrassed about my own humble and absurd beginnings.

Almost immediately this cathartic moment triggered an idea: perhaps all of the other great players had daft stories too? The phone calls began... At first I felt like a cub reporter: phoning musician buddies may have been easy, but extracting information through artists' management channels sometimes necessitated a certain degree of subterfuge. I was therefore delighted when so many musicians submitted their own highly literate and amusing accounts (some of these interviews first appeared in *Guitarist* magazine in 1989).

Roger Glover told me: "We are the last generation that can remember what life was like before rock 'n' roll." He was, of course, referring to a time when LSD only referred to pounds, shillings and pence, and when everywhere in England seemed to be closed on a Sunday. It was also a time when all American goods, including guitars, were totally unavailable; savants spoke in hushed tones of a revolutionary new instrument known simply as a "Fender", although it was beyond me why anyone should want to play the mudguard of an American car or the protective surround of an open coal fire! All was revealed, however, on the sleeve of the LP *The Chirping Crickets*, upon which stood Buddy Holly and his chums, grey-suited and silhouetted against a blue Texan sky. In Buddy's hand was the object that inspired such awe: the Fender Stratocaster. The first "Strat" to reach the UK was imported by Cliff Richard for Hank Marvin in 1959, and the rest is history.

Today's guitar heroes and top session players were once mere mortals struggling to buy or build their first guitar. Much experimentation was involved, a lot of it crazy and even futile, but mostly it was just good fun. The history of

British rock 'n' roll owes a huge debt to these visionary players who produced some of the most powerful and memorable music of the last five decades. But this debt, it transpires, should also be extended to a lot of dads, a lot of red paint, a lot of radios, a lot of ukuleles, a lot of junk shops, and even a lot of tea importers.

Although I originally studied physics at the University of Sussex, I have been a studio/touring bass player for most of my life. Inevitably in the course of writing, recording, producing, and touring more than a few stories have emerged.

When I first began writing this book – almost twenty years ago, and mostly in longhand – interviews were almost always face-to-face, or one-to-one on the telephone. By the early nineties we did have fax machines, but it's hard now to imagine that at that time Google had not been invented, there were very few mobile phones (all of which were huge), there were no websites, and only a few people – mostly women doing secretarial work – could type. There was no email, no texting, no scanning, no Facebook or MySpace or Twitter, and the internet was a concept understood by only a few scientists, the military, and specialist nerds. How that would change in the next few years!

The stories in this book chronicle the formative period during which the excitement of discovery, the naïvité, and the insane struggles gave birth to the rise and development of rock guitar in Britain, and helped to shape the way in which we perform and record today. These stories are idiosyncratic, charming, and optimistic, but above all, they are very funny.

Assembling such a rich tapestry of how it all began has been nothing short of joyous, especially as I compared others' early experiences with my own. Whether household names, or unsung heroes, I've chosen the cast for their important observations and contributions to this fascinating story. I've heard it said that when a person dies, it is as though a library is burning down. Since I originally wrote my book, many of the contributors have sadly died, and their stories – had I not jotted them down – would have been lost forever. But the love and respect of their friends and families will ensure that their stories will live on.

The second half of British Rock Guitar is devoted to the rise and eventual demise of the London studio session scene. I've tried to present an insider's view of this creative world, and the wonderful absurdity of musicians' humour in general. As a bonus I have also learnt how to spell ukulele, bouzouki, and *oud*.

My 42 years as a professional musician have been far more fun than they could possibly have been had I pursued my intended career as a physicist. But I still subscribe to *New Scientist* magazine.

Mo Foster,
Hampstead, London
August 2010
www.mofoster.com

FOREWORD

It seems a lifetime ago that an enthusiastic cub reporter (whom I later found out to be Mo Foster) called me up to tell me about the marvellous idea he had for a book based on the first 20 years of British rock guitar, and asked if I would contribute anything towards it. I explained that I was a bit short at the time but would send him a postal order when my next royalty cheque came in. "No, no, no," he said. "I'm not asking for money, I'm a bass guitarist. What I need is some information, like when did you get your first guitar? What was the make? How much was it? What did it mean to you? Do you still have it... and is Elvis still working in a chip shop?"

These questions brought back to mind a particular day in 1973 when Mo (whom I have in fact known since that time and would never really mistake for a cub reporter) was rehearsing with me. I clearly remember Mo struggling with the bass part for "FBI" and thinking to myself that one day this red-headed young man with his engaging personality and blistered fingers would write the definitive – if not the only – book on early British rock guitar. And, Mo, you've done it.

May I take this space to thank you for the belief and tenacity you've shown in bringing your concept to fruition, and so enabling myself and countless others to share in the funnies and frustrations, and the hopes and aspirations of my fellow British rock guitarists. It's a great read.

Hank B. Marvin,
Perth, Australia
March 2011

Mo Foster (second left) playing 'lead descant' with the Old Fallings Junior School recorder consort. His friend Ronald Powell (extreme left) was not to know that it would be another fifty years before his trousers would become fashionable.

PART ONE: GROWING PAINS

CHAPTER 1

IN THE BEGINNING

Houses were quiet in the early 1950s: no all-day radio stations blaring away, and until 1955 there was only one TV channel, which transmitted until 11pm and which was off the air for an hour each weekday between 6pm and 7pm so that young children could be put to bed without complaint – it was known as 'the 'toddler's truce'. The 24-hour broadcasting that we know today was unheard of.

At first we didn't own a radio, a TV, a gramophone or a piano. You could hear clocks ticking.

Until I was about nine years old I wasn't really aware of any music at all, unless one acknowledged BBC schools' radio programmes such as *Music And Movement*, in which a disembodied voice might ask us to 'play games with our balls' or to cavort leadenly around the room, inspired by the music of tunes like Grieg's 'In The Hall Of The Mountain King'. I was quite a good troll.

In the fifties there were only three national radio stations available in Britain:

The BBC Home Service (now Radio 4), which was for plays and talks.

The BBC Third Programme (now Radio 3), which was for classical music.

The BBC Light Programme (now Radio 2), which was for the more popular music of the day. My parents seemed to prefer this station, a station which seemed – to me – to play mostly pointless drivel. The only pop songs I can recall on the family radio from that time were tacky novelties. Here are a few awful examples:

- "I'm a Pink Toothbrush"
- "How Much is that Doggie in the Window"
- "Shrimpboats Are a-Comin"
- "Two Little Men in a Flying Saucer"
- "Twenty Tiny Fingers"
- "Seven Little Girls Sitting in the Back Seat"
- "The Runaway Train"
- "The Three Billy Goats Gruff"
- "I Am a Mole and I Live in a Hole"
- "Bimbo, Bimbo, Where Ya Gonna Go-e-o"

Some I could just about cope with:

- "Sparky's Magic Piano" (this was actually rather good and featured the Sonovox, an early vocoder)
- "Tubby The Tuba" (quite emotional in places)
- "I Tawt I Saw A Puddy Tat" (okay, it's fun)
- "The Teddy Bears Picnic" (quite good really – nice bass-saxophone)
- "The Laughing Policeman" (nice tuba)

This is what we had to listen to at 9 a.m. on Saturday mornings on *Children's Favourite*s in 1954! They certainly weren't *my* favourites. It's very weird to think back and realise that the only music that made any sense to me was hymns, which I would hear at school assembly every morning or – on special, but always bewildering occasions – at the local church. I loved the harmony and the bass-lines that were played on either the organ or the piano but I loathed the dreary singing and incomprehensible lyrics. To this day I can only be in a church as long as *no one* is singing.

In later years I began to envy American musicians who talked about listening to, and being influenced by, powerful local radio stations playing rock, blues, country, bluegrass, jazz, gospel, etc. Lucky bastards. For us in the UK all we had was the idiosyncratic Radio Luxembourg, and it would be a while until pioneering DJs such as Jack Jackson and Brian Matthews began broadcasting their wonderful programmes on the BBC in the early sixties. Eventually, of course, the pirate radio stations – such as Radio Caroline and Radio London – would come to the rescue.

RECORDER

One day, when I was nine, my primary school teacher, Miss Williams, brought a "descant" recorder into class, played it for a couple of minutes and asked if anyone would like to learn to play and form a recorder consort. I was mesmerised. My parents didn't take much persuading to buy one and, having presented it to me one afternoon on a pavement somewhere in Wolverhampton, were amused that in my zeal to open the white cardboard box, I had read the label a little too quickly and proceeded to thank them profusely for buying me a "decent" recorder.

I became fascinated with instruments that I saw in marching bands – such as the trumpet – which had music stands shaped like lyres fixed to them. Inspired, I carefully bent a convincing music stand out of stiff wire and fixed it to the end of my recorder with Christmas Sellotape (it was white with lots of holly and berries, and the occasional robin). I was quite pleased with it, even though it was totally unstable, and the music kept falling on the floor.

After devouring tutor books I and II, I later listened to the radio with increasing interest as I picked up by ear the instrumental hits of the day, including "Cherry Pink Mambo" and "Swinging Shepherd Blues" complete with bent notes. Was this blues recorder?

SUMMER CAMP

My father was a PE teacher at a boys' college in Tettenhall, near Wolverhampton, and every summer during the 50s we would take a succession of trains to Salcombe, in Devon, where 120 boys and seven or eight teachers with their families would spend a pleasant two weeks under canvas in a farmer's field near a sandy bay. On particularly wet days everyone would assemble in the central marquee to be entertained with a sing-song, or by anyone with a talent for playing a musical instrument.

One boy played the accordion; he was good and had a fine repertoire of folk tunes. I was seized by the desire to accompany him in some way, but this momentary eagerness was rendered futile by the realisation that the only instrument I could play convincingly was the descant recorder, and then only from sheet music. The damp throng would certainly not be interested in hearing my unaccompanied selection from *Swan Lak*e. Nevertheless, the seed of desire to be part of a music-making team had been planted, although for this to happen convincingly I would have to wait for the advent of rock 'n' roll... and the guitar.

VIOLIN

A little later I was given a violin, a shiny instrument in a drab black case which had been handed down to me by my grandfather. By now I was eleven years old, the top recorder and violin player in the school. I would play violin concerts accompanied by my teacher, Miss Williams, on the piano. In my innocence I thought I was pretty good, but I was sadly deluded and, after one particular recital, I went to the back of the hall where an older man was engrossed with a machine that had two spools on top. This was the first time I had ever seen a tape recorder (there weren't many around). Having rewound the tape, he pushed a button and I was surprised to hear the ambient sound of someone playing a violin rather badly, and with a pitching problem in the higher registers, about 100ft away. It became obvious that the offending violinist was me: I had experienced my first lesson in objectivity.

I studied violin privately for a while with a proper music teacher, Mr George Schoon at Tettenhall College, and even joined the Wolverhampton Youth Orchestra for about half an hour. But when I graduated from my primary school in Wolverhampton to the village grammar school in Brewood, Staffordshire, the long bus journeys involved meant that it was impossible to continue studying. Sadly I had to give up the violin.

In 1956 I arrived at Brewood Grammar School – where I would spend the next seven years – and discovered to my dismay that there was no music department and no orchestra; music was not even on the syllabus. In retrospect this was an unforgivable omission: we could study Latin, art, and agriculture – but not music.

The few token music lessons we did have were chaotic and pointless, and consisted of the class being cajoled into singing obscure folk melodies. I have this memory of the teacher leaning on his desk and staring into the middle distance, bored shitless as he picked his nose. Mercifully, this terrible waste of time and energy lasted no longer than a year.

CHAPTER 2

THE OUTBREAK OF SKIFFLE

"I think I was about 15. There was a big thing called skiffle. It's a kind of American folk music, only sort of jing-jinga-jing-jinga-jing-jiggy with washboards. All the kids – you know, 15 onwards – used to have these groups, and I formed The Quarry Men at school. Then I met Paul."

(John Lennon)

When I was 13, my schoolfriend Graham Ryall and I went cycling and youth-hostelling around North Wales. In those days there were strict rules about vacating the hostel in the morning, and as we were leaving a hostel one Saturday, I remember hearing a couple of older boys pleading with the warden to let them stay and hear the BBC radio show *Skiffle Club* (which became *Saturday Club* on 4 October 1958, and was at that time the only thing worth listening to apart from Radio Luxembourg). I had no idea what they were talking about.

Skiffle, however, was a short-lived phenomenon. Although its widespread popularity lasted only 18 months, it served both as an influential precursor to the forthcoming rock 'n' roll craze and the catalyst behind many a British youngster's discovery of active music-making. Like punk 20 years later, skiffle was of critical importance to British rock 'n' roll, but was forced to endure a love/hate relationship with the music business. Inexperienced would-be musicians loved skiffle because they could at last approximate a melodic or rhythmic sound with makeshift instruments and without any real skill, but purist aficionados of "good" music detested it with a vengeance. Some journalists were wont to label the style "piffle" – and that was when they were feeling charitable.

Mike Groves

As a skiffle player, Mike Groves of seminal folk group The Spinners encountered a polite line in bureaucratic etiquette when he applied for his Musicians' Union membership: "I was the first washboard player to join the MU. They sent a nice letter to thank me for joining but didn't think they would be able to place a lot of work my way." In households up and down the country, mums would be baffled by the constant disappearance of their thimbles – the washboard player's vital tool. For Ron Wood, the instrument was simply a way of getting started in front of an audience. He says: "One day I spotted something I could really make my mark with, that took no book learning (you either had rhythm or you didn't) – the washboard. Inspired by various American country pickers, Chris Barber, and Lonnie Donegan, my first stage appearance (aged nine, at the local cinema, the Marlborough) was playing live skiffle in a band with my brothers between two Tommy Steele films, and playing washboard made me nervous enough to want to take this experience further."

Bruce Welch

Shadow Bruce Welch observes that, "In the early skiffle days, everything was in the key of G, with discords down at the bottom end." This simple form of music, however, had an interesting social history. It originated during the American Depression of the 1920s, when groups of people would organise "rent parties" between themselves to help clear their mounting debts. At such get-togethers, "instruments" such as washboards, suitcases and comb and paper would be used to create an uplifting blend of blues and folk, marrying tales of farm labour with those of city materialism.

Lonnie Donegan

Similarly, the spiritual void that hung over Britain following the end of World War II was filled by this new "happy" sound, and the man who spearheaded the skiffle craze, like a rough-and-ready Pied Piper, was Anthony Lonnie Donegan. In 1952, Lonnie joined Ken Colyer's Jazzmen, in which he played guitar and banjo, and was reunited with army colleague and double-bass player Chris Barber. Chris subsequently left and formed one of Britain's top New Orleans-style trad jazz ensembles with Lonnie, his own Chris Barber's Jazz Band. On recording dates, however, Lonnie was employed by Decca only as a session player.

The Lonnie Donegan Band. L-r Jimmy Currie, Lonnie Donegan, Nick Nicholls, Mick Ashman

During a session in 1955 for the band's ten-inch LP *New Orleans Joy*, Lonnie wanted to record "Rock Island Line", an old Leadbelly song, but the producer was reluctant and refused to do it. The engineer agreed to stay on during a break, however, and recorded the song with just Lonnie's vocals and guitar, double-bass, and washboard. Credited to Lonnie, the track was released as a single in February 1956, hit number eight in the UK chart and launched a nationwide skiffle boom. "Rock Island Line" also climbed to number eight in the USA, helping to boost its cumulative sales to over one million. Unfortunately, Lonnie wasn't a contracted Decca artist and received a mere £4 session fee. (Forty years later Decca eventually agreed to pay him a royalty, but sadly for Lonnie this wasn't backdated.) Lonnie's response, in 1956, was to sign with rival label Pye-Nixa, and on 24 March 1960 he was the first British artist to have a single shoot straight to number one with "My Old Man's a Dustman". Recorded live on tour in Doncaster, the song was an adaptation of the old and arguably rude Liverpool song "My Old Man's a Fireman on the Elder-Dempster Line".

ALL ROADS LEAD TO LON

During my conversation with Lonnie Donegan at his Malaga home – some time before he died – we discussed the often hilarious experimentations and innovations which accompanied the non-availability of decent musical instruments in the 1950s and early 1960s, and cited Vic Flick's use of a tank commander's throat microphone to amplify his guitar as but one example. There follows the complete transcript of our illuminating interview:

Lonnie: "The thing about the tank commander's throat mic was that it in fact came from me. I was the first one to do that in about 1950, and it wasn't a tank commander's throat mic: it was a pilot's throat mic. The surplus stores were selling everything from the army in those days, and we used it as a contact mic. We strapped it to the front of the guitar – it was all rubber – and we played through the radio because we didn't know anything about amplifiers. In fact, I doubt if you could have even bought one then. We certainly couldn't have afforded one."

Where did you buy records?

Lonnie: "In second-hand shops. We had to search very hard for any American jazz or folk music of any type whatsoever in those days, and the source of supply was principally Collett's book and second-hand record shop in Charing Cross Road. It was in fact a communist shop, and the reason why they were stocking jazz and folk was because it was music of the people – 'right on brother'. They used to get a fair little stack – only small stuff, I suppose, now I come to think of it; there probably wasn't more than 20 records in the shop at any one time. We kept our eagle eyes on the shelves, you know, and any time anything came in, we grabbed it. And the manager at that time was a man named Ken Lindsay, who later became a jazz club operator in St Albans. The assistant manager was Bill Colyer, who was jazz trumpeter Ken Colyer's brother. It's a funny old world, isn't it?"

Where did you find your first guitar, and who taught you? You're a very good rhythm player, so someone must have shown you the right things.

Lonnie: "I got my first guitar when I was 14, which is when I had my first job, in Leadenhall Street. I was a stockbroker's runner, and a 17-year-old clerk in the office was an enthusiastic amateur guitar player – played in dance bands, you know – and he wanted to get rid of the guitar he'd first learned on. So he set about interesting me in guitar by sitting in the little cafés at lunchtime and in coffee breaks [with great animation, Lonnie impersonates rhythm guitar sounds: ching, ching, ching!], showing me what the chords looked like, and he got me so fascinated by it all that I prevailed upon my mother to pay the 25/- (£1.25) for the guitar for my Christmas present. Eventually my mum paid some of it. It was really a Spanish guitar, and it wouldn't tune up – I broke its machine-heads trying to get it in tune. I then went out and found a £12 cello-top guitar at a music shop in East Ham High Street. My dad funded that guitar – in fact, he loaned me the £12 so that I would pay him back at half a crown a week, which I did, right to the last penny.

"Thank you for your comments about my rhythm playing. No, the answer is I never had any proper lessons, ever. I did try in the early stages to find a teacher, but of course no guitar teacher knew anything more southern than 'Way Down upon the Swanee River'. I didn't want to learn the scale of C; I wanted to learn three chords so I could play blues, and none of them even knew what the blues were, so I didn't get any lessons whatsoever. I picked it all up by ear, as you could probably tell if you had an a'poth [half penny worth] of sense!"

Could you tell me a bit about your first band, and how your music progressed into the blues?

Lonnie: "You've got that the wrong way around. It wasn't the band that came first, it was blues that came first: blues, country music, folk songs, almost exclusively Afro-American folk music I heard on the BBC. They had a programme once a week on Friday evenings called *Harry Parry's Radio Rhythm Club Sextet*, and they'd play a couple of records per week, which were either jazz or blues – maybe Josh White's 'House of the Rising Sun', or Frank Crumett's 'Frankie and Johnny', or something like that. And that's how I started getting interested in guitar and American music. Later on came the jazz. I stumbled across a jazz club when looking for blues singer Beryl Bryden, and upon finding a jazz band – Freddie Randall's – I was bowled over by the jazz. So the two things then went hand-in-hand together until eventually, when I came out of the army in 1950, I formed my own little jazz band called The Tony Donegan Jazz Band, in which I used to play the banjo and sing a couple of jazzy-type songs and also stand up and sing some blues things, which became known, to my everlasting regret, as skiffle. If I'd only just called it Lonnie Donegan music, I'd have made a fortune."

This music, known perhaps unfortunately as skiffle, inspired a whole generation of young musicians to play, from The Shadows to The Beatles. It was a very important part of the process in the development of British rock.

Lonnie: "It wasn't an important part; it was the beginning of the whole process – all roads lead to Lon. I was the first to do that. Nothing very clever in that; I just happened to be chronologically number one and all the others you have mentioned, the Eric Claptons etc, were very, very much younger than me, and so they came along as little boys to hear what Big Lonnie had started to learn. Of course, they vastly improved on it at a rapid rate. It's much easier, of course, to improve when you're given the example in the first place, but my whole early life was involved in evolving the example."

It was bad enough in the 1960s to get hold of decent instruments, but what was it like when you started in the 1950s?

Lonnie: "It was a great struggle to get anything related to the guitar at all, including the guitar itself. At that time about the only guitars you could buy were the imported German cello-type guitars, like the Hofners, or some second-hand Gibsons and Epiphones, things like that – all jazz-orientated guitars. It was very rare to find a round-hole guitar. We didn't even have Spanish guitars, let alone country and western guitars – they weren't even dreamt of.

"The first proper country-type guitar I got was a Gibson Kalamazoo, which I found in Selmer's in Charing Cross Road – that cost me, I think, £20 [a lot of money] – and I took that with me into the army for my National Service and took it around everywhere with me. And when I came back from National Service, having met a lot of Americans in Vienna playing country music, bluegrass, and stuff, and having pinned down my hero worship to Lonnie Johnson, who I found was playing a Martin guitar, I then stumbled across a mahogany Martin guitar on a market stall in Walthamstow for £6. It was strung up like a Hawaiian guitar – you know, with the metal bar under one end to raise the strings up. Of course, the strain of doing that had bowed the arm completely, so to all intents and purposes to look at it you'd think it was useless. Well, I bought it, took the bar out and gradually the arm resumed its proper shape, and I used that guitar for a long time.

"Strings were almost entirely unobtainable. The only ones you could get were very old pre-war strings, Black Diamond, which I found a stock of in Aldgate, in a music shop which had a very, very old stock. I used to replenish from there. And then a company called Cathedral started producing guitar strings, and we all had to switch to Cathedral 'cause they were the only ones you could get – until, of course, the pop explosion, and then everybody had guitars, and strings came pouring in from everywhere. I was given my first set of Martin strings by Josh White, when he came over to play at Chiswick Empire. Nobody knew he was a blues singer; they all thought he was a variety performer because he'd got a hit song called 'One Meatball' – a total accident, 'cause it's an old folk song, you know, like everything else in this business – all accidents. I went to see Josh every night, and he eventually presented me with a set of Martin strings which I cherished for years before daring to use them. So that's how things were, and stayed like that until... really about the time I hit with my records, and then everything exploded after 'Rock Island Line in 1956."

INSPIRATION

Tony Hicks

For many the sight of skiffle groups on television signified their first awareness of the guitar. One such person was Tony Hicks who, many years before he would rise to international fame as a key member of The Hollies, was inspired by a particular guitarist in the background of Lonnie's band. "My sister Maureen used to buy Lonnie Donegan records. Although I liked the songs, when his group was on TV I never looked at Lonnie himself – I was always attracted to the sight and sound made by the man at the back, and this funny little box he had with a wire going to it. I initially cut out what looked like a guitar in plywood – the shape sort of appealed."

Peter Watkins

Another similarly affected person was Peter Watkins, with whom I would later team up at school to form The Tradewinds. Peter says: "I suppose I first noticed the guitar when I saw Lonnie Donegan on what was probably the TV show *Sunday Night at the London Palladium*. I quickly observed that there were two distinct types of guitar: the one with the round hole and the tear-shaped black thing around it, and the one with the ornate f-shapes and knobs and things. I made both types out of cardboard – no cricket bats for me – and posed in front of the mirror. The round-hole type was the more important – the star played that one. The other sort was played by the man at the back."

Les Bennetts

The guitarist in question, who now appears to be forever immortalised as "the man at the back", was Les Bennetts. Les' first guitar was made from a cigar box, a pencil case and some fuse wire, and featured just two strings. From records, his early inspirations were Les Paul, Charlie Christian and Django Reinhardt, and later Wes Montgomery and Barney Kessel. Ironically, despite earning his living by playing skiffle and rock, he vehemently hated the music ("I couldn't stand the 'Coke bottle down the trousers', a device some singers used that they hoped would arouse the girls in the front rows") and deemed it "crap". He was a jazzer, you see, but the good stuff paid no money. His band, Les Hobeaux, regularly played the 2i's club in Old Compton Street, where there was always lots of jamming going on, and new players like Big Jim Sullivan and Hank Marvin would while away the hours watching him from a crouching

Les Bennetts, 'the man at the back', playing at the Earlswood Jazz festival, Birmingham, in 1963

position. Earlier, Les had taken a couple of lessons from guitarist Roy Plummer, who encouraged him to play melodies with two or even three strings – he reckons Hank learned that from him.

When Les Hobeaux recorded for HMV producer Norman Newell, he had a problem with Les' playing ("You're playing too much jazz"), and brought in a staff guitarist: Bert Weedon!

After the 2i's, Les toured the Moss Empire circuit alongside Tommy Steele and The Vipers. On one night his

Skiffle Group Les Hobeaux, with Brian Gregg (standing, right) on Double Bass, and Les Bennetts (seated, centre) on lead guitar

agent asked him to stand in for Lonnie Donegan, who had the 'flu. They liked him, and he later auditioned for Lonnie at the ABC Blackpool.

Les: "When do I start?"

Lonnie: "You've started."

He subsequently played on and arranged all of Lonnie's big hit singles. "Yet again, the irony of a good player playing simple music, and occasionally playing a dustbin, in order to survive," said Les, who continued to play skiffle up until his sad death in 1996, not long after I had interviewed him.

Chas McDevitt

Another artist who became synonymous with skiffle was Chas McDevitt, who recorded "Freight Train" at Levies' Sound Studio in Bond Street, with Nancy Whiskey on vocals. It was one of the foremost hits of the genre and a number five single in April 1957. When he was 16, Chas became very ill and was sent to a sanatorium for nine months, where he became interested in jazz and blues and began playing the ukulele. When he regained his strength he went back to college and joined a jazz band, playing mostly banjo. He took up the guitar and joined the Crane River Jazz Band (which had originally been formed by Ken Colyer), playing gigs in jazz clubs and coffee bars. Their set also featured skiffle numbers, and it wasn't long before The Chas McDevitt Skiffle Group was formed from within the Cranes. Liberal in their musical tastes, Chas' group epitomised all that was skiffle and drew on folk roots, blues, jazz and mainstream pop to develop their own infectious formula.

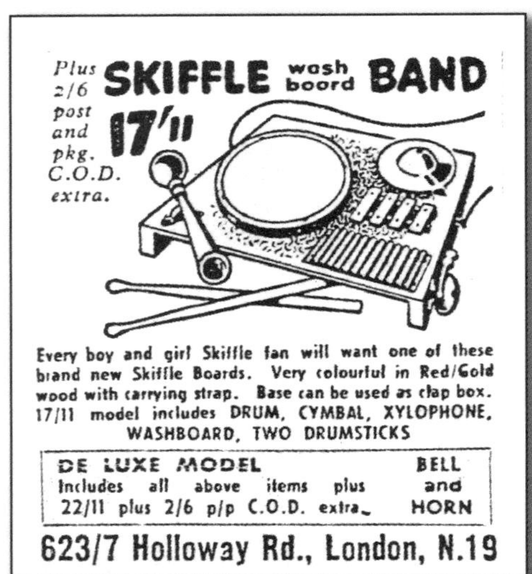

The De Luxe Washboard

Capitalising on the success of his single with Nancy Whiskey (who was soon replaced by Shirley Douglas, one of the first female bass guitarists), in 1958 Chas founded the Soho nightclub, Freight Train. This popular venue for live music ran for ten years, during which time it was the favoured haunt of many London musos, before it eventually became a "jukebox dive".

DISCOVERY

Many of the rock stars of the 1960s and 1970s born around the time of World War II came to develop their love of the more energetic and dynamic rock 'n' roll through an earlier appreciation of skiffle. Deep Purple's Roger Glover was one of several such musicians, and has a vivid memory of the time when he was "baptized" through his confrontation with a skiffle group.

Roger Glover

"In 1955," he says, "I was living above a pub that my parents managed in Earl's Court, in London. I was nearly ten years old. No doubt to attract new custom they started getting skiffle bands to play in the saloon bar on certain nights. Picture me one night, in pyjamas, wondering what the sound was, creeping down the stairs, inching open the door that led to the bar and finding myself almost in amongst a skiffle band as they played. Revelation! Live music! There would be about five or six of them: several guitarists; a banjo or ukulele player; a percussionist, whose main instrument was a washboard with all kinds of bells, cymbals, hooters and whistles attached; and a bass player using a tea chest bass. There was a furious strumming, banging, thumping and a lot of hollering, followed by applause. Then it would start all over again. My eyes grew wide that night.

"Every night that they played I would be there, an unknown fan, peeking in on what grown-ups did and wanting to be part of it so much. Because the bass player was at the back he was the one I was closest to, and I loved that sound. It was almost magic, the way an upturned tea chest with a bit of string secured in the middle and tied to the end of a broomstick could make such a deep, driving, thumping sound. It swung so much, and all the other instruments seemed to be driven by it.

"So skiffle music became my first love. The charts were full of songs by people like Anne Shelton, Kenny Ball or Dickie Valentine, but for the first time I was aware of the existence of music other than what was in the Top Ten. I stumbled across it, and my record collection was started. The first 78 I conned my parents into getting me was 'Cumberland Gap' by Lonnie Donegan, and I also owned 'Streamline Train' by The Vipers Skiffle Group, 'Big Man' by The Four Preps and 'Singing the Blues' by Guy Mitchell. As one can see by these choices, I was either broad minded or confused. Ken Colyer and a few others were good, and I remember wanting 'Freight Train' but I guess we couldn't afford it. For some reason – probably lack of the readies – these four records were the sum total of my collection for years. It wasn't until years later, when I was doing my first summer job – mowing grass for the council – that I bought Chuck Berry's first album.

"I didn't like trad jazz very much, except for the fact that skiffle had emerged from it, but not far up Old Brompton Road was The Troubadour – a favourite hangout for beatniks with their folk music. I never went in, and subsequently it held me in thrall. I heard the music, though, and I was fascinated. The line between skiffle and folk was vague; sometimes the music was interchangeable, so I liked them both."

The Bluetones Skiffle Group, featuring Jim Rodford on tea-chest bass, playing at a St Valentine's Day dance in a printing firm's canteen in the mid 1950s. Jim Rodford: "That night we had the rare luxury of using the in-house public address system for vocals." L-r Mick Rose, Jeff Davies, Jim (partially obscured by tea-chest with a broom handle), Bill Bennet and Geoff Pilling

Andy Summers

Andy Summers, who went on to play guitar with Zoot Money and The Police in the late 1970s and 1980s, was at one time a member of two or three skiffle groups who practiced in various mums' and dads' front rooms, boys' bedrooms and church halls, and always with the admonition to "Keep it down!".

He recalls: "Our guiding star was Lonnie Donegan, and the repertoire consisted of songs such as 'Midnight Special', 'John Henry' and 'St James Infirmary'. The ultimate moment for me came when I was allowed to sing and play 'Worried Man Blues' and 'Tom Dooley' in front of the whole school. When I had finished my performance, there was an audible gasp from the audience. Whether it was in disbelief at the ineptitude of the performance, or horror at the ghastly American row that had just sullied the school assembly hall, one will never know. However, the result was that my status went up ten notches in the school, and I was constantly followed home by adolescent girls – my career in rock had begun!"

Andy Pyle

Meanwhile, when Andy Pyle decided to jump on board the skiffle bandwagon, his problem was not a lack of ingenuity but one of bad timing. "From an early age I'd been treated to a diet of Elvis, Little Richard, Eddie Cochran, Buddy Holly, The Everlys, and Gene Vincent thundering from the radiogram, courtesy of my teenage brother and his dodgy pals. Determined to be a part of this phenomenon, I repeatedly asked my parents for a guitar. They repeatedly said no. By the time I was twelve, skiffle was all the rage, and as a couple of my friends had guitars I thought I was in with a chance. It was pointed out to me, rather cleverly, that two guitars were enough, and that the last thing needed was another one. This revelation led to my first bass, which I made one Saturday morning out of a tea chest, a broom handle and a piece of string. We 'practised' all that afternoon, and by tea time my fingers were bleeding, the neighbours were complaining, Mum wanted her broom handle back, and anyway the tea chest had been promised to an aunt who was emigrating."

TRANSPORT PERILS

The tea-chest bass, although a cheap and functional alternative to the expensive and technically demanding double-bass, presented a whole range of problems when it came to transporting it from gig to gig. Of course, these were the days when privately owned vehicles were still rare luxuries, and public transport was often the only option – although not all bus conductors were sympathetic.

Dave Lovelady

Dave Lovelady, of successful Merseybeat combo The Fourmost, remembers: "One conductor was very loath to take our tea-chest bass on the bus. After we pleaded with him, he agreed to let us stand it on the platform, right on the edge. As we were pulling off from the next stop a chap came running full pelt for the bus. He made a frantic leap for the platform but grabbed the broom handle instead of the pole. He went sprawling into the street and the tea-chest bass went all over the road."

Jim Rodford

Jim Rodford, who was yet to experience acclaim as the bass player with Argent, faced similar difficulties. "The skiffle group I was in, The Bluetones, was on a double decker bus going to a youth-club gig in Hertfordshire. I was sitting on the long sideways seat at the back by the door, with my foot against the upturned tea-chest bass, with drums and broom handle inside, lodged in the well under the stairs to the top deck to stop them falling out of the bus when we drove around corners. Bus stops were very rarely anywhere near the gig, and the argument was about whose turn it was to carry the loaded tea chest on his shoulder, up the road to the youth club. It was always me or the drummer, but we felt it was unfair that the guitar players, with their light Spanish acoustics (no cases, not even soft), didn't take a turn. This was the extent of our equipment: no microphones, amplifiers, PA – nothing. Just acoustic guitars, tea-chest bass, drums and washboard. It didn't matter, because that was then the state of the art for all the emerging skiffle groups up and down the country."

Danny Thompson

A stroke of genius from upright bass-playing legend Danny Thompson cured most of his tea-chest transport problems. He and a friend formed a skiffle group after having been inspired by the blues that they heard on Alan Lomax's radio programme *Voice of America*, and Danny built a collapsible tea-chest bass (five sheets of hardboard with a bracket) which could be folded down for travel on buses. The solitary string was in fact a piano string, "borrowed" through a friend who was a tuner. Like many kids with stars in their eyes, Danny's group entered many skiffle contests, and at the age of 14 they were singing songs that they couldn't possibly understand, such as "Rock Me Baby". Danny, however, didn't sing, and admits: "I don't even talk in tune."

Licorice Locking playing tea-chest bass with The Vagabonds in Grantham, 1956. The secret of his sound was to use GPO string, although the tufted headstock may have contributed.

Hank Marvin

Even the sophisticated tones of The Shadows had skiffle origins, as did the music of The Beatles, in their first incarnation as The Quarrymen with Paul McCartney on lead guitar. Hank Marvin, meanwhile, was developing a passion for jazz and folk music, and taught himself to play with the aid of a chord book and many visits to a happening local jazz club called the Vieux Carré, down near the Tyne. Whereas many guitar players in later years would dream of Fenders with pointy horns and scribble them absently in their school books, Hank would draw the instruments associated with skiffle groups, such as washboards, banjos, double-basses and acoustic guitars. Hank's own team, the Crescent City Skiffle Group, entered a skiffle contest at the Pier Pavilion in South Shields on Saturday 18 May 1957, and in spite of stiff competition, and to their great surprise, they won!

Bruce Welch

That summer, inspired by their mutual interest in music, Hank teamed up with a friend from school, Bruce Welch. Bruce had his own band, The Railroaders, who played more commercial music – the revolutionary rock 'n' roll genre, which was then traversing the Atlantic at great speed to capture the hearts and imaginations of British skiffle lovers. He had now discovered – and indeed wanted to be – Elvis, whereas the young Hank was "more the jazz/blues purist. He wore a duffel coat with a long college scarf. Hank was a much more serious player; he played banjo with real chords!"

A year or so previously, Bruce had queued for ages at the side door of the Newcastle Empire to catch a glimpse of 'The King Of Skiffle', Lonnie Donegan. "I nervously handed him my autograph book, and he spoke to me. Even now, I can remember my hero's words like it was yesterday: 'Fuck off, son, I'm in a hurry.' I was absolutely choked."

What Bruce didn't realise was that the Donegan Band were exhausted. It was Saturday night, they'd finished a week's work, and they had to race across town to avoid missing the overnight sleeper train back to London. When you're 15 you don't know about such things, but Bruce has

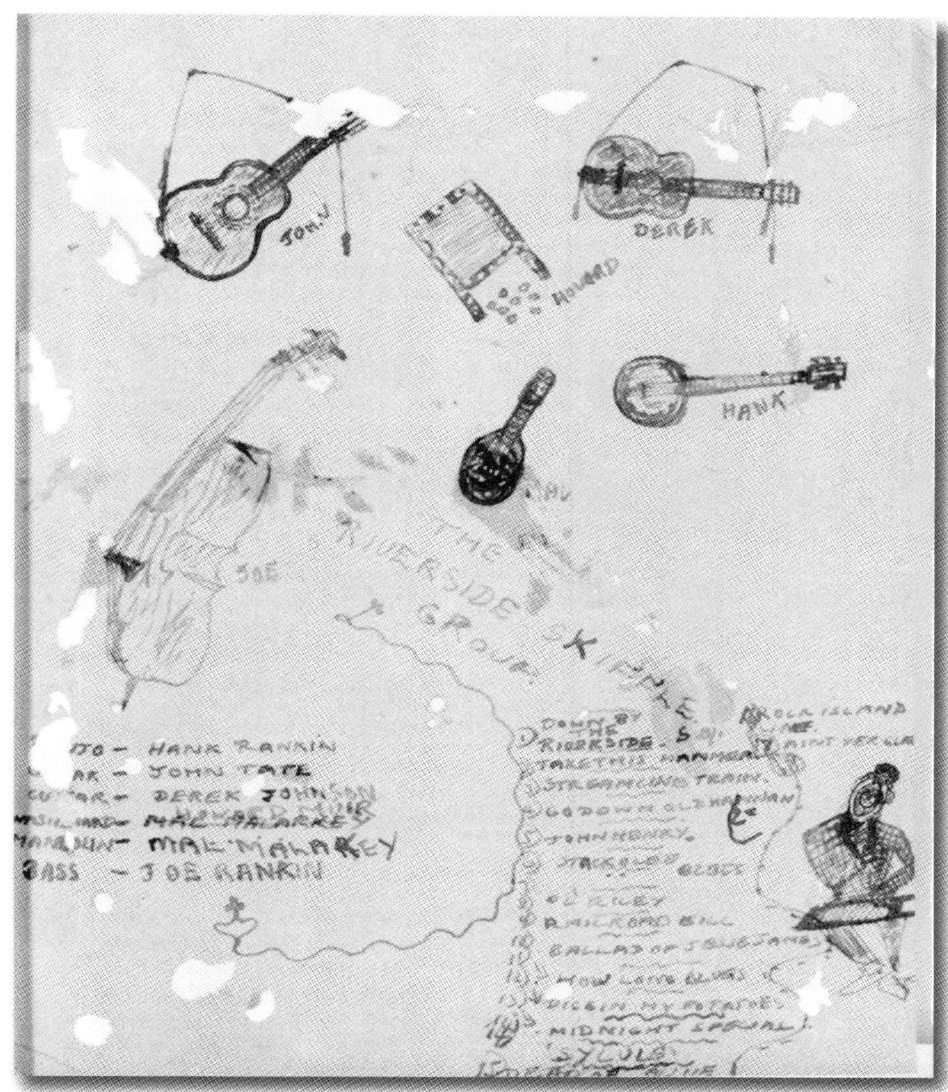

Hank Marvin's schoolday scrapbook

since learned all about tight schedules and the problems of touring. He and Lonnie later became good pals.

Like all of his peers and contemporaries, Bruce learned guitar by listening intently to the artists of the day, imitated them, and then gradually added his own personality to develop a unique style. There were always areas of mystery about the records he heard: "Nobody realised that Buddy Holly used a capo on things like 'That'll Be the Day', so we learnt the hard way – without." It was through manfully dealing with such struggles that Bruce later inspired a nation of rhythm guitar players. For now, though, Britain's youth was in the grip of the second phase of its spiritual re-awakening: the birth of rock 'n' roll.

Skiffle was a blend of country music and the blues, a craze that had swept the nation. But it was soon followed in Britain by trad jazz – a sanitised version of New Orleans jazz. And as music evolved from the dance band-led fifties to the rock band-led sixties the main music paper – *Melody Maker* – imperceptibly changed its content from trad jazz to pop and rock. As a consequence the front page – which once featured men with shiny brass instruments and women in bathing costumes – now featured strutting men with guitars and women in flowing costumes.

But it wasn't until the advent of amplified instruments that the music really became exciting, made sense, and was of any interest to the new teenagers.

CHAPTER 3

ROCK 'N' ROLL 'N' RADIOS

Britain was still suffering from the aftermath of food rationing and post-war reconstruction when rock 'n' roll hit its shores. America remained a mystery, a sprawling continent where oversized fin-tailed cars filled the streets and the people seemed larger than life. In sharp contrast to our permanently grey and uninspiring environment, America seemed to be fuelled by the Technicolor™ of Hollywood movies. It was an exciting, exotic, and impossibly distant place, the stuff of dreams.

The first artist to break into the British market with a rock 'n' roll record was Bill Haley and his Comets, with "Rock Around The Clock" on 15 October 1955. When an identically titled film was shown for the first time in British cinemas the following year it incited unprecedented youth riots. Cinemas were literally torn apart. Parents were horrified. Bizarrely, the singer responsible for cooking up this storm was a chubby 30-year-old man with an out-of-place kiss curl. Haley looked more like a school-teacher than a rock star, and certainly not the kind of person one would associate with revolution.

Although this country perceived the birth of rock 'n' roll to be a sudden event, in truth it had evolved slowly over the previous ten years, absorbing the flavours of jazz, R&B, country, and bluegrass, but for the first time the music was allowed to be a channel for raw emotion. Unlike Bill Haley, Elvis Presley was young, soulful and, more importantly, dangerous, seeming to sing with the voices of both God and the Devil. At first, with his smouldering, hip-swivelling movements, he was perceived as a threat to the American youth, and could only be shown on TV from the waist up. The moment when Britain began to divert its attention away from skiffle came on 19 May 1956, when the dark and sinister ambience of Elvis' "Heartbreak Hotel" entered the chart on its way to the Top Five. To some the record was incomprehensible, particularly its lyrics, while others marvelled at this new and original sound. Nevertheless, this was only the beginning.

Judd Procter

It was around 1956 that Judd Procter felt the first tremors of rock 'n' roll, coinciding with the publication of photographs of Elvis and Tommy Steele in *Melody Maker*. He and his mates thought that the rock 'n' roll and skiffle they heard on the radio was: "A load of crap. Musos had an uncommercial view of music, and they played the stuff under duress. Where were the lovely chord changes?" Perhaps a restricted viewpoint from someone of only 22, but 30 was considered to be very old then.

Roger Glover

Roger Glover recalls what he describes as the "sudden impact" of rock 'n' roll: "*6.5 Special* on TV was kind of old fashioned, or maybe that's my memory playing tricks, but it was the only place you could see the new stars. It's hard to imagine now but Wally Whyton, hitherto a gentle folkie, was the presenter of this rebellious new music! 'Rock Around the Clock' reminded me of skiffle in a way: it had the same exaggerated backbeat, and I liked that but Bill Haley's voice and his silly hairstyle didn't turn me on.

"Then I heard Elvis Presley: 'Hound Dog' did it. I strained to catch every word, every breath, every detail. I'm sure that for all of the musicians of my generation that snare drum sound is, even to this day, a benchmark. When the follow-up, 'Jailhouse Rock', was released, I was ready for it. I recall my friend Keith and I listening to it repeatedly for an entire afternoon. Then we'd flip it over and listen to 'Treat Me Nice' until bedtime. It was exhilarating stuff."

Chris Spedding

When Chris Spedding discovered rock 'n' roll he couldn't wait to lose the violin and get a guitar. He observes that a 12-year-old guitar player in those days stood a better chance with the girls than a 12-year-old violinist. "My parents were aghast, and thought that guitars and rock 'n' roll were synonymous with teenage delinquency – they were actually pretty well informed," says Chris, "and, having just bought me an expensive violin, they weren't about to indulge this latest fad by buying me a 'horrid, beastly guitar'."

Jeff Beck

Jeff Beck's devotion to the electric guitar began at a very early age. "I can remember just being very impressed with the sound of the thing. Les Paul was the first player I singled out, I think, because he played the signature tune on some radio programme. My elder sister also influenced me. She listened to Radio Luxembourg. She would never say 'Oh, I love this guy', or 'Elvis is great'; she would point out a guitar solo. I was most interested in bands that used the guitar to great effect, people like Scotty Moore, Cliff Gallup and Gene Vincent – all of them in the States, which is where my musical roots are.

"After Les Paul, the next important influence – and it was some time later – was 'Hound Dog'. Not so much Elvis himself, but the guitar solos – they put me on the floor for several months. Then I started to take in what rock 'n' roll was about: the outrage of it, hips wriggling, greased-back hair."

John Lennon

For John Lennon rock 'n' roll signified a major turning point as he approached adulthood. He once said: "I had no idea about doing music as a way of life until rock 'n' roll hit me. Nothing really affected me until Elvis. That changed my life. The idea of being a rock 'n' roll musician sort of suited my talents and mentality."

Tom McGuinness

Lonnie Donegan and skiffle opened the door for Tom McGuinness, starting him on the 'three-chord trick'. Buddy Holly proved to him that he could do it wearing glasses, and Hank Marvin showed him that he could wear glasses and be born in England and still play rock 'n' roll. "Without those people I might never have become a musician," says Tom, "but hundreds of others have contributed to making me what I am today: a guitarist still learning his trade. And I've only found one other thing that I enjoy as much as making music, but that usually involves being horizontal!"

EARLY DAYS

Although the rock 'n' roll phenomenon swept through most of Britain like a hurricane, by 1958 I was still to be affected by its excitement. Tom, who lived in the suburbs of London, says that this new craze appeared "slightly alien" to him. Living in a tiny village in the Midlands, it seemed all the more distant to me – almost like it was happening on another planet. True, I had heard the phrase "rock 'n' roll" many times, and read about it in the newspapers, but I had somehow mixed it up with Teddy boys and their penchant for Edwardian fashion. As there were no Teds in my area, nothing about the craze made any sense to me. On the bus home from school one night my friend Richard Hallchurch mentioned the name Elvis Presley, but in my ignorance I corrected him "No, it's Priestly." That's how much I knew. Musically I made more of a connection with the more jazzy records of the day, like Peggy Lee's "Fever", which had a tremendous atmosphere and a great bass and drum sound.

Nevertheless I was too busy immersing myself in a new hobby that, unbeknownst to me, would be of enormous benefit to my early days as a musician. I had always enjoyed science, and as a child I had an inquisitive mind, asking questions such as "What holds the sky up?" Looking back, it was natural that I would develop a keen interest in electronics.

RADIOS

When I was 14 my dad brought home a copy of the monthly magazine *Practical Wireless* for me, possibly in an attempt to rid me of a perceived aimlessness. Some neighbours said they had some old radios that they no longer needed, so I collected them and discovered that they were American. The valves were made by Sylvania and Brimar, not the English company Mullard, and the dial was FM, from approximately 95–107MHz. This was particularly exciting, since in the UK at the time we could only listen on the AM radio band, medium wave 520 kHz–1,610 kHz and long wave 148.5 kHz–283.5 kHz. At 110v, these FM radios were at the wrong voltage and in the wrong country, and I tried to imagine the stations they could pick up. It was an early instance of my fascination with the mystery of America, even before I'd actually heard any of the music.

In this picture of the Talismen, Tom McGuinness is at the back playing his Hofner Club 40 though a Watkins Westminister. The bass player had enterprisingly built his own instrument using the neck of an old banjo

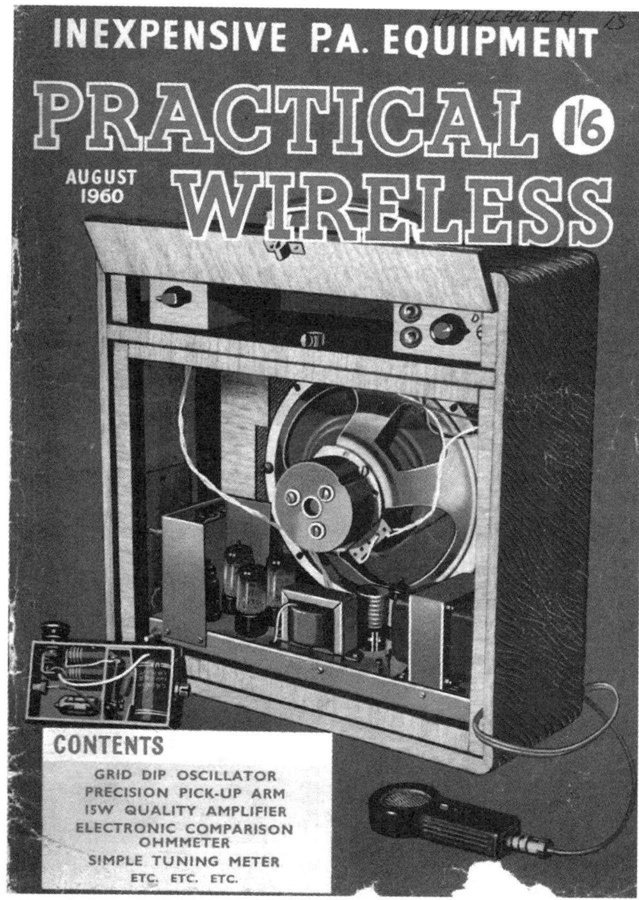

Practical Wireless *cover August 1960. This is what PAs used to look like*

When my fantasies exhausted themselves I ended up dismantling the radios, and later used one chassis in the construction of a three-valve tremolo unit. A little later, spurred on by my growing reputation for making use of old American radios, other neighbours in the village began to realise that they could offload their dud gear onto me. At one point I had accumulated several radios, various odd bits and pieces, and ten televisions, none of them working! I didn't have the patience or the knowledge to fix them, but I did realise that they all had components such as volume pots (potentiometers) that I might use to construct a sound mixer. More dismantling followed, and I drove my parents crazy by littering the house and attic with countless disembowelled televisions. My dad eventually buried them all in his back garden, along with an old iron water pump. Archaeologists of the future will have great difficulty interpreting this collection.

One of the more successful results of this orgy of deconstruction was a passive four-input mono mixer, which I had assembled from four TV volume pots, four resistors and four jack sockets, and had built into a metal toffee tin covered in black star-speckled Fablon. This device amazingly lasted for many years, and I still have it.

I developed a strange obsession with "concealed wiring". My hideous lime-green-painted bedside cabinet wasn't normal: it was drilled with holes in strange places, and twisted flex seemed to run all over inside it. Crystal sets, plugs and sockets, one-valve radio chassis, massive batteries, field telephones, buzzers, large toggle switches and even a Dinky toy's moving searchlight all seemed to occupy the spaces where books or shoes ought to be. Some time later my discovery of the electric guitar was made especially exciting by the instrument's concealed wiring. The mystery of this wooden instrument with a shiny pickup and magic tone and volume control knobs, all without a wire in sight, was all-consuming.

HI-FI

For my fifteenth birthday my parents bought me a two-tone red-and-cream Dansette Minor record player. It was sonic heaven: the cartridge could rotate through 180° with one stylus for 78s and the other for single 45s or LPs at 33 r.p.m. Since I only had one single to play, Duane Eddy's "Forty Miles of Bad Road", my schoolfriend Peter Watkins (who would become our lead guitarist) lent me his priceless collection of 78s by Duane Eddy and The Rebels, Johnny and The Hurricanes, Bert Weedon, and many others.

Whilst carrying them up the stairs I tripped, dropped them, and broke the lot – a very depressing sound. Regrettably, the replacements I bought had to be 45s, because by the early 1960s shops no longer stocked 78s. (In January 1959 *Practical Wireless* predicted that the 78 would die out within ten years. In reality its demise came almost immediately.)

(Although it was indeed a fine machine the Dansette had only a very small speaker, and to learn a bass part from a record I would play 45s at 78, practice the line, and then transpose it to its normal pitch and speed. This was a method of familiarisation which was also used by Sting during his formative years. Our Murphy Radio, conversely, had a great sound for bass, with its ten-inch speaker, and I would absorb music from Peggy Lee, Perez Prado and His Orchestra, Eddie Cochran, Buddy Holly, Duane Eddy and, eventually, The Shadows.)

Four-Input toffee-tin mixer

Inside view

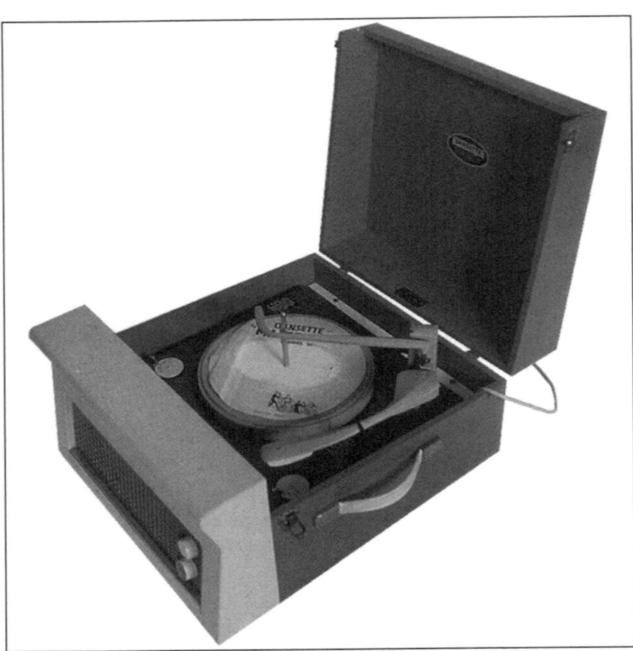

The Dansette Major record player

REVELATORY MOMENTS

On the bus home from school one day, my classmate John "Tub" Freeman suggested that I interrupt the journey in order to hear his dad's new radiogram. Since the only other choice was maths homework, it seemed like a good idea. John carefully placed a shiny new 78 on the turntable of this very large piece of polished-wood furniture – the size of a small jukebox – and music filled the room, obscuring my senses. The floor vibrated. The record was "Rebel Rouser' by American guitarist Duane Eddy. What was it that made these intoxicating reverberant sounds? I was hooked.

The mighty radiogram

John Paul Jones

Some time later John Paul Jones accompanied his parents, who were entertainers, to Ramsgate, where they were playing a summer season, and it was there that he experienced a revelation of his own: "While walking along the seafront, I heard – or rather felt – a vast rumbling sound. It was a jukebox playing the hit of the moment, 'Shakin' All Over' by Johnny Kidd and The Pirates. What was making all that fabulous stomach-churning noise? A bass guitar. I wanted to do that! The next track up was 'Lucille' by The Everly Brothers. It was a sign from the gods. I couldn't wait to get home and try this out on my new-born axe of destruction. I'd mentally learned and rehearsed both bass-lines (you get some funny looks marching along going boom-boom, boom-boom, boom-boom, boom-boom), and was now listening out for more low frequency pearls."

Snail's Pace Slim

It was the surprise purchase of a classic record that converted The Hamsters' Snail's Pace Slim to rock 'n' roll: "My dad brought home a Little Richard EP with 'Tutti Frutti', 'Rip It Up', 'Ready Teddy', and 'Long Tall Sally' on it. KABLOOEY!! I've still not recovered, and the nearest I've ever come to having a religious experience was when Richard appeared on TV around 1962. I must have been nine, and sat right in front of the box with jaw on the floor as the man stood on his piano, shirt soaked with sweat, screaming 'Lucille' while the fab Sounds Incorporated rocked 'n' rolled behind him. Little Richard – there will never ever be another. The greatest."

John Gustafson

The Big Three's bassist, John Gustafson, was also moved by that great American rocker. He says: "When I was a kid, my sister let me stay up and listen to the radio while my mum and dad were in the pub. The radio was normally on too late at night, and I was never allowed to listen to it. She let me stay up this one night and on came a record by Little Richard called 'Rip It Up', and that changed my whole life, I tell you. I thought: 'What is this? Music from outer space or what? What is it?' I was so excited that I couldn't sleep at all that night. To cap it all, I didn't even have a record player, but I went out the next day and bought that record and I sat in the house just reading the label over and over again for about three months. And that's it – that's how I started. That simple thing. It was gospel."

Roger Glover

Roger Glover was never quite the same when, in 1961, he heard loud music floating out from the gymnasium at Harrow County School. His curiosity was aroused: "I peeked through a door and saw a mesmerising sight: The

Lightnings – the school pop band, a year above us – were practising 'Poetry in Motion' by Johnny Tillotson, and from that moment on I wanted nothing else but to be in a band." He continues: "Although I didn't have the money to actually buy them, I knew every record in the charts. My information was gleaned from the music papers, whose charts I committed to memory far more easily than any schoolwork. I also listened to the radio and to the school scuttlebutt. It became cool to like certain kinds of music; for instance, it wasn't cool to like the British cover version of a particular song – the original American one was always much better. We learned how to be musical snobs, and the coolest kid was the one who was the first to rave about some obscure American artist, and even lie about having heard them."

Billy Connolly

In 1967, folk singer Alex Campbell played a Glasgow folk club wearing a typical outfit comprising of a denim jacket and cowboy boots. In the audience was a young and impressionable Billy Connolly, who was so moved by the image and power of the man that he exclaimed: "I want to be one of them." A fair banjo player, Billy quickly teamed up with guitarist Gerry Rafferty to form a folk duo known as The Humblebums.

Billy Connolly and Gerry Rafferty: The Humblebums. London, 1967

Martin Taylor

A wonderful insight into the playability of guitars comes from Martin Taylor, whose first guitar was a very clumsy looking three-quarter-size Russian instrument, the kind that proliferated in Britain during the late 1950s and early 1960s. According to Martin, they were responsible for starting – and ending – the careers of many guitar players: "With a neck the size of a felled mature oak tree, and strings at least three inches off the fretboard, you needed an almost toxic level of testosterone to gather enough strength to press the strings down. It was a truly awful instrument of torture, but

Martin Taylor aged four in 1959 with "That awful Russian guitar"

I fell in love with it and, at the risk of doing myself permanent physical damage, practised non-stop for hours and hours.

"Having never played another guitar, I thought it quite normal to break out in a sweat while playing a C major chord in the first position, and remember being totally amazed when I heard guitarists fly about all over the fretboard on records, knowing just what a difficult instrument the guitar was. The first time I played a real guitar was four years later, at a local music shop. It was a Gibson 335 and it was so easy to play that I honestly thought it was some kind of revolutionary guitar concept for disabled people to share the joys of guitar playing."

Hank Marvin

While still members of The Railroaders, Hank Marvin and Bruce Welch performed a gig at Newcastle Palace. At the rehearsal, Hank accidentally touched his guitar against the mic stand. There was a bang, lots of sparks shot from the guitar, a singer in the show flew into the orchestra pit, and three strings broke. Hank remembers thinking: "So that's what happens when you break a string on an electrical guitar!" It was the first time he'd played one – he wasn't sure which was cause and which was effect.

Andy Summers

Discovering the bending of notes came as an immense surprise to Andy Summers, who recalls listening to the BBC radio programme *Guitar Club* every Saturday night, which was presented by Ken Sykora and featured such people as Ike Isaacs, Diz Disley and Dave Goldberg. "After a while I noticed what sounded like a crying or laughing sound that would occur in solo passages. I often wondered what that sound was, and how they got it," says Andy. "One day while practising I accidentally pushed the B-string over sideways and then released it to its correct position on the fret. I heard the string make that crying sound which I'd heard on the radio. I was knocked out! I'd just played my first blues note."

Chris Rea

Blues, it seems, featured prominently when Chris Rea had his first encounter with the bottleneck slide sound that was to become his own guitar trademark: "I remember everything about that day in 1973. I can remember what I was looking at, the weather, even the time – it was 6.30 p.m. I was more or less a non-musician waiting for his musician friend to take him to a gig when I heard Joe Walsh on the radio, and rushed out the next morning to buy his record. I didn't even know that the sound which was to change my life was called slide guitar. Now all I ever want to be is a good slide guitarist. I still have no desire to be a rock star."

Graham Gouldman

Graham Gouldman remembers a particular moment at the age of seven when a change of "instrument" was required. "I wanted to be a drummer, and would get up extra early on Saturday mornings to listen to dance-band-style music on the radio. I would use clothes brushes and one of my mum's handbags – which had a rough surface – as my snare drum. I even had lessons from the late Dave King, who played with The Joe Loss Orchestra, but after a while I realised that playing a handbag was not for me."

Gary Moore

For blues guitar maestro Gary Moore, however, the discovery of his true strength in life came from a simple admission of failure: "The reason I started playing was because I was so crap at everything else, whether it was Boy Scouts or football. I was a total misfit, always on my own. I felt that I didn't belong anywhere, but as soon as I found music I felt that I'd come home – and I wasn't leaving!"

Although the aluminium disk that I'd cut in 1959 had (by accident) similar dimensions to a modern CD, its restricted bandwidth (about 1-5kHz if I was lucky) meant that it wasn't destined to be a major format. Surface noise was also a problem

Grundig TK5 tape recorder

Grundig TK5 Microphone

RECORDING EXPERIMENTS

Among all the cast-off clutter donated by our neighbours I found a portable wind-up gramophone and a collection of old 78 discs. Now this was exciting, though not necessarily because of the music itself. (It's only possible to listen to a brass band playing 'Blaze Away' three or four times without feeling that there really is something more important to do.) What grabbed my attention was the whole mechanical process, from the grooves on the record and the shiny metal of the arm to the way the record sounded less scratchy when the lid was closed and the comic effects from the clockwork motor slowly running down.

A couple of months later I was even more excited at the appearance of an electric gramophone, with a magnetic cartridge and a steel needle. As I stared intently at the grooves of a 78 I envisaged great possibilities. You could really see the different patterns caused by different frequencies, such as long, wavy lines for the bass notes. Between the run-out track and the label was a shiny blank space. I figured that if I softened the shellac in this area with a Bunsen burner from my home chemistry set then I could record onto it.

Using a small loudspeaker as a microphone and part of an old donated radio as an amplifier I was able to drive the magnetic cartridge and make the needle vibrate. With an old 78 rotating on the turntable, and the burner softening it from a few inches away, I lowered the arm and cut a new spiral for about five seconds. Immediately after the cut was finished I grabbed the record and shoved it under the running cold-water tap in order to re-harden it.

To my immense surprise and joy it played back! This whole process drove my mum crazy, since it all took place in the kitchen while she was trying to do the ironing, and she had to talk or sing or whistle into the mic between pressing shirts. I later progressed to recording onto sheet aluminium, which also worked, and a disc survives to this day.

Perhaps in response to my ludicrous attempts to be a cutting engineer in the kitchen, my dad surprised me one day by bringing home a tape recorder that he'd borrowed. It was a Grundig TK5, and had a large brown circular microphone protected by gold mesh. This was the first time I had seen such a contraption since my primary school days, but this time I saw a real purpose for it.

THE BAND

In my third year at school I had met three friends who shared a common interest in popular music. Out of our many discussions emerged the idea of forming a band, something that no one at the school had ever attempted before. It was a great idea but it was, nevertheless, a struggle since between us we had almost no equipment: Rick Hallchurch could play fairly good piano and a little guitar, Patrick Davies suggested that he would like to play drums but hadn't got any, Roger Swaab owned a guitar and could play a few chords, and I could play descant recorder and violin. We were enthusiastic but it was hardly the stuff of rock 'n' roll!

When we were very young, Peter Watkins and I both lived in the same village, Bilbrook, in Staffordshire. We would often re-enact scenes from TV programmes such as *Rin Tin Tin*, the series about a dog in the US cavalry. Peter's collie, Lassie (who was older than him), was unfortunately useless, refusing to act the part of an Alsatian who was happy to obey orders. In time Peter and I drifted apart, but we were reacquainted years later when he was about to join my school. One afternoon in 1958 I popped round to his house to say hello again and I was stunned to see him playing simple melodies on a big black guitar. To see someone I actually knew playing a guitar convincingly was a revelation. He had the knowledge.

THE AUDITION

I couldn't wait to tell the other guys about this guitar virtuoso (well, he was to me) who would soon be starting at our school. Two weeks later Rick (aged 14) chanced upon Peter (aged 11) in the (less than impressive) outside school urinal. The following conversation ensued (and I should explain that at grammar school everyone was known by their surname):

Rick: "Is your name Watkins?"

Peter (terrified, and assuming that Rick was a teacher): "Yes, sir."

Rick: "Are you a friend of Foster?"

Peter (still worried): "Yes."

Rick: "He says you can play guitar."

Peter (calming down): "Yes."

Rick: "Do you want to come to my house on Wednesday afternoon for a 'session'?" (rehearsals were called sessions)

Peter (delighted): "Yes!"

That was essentially Peter's audition and we soon discovered that – although he was three years younger – he could still play better than any of us.

We assembled in my bedroom one day at our house in the village of Bilbrook. Whilst Roger, Rick, and Peter may have been less than professional, they could at least play guitars, whereas I couldn't at all. What I could contribute, however, was the tape recorder. And so by default I became the engineer/producer (which meant that I held the mic and moved it nearer Peter Watkins' guitar during his solos).

Skiffle was in the air, and the first songs we interpreted were bold choices: "Living Doll" by Cliff Richard and The Drifters (produced by Norrie Paramour, and recorded in the now-legendary Studio Two at EMI's Abbey Road Studios), and "The Ying-Tong Song" recorded at Decca Studios West Hampstead by The Goons.

(Whilst George Martin had produced Peter Sellars at Abbey Road as a solo artist, it was Decca Records' music director Marcel Stellman who wanted to record all three Goons together – Spike Milligan, Peter Sellars, and Harry Secombe – for his label. But there was a problem: Harry Secombe was already signed to the Phillips label as a light tenor. A meeting was convened with MD Johnny Franz, and a contract was drawn up such that the three guys could perform together, but whereas Spike and Peter were allowed to sing, Harry could only shout and blow raspberries. Now you know. I'd really love to see that contract.)

Ambitious is perhaps an inadequate word to describe our attempts to recreate these two hits with just three cheap acoustic guitars, shrill pubescent vocals, one tape recorder, one microphone and lots of silly sound effects. But during that afternoon we were so happy.

HOME RECORDING

Although we continued to improve, I found that recording the band at home presented many problems, especially since I had now become both musician and engineer. Live fades were especially difficult and unpredictable, and had to be performed by slowly rotating the very large input-volume knob of the tape recorder with my right foot. Good takes were often ruined when I fell over at the end of a slow fade.

THE SEARCH FOR ECHO

Even when music was first recorded it became evident that the use of reverberation, ambience or echo would dramatically enhance the "reality" of the recorded performance. At first, such enhancements could only be achieved by situating the artist in a naturally reverberant space such as a church. Unfortunately, while the effect was rich and beautiful it was also uncontrollable, and it wasn't until the advent of electronics that any form of sophisticated control became possible.

Among the first studios in the world to have its own echo chambers were EMI's studios at Abbey Road. These were separate tiled rooms, built onto the actual studio, with a large speaker at one end and a microphone at the other. Bruce Welch recalls: "The echo chamber at Abbey Road was outside the building. During the early 1960s, complaints about sound leaking from it (from the apartments all around) meant that sessions stopped promptly at 10 p.m." In desperation, other means were sought. "It was common to find the long corridor outside the studio door being used for echo in the late evening."

The chamber of Studio Two had a sumptuous sound and contributed greatly to many early English rock classics, such as "Move It", "Shakin' All Over", "Apache", and "Love Me Do". Other studios which used natural spaces were Atlantic in New York City (a tiled chamber "designed" by engineer Tom Dowd) and Kingsway in London (a large underground car park).

Duane Eddy

Some studios had a recognisable sound of their own, and many industry professionals were able to identify the venue of a recording just by hearing the first few bars of a track. In the late 1950s, Duane Eddy recorded most of his big hits at Audio Recorders in Phoenix. Studio boss Floyd Ramsey and producer Lee Hazlewood found a 2,100-gallon water tank with good natural echo and moved it into the studio parking lot. As engineer Jack Miller recalls: "We took the signal from the board (after the EQ and limiting), fed that to a secondary Amphonal mixer, then to the ten-watt PA amp that fed the speaker in the tank (an eight-inch Di-cone Lansing). The mic in the tank picked up the signal and brought it back to another pre-amp to bring it back up to line level, and we mixed that into the board. We added more 'water tank' to the slapback than we did to the original, so the original had cleaner pop."

In 1975, Duane Eddy said of his own experience of this echo-tank: "Sometimes if a siren went by from the fire company or a police car we'd have to stop recording until it passed, and then in the morning we'd have to go out and chase the birds off it because we could hear them in the echo chamber. That was kinda fun."

Joe Brown

Meanwhile, back in England, Joe Brown had just introduced the idea of a guitarist's echo box to Hank Marvin. Prior to this, slap echo was always created in the control room by means of an intermediate tape machine. Hank: "Actually, the first box I had tended to wow and flutter a bit, which was quite interesting because, instead of the echo coming back as a straight repeat, you had a slight wobble on it, almost like a chorus."

Dick Denney

Dick Denney of Vox remembers the actual box: "It was imported from Italy, a Meazzi. It had a rotating aluminium drum, coated with ferric oxide, surrounded by erase, record and replay heads. Unfortunately the oxide wore off, so I wound quarter-inch tape around the drum, adhesed by three-in-one oil. It remained faithful for hundreds of shows."

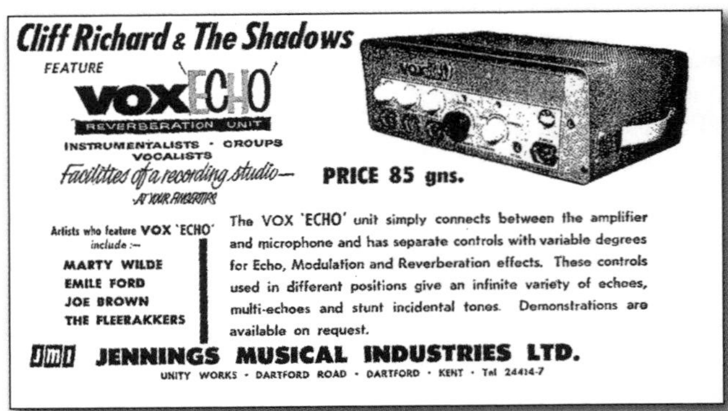

The Vox Echo – a fine machine, but what exactly are 'stunt incidental tones'?

Joe Meek

Joe Meek was a recording engineer with a flair for the original and a passion for innovation. He recorded the song "My Dixie Darling" for Lonnie Donegan at a British Legion drill hall in Plymouth. To achieve his beloved echo he recorded the sound in the gents' lavatory, with a speaker at one end and a microphone at the other. Joe, who had refined his engineering skills at IBC studios* began making recordings at his flat with an alarming mixture of second-hand equipment. When it came to adding his magic touch to recordings, without doubt his favourite effect was reverberation. At home he was forever sniffing out new places to produce echoing sounds. When singers weren't being pushed into the bathroom to achieve optimum resonance they would be singing across a jug or a cigar box.

**For many years after the war, IBC (Independent Broadcasting Company) was the only independent recording studio in London. In the unlikely setting of 35 Portland Place, and surrounded by embassies, this studio was the birthplace of many famous early singles from The Who, The Faces, The Kinks, Jimi Hendrix, Elton John, Duane Eddy, and countless others.*

Guy Fletcher

Guy Fletcher, Joe's one-time vocal arranger, has his own recollections of the producer's techniques: "Joe used the tiled bathroom in his flat as an echo chamber with a speaker at one end and a mic at the other. Although it never seemed to bother him, the yip-yip of the neighbour's dog could often be heard on the echo return of the vocal channel. It was certainly audible on tracks by Heinz and Gene Vincent.

"When he had a sound already down on tape the scope was wider. Not content with just sticking a speaker and a microphone in the bathroom he would try them out inside a dustbin or down a drainpipe and record what came out the other end. He had also built two echo devices of his own, one of which was just a garden gate spring with a transducer at either end: simple but effective. The other one was his 'mystery' echo chamber. He was sure that no one else had one, and had been intending to get it patented. It was built into a small metal case and was taped up to prevent anyone from discovering its contents. If it was accidentally knocked it made a loud, resonating yoing-yoing sound, because it was made out of springs from a broken fan heater. The secret of this little piece of top-secret equipment was only revealed when Adrian Kerridge, still his assistant, risked life and limb by untaping it to peek inside. Fortunately Joe never found out."

Rick Parfitt

Rick Parfitt used to visit Butakka, a trendy club in Woking, where he was fascinated by the resident band and would stand with his face inches from the guitarist's left hand. He would memorise a shape and learn a new chord every week. (I said to him that he must only have gone for three weeks – sorry Rick.) On one occasion at the club there was the announcement: "Next week we have appearing here a group with an echo chamber," which was followed by a ripple of excitement and confusion. Rick pondered: "Does that mean they're bringing a special room with them?" The next week he eagerly turned up again at the front, but of course the echo chamber was simply a Watkins Copicat tape echo!

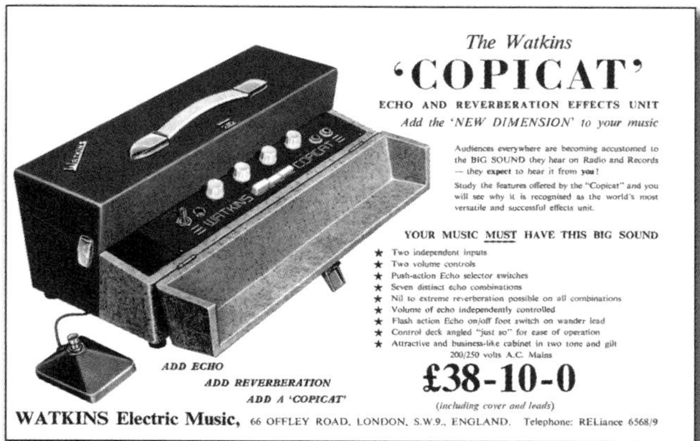

The ubiquitous Watkins Copicat Tape Echo. When the Copicat first went on sale at his South London shop, Charlie Watkins was surprised to notice a queue stretching down the high street. "I thought it was for the grocer next door – I thought he had a special offer on!" Charlie is pretty sure that Johnny Kidd bought Number One. Over the years many people have tried to improve the machine, and even steal the design, but the Copicat had a magic sound and feel which Charlie concedes was due to his "dreadful engineering design and the little 'bonk' as the tape went round."

Adrian Lee

When Adrian Lee was 13 he was the proud owner of a red-vinyl-covered Hofner Colorama with white edging. Outside his bedroom window was a garden, then a fence, and then the opposite row of terraced houses. He discovered that if he suspended his WEM amp out of the window and played the guitar he got a terrific echo off the opposite houses. This effect was inspirational for his renditions of "Apache" and other instrumental hits of the day. He thought all was fine until one day a pair of strong hands gripped the top of the fence and a face appeared: "Oi! Shut the fuck up!" Adrian slunk down out of view and withdrew the amp for good.

ECHO AND REVERB

As a schoolboy I was fascinated by echo and reverberation, and couldn't resist clapping, whistling or finger-popping when walking under arched canal bridges, for example. The sound was a source of constant surprise and mystery. There is also a wonderful ringing sound called the echelon effect, which can be heard when approaching a long stone stairway.

I'd noticed that records definitely sounded better if the reverbs were interesting, and tried to capture an element of this spatial characteristic by recording the band in the school gymnasium, an inspirationally ambient room. We chose to record a Jerry Lordan composition, "Mustang". With a logic that escapes me, the guys were arranged so that the rhythm guitar and the bass guitar were positioned near the tape recorder's solitary microphone, and the other musicians were placed further and further away in order of volume. The drums, being the loudest, were about 30 feet away.

I was so eager to hear the playback, and yet so hurt when I did. It sounded like an animated basketball game with instrumental accompaniment. Why was it so awful? Further reading provided me with information about how the real studios dealt with echo by using separate chambers, delays, and microphones, and I became mesmerised.

We had just moved to a new bungalow (one of nine, which my dad and eight other guys had just finished building for themselves over a three-year period) in the village of Brewood itself. Perfect! I would wait until my parents had gone out, take up the carpet in the shiny tiled hall and use this empty space as a reverb chamber, with a speaker at one end and the microphone at the other, whilst recording the band in my bedroom. It was sheer joy – at least, it was until someone rang the doorbell during the best take. But I was in good company – even the great Les Paul would suffer from being plagued with fire engine sirens and noisy neighbours during his pioneering multi-tracking sessions at home in the late 1940s.

Brian Coombs

Brian Coombs of Bristol Musical was yet another victim: "A little knowledge is a dangerous thing. Somebody had told us that the echo effect was achieved by running the sound down very long cables to slow it down. It seemed logical, we all agreed. So at practice that Saturday, in order to echo the whole band, we ran our mains cable outside and wired up the chain-link fence that ran around the shed, and then rewired the other end to our amplifiers. With a sound like a small atom bomb the fuse box blew itself off the wall and ended our association with that particular place for all time."

Linda Hoyle

Of course, it wasn't just young instrumentalists who joined in the great search for echo – singers were at it too, one of them being Linda Hoyle, the singer in my band Affinity, who found an ingenious alternative use for an everyday household object: "My sister Wendy and I grew up singing together. At five and six years old she was harmonising to the Fats Waller tunes I sang. We would lie in bed and sing into the night – great songs, old songs, songs that beat the Kaiser, 'Lulu's Back In Town', 'Shine', 'Nobody Knows What a Red-Hot Mama Can Do' – do doodlie-doo de-doo. We longed for microphones and speakers, tape recorders and electric guitars. What we got was a Valor convector heater.

"It was the first item that was put into the bare-boarded empty front room of our new house (we moved from one end of the street to the other when I was 13). We discovered that it picked up the sounds in the room and reverberated in a pleasing, hollow kind of way. We sang at it, harmonised into it and did a concert on the spot. About three feet tall with a black grille in the front at the top and the rest a hollow box with a flue inside connected to a paraffin tank, it was our own echo chamber. It improved the sound of our voices so much that we even sang into it when it was on, its bright blue flame burning beautifully from all my father's attentive wick trimming. It was a hot and rather dry inhale, but the tone improved. I think it was this that drove Wendy and I to join bands later on, searching for the progress of technology, but never quite finding the same wonderful, intimate, cosy tones that the Valor offered us."

LATER DAYS

It's a good deal easier now. With the advent of the echo plate and affordable digital reverberation – now as a computer software option – we no longer have to sing into heaters, shoo away birds, curse at barking dogs, wait for the fire engine to pass, or pray that the neighbours won't come around. When a young guitarist – or engineer – plugs into a multi-effects unit today it probably never crosses his mind just how difficult it used to be, and how hard the pioneers had to struggle.

CHAPTER 4

THE FIRST GUITAR

If there is ever a subject that summons up horrific, but fond, memories among seasoned musicians it is that of the first instrument. When I was about 15 I bought a round-hole Egmond Frères acoustic guitar for £2 from Dave Left, who became one of the singers in my first band. It had five cream-coloured tuning pegs and a white one which, since it didn't grip the spindle at all, was really only cosmetic. Tuning was effected by an old clock key.

Almost immediately I contracted chicken pox and was confined to the house for the next two weeks. This time was not wasted, however, and I could soon play a few basic chords, plus the main riff from Duane Eddy's version of "Peter Gunn". To this day I'm convinced that anyone who catches chicken pox will be able to play guitar once they have recovered.

Peter Watkins

Schoolfriend Peter Watkins' tenth birthday present was his first guitar: a four-string plastic "Elvis Presley" model, with a plastic "chord machine" (which did the fingering for you). It was bought from Woolworth's for four guineas in 1957. Five years later, the same item was a "Beatles" model. Peter recalls: "I remember liking the sound of the unwound B and E strings, and asking my dad if he could get me all of the strings like that. But after school one afternoon it fell off a chair and the neck snapped. All the Bostik in Wolverhampton couldn't mend it. I was devastated. Eventually I acquired a six-string guitar which had been made by my friend Robert Evans' dad and it cost me 10/- (50p). The action was ideal for playing slide guitar... under the strings.

"Not long after that, my dad came back from town with a sorry-looking black guitar which he claimed was his. Even as a gullible 11-year-old I was suspicious, and sure enough, before long the secret was out: this guitar was for me. It was a cello type, f-holes and all. We painted little silver notes on it, so that it looked cool. I had been promoted to the man at the back, and – even more impressively – I now had two guitars! Dad's famous comment at around this time, however, was: "Guitars? Pffff! They'll be giving them away in a couple of years."

At just under £4 this was clearly a quality instrument.

Peter Watkins (aged 12) and his 'black guitar'

FIRST GUITARS

- Eric Clapton wanted to be a drummer, but his granny thought better ("I'm not having noisy drums in this house!") and bought him a little acoustic guitar for £14 on HP from Bell's Music Shop in Kingston-upon-Thames. Eric soon swapped the acoustic guitar for a £100 double cutaway Kay electric guitar that had a thick neck and a very high action which couldn't be lowered. It was, he says, "a bitch to play."
- **One day, Jimmy Page discovered a round-hole acoustic guitar lying around the house that had been brought back as a present from a Spanish holiday by a relative. He liked the sound and feel of the instrument, and took it to school so that a friend could show him how to tune it.**
- Looming large at the beginning of John Etheridge's career was a Russian-made acoustic guitar which he bought from his local store for £3/2/6d (£3.12½). On it he achieved vibrato by "bending the neck backwards and forwards. You could drive a bus under the twelfth fret!"

John Etheridge and his 'Soviet' guitar in 1962

- **Pedal-steel guitarist Pete Willsher's first instrument was made from his mum's old ironing board.**

Pete Willsher in 1959 at Southend-on-Sea with the lap-steel that he and his dad made from his mum's old ironing board

- David Gilmour: "The first few guitars I had were all a bit makeshift: a nylon-strung one, then it was a Selmer Rex and a Burns Trisonic. But around 1963, I saw a Hofner Club 60 with a broken neck in my local music shop. It was in for repair but I persuaded the bloke to let me buy it for £30."
- **David's touring colleague with Pink Floyd, Tim Renwick, felt that, with the arrival of long trousers – which was a significant moment for young teenage boys in the fifties/sixties – his image was incomplete without the additional fashion accessory of a proper guitar. He bought a nameless Japanese-built blonde semi-acoustic with a pickup, a guitar he found to be reasonable when played acoustically but disastrous when amplified. Tim's first serious guitar was an Italian-built Eko with a silver-sparkle formica front and strange cutaways. It had four pickups and six selector push switches: "It didn't matter which button you pushed; the vibrations generated by playing caused the buttons to move up and down quite randomly."**
- Bruce Welch splashed out £4/19/6d (£4.97½) for his first acoustic from a sports shop in Newcastle upon Tyne. The action was interesting: he couldn't play past the fifth fret.
- **Terry Walsh started on banjo but switched to guitar when a relative observed: "They're not using banjos any more." He bought his first guitar from Hessy's in Liverpool and had six free lessons from Bob Hobbs.**
- Spotting a newspaper advertisement, Brian Odgers bought a £13 guitar – it took a month for this virtually useless lump of plywood to arrive, and he sent it straight back.

The EKO Italia, with 'tap – tab' tone changes

Dave Gilmour in 1965 playing his Hofner guitar on stage with Cambridge band Jokers Wild

- **Laurence Juber: "I nagged my parents for about a year to get me a guitar. What I ended up with wasn't very special – it had a bolt-on neck with the bolt on the outside. Very bizarre! I had to put scrunched-up cornflakes packets underneath the neck to get the action playable. It had a kind of floating fingerboard."**
- Denny Laine: "My first guitar cost £3. It was a flat-bodied acoustic of a dirty red/brown colour and it wouldn't stay in tune. Next came a Framus f-hole round-bellied Sunburst for £15, but this wasn't used as much because it wasn't loud enough. So now I had a two-guitar collection, and I tuned to an open chord until I was shown the correct tuning by an older schoolfriend who was taking jazz lessons."
- **John Etheridge finally hit the big time with his Hofner V3, which featured three pickups and a tremolo arm.**

Roger Swaab

Roger Swaab, the future rhythm guitar player in The Tradewinds, observed that: "The most memorable feature of Peter's new instrument was its colour. Well, not so much its colour – which was black – but more its finish, which had the texture of a medium-grade sandpaper, and it was carried in a strange-looking home-made bag, fashioned from what appeared to be an unwanted Mackintosh."

Bert Weedon

In 1933, when Bert Weedon was 12 and growing up in East Ham, there were no guitar heroes, no role models and certainly no electric guitars, but Bert's attention was grabbed by the thrilling sight of a round-hole acoustic guitar on a market stall a few miles away, in Petticoat Lane. Every Sunday he would return to this same stall to find the same guitar still there. He could stand the temptation no longer and eventually persuaded his father to buy it for him. The guitar cost 15/- (75p) and Bert carried this rather battered old instrument home, wrapped in brown paper, caressing it all the way. To make it even remotely playable, Bert slowly improved the instrument by lowering the impossible action, unstiffening the pegs, and removing the strings of unknown parentage.

1938 saw 17-year-old Bert Weedon thrill at the sight of Jack Abbott constructing his first-ever hand-built guitar: the Abbott Victor. (There's enough material for another suit in those lapels)

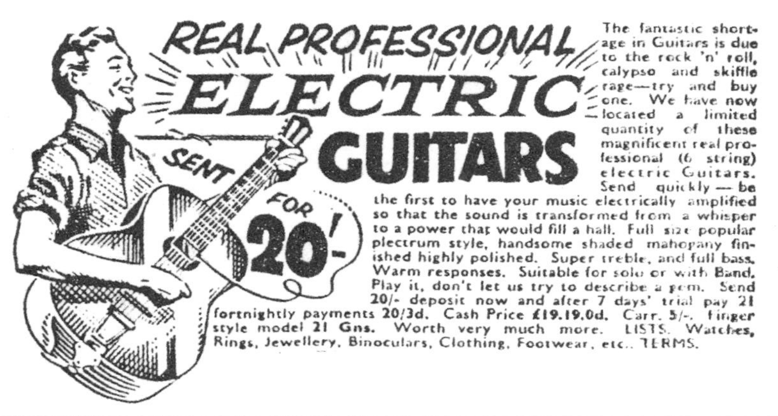

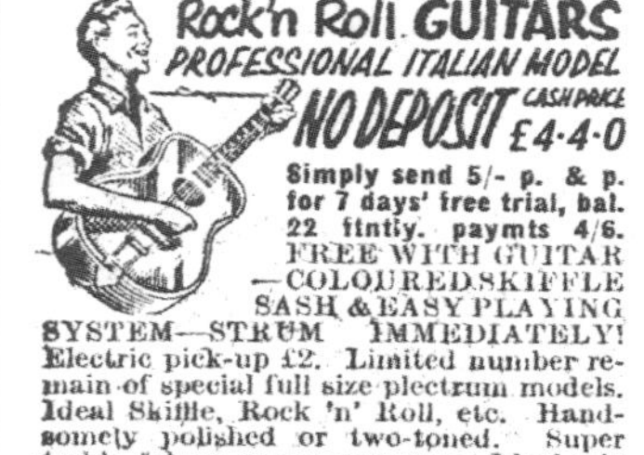

This remarkable sequence of adverts ran between 1957 and 1964 – always the same grinning oaf, and always the same trashy instrument

Capture that Beatles' sound in 1964

Joe Brown

A stone's throw away from Bert in the East End of London lived the Dance family, who were famous for their considerable musical talents and for owning a telephone. The family consisted of two sisters, Bubber the pianist, Arthur the accordion player, and Georgie Dance, the guy notable for being the first guitarist ever noticed by neighbour Joe Brown. Joe remembers: "Georgie used a matchstick as a pick, and it produced the strangest sound. All that was a long time ago, but I can see him now, leaning against the corner on the street, stoned out of his mind, singing his head off and doing all these runs out of time.

"Well, I bought that guitar from Georgie Dance for a pound. I didn't know it then but he always tuned the guitar to an open chord, and of course I thought that was the way to tune it, so if ever I broke a string I'd put another on and tune it the same. I think I played the bloody thing like this for five years until I suddenly realised that I'd better do something about it and start again. The trouble was that, in those days, the guitar wasn't about, really. Not with kids."

(NB this is what Joe said – I thought the meaning was obvious. To define it would be embarrassing.)

Bryan Daly

Bryan Daly's first attempt to get his hands on an instrument came in the form of a specific request as a four-year-old for a toy tin banjo which he assumes must have been totally unplayable. After hounding his parents, he was finally given a small but authentic ukulele banjo at around the age of eight. Then, a year or so later, there followed a deluxe version, complete with a velvet case. "We lived in the country, near Oxford, avoiding the bombing during the war, so I was lucky to get such a prize. A proper banjo followed at around eleven, but the sound was not to my liking. By then all that interested me was the guitar. I had seen one at my cousin's house and that had settled it."

Albert Lee

It was the piano which triggered Albert Lee's initial musical journey at the age of eight, but the desire to play the guitar eventually reared its head just as he was reaching his teens. "A schoolfriend and I started to play together on a very cheap arch-top with an horrendous action. We must have been 12 or 13 at the time – it was around 1957. I played for the next 18 months or so on borrowed guitars, and my friends' parents would understandably get quite irate. They would demand the guitars back. Imagine that!

"I was in one group playing a guitar belonging to Bruce 'Bugs' Waddell; it was a small Victorian model – I guess you'd call it a ladies' model. We bought a £3/10/- [£3.50] Hofner pickup for it and plugged it into radios, but before long my folks bought me a Spanish guitar for about £5. This was okay, but I immediately put steel strings on it, of course. I played this until Christmas of 1958, when my folks spent nearly all of their Christmas club money on my first good guitar, a Hofner President with the add-on pickup at the end of the fingerboard. I remember it was easy to pull the wire out of the pickup by stepping on it."

Albert Lee (r) in his back garden in Kidbrooke, London, in 1959. The bass player is Bruce 'Bugs' Waddell, who also later played in the Thunderbirds

Mike Read

DJ and Shadows' fan Mike Read started out playing a Broadway, but his first serious guitar was a twelve-string Hoyer with an impossible action which prevented the playing of *barré* chords – except when posing for photos! In his early days he used to walk up and down the Charing Cross Road and sit in cafés, all the time with his guitar in its

Mike Read (back row, second left) playing his first guitar, a Broadway. The headstock reads 'Mick'

case. One day, in the corridor at Woking Grammar School, a friend asked him: "What do you play?"

Mike: "Lead guitar."

Friend: "Oh, you must know lots of chords then."

Mike: "No, I play lead guitar."

Mitch Dalton

A related confusion affected Mitch Dalton, who idolised Hank Marvin and the sound he produced from his guitar. In his quest for knowledge he avidly read the sleeve notes on the backs of Shadows' albums, and it was on one of these that he noticed a clue: Hank played lead guitar. Mitch, who played guitar from the age of ten, became convinced that the secret of Hank's sound was the lead – the metal – out of which his guitar was constructed. (Can you imagine the weight?)

Mitch Dalton (far right) with his R&B band – Five Months of Dusk – gigging at the church hall, Ickenham, in 1964. Mitch recalls that his father would drive the band to rehersals. "Imagine three twelve-year-old boys, two amplifiers, and one drum kit – plus my dad – all packed in a Mini!

His first electric guitar, bought for £30, was a blonde Emil Grimshaw EG Hertford 10. The pickup was visually an extension of the rosewood fingerboard, and only the six-pole-piece screws were visible. His £12 amp was a Besson, of which he says: "My only memory of it was that it looked like a radio, was completely dangerous, had no earth, and I was electrocuted on at least three occasions!"

Hank Marvin

Hank himself was just 14 years old when he bought his first instrument, in 1955. "It was a Windsor G five-string banjo that I bought from James Moody, a school master at Rutherford Grammar School. The deal we struck was £2/10/- [£2.50], repayable at half a crown a week out of my pocket money." For his 16th birthday, in October, Hank was delighted to receive a Hofner Congress cello-body guitar from his dad. He added a small pickup, which was joined by two arms to the neck at the end of the fingerboard, and borrowed a small amplifier from a friend. "It was about the size of a cornflakes packet – and sounded like one!" Nevertheless, he was thrilled at how different the guitar sounded when it was amplified.

Tony Hicks

Tony Hicks had a job on his hands when his aunt kindly gave him a large-scale Tex-Mex guitar that had been made by a friend. Being only twelve years old, Tony remembers that he looked ridiculous wearing such a comparatively huge instrument, which he describes as resembling a *guitarrón*. "My first proper Spanish guitar was bought, yet again, by my auntie from a shop in Nelson, Lancashire, where I lived. The guitar was supported by a silk cord with a choice of colours, and I chose a blue one. Although it was wrapped in brown paper, I distinctly remember insisting that they tied it to the shape of the guitar so that when I walked through the town centre everyone would be impressed."

Rick Parfitt

Before the days when Rick Parfitt's wardrobe consisted mainly of denim, his first guitar was a £13 sunburst Framus. "It had a smell of varnish, especially when you opened the case. It also had a sash with a tassle which cut into your shoulder." This was swapped for a beautiful Martin Collette, but he later went with his dad to Selmer's, where he was bought a beautiful blonde Hofner acoustic. It needed a pickup, so a particularly dim assistant in the shop screwed one straight into the body, and the dangling wires were shoved into the f-hole. His dad also bought him a Selmer Truvoice (with tremolo). When Rick got back home, he was in heaven.

Andy Fairweather-Low

When asked about his first guitar, a wide-eyed Andy Fairweather-Low delivered an emotional and poetic reply: "My first close encounter with the drug called rock 'n' roll

DOODLES

- **Whilst at school Hank Marvin – who was passionate about jazz – used to draw and doodle banjos, double-basses, trumpets, clarinets, and skiffle instruments in his rough exercise book.**
- Eric Clapton showed promise at drawing from an early age, and at school he drew "pointy" guitars. He later studied graphic design at Kingston Art College, but the guitar was his passion – he played all the time.
- **Mike Read drew guitars in his school note-books, "the pointier the better." Meanwhile, at home, Mike's father was convinced that electric guitars played themselves, and to this day he still refers to guitars as "banjos".**
- John Etheridge's heroes included The Ventures and Hank Marvin, and he would spend hours drawing pictures of fantasy electric guitars: they had horns and were always plugged into the wall socket.
- **John Paul Jones: "At 15 I was still going to school, in theory. When I wasn't doodling at my desk, drawing hundreds of bass guitars in ever more fantastical shapes, I skipped off school to go to the West End of London. There I supplemented my education at art galleries, museums, free lunchtime organ recitals and just plain walking the street"**
- At school, all Roger Glover could think about was music. "The only two subjects I had any interest in at all were English and art. Wednesdays were sports classes and I invariably skived off, and anyone who knew me knew where to find me: in Lyons Tea House in Harrow, idly filling my exercise books with stage designs full of towering amplifiers and expensive PAs, or drum front patterns, or just filling my head with dreams. Little did I know... "

probably gave birth, if I'm lucky, to my equivalent of Citizen Kane's last utterance: 'Rosebud'. 'Did he say anything before he passed away?' they'll ask, and with a bemused look they'll say, 'Futurama... he said Futurama.' I can see it now. Ice blue, a small grille between two pickups and a black neck and headstock. Oh, my, my, my. Hmm, oh yeah, ooh bloody yeah, yeah, yeah! 'I want, I want, I'd be the happiest boy in the world if...' Now where was I? Ah yes, in an arcade in Cardiff, 1963, looking through a music store window. As it happens I never did get to own a Futurama guitar. My first guitar was a Hofner Verithin, a poor boy's Gibson and I was a poor boy. My father signed the HP agreement and my fate was sealed."

Roger Glover

After experiencing the exuberance of skiffle, the young Roger Glover fell in love with the acoustic guitar. He once spent all night strumming a borrowed one and "getting off on the jangle", but it was a few years before he acquired his own. "It was a Christmas present, and it cost £2. It was horrible. I can't remember the make, and the action would have been good for Robin Hood, but it was a prized possession. I learned how to play the basic chords on it, but I couldn't play an F major. It was only when I was in a guitar showroom in Harrow, and was cheekily trying out a beautiful cherry-red guitar – Italian, I think – with fancy looking f-holes and a floating pick guard, that I found I could play F. Unfortunately, the guitar was £12 and way beyond my means so all I could do was dream about it until I resolved to buy it through saving my paper-round earnings. I used to walk to school past the shop and see it in the window waiting for me. Eventually I bought it with the help of my parents and the old guitar just faded away."

Ritchie Blackmore

Roger's future Deep Purple colleague, Ritchie Blackmore, was inspired to take up the guitar after seeing a schoolfriend playing one. "It was a Spanish model and cost about £5. I was ten years old so I asked my friend to come to my house and show my parents the guitar. I was hoping and praying that it would prompt them into buying one for me. Just holding this instrument gave me shivers up my spine. I begged my mother and badgered her for about three weeks. When she couldn't stand it any more she approached my father. Knowing it was either buying me one or hearing both of us nagging, he gave in.

"We all went to the music shop in Hounslow called the Bell Music Shop, where there was this amazing guitar in the window. It was a dark, almost black Framus, but it was not £5; it was seven guineas. This posed a problem: it was £2 more then we had anticipated, and I thought it was all over. But luck was with me. My father bought it for me on HP and I remember carrying the guitar out of the shop, floating on air. This was the present to end all presents!

"As we walked back to take the bus home, my father turned and wryly said to me, 'If you don't learn how to play this guitar, I'm going to put it across your head.' (I had a habit of not following through with any worthwhile ventures. Also, my grades weren't what they should have been in Berkeley Junior School.) When I got home I held the guitar in front of me and posed in the mirror, pretending to be Tommy Steele."

This picture of Mark Knopfler and Steven Phillips shows their group – The Duolian String Pickers – at a party in February 1970, wearing the gangster-style hats which they adopted to emulate the illustrations of black blues men as seen on old blues albums. The very name of the band came from an American National steel guitar, as played here by Steven, and a photo of which later appeared on Dire Straits' 1985 album, Brothers In Arms. Mark faithfully copied the finger-picking style of Lonnie Johnson (from whom Lonnie Donegan was to take his name), and Mark is seen here playing a Zenith 'Josh White', imported by Ivor Mairants. In an early ad for this guitar, the caption read: 'Ideal for skiffle groups'

Mark Knopfler

Mark Knopfler went through a similar posing phase in his youth, often with that king of props, the tennis racquet. He finally persuaded his dad to fork out £50 for a red Hofner V2 solid body (it had to be red), and as he and his dad left the shop with their prize the shopkeeper advised "Stick at it!" However, Mark didn't have the nerve to ask for an amplifier as well, and so he continued to plug the V2 into the family radio until the speaker finally blew.

Richard Brunton

Richard Brunton first played a gimbri, a three-stringed instrument with no frets, which had been bought for him in Morocco by some friends. Undaunted, he played the theme from the TV series *Z Cars*, with such monotony that his father, faced with certain madness, went out and bought a Romanian acoustic for £6/10/- (£6.50) which had been reduced in price because of faulty varnishing. To reinforce the sound, a Hofner pickup was finally fitted in the sound hole.

Mel Galley

Having an older brother with impeccable musical taste, Mel Galley was weaned on Buddy Holly, and by the time The Shadows appeared he knew that he absolutely had to play the guitar. "My brother was supposed to have been going to piano lessons for two years, but my mum and dad found out he was instead going to the pictures, so they were quite reluctant to give me the opportunity to learn. But after continued cries for a guitar I finally got one. After a while, I was left with only three strings and the only way I was going to get a better instrument was to be able to play 'Apache' on the remaining strings. Having seen an advert in the back of the *NME* for a Rosetti Lucky Seven, I remember thinking '£7/4/6d? [£7.22½] – I'll never be able to afford that.' But after paper rounds and grocery deliveries, I finally got one. Fortunately there was a chap, an electrical 'whizz', who lived in the prefab at the top of our garden, and he fixed up an old radio so that I could play through it. My music teacher told me how disappointed he was because he thought I could have been a serious musician."

Graham Gouldman

Graham Gouldman's big moment came in 1951 when his cousin Ronnie brought him a second-hand guitar back from holiday in Spain. "It cost £5 and had a terrible action, but it changed my life. By the end of my first day with it my fingers were sore, but I was overjoyed. The first proper electric guitar I had was a Star. I have no idea who made it but it looked great. It was small and black, with sparkly bits around the pickups. We parted company one night when the tremolo system disintegrated during a gig with one of the groups I was in."

Richard Brunton enjoys playing his Romanian acoustic, in spite of the 'faulty varnish'

Phil Hilborne

In his early teens, Phil Hilborne discovered the guitar after hearing acoustic guitarists practising at his school. "Apart from the marvellous sound, it was the percussiveness and attack of the notes that actually attracted me so much. My first guitar was an acoustic of unknown origin, with the obligatory mile-high action and strings that bore more than a passing resemblance to ships' mooring lines. With this guitar I learned my first few chords, and I was on my way."

Phil Hilborne, aged 16, with his first twelve-string guitar, a Kimbara. Note the unfeasibly large flares

Mickey Moody

Mickey Moody entered the world of rock 'n' roll after acquiring a pink plastic guitar which had a photograph of Elvis Presley emblazoned on the front. This was eventually replaced with a guitar bought by his father from a second-hand shop, and on one string he learned to play 'Apache'. "It had a four-inch action, and the scratchplate was adorned with a large butterfly."

Joe Moretti

One of seven children living in a crowded Glasgow tenement, Joe Moretti's first instrument was not a guitar but an accordion. His father acquired it in exchange for a horse harness, but was so hard up that he had to sell it soon afterwards. Struck down by chest trouble, Joe was out of action for nine months, but came back fighting and bought a guitar and a concertina in a package deal costing £5.

Jim Mullen

Jim Mullen started playing on an Egmond, which had a cello body of shaped plywood. It cost £10, but it took him two years to pay for it on hire purchase. He went electric with a red Hofner Colorama, which he found to be almost unplayable, although two years after he had sold it he played the guitar again and was reassured that the fault was not his!

Alan Parker

Despite his yearning to play the trumpet, Alan Parker's parents couldn't afford one, although they did know of an uncle who had an old guitar in his loft. Alan cycled to his house to discover it was an old Gibson Kalamazoo. He cycled home with it on his back, with fresh motivation.

Gary Moore

Gary Moore's father was a promoter in Northern Ireland, and this guaranteed him an early exposure to live music – at the age of five! "I have this vague recollection of seeing bits of drum kits and PA stuff around the house. I think it was just meant to happen. He came home one day and asked if I wanted to learn to play the guitar, so I said yes. I'd always had a lot of music in my head. A friend of my dad's bought me this Framus guitar – a cello-bodied f-hole, it was. It literally was like a cello against me, 'cause I was so small and I could hardly get my fingers around the neck. By the age of around ten or eleven I was seriously into playing the guitar."

Gary Moore in 1960, aged about seven or eight, in the garden of his grandma's bungalow in Mill Isle, County Down. The guitar belonged to a friend of his uncle. (What great knees – watch out Angus Young)

Ray Russell

Guitar was always a passion for Ray Russell, and he knew from a very young age that his career was destined to be in music. He started playing on a four-string ukulele before acquiring his first Spanish acoustic guitar. He then acquired a Hofner President with an added-on 14-guinea tremolo, and went electric by adding a DeArmond pickup, the kind that slid along a fixed metal rod so that the pole pieces could be situated anywhere from the bridge to the neck. "The wire that followed the pickup along was never long enough, so the braid was always fracturing," His next move was to progress to a Hofner Verithin, with a Selmer Truvoice amp.

Jullian Littman, playing a Chinese ascoustic which was hired by his father while they were on holiday in Austria in 1962

Julian Littman

Julian Littman still has his first guitar, a nylon-strung Kapok, which was bought for him by his father from a music shop in Dun Laoghaire for £4/10/- (£4.50). Its label reads "Canton Musical Instrument Manufacturing Institute'. He began playing guitar seriously on a Rosetti, and in a demonstration of hero worship he used to suck in his cheeks in order to look like Keith Richards.

Keith Richards

When he was younger, the Rolling Stone himself was fascinated by the image of Roy Rogers with a guitar. Keith acquired a Rosetti acoustic Spanish guitar for £10 on HP, which was paid for by his parents. He taught himself from Chuck Berry records, a basic chord tutor, and with some help from his grandfather, who had also been a musician. By the age of 15 he knew most of Chuck Berry's solos. Keith also cites Buddy Holly as a big influence on his playing, and admits to "nicking" all of his solos.

Andy Summers

Andy Summers recalls: "My first guitar arrived via a mysterious 'Uncle Jim', when I was 14 years old. It was a small, battered Spanish guitar, with only five strings. Six months later it still only had five strings. It dawned on me later, after staring at several acne-ridden guitar-playing youths at my local school, that I was one string short. Such is life! Eventually, one of these guitar giants took pity on me and made me a present of the sixth string. Thereafter began my first painful steps upon my chosen instrument.

"I didn't have a clue how to get it in tune. Six months passed and I was getting nowhere. Luckily, my mother took in a lodger, a six-foot-seven-inch ex-RAF serviceman known as Cloudy. Fortunately for me, Cloudy had a bit of an ear for music, and was able to tune my guitar via the family piano. Once I had the guitar in tune I could get from D7 to G, sounding only just slightly more pleasant than a cat being struck by a moving vehicle."

Phil Manzenera

Rock 'n' roll took a while to reach the exotic climes of Venezuela, but by 1961 it had captured the imagination of ten-year-old Phil Manzenera, who attended boarding school in England. Phil says: "An English friend sold me his Framus cello acoustic with a Hofner pickup on it. He showed me a Chuck Berry riff, and I was off. Next birthday, in London and using my £5 birthday cash as a deposit at the grand age of eleven, I entered into a hire purchase agreement with Bell's of Surbiton via their mail-order catalogue for the

Phil Manzenera (centre) playing a Hofner Galaxy with The Drag-Alley Beach Mob

flashiest red Hofner Galaxy guitar, with an incredible tremolo arm (price: £55). Ten years later, and in Roxy Music, I bought a red Gibson Firebird. Plus ça change!"

Bernie Marsden

The very mention of the Bell Music catalogue reminds Bernie Marsden of just how much he lived in fear of it. This publication always claimed to be "just off the press", but every few months Bernie sent off his coupon for the new one only to receive the same one again – foiled every time. He ploughed through all of the delicious photos of Fenders to find, at the back, a Hofner Colorama. It was red. Inspired, he persuaded his dad to put down the deposit on his first purchase. A visit to Selmer's was the turning point (not only that, but Jimmy Page also happened to be in at the time). For 23 guineas Bernie bought a double cutaway Hofner Colorama with chrome-look humbuckers and a Bigsby-type tremolo, and the generous inclusion of a plectrum. A while later he painted the guitar with flowers. Eventually he had the courage to say to his dad: "I need an amp!" "You never said anything about that!" said his surprised dad. Nevertheless, the amp was bought for him. It was a five-watt Scala, with only one input – a selfish choice so that nobody else could use it!

The Bell Music Catalogue

Bernie Marsden and the Hofner Colorama which he painted with flowers, presumably to match the curtains

Martin Barre

Jethro Tull's Martin Barre painfully remembers his early 1960s Birmingham youth. "I used to be a ridiculously shy teenager, totally lacking in the basic rhythm and confidence needed for dancing and thus meeting females. The answer to this problem came when my sister took me to see a local group, Mike Sheridan and The Nightriders.

"The guitarist played a Gibson 345, wore winkle-picker shoes, sported a bunch-of-grapes hairstyle, and had a cigarette permanently lodged in the corner of his mouth, with the ash dangling at an impossible angle. He was completely surrounded by adoring girls! This was it. If I could be like him, I would never have to dance again!

"The solution was hire purchase. With it I bought a red Dallas Tuxedo guitar, a very basic instrument which was, to me, a thing of infinite beauty. It was amplified by a Watkins Dominator. My dream finally materialised when I saw a brand-new Gibson 330 TD in a music shop window. My dad's signature on the credit form (thanks, Dad!) secured the guitar and a Vox AC30 amp. The hairstyle and the winkle pickers I already owned, but I always found it impossible to smoke while playing, and my dancing never improved."

Joan Armatrading

Britain has produced some wonderful female rock musicians in recent years, but in the 1960s, when Joan Armatrading began her long climb to recognition, there were few female guitarists. It was her dad's influence and her mum's selflessness that triggered her love of the instrument. "My father showed me how to tune his guitar, and I still tune it that way now, which is to play a sort of tune on the six open strings. After that he seemed to not want me to play the guitar at all and used to hide it in very strange

Martin Barrie demonstrates his impressive collection: "Watkins Dominator, Fenton Weill 'Solid Special' made by Dallas, acoustic guitar with drastic octave adjustment to bridge, home-made twelve-inch speaker cabinet on coffee table-legs"

LEARNING GUITAR

- Pete Townsend: "When you're learning, it's very difficult to realise that what you're suffering from is a very bad guitar."

- **Evidence of Bert Weedon's continued search for musical knowledge comes from an entry in Ivor Mairants' diary: "Sunday May 3rd 1938. H.M. Weedon (Bert) of 1 Ashland Road, East Ham. E6. £4 for term of six sessions."**

- David Gilmour's parents' gift of a Pete Seeger instructional record and the influence of Bob Dylan and Leadbelly were the catalysts behind his interest in the guitar as he entered his teens.

- **Laurence Juber: "After I took up the guitar I learned to read music almost immediately. I had some lessons and progressed with the aid of Bert Weedon's Play in a Day book. I sat down one day and figured out how to play 'When the Saints Go Marching In' and kept going from there."**

- Noel Redding: "I was at a bus stop going to school, and a lady across the street had something in a brown bag. I asked what. She told me it was a guitar, and revealed to me a normal Spanish-type acoustic. She said that later that day after school she'd show me some chords – which she did!"

- **At the age of 14, Jim Sullivan bought his first acoustic guitar from a pawnshop for £1. Undeterred by the visual impact of its orange boxwood, and the fact that it was incorrectly tuned, he taught himself to play one of the hits of the day, "Zambezi", on the tube journey home between Notting Hill Gate and Hounslow stations.**

- Ron Wood: "Thanks to the efforts of my brothers, Art and Ted, banjo and guitar player Jim Willis, and expert Broonzy-style picker Laurence Sheaff, my early guitar guide took the form of the fretboard with lines and dots drawn to show me how to make basic chord shapes."

- **Mickey Moody's father recognised his son's talent and organised guitar lessons for him with a local teacher, Johnny Griffin, who taught using the Mel Bay method. "It took ages," he says. "It seemed like I learned only one tune a month."**

David Kossoff
May 94

Paul began lessons on guitar when he was eight. His teacher was a widely respected miss Munroe. She taught only classical guitar in very orthodox fashion. A great bond grew between them. She knew that he would not stay 'classical' and knew that his careful training would play its part in whatever field of music he found himself. She was right. At 16 he was backing champion Jack Dupree like a Louisiana blues man!

When Paul, at 11, decided he wanted an electric guitar, he knew which one; where to buy it, and how much it would be. This final piece of information he withheld from his father until they were in Selmers. It was a shock, but Paul had a soft-voiced reasonableness that covered a will of steel. He also knew his father very well; that he was a perfectionist, who liked the best. They were alike. They left with the guitar.

Actor David Kossoff talks with love and humour about his late son, guitar legend Paul Kossoff

- Pino Palladino: "I got interested in music shortly after my sister Andreina started strumming a Spanish guitar in the school folk mass. I was aged 13 or 14 and learned the basic chords and fingerings from a Catholic priest at Bishop Hannon School in Cardiff, named Father Delaney. I then went on to play at the folk masses every Sunday."

- **Brian Odgers bought a ukulele and Bert's Play in a Day, and was surprised and pleased to discover that he could play a G chord with one finger He then bought whatever books were available at the time, such as Ivor Mairants' series, and learned proper chords.**

- Dave Richmond: "At the age of twelve, I started playing ukulele with the help of my father and a 'First Step' tutor book (as seen in the sleeve photo of the debut album by The Faces). My parents then paid for Hawaiian guitar lessons when I was 13, before I graduated to plectrum guitar"
- **When Alan Jones was 13, his carpentry teacher offered to give guitar lessons to anyone interested. Alan and two of his mates applied and soon learned the basics of the instrument and progressed by copying American rock 'n' roll records.**
- B.J. Cole was left-handed, which made him feel insecure and demoralised, but it was Hank Marvin's sound, not country and western, that led him to the steel guitar: "I wanted to sound like Hank, only more so."

Paul Kossoff on acoustic guitar in a double act with his father, actor David Kossoff. In attendance are his mum, Jeannie, and his brother, Simon

places. In fact, when we moved house he forgot to take the guitar with him from his hiding place. I'm sure I developed the craving for it because it was denied me.

"One day I was walking past a pawn shop and in the window I saw a guitar. I thought 'Right, I'll have that.' I went home and told my mum about it and asked her for the £3 to buy it. She said I could have had it if she had the money, but she didn't. Then she said 'I've got your sister and brothers' old prams sitting there doing nothing. Why don't you see if the lady in the shop will have them in exchange for the guitar?' She did. I got my first guitar. I don't know why I developed such a strong rhythmic guitar style, or how, because that guitar was a monster. It had a neck as wide as the body. I still have it, and wonder how I ever managed to play the thing, because I can't play it now."

TUITION

Today, if you should want to play the guitar, as long as you persevere and have innate talent there is theoretically nothing to stop you. The market is almost overloaded with good advice, as never before. There are guitar colleges in many major cities, residential summer courses, freelance teachers, dedicated magazines, improvisation classes, degree courses, tutor books and videos, chord dictionaries, CDs, and even guitars which have fingerboards that light up to guide your fingers to the appropriate scale! The rate of progression in this area has been nothing short of astonishing, and yet 40 years ago the prospect of there being so many and varied aids would have seemed a far-fetched dream.

According to *The Oxford Companion to Music*, the first British guitar tutor was published in 1758. Before the 1950s few people in Britain were motivated to learn to play the guitar, an instrument whose use was mostly restricted to dance bands. The emergence of skiffle and then rock 'n' roll, however, witnessed an explosion of interest in the guitar, and the few professional guitar teachers who were out there suddenly found themselves with too many pupils. To complement one-on-one teaching, a few astute musicians spotted a gap in the market for easy-to-understand tuition books.

Among those guides published in the 1950s and 1960s were Ivor Mairants' tutor, Mel Bay's *Modern Guitar Method*, Shirley Douglas' *The Easy Guide to Rhythm and Blues for Bass Guitar*, and, for advanced players, *Dance Band Chords for the Guitar* by Eric Kershaw, which many skiffle players – including Les Bennetts – preferred above all others.

Bert Weedon

By far the most popular guitar tutor of all time is Bert Weedon's *Play in a Day*. A truly legendary publication, written in 1957, it has been cited by countless top professionals as the book that gave them their first glimpse into what guitar music actually looked like. It has since sold

Bert Weedon's legendary tutor *Play In A Day*

over two million copies, for which Bert was awarded two Golden Pages, the literary equivalent of Gold Discs. Extending his role in education still further, for a while Bert appeared on the children's TV show *Five O'Clock Club*, where he would demonstrate a new chord each week.

When Bert's father bought him his first guitar at the age of 12, in 1933, he searched around for a teacher, of which there were very few, and finally found an elderly man, James Newell, who said he would teach Bert, but only classical guitar. This was a disappointment, but when Newell sat down and played an arrangement of a Chopin prelude it opened a fantastic new world of music to the cockney kid, and right away Bert decided that the study of the guitar would be his life's work.

Bert's contribution to the guitar and the entertainment world – not to mention his enormous influence on a whole generation of guitarists – was honoured in October 1992, when Thames TV dedicated an edition of *This Is Your Life* to him. Among the people paying tribute to Bert were Eric Clapton, Brian May, Hank Marvin, Phil Collins, Adam Faith, Val Doonican, Joe Brown, Lonnie Donegan, Marty Wilde, Frank Bruno, Henry Cooper, Paul Daniels and many other stars from the world of showbiz.

Dave Pegg

Dave Pegg says: "My first influence, really, was good old Bert Weedon. I watched him on TV in black and white, with his big Hofner, and decided I had to have a guitar. Luckily, I had a truly great dad, and I persuaded Albert to part with £5 (probably his week's wages) to buy me a second-hand Rosetti Lucky Seven and Bert's *Play in a Day* from Woodroffe's in Navigation Street, Birmingham. I took them home and spent six weeks trying to tune the thing and dressing my blisters, as the action was half an inch high at the fifth fret."

Mike Hurst

It was 1955. Bill Haley was big news on Radio Luxembourg when, at the age of 13, Mike Hurst received his first guitar, a £4/10/- (£4.50) Framus acoustic, from his mother. Having no idea where to begin, he bought an Ivor Mairants book, which he says utterly confused him: "The real problem was that I didn't know whether to be a lead or rhythm guitarist, because all of the records I heard featured lead-heavy band guitarists," says Mike. "But the problem was solved when Elvis turned up the next year and I found a book quaintly titled *Skif-Rock*. This book showed the simplest way to play chords and I realised that I basically wanted to accompany myself as a singer. Having mastered the necessary three chords – E, A and B7 – I was raring to go."

Phil Chen

Across the ocean in Kingston, Jamaica, in the early 1960s, Phil Chen was burning the midnight oil after borrowing a copy of the Mel Bay chord book. He remembers "staying up many nights drawing the fingerboard and copying the sixth, ninth and thirteenth chords on the empty pages of my geometry book, till the cows jumped over the moon. When the book was confiscated or lost, I would call it my punishment for not addressing my real homework. This crisis I turned into an opportunity because, by the constant writing of the chords, I had remembered them. They were

Dave Pegg aged 15, in his back garden at Acocks Green. Could this really be the future Victor Meldrew impersonator?

ingrained in my brain. My pre-requisite for playing guitar was to harden my fingers, which I did on my way to and from school by finding the longest serrated concrete wall to drag my fingers across. Then I would cut the calluses with razor blades to make them even harder."

All of the theory he had learned from the chord book began to make practical sense when he and his cousin, Colston, attended the band rehearsals of The Vagabonds. "I intently watched the guitarists, Trevor Lopez and Wallace Wilson, and they each gave me pointers on technique, which I was anxious to try out. I remember sometimes hoping that one of them would be a no-show, so that I would have a chance to fill in for them and practice what they had taught me. My passion and ambition made me anxious for opportunity. Finally, after a brief stint with rival group The Mighty Vikings, my dream came true. I was asked to join The Vagabonds as a spare guitarist, bassist and glorified gofer. I was thrilled."

Clem Clempson

When Clem Clempson got his first proper guitar, the first six months of playing were completely wasted because he didn't have a clue how to tune it. "Where I lived in Birmingham the only guy I knew who knew anything about guitar was an Hawaiian guitarist who played at the local working men's club. So I borrowed his books and they showed me how to tune the guitar – the Hawaiian guitar! I spent the first six months learning B.B. King solos with my guitar tuned to an open chord. I knew how chords were made, and what the notes were, so I worked out the chord shapes for myself. Then I got hold of the Bert Weedon tutor, and none of the chord shapes matched up! I sorted out what I was doing wrong, and I had to decide whether to carry on as I was or to start again. I started again and carried on teaching myself."

I was once on a session with Clem at Westside Studios. He was playing mandolin – an instrument I'd never heard him play before – and he sounded great. Because of the acoustic screens between us I could see only his head, so during a tea break I wandered over to have a chat. I noticed to my surprise that on his music stand was not only the music we were playing but also a copy of *How to Play the Mandolin*. He'd never actually played one before – now that's high-order bluffing!

Chris Rae

Chris Rae has been a professional guitar player for over 30 years, and says that he owes his trade to Bert Weedon (whom he has never met) after learning to play from his great book. "You can actually play 'Jingle Bells' in a day!" he observes. This and a fair amount of self-tuition led to Chris turning professional at the age of 17, when he found his first job in a palais (dance hall) band because he was "the only guitar player out of 60 who could read and play 'Moon River' and do a rock solo that sounded like Bert."

Chris Rae in the back garden with his Watkins Rapier. Charlie Watkins recalls: "My brother, Reg Watkins, missed being Britain's first solid electric guitar maker by a day! His Watkins Rapiers were beaten to that particular post in history by Dick Sadlier's Tuxedo Solid. Dick had them produced by Dallas, one of the biggest musical wholesalers of the day, ahead of both Burns and the legendary Grimshaw. The first models were put on sale in 1958"

During one recession, Chris continued to earn a living by harnessing all of his acquired knowledge of guitar technique (Bert and all!), and after placing an ad in *Melody Maker* he began to develop a sideline career as a guitar teacher. "A guy from a college in Hertfordshire telephoned, begging me to take a class of students as their tutor had suddenly left. On the first night I nervously faced my class of 18 students, who mostly had new guitars with strings not tuned to concert pitch. I spent quite a while pulling the strings and tuning these 18 guitars before attempting to start the lesson.

"I directed, 'On the count of four, with your first finger, thumb or plectrum, pluck the thinnest string (the E). The notation looks like this on the blackboard.' I counted four and heard a sound that still haunts me to this very day: 18 guitars all tuned somewhere between C sharp and E. I nearly burst into tears. I now know why the last guitar tutor left. I used to put the pupils of different standards in different rooms and run to them throughout the lessons. I am most pleased to say that one of my ex-pupils is one of the most sought-after insurance consultants in England. He gave up the guitar after only one lesson."

The problems that Chris encountered reminded me that in 1975 I had a call from a friend at Goldsmiths' College, which is part of the University of London. We discussed the idea of starting an adult bass-guitar course, just one afternoon per week. As far as I know this had never been done before in the UK. I like a challenge and agreed to try it for one year. On day one I had a similar experience to Chris: spread out in front of me were 30 eager bass players, with their instruments plugged into their amplifiers – 30 twinkling red lights. I played my bottom string and said: "Here's a low E. Let's start by tuning to this." Suddenly I was transported to World War II, with squadrons of Lancaster bombers passing overhead, their Merlin engines generating low rumbles as their different frequencies clashed with each other. Windows rattled, ornaments fell off shelves, and I might possibly have ducked a little. It was evident that a decision was required: no more amps from now on.

I finished the year, made some good friends, but finally decided to quit, mainly because I was losing money by cancelling session work. I found an excellent replacement – bass player Laurence Canty – who continued the course for another 21 years!

Ray Russell cradling his Burns Guitar at Ronnie Scott's Jazz Club on 13 August 1967. Alan Rushton is on drums

Ray Russell

Ray Russell used to live in a ground-floor flat, above which lived a neighbour who would regularly complain about the noise whenever he practised his guitar in the evening. One night, with his own jazz group, Ray played on the prestigious BBC2 TV show *Late Night Line-up*. A while later the neighbour knocked on his door and pleaded, "I've always wanted to play guitar. Can you teach me?" Ray was confused and asked about the noise problem. "Oh, it's okay. We didn't know you were famous!"

Judd Procter

Whether given by a relative, friend, lodger or formal music teacher, the personal lesson has often been the more practical method of learning to play the guitar. After Judd Procter's mum surprised him by buying him a G-Plectrum banjo he initially had lessons from Ronnie Smith, a coalminer who lived in the local village of Goldthorpe, in Yorkshire, and learned to read from Edwardian song copies while listening to Big Bill Campbell and his Rocky Mountain Pioneers (who were actually British) on the radio. For added inspiration, Judd would seek out live music at the Baths, or the Corn Exchange, especially the Len Boote Doncaster Municipal Dance Orchestra. He noticed the rhythm guitarist playing four in the bar (comping), and that he played Hawaiian lap steel guitar. His interest was fired.

Judd bought a Resonator guitar for £10, but the action was so hard his fingers bled. Persevering, he ordered Ivor Mairants' transcribed guitar solos, after seeing a *BMG* (*Banjos, Mandolins & Guitars*) magazine ad, and took private lessons from Len Boote's guitarist. A guitar was a very unusual sight in Yorkshire, and as he carried around the shaped cardboard case people would call out, mistaking it for a cello, a banjo or even a shovel! He diligently worked through a chord book, and although there wasn't as much real literature around like there is today he felt driven. Understandably, for the time, his dad was insistent that he learned Hawaiian style, but Judd couldn't face it.

Bryan Daly

Bryan Daly's mother had already bought him a guitar, and at the age of 14 he was given private lessons by local musician Ray Webb, who insisted on taking no payment. "When the chance came later I started to pursue the classical guitar, taking lessons from an old Russian medical doctor, Dr Perot, founder of the Philharmonic Guitar Society. Through this deceptively small organisation I progressed and started at last to meet other players. We gave small concerts and played to the other devotees. I came to meet Len Williams and his son, the now famous guitarist John Williams, with whom I still keep in touch."

John McLaughlin

The piano has always been a useful instrument upon which to obtain a grounding in music theory, which can then be adapted to any other instrument. As an eight-year-old boy, John McLaughlin asked his mother, an amateur violinist, if he could take piano lessons. His wish was granted, although John remembers that "I had this dragon of a piano teacher." His new-found knowledge wasn't wasted, however; through playing the piano he developed an ear for music, and was later influenced by Mississippi blues, flamenco and jazz. "The greatest thing about my school was my music teacher, who taught classical but also encouraged us through his love of all music."

Bryan Daly, aged 20, dreaming of the Wigmore Hall but apparently sitting in a fireplace

Andy Fraser

Unlike John, who took a genuine interest, music was virtually forced into Andy Fraser's lap at the age of five, when he began studying classical piano. He did so until he was about 11, and took all his Royal Society of Music grade exams, but it felt like extra homework. "I could play Beethoven like a parrot, but had no real feeling for it," he remembers. After hearing The Shadows and other rock 'n' roll bands on the radio, a sudden act of rebellion saw Andy buying a guitar and quitting his piano lessons, even though it soon occurred to him how useful they had been. "I was quite surprised to discover how much music I actually knew – I just had to figure out where the notes were and then transpose the ideas."

Alan Parker

Alan Parker studied with local teacher Charles Johnson for around four years, and it was through Charles' input that he eventually obtained scholarships with *BMG* magazine, which led to competitions held at the Wigmore Hall and the Festival Hall in London. At one of these events, one of the adjudicators was the classical guitarist Julian Bream, who approached Alan afterwards, and told him "I don't teach as such, but if you wish for some extra coaxing and help in your studies, come around." Alan learned much from this hand-holding, but at the age of 15 he left school and took a job as a book-keeper. What he really wanted, however, was to be a professional musician. Through conversations with Julian he had realised that there was little work in the classical field, so he investigated the transition to the electric guitar.

Bernie Holland

When Bernie Holland was about six he loved to listen to his elder brother playing George Formby rhythm patterns on his ukulele. He was even more thrilled when his brother showed him how to play a few simple two-finger chords, and he soon immersed himself in skiffle music: "That's what got me going." Bernie graduated to a six-string steel-strung guitar, and was partly taught by a friend of his father. However, he also admits his recourse to "that classic of tutors, Bert Weedon's *Play in a Day*. I worked my way right through it."

Allan Holdsworth

For those who couldn't afford private lessons, had no access to free training, or were put off by the formality of tuition, the only way to learn was through the process of teaching themselves. Allan Holdsworth tried for a while to study from one of Ivor Mairants' tutors, but "I could never get on with books. I always found myself dissatisfied with my progress. I preferred to find my own way."

Alan Parker proudly displays his prizes and his Martin Colette

Gary Moore

Gary Moore started purely as a result of listening to The Shadows. "From the word go I was never interested in playing rhythm guitar. I always wanted to be a lead guitarist; that was my big thing." He recalls trying to learn his first tune: The Shadows' "Wonderful Land". "I wanted to play it on only the top E and B strings. By de-tuning the B through several stages I finally got to the point where I could play it." He eventually got around to taking lessons, however, and his teacher, amazed by the route his pupil had taken, showed him how to tune the guitar properly.

Tim Renwick

An undercover operation was required by Tim Renwick when he began learning. "I began to learn how to play the guitar on a plastic instrument, ukulele style, with four strings. Unfortunately, it bore the likeness of that lovable icon Mickey Mouse, which meant that I had to practise in bed under the sheets so that no one would know, not even my brother, to hide my potential embarrassment! When I finally stood in for a local band in a talent competition and we won, my friends were amazed to note that I'd only had a real guitar for two weeks!" Little did they know that Tim had been practising under the sheets for several weeks, playing and listening to Radio Luxembourg way into the night.

Joan Armatrading

Joan Armatrading's musical awareness began through having a piano in her family home. Her mum and dad arranged private tuition for her, which sadly came to a premature halt when her teacher died after only one lesson, and it was then that she took up the guitar. "I would just make things up. I never sang other people's songs; I started straight in with my own compositions. I was always a loner, working by myself, knowing that songs had a bass and drums and piano under the vocals, and that's what I tried to do on the guitar. I tried to play everything all at once while I sang the song. That's how my style developed, but when it was time for my first album, in 1972, I was in everybody's way with my playing. I had to work out a way of keeping my style but allowing room for the other players."

Phil Hilborne

With his trusty Gibson SG copy, Phil Hilborne would sit for hours on end trying to work guitar parts out from records. His mum, who was for many years a professional pianist, thought that this was a long-winded method and asked him why he didn't just go to the music shop and buy the sheet music. Theoretically this would seem to be a helpful suggestion, but as Phil explains it wasn't that simple: "Most of the blues, rock, and pop sheet music that was around in the early 1970s was very inaccurate, and was mainly piano arrangements that had a few arbitrary chord diagrams stuck on more or less as an afterthought. With hindsight I can clearly remember seeing songs written in keys that were actually disastrously wrong – for instance, Deep Purple's 'Smoke on the Water' in A flat, and even The Beatles' 'Day Tripper' in F [a guitarist's nightmare!]."

The pitfalls of sheet-music negotiation made Phil Hilborne – now the music editor of *Guitar Techniques* magazine – even more keen to listen to his favourite music and work out the parts for himself. "As I could read and write music it seemed like a good idea to keep a record and jot it all down, but I mistakenly thought that this was what everyone did! Little did I realise that I was actually giving myself an apprenticeship for my later career as a guitar teacher, music-book author, magazine contributor, music editor, and transcriber."

Geoff Whitehorn

It was a problem that also affected Geoff Whitehorn and thousands of other frustrated guitarists. "At school we used to swap sheet music of the hits of the day, which was never much use because they were usually transcribed by piano players into the wrong key. You try playing 'Apache' in B flat minor!"

Joan Armatrading, Ovation guitar, and front-door key

Geoff Whitehorn recalls: "When I was aged fourteen, in 1965, the singer of our group, The Sunbeats, used to use a Kent County Council Record Player to sing through, so needless to say he could never be heard, which was just probably just as well. We also used to borrow the record player from our school with fervent promises to return it every following Monday. We were very good with matchsticks and silver paper in those days – note our interesting power arrangement with an unplugged heater. Notice also the Watkins Dominator amp with two ten-inch speakers and 17 watts - oh the thrill of all that power! It was all very well but the bass, the rhythm guitar, and I were all plugged into it"

BAND PRACTICE

Ronnie Caryl

Imagine the scene: the Strand Theatre on the opening night of *Good Rockin' Tonite*, a show about the life of Jack Good, the original producer of legendary TV shows *Oh Boy*, *6.5 Special*, and the US show *Shindig*. Ronnie Caryl had made a speech in front of a thrilled audience and sung "Born to Rock and Roll', the big-ballad reprise, when Jack rose to the occasion and invited Cliff Richard, Marty Wilde, Don Lang, Joe Brown, Lonnie Donegan and other 1950s luminaries onto the stage.

Ronnie says: "The curtain came down. Lonnie rushed over to me and said 'You were great, played great, sang great, just great.' I said 'Thanks a lot, but we've met before. Do you remember coming to a house in Hounslow, where I was rehearsing

As far as the sheet music of The Beatles was concerned, the fault lay with an ageing jazz musician on the top floor at Dick James Music, who would listen to an advance tape or acetate of a new record by the group just before it was released and use his jazz expertise to estimate which chords were used. These chords – often in the horn-friendly keys of Bb or Eb – were often a far remove from what actually featured on the records, and the problem wasn't fully addressed until the late 1980s, when the entire Beatles canon was re-transcribed by someone younger and more guitar-friendly.

Peter Watkins

Back in Brewood, it was during Peter Watkins' ownership of his black f-hole guitar that he changed schools and met the fellow who was to change his life: his mentor, Richard Hallchurch. "I had previously been under the impression that the guitar should be tuned to an open E chord, in spite of my dad's insistence that 'that's not what it says in the book'. Richard actually persuaded me that my dad was right, and taught me two chords: C and G7. I remember it was a Sunday evening when I sat down, determined to master these chords. I played them alternately, and soon began to hear in my head several tunes to which they would fit. The seeds of playing by ear were sown. More chords followed, and by the time "Apache" came out I was ready, although the F chord was hard to master."

Brian Chatton on keyboards, Flash on guitar, Ronnie Caryl (unusally) on bass, and a very young Phil Collins on drums – this was Flaming Youth being filmed in Trafalgar Square

Hugh Burns (l) in his band, The Tearways

with a drummer in the front room? My Levin was plugged via a Fuzz-Face into a one-input Wallace amp, which was powered from a light socket, while the drummer had an extra bass drum to make up for the lack of a bass player. You came in and said to me 'You are nothing without your volume,' and, to the drummer, 'If you can't play a paradiddle – a snare drum rudiment – you'll never get anywhere.' Well, that drummer was Phil Collins, then 15, and the guitarist was me! That's showbiz!"

Whereas acoustically designed rehearsal complexes have now sprung up all over the country, offering professional-quality facilities such as 24-channel PA mixers, monitoring and a full range of excellent microphones, all at rates affordable to young bands, most of my generation got our acts together in bedrooms, living rooms, and even pigeon lofts.

Ron Wood

Ron Wood was eight years old when his elder brothers needed a space to practice their music and entertain art-school friends. His parents had set aside their downstairs back room next to the kitchen, which had a door connecting the two. To provide privacy this door was bricked in, and the only way in was from the front hall, at the foot of the stairs. Uncle Fred made a small hatch from the kitchen just big enough for food and drink to be passed through. "This room was my first introduction to having free access – when everyone was out – to a showcase of instruments, such as drums, woodblocks, tea-chest bass, kazoo, comb and paper, cornet, clarinet, harmonicas, banjo, guitars, and trombone and, when all the art-school crowd came in, to observe girls and listen to live music, plus take part in their early tape-recorded 'mad' comic shows and plays. It was a magnificent spur to learning to play something – any instrument would do, just as long as you could bluff it enough to gain their respect. Being so young, making some sort of contribution made you less of a pain in the neck to the art-school crowd."

Hugh Burns

Rehearsals with Hugh Burns' first band centred around discussions about how they could plug their two guitars, bass and vocals into the same amplifier. Since the bass control was clearly for the bass guitar (or so they thought), and the treble clearly for the lead guitar, their solution was both simple and elegant: all of the controls should be on full, so that everyone was covered! Hugh says: "The lack of inputs was solved by instigating a rota basis, where firstly bass and vocals played in glorious 'sound around', with the two guitars unamplified. We refined this rehearsal method even further with the discovery that, if you positioned a table at a right angle to a door and placed the edge of the guitar body on the table with the end-pin against the door, this increased the volume and resonance of the guitar by at least one watt!

"Apart from the usual round of bedrooms and kitchens as rehearsal rooms, one memorable day was spent in the bass player's father's back garden pigeon loft – or 'doocot', as it is known in Scots. The group set up in a straight line in this long, narrow building, and looked out at eye level through the slit at the front where the birds landed."

Andy Fairweather-Low

Welshman Andy Fairweather-Low's first band was The Firebrands. "Our drummer was in the Boys' Brigade, so everything tended to have a military feel about it: 'Hey, Bo Diddley – left, right, left, right.' Our first rehearsal was in the front room of a terraced house with a sturdy Watkins Dominator amp doing the necessary for guitar and bass. I moved on quickly to another band, The Taffbeats, who later became The Sect Maniacs (Cardiff's gift to lonely women). Sometimes I wonder about my mental state at that time, but a band must have a name. I auditioned for The Taffbeats in the guitarist's house, this time playing through his Bird amplifier, which I later used, and I've never seen another one to this day."

Paul Rodgers

Paul Rodgers recalls: "There was a local band, a class band, and eligibility was assured by owning a guitar – you didn't have to be able to play it or anything! Well, I happened to have a twelve-string acoustic. I couldn't play it, but it made me eligible to join the class band. We did horrible things like 'If I Had a Hammer'. Mickey Moody was in that band, and we used to practice at his house and drive his parents nuts. I then decided that bass would be easier to play, because it only had four strings, so somebody brought along a bass. It wasn't any easier to play, actually, but I enjoyed it. And then one day we finally got a PA system – a microphone, some speakers and an amp."

Richard Thompson

Following a brief flirtation with the obligatory tennis racquets, Richard Thompson and his friend Malcolm graduated to playing Shadows' numbers at first on Spanish guitars, and then finally on electrics. "We then got guitar straps – it's easier to do the Shadwalk with guitar straps – and I teamed up with bass and drums from his school chums at St Aloysius in Highgate, and then rehearsed every Sunday for about two years. The bass player's house was our favourite because his mum, being Polish, supplied amazing cream cakes. We'd rehearse for about an hour, and then try to think up a group name for the next four hours. I had a group at school after that with Hugh Cornwell [the future Strangler], and we rehearsed in the Mormon church in Archway for free in exchange for playing and opening for the puppet show at their annual dance!"

Steve Marriott

Shortly before his untimely death, Steve Marriott described The Small Faces as the band that was formed with the intention of fronting mod culture in the mid 1960s. "We got pilled up and bounced off the walls of nightclubs, high as kites! Then the music started becoming more important. I jammed with Ronnie Lane's band at some gaff just south of the river [Thames], and I probably ruined the night for them, but then we decided to form the band and it was a time of great excitement. We got our act together, rehearsing in the Ruskin [the Ruskin Arms pub in Manor Park], and the fact that we became successful was a bit of surprise to us because we were only in it for a laugh and the birds!"

L-r: Mickey Moody playing a Harmony ("It had switches like those on a hairdryer"), Colin Bradley supporting a Hofner Verithin, and Paul Rodgers attempting to play a Vox bass (he's much better singer)

Andy Fairweather-Low looking cool with his Bird amplifier

CHAPTER 5

THE FIRST EXPERIMENTS

DIY

Vic Flick

Vic Flick's musical interests began at the age of seven, on the guitar rather than on piano, on which he achieved about grade eight status. Looking for a change of direction he played banjo for a while, but at around the age of 14 he swapped it for an obscure Gibson round-hole Kalamazoo guitar to enable him to take part in a dance band. In an attempt at amplification, an army-surplus throat mic was strapped to the machine-head, where the resonance was most prominent. "The resultant freaky tone was then shoved through the aux input of my father's Mullard 'The World through Your Speaker' radio. It helped, but I eventually spent all of my savings on a Hofner President."

War surplus Throat Mic

Jim Cregan

The main source of entertainment in Jim Cregan's family home was the wireless. Theirs was a vintage specimen that sat in the living room on a table near the open fireplace. It was the size of a small wooden suitcase, with two doughnut-shaped knobs on either side of a glass window that listed exotic faraway places like Hilversum and Antwerp. The cloth speaker grille resembled a large watermelon, and at first was very impressive; but as time and grubby fingers took their toll, the real dimensions of the speaker were revealed: it was the size of a grapefruit.

"Somewhere in the garden shed I found some bakelite headphones, undoubtedly stolen from the military by persons unknown," says Jim. "I discovered, in my curious schoolboy way, that if I plugged them in the back of the radio and shouted into them I had the makings of a primitive microphone and amplifier. Armed with a roll of sticky tape and my £3/10/- (£3.50) acoustic guitar, I taped one of the earphones solidly onto the inside of the guitar and played a very shabby version of 'Shakin' All Over' by Johnny Kidd and The Pirates. It worked! My joy was complete. I now had an electric guitar. Little did I know that I had taken the first step on the never-ending slippery slope of musical equipment.

"All was well until my family wanted to listen to *Round the Horne* or *The Billy Cotton Band Show*, and I had annexed the radio for some serious Duane Eddy practice, or working out the intricacies of 'FBI'."

Gerry Rafferty

Up in Glasgow, Gerry Rafferty and his pals clubbed together to buy a communal guitar after reading a newspaper advertisement sent in by a guy who was emigrating and selling anything that would raise instant cash. "The item in question was a well-scuffed f-hole semi-acoustic job, with the legend 'Big Timer' emblazoned on the head and an action set high enough to induce repetitive strain injury; but it was ours, and in one fell swoop we were up there with Chuck Berry, Chet Atkins, Gene Vincent and the rest. I had an acquaintance of mine build a pickup with an enormous volume control, probably salvaged from a wireless, then we acquired – on the cheap – an ageing Selmer amp with two inputs and a solid-body bass guitar of an uncertain provenance. In short, we were in business."

Alan Murphy

Obsessed with The Rolling Stones, Alan Murphy attempted to emulate their instruments by taking his odd-shaped sunburst Futurama, sawing the points off, sanding the body and painting it lilac. This whole process took three weeks.

The result? "The finish was disgusting and grainy, like wood filler." Initially, this transformed instrument was played through his home radio, but Alan made the remarkable discovery that if a transistor from his box of components was inserted between the amp and the speaker, the unit became an appreciable fuzzbox! Eventually this had to go, and was replaced by a Selmer Treble and Bass 50.

Ritchie Blackmore

Ritchie Blackmore's acoustic guitar obviously didn't have any pickups, but for his next birthday he received one, which he then attached to the guitar. His immediate problem was how to amplify it. "My dad had an old Sobel radio in the house. I plugged in my guitar and it became electric. I could just hear the strings resonating through the speaker. Two watts of power – this was it! I could rule the world."

John Paul Jones

John Paul Jones had earlier been experimenting with electrifying instruments, and his first attempt involved the banjo-ukulele that his father had used in his Vaudeville days. "I had acquired a telephone operator's headset, and jammed the microphone under the vellum. Hank B. it wasn't, but I had caught the bug. My next instrument was a pink plastic toy guitar that I fitted with magnet and coil. I was getting closer."

Colin Green

Colin Green's dad, who was killed in World War II before his son was born, had left a ukulele lying around the house, and occasionally Colin would idly strum a few chords on it. Later, when he discovered his dad's old plywood guitar, he was off and nothing could hold him back. Colin instinctively knew how to tune the instrument without any guidance, and to expand his knowledge he learned a few more chords from an Ivor Mairants book.

To make the guitar more slimline he removed the back, cut away half the width of the body, and then replaced the back. Even a cutaway was engineered, and he covered the guitar in white melamine. A grammar-school boffin friend wired a pickup by hand and fitted it diagonally in the round hole, even though the string spacing was hopeless. They plugged it into a Dansette record player and, to their amazement, it worked.

Brian May

Skiffle was Brian May's early passion, and in his first bands at school in Middlesex he played an old acoustic with a pickup that he had made himself. "The main thing that I remember about equipment, in the days when I was starting to play guitar, was that I couldn't afford any of it. I managed to figure out how to wind some wire around some Eclipse magnets and strap the thing onto an acoustic guitar, and this was my entry ticket to the (very illegal!) guitar club at Hampton Grammar School. It's strange why rock 'n' roll was so totally frowned upon in this school, and yet the place managed to spawn such musicians as Paul Samwell-Smith and Jim McCarty of The Yardbirds, Murray Head, and also yours truly, a boy who even in those days dreamed of those Queen-like guitar harmonies."

Colin Green playing a Harmony Sovereign in 1962. Colin notes "very correct hand positions, short hair, regulation one inch of ash on the cigarette, and a tie – all very rock 'n' roll!"

Mike Jopp

Mike Jopp: "My dad gave me an old acoustic guitar, which he had owned for many years. It was a flat top that had suffered years of abuse, having been lying around the house without a case, and it had a crack all around one side caused by leaving it out in the garden overnight. This guitar had seen some life!"

Mike had no idea that his dad's old guitar was anything special. "It was so warped that the action was very high, and as my playing matured I began to find this a limitation. I worked out a brilliant way of improving this action by fitting a tailpiece and drilling holes in the top so that the strings threaded under the fixed bridge and came out onto the top. This sorted the action but completely fucked up the scale length and intonation.

"After a while I realised that it needed a proper repair, and took it to Harry Webber, who owned King Street Music Stores in Chiswick. He immediately identified the guitar as a Martin, information which, at the time, meant nothing to me. Harry found a violin repairer who fixed it up and was keen to buy it. It was now beginning to dawn on me that this guitar was a bit special. Over the next two months I found out more about Martin guitars, and wrote to the company describing my model. In due course I had a letter back from Mike Longworth, identifying it as a 1930 OM28, an extremely rare and desirable model with herringbone inlay and Grover banjo-type tuners.

"When I think of all the abuse my dad and I heaped on this guitar, even leaving it out in the garden overnight, it's amazing that it survived. I was only twelve when I started repairing it with a drill! Over the years I've used the guitar a lot, and studio engineers always remark on how well it records. If only they knew!"

HOME-MADE GUITARS

The attraction of rock 'n' roll led to Britain's youth taking desperate measures as they sought to own the types of guitars they saw their new heroes playing on TV. Good guitars were often prohibitively expensive, but those who possessed construction skills and/or helpful parents were in some cases able to produce an approximation of the real thing. Sometimes the results were disastrous, whereas the efforts of Brian May and his dad led to a legendary instrument which was crucial to the Queen sound and, more than 40 years after its creation, remains an icon of British rock.

Brian May

Brian, noteworthy for his use of old silver sixpences as picks, says: "I drooled over John Garnham's gleaming Hofner Colorama and his Watkins Copicat echo chamber, coveted Woolly Hammerton's V3 – cherry red with a chrome tremolo arm – and spent hours poring over catalogues which showed us the Fender Stratocasters, Telecasters, Gibson Les Pauls, and such like, which we all played only in our dreams. But not being able to afford all this stuff was, I guess, the main impetus behind my dad and I deciding to make a guitar." The neck was part of an old fireplace that was lying around a friend's house, while the rest of the body was blockboard glued and screwed to oak. "It took us two years of spare time, but at the end of it we had something which incorporated features, some of which have only recently been absorbed into the mainstream of guitar-making. We tried lots of experiments with truss rods and tensioning, and I spent a long while on the calculations involved. My strong subject at school was maths, and I had got to know quite a bit about acoustics, so I deliberately set about designing the body to give me the feedback I wanted.

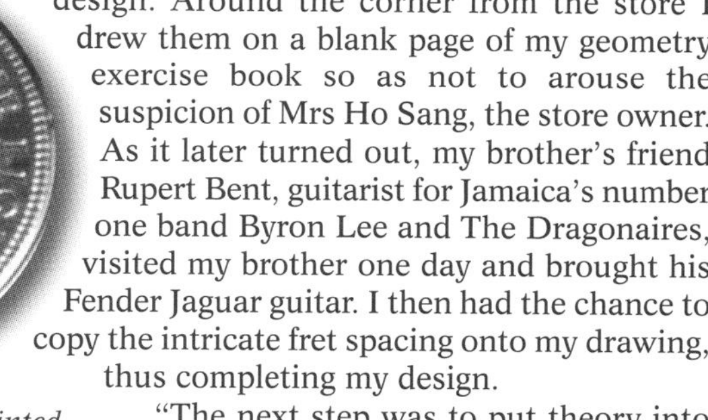

Brian May uses specially-minted reproduction sixpenny pieces for his plectrums

"I built the guitar with small acoustic pockets in it, and rigidly mounted the pickups to the body so that the whole thing interacted with the air. Originally I made the pickups myself, but found that they were too uneven in their response, so I bought some Burns Tri-Sonics and rewound them to get the sound I wanted. We designed a knife-edge tremolo unit with almost no friction, I fashioned a system of rollers for the bridge which could be adjusted in position for intonation, and we designed our own system of switching to give a wider range of sounds than anything else out there. By some miracle the guitar even survived being beaten to death all around the world several times, as I toured with Queen, and now with The Brian May Band. Still, it hangs in there, and looks like it will just about see me out!"

Phil Chen

Years before Phil Chen became the "Bruce Lee of the bass", he also turned his hand to making his own first guitar in his home town of Kingston, Jamaica. Music was always a part of Phil's life, and his daydreaming of a future career would often give his school teachers cause to reprimand him. He remembers receiving a demerit in geometry for playing the banjo on his geometry set with a rubber band! "At every opportunity I would look for an excuse to get out of school so that I could go to Music Mart, the only music store in Kingston, to be mesmerised by the Fender Jaguar guitar so graciously showcased there. I couldn't afford to buy it, but I memorised the minute details of its design. Around the corner from the store I drew them on a blank page of my geometry exercise book so as not to arouse the suspicion of Mrs Ho Sang, the store owner. As it later turned out, my brother's friend Rupert Bent, guitarist for Jamaica's number one band Byron Lee and The Dragonaires, visited my brother one day and brought his Fender Jaguar guitar. I then had the chance to copy the intricate fret spacing onto my drawing, thus completing my design.

"The next step was to put theory into practice and build the guitar. My mother took me to see Uncle Luther [Alfred] Chen

Brian May and his pal Tim Staffell gigging in 1965

Phil Chen, the Bruce Lee of the bass, with his gorgeous Fender amp

at his furniture shop to ask if he could help. At the time he didn't have any extra wood, but after six weeks of helping him and clearing up the shop he gave me some that was left over from one of his customer's orders. I look back in appreciation to that customer and my uncle, since they so generously provided me with the wood for my first guitar. I bless them and am very grateful.

"The body was spray-painted by a friend of a friend whose day off at the body shop was a great welcome. I had to wait to get the right colour, depending on what was left over from the last paint job. With the help of my friend and mentor, a tall dark guitar and bass player of Arawak Indian descent from the Rainbow Club next door who rode a shiny motorcycle and sported a neatly Brylcreemed hairstyle, I made the pickup. Together we would rewire the magnets from an old bicycle generator, and for frets we used the excess clothes line from a neighbour's yard on Eastwood Park Road. We worked so hard beating the hell out of it to get it to fit the delicate, precise grooves of the fingerboard. No detail was overlooked. The scratchplate came from kitchen countertop off-cuts found at the nearest construction site, while the shiny metal hand-rest was neatly salvaged from the chrome bread toaster at my uncle's KG Records shop."

Phil's imagination excelled itself when it came to guitar picks. "I requested tubs of Creamo ice cream, which mounted up uneaten and topless in the freezer, so that I could obtain the plastic container tops which I used to produce the choicest handmade plectrums. Selling them gave me a small source of income on the side to finance strings. (John McLaughlin once took home a plastic Pure Wool logo window display and cut it up to make his own plectrums.) The strings, tuning pegs and tail piece were ordered while we wired our own circuits with 250K log pots. For an amp, my brother Pat and cousin Colston would modify salvaged amps from jukeboxes for their great bottom end, and with the KT88 or 6550 tubes (valves) glowing at us we would plug into our home-made 30-watt Celestion plyboard enclosure and pretend to be The Beatles.

"While the older teens were chasing the girls of their dreams, I was sleeping with mine. B.B. King called his 'Lucille'. Secretly, I had named my shapely creation 'Ursula', after the stunning actress from the James Bond movie *Dr No*, which had been filmed in Jamaica. In one scene, Ursula Andress was filmed on the beach collecting sea shells. This was the same beach where I would play and swim almost every weekend while growing up."

Phil Palmer

Inspired by his uncles, Ray and Dave Davies of The Kinks, Phil Palmer took up the guitar. He had to have a Flying V, so he built one himself in 1967, at the age of 15. "My custom Flying V was made from an old wardrobe door – solid mahogany, I think – with two pieces glued like a sandwich, roughly cut out and then sanded down by hand. The neck was from a Vox Phantom (horrid) and electrics and pickups from a Harmony Roy Smeck model, which was later re-assembled and which I still have. It sounded alright through that lovely old AC30, but it was really a piece of shit, a bitch to play and tune and it weighed a fucking ton! Hence the lower back problems now." Phil nevertheless loved playing it, and a little later his Uncle Ray brought him back an extremely rare Fender No-Caster from America – one of only a limited number of transitional models between the Broadcaster and Telecaster. No-Casters were made for just a few months in 1951, and were so called because there was no name printed on the headstock.

Phil Palmer in 1967, at the age of 15, with his incredibly heavy home-made Flying V. "As you can see the audience was on its foot!"

Clem Clempson

Clem Clempson studied classical piano from the age of five, and by the time he was 15 he had progressed as far as he could go without actually going to the Royal College of Music, but he was not yet old enough to leave school. However, it was his earlier passion for the guitar which had begun to occupy his imagination. "At this time I was always building guitars from bits of wood, with rubber bands for strings, stretched between nails." Then came the big day: he sold his train set to pay for a £5 acoustic, and to make it look more 'electric' he cut a piece of plastic for a scratchplate that covered the hole. He eventually added a £2/10/- (£2.50) Hofner pickup, which he plugged into his home radio. Frustratingly he found it very hard to play, but didn't realise that it was the guitar that was at fault. "I cried when I couldn't play Chuck Berry riffs at the fifth fret."

BJ Cole in 1964 with his first Fender 1000 pedal steel

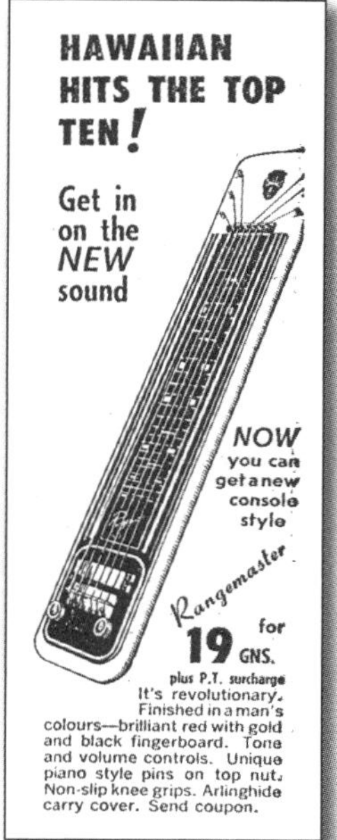

BJ was an avid denizen of Charing Cross Road, and on one occasion he spied a Dallas Rangemaster lap steel (a man's colour? knee grips?), which was basically a red plank with fittings and strings. He sold his Scalextric set and bought the Dallas, along with a ten watt Selmer Truvoice amp, but was confused at first and played with the steel between the fretmarks

B.J. Cole

B.J. Cole's dad, who played guitar and mandolin, made his son a solid guitar body from the back of a piano, while the neck was constructed from the various struts and the frets copied roughly from a Fender Stratocaster. When finished and varnished, its image was futuristic, with long pointy horns – a vision of half reality and half fantasy.

Mick Grabham

Mick Grabham built his first guitar as a copy of a Gibson 335, or rather, as a young lad's impression of this instrument obtained from pictures of Joe Brown. It featured a mahogany neck, frets measured from information in a library book, and a Hofner pickup with a little thumb-wheel volume pot. The socket on the instrument was co-axial, similar to a TV aerial connection. His dad's friend expertly french-polished the neck and painted the body bright red.

Martin Kershaw

As a kid with a musician father, Martin Kershaw remembers being surrounded by myriad bits of dismembered banjos and ukuleles. He was fascinated by these parts, and began assembling them into workable instruments by adding pegs and strings, made from braided fishing line. He practised in the school changing room because of the echo. His first proper guitar was a hand-built Abbot Victor, an acoustic which featured a bent neck and pickup made from the cockpit mic of a German aircraft.

Adrian Legg

Adrian Legg, guitar maestro extraordinaire and author of *Customising Your Electric Guitar* (Amsco, USA), is a source of sage advice and information on guitar "technicalia" for both acoustic and electric guitars because of his own ceaseless experimentation and innovation with the instrument. He is pictured in his photo at a tender age with one of his early creations, "experimental planks", which embody his adolescent rebellion against both profound parental disapproval of the guitar and compulsory

This photograph circa 1961 features Martin Kershaw (far right) playing in the Dennis Langfield orchestra dance band in Burnley. Dennis lent Martin the money to buy a Gibson Barney Kessel – he paid it back at £1 per week. Note the crest above the drummer

Adrian Legg, playing an instrument of his own design

oboe lessons. These instruments were essentially string billets with frets; the bodies were purely incidental and probably pioneered the straight-through-the-body neck. Certainly Adrian used it again when designing the Vox guitars of the early 1980s. The scale lengths of various early attempts were lifted from other guitars and basses with the aid of a ruler and a biro, and frets were hammered straight into the neck. Adrian added three or four strings, home-made tailpieces and contact pickups (such as record player cartridges) plundered from a variety of unlikely sources – including junk shops – in his efforts to get closer to the desired twang. Occasionally, the thumbscrew button mountings used to retain the anti-macassars on coaches were pressed into service as string anchors.

The pictured example is a "thru-neck" model, made of nato (*palaquium luzoniensis*) filched from school woodwork shop bins. (Nato is a general utility timber mainly used by Filipino and Chinese cabinet-makers for manufacturing the sides of drawers. It's also said to be rarely attacked by beetles.) It's a four-string guitar, probably with a magnetic pickup acquired in a later phase of technological progress (i.e., swapped for something), and probably tuned with the bottom string at C and string intervals rising in fourths.

The biggest problem Adrian and his contemporaries faced at that time was the necessity of tuning some strings with pliers, because of the regular failure of plastic machine-head buttons. The overall pitch of a piano-less gathering of string neophytes would frequently be dictated by the player with the worst machine-heads and no pliers, and sessions with the piano required a preparatory trip to the tool shed.

Adrian eventually hit the big time with the arrival, via mail order, of an El Chico, a very cheap Eastern European six-string plywood acoustic horror made from banana crate and plywood, and a copy of the sheet music of Duane Eddy's "Shazam". He is now one of the most innovative and exciting guitar soloists ever to come out of Britain, and his continuing tinkerer's urge makes him a regular collaborator with the Ovation R&D department in Connecticut.

John Etheridge

Success as a luthier-by-necessity didn't come to everyone. In 1962, John Etheridge and his brother Hugh built a guitar that was meant to be a round-hole acoustic Stratocaster. When it was completed they fitted the strings, but to their immense frustration the neck bent to a right angle.

Allan Holdsworth

The purchase of a 10/- (50p) nylon-strung Spanish guitar from his uncle inspired Allan Holdsworth to make his own guitar. Unfortunately, this was not a happy event, as he could never get the frets in the right place, and when he did they tended to rip his fingers to pieces. Sensing Allan's dedication and desperation, his dad bought him a Hofner President f-hole acoustic, to which Allan added a Hofner pickup and a scratchplate. His first amp was a copy of a 15-watt Selmer made by his dad's friend.

The acoustic Strat built by John Etheridge and his brother Hugh in 1962

Allan Holldsworth at home with his Hofner guitar and Dulci amplifier

Chris Spedding playing with Pete Brown's Battered Ornaments in Trafalgar Square, 1968

Chris Spedding

Chris Spedding's pocket money didn't stretch to a brand-new, ready-made guitar, and the second-hand market was at that time almost non-existent, but on scanning the ads at the back of the paper one day he found the answer to his problem. "For only a few shillings I could send away for a 'Make Your Own Guitar Kit'. Now, my handicraft skills are nil, and I was very impatient to get the strings on and get to playing this bizarre plywood monstrosity I'd created, but I never got to play this – my first guitar – because, as soon as I tried to put the first string on and bring it up to tension, the whole sorry thing collapsed. I hadn't had the patience to wait for the glue to dry. I was heartbroken."

Ray Fenwick

Ray Fenwick once had a schoolfriend who, with seemingly mystical powers, had made a guitar. He would visit his friend's house and stare at this guitar as if it were pornography. As a result of this experience he plagued his dad to help him to make a guitar of his own. They started construction, but their enthusiasm was tempered by ignorance. The neck was a broom stick cut in half.

"It needs frets," Ray observed.

"How many?" enquired Dad.

"Oh, about 20."

"Where?"

"Just make them closer together as it gets higher," said Ray, displaying a weak knowledge of the luthier's art.

The instrument featured an old Selmer pickup with dangling wires. A while later, his mum bought him a nylon-strung acoustic, but even with this sophistication he could still only play the chords of E and C. For Christmas that year, however, Ray received a blue Hofner Colorama (valued at 18 guineas), which he played through a succession of Linear and Elpico amps, and a five-watt Selmer Little Giant.

Much later, on an early rock 'n' roll package tour, the Vox AC30 Ray had progressed to broke down. A roadie dismantled it and then reassembled it, but with a few parts left over. "Aren't those important?" asked Ray, pointing at the stranded components. "Nah, those parts are moody, man!"

Jeff Beck

Failure is not a word that can be associated with Jeff Beck's guitar skills, but his early attempts at creating a playable home-made instrument were another matter. Jeff's dad wanted him to play a "proper" instrument, like the piano, but Jeff had a fascination from an early age for the shape and sound of the guitar. His initial construction endeavours involved lots of cigar boxes for a body and a piece of unsanded fence moulding for a neck. The nuts and bolts that joined the two had no washer and subsequently sank into the wood. The strings were aircraft control line wire, single or double strand as required. And the frets? They were painted on! (Could this have been a fretless guitar?)

More experiments followed. Jeff designed a guitar body which he had meticulously cut by hand from very thick wood. Unfortunately, when he built the neck his measurements were taken from memory, and worse, from those of a bass guitar. "The scale was so bad that it was only playable with a capo at the fifth fret. I was interested in the electric guitar even before I knew the difference between electric and acoustic. The electric guitar seemed to be a

Ray Fenwick playing a Gretsch Corvette with Rupert And The Red Devils

totally fascinating plank of wood with knobs and switches on it. I just had to have one."

The Pye Record Maker. After driving his neighbours mad by "endlessly playing the theme from The Third Man" on the zither, Jeff Beck was inspired when a friend who owned an Egmond electric guitar invited him to his house to record on a Pye Record Maker. This device was the size of a radiogram and was contemporary with the first domestic tape recorders at around 1953. The difference was that, although it looked like a record player, and did in fact play records, it was also a mono recorder. The arm of the four-speed changer had plug-in cartridges, one for 78s, a second for 33rpm LPs, and a third option, a tape head for use on a specially-coated magnetic disk. This disk had a box-shaped spiral groove, one tenth of an inch wide, with brown ferric oxide coating the bottom. The tape head sat in the groove in contact with the oxide

TREMOLO TALES

For some time I had loved the soulful sound that is made when a tremolo arm is used to enhance a long note. Guitars that featured this device, such as Gretsches or Fenders, were now finally available in this country, but were still prohibitively expensive, so I thought I'd make an arm for my acoustic guitar.

I'd spotted some old hinged-lid desks being thrown out at school, and it was relatively easy to remove the steel edge strip from the side of one of the lids with a hacksaw, and this, along with some springs from a junk shop, was fitted carefully to the front of the acoustic to effectively become a "rocking" bridge. Having part of a school desk sticking out of the instrument did make it look slightly ridiculous, but it worked as I bent notes up or down. At least, it worked until I foolishly dared to bend the strings beyond a quartertone. With an ear-splitting crack the whole front of the guitar came off in a shower of sawdust, plywood, and fish glue. Oh, the depression!

Geoff Whitehorn

As an eight-year-old boy, Geoff Whitehorn took violin lessons, and despite hating them then he now appreciates how they helped him to read music. In Geoff's mind, the marriage between rock 'n' roll and his formal musical education formed an interesting concept. "I vividly remember putting a tremolo arm made from a strip of Meccano on the violin after seeing The Shadows on TV, but that didn't go down particularly well with the violin teacher. My very first guitar I actually made from Meccano and fishing line – a Dalekcaster, possibly."

Alan Parker

Alan Parker's first electric guitar was a red Vox copy of a Fender Stratocaster, which he used with his trusty Watkins Dominator. "The main difference between the two guitars was that, whereas the tremolo arm on the Fender was an engineering masterpiece of essentially frictionless pivoting, the arm on the Vox was welded onto a solid plate with a rivet. Underneath, instead of return springs there was a thick piece of rubber which would jam solid at unforeseen moments, and if this wasn't bad enough, after a while the rivet would wear through and the arm would snap off. Chaos!"

Hank Marvin

One night, when he was lifting up his Burns guitar in a dramatic position, the tremolo unaccountably locked out of tune – it sounded awful. It happened several times that week, and neither Hank nor designer Jim Burns could solve it, until Hank noticed that the back plate of the tremolo had a slit in it, and his suit button was entering the tremolo housing and locking. Solution: they changed the back plate and all was fine.

Julian Littman

Rarely does one perceive the guitar itself as a risk to physical well being, although Julian Littman might disagree. He was the guitar player in the band of an all-nude musical called *Orgy*, which was directed by Michael Bogdanov and staged at a repertory theatre in Newcastle upon Tyne. It was one of many such bizarre shows that followed in the wake of *Hair*, the first musical to feature nudity on stage. The action took place on a giant inflatable cushion, and seemed to feature predominantly naked, writhing bodies. The choreography demanded that, at a special moment in the play, Julian (also in his birthday suit) would leap onto the giant inflatable and play a Hendrix-like screaming solo on his Fender Stratocaster. On one afternoon his Strat needed some minor repairs, and Julian had removed the back cover plate to expose the four tremolo springs. He completed the adjustments, but with an unforgiving lack of vision forgot to replace the plastic cover.

That night he chose to play a particularly dexterous solo, making plenty of dive-bombing use of the tremolo arm. This was really unfortunate: what the audience heard was plenty of screaming guitar and feedback uniquely blended with Julian's own impromptu screaming as his pubic hair became caught in the springs. His pain was followed by indignity when, in front of the whole audience, he was extricated by two scissor-wielding naked handmaidens (one of whom was singer Charlie Dore) while he pulled and pushed the arm to slacken the springs. A part of him remained forever enmeshed. Leo Fender could never have anticipated such a design hazard.

Pete Townshend

Not so long ago, as a result of poorly negotiating his Strat, Pete Townshend was also maimed – not by the tremolo springs but by the whammy bar itself. He is world famous, of course, not only for his relentless destruction of his guitars (which must have enraged thousands of kids who couldn't afford even one!) but also for his right arm windmills, an image that has become synonymous with both the awesome power of The Who's music and all things mod. Roger Daltrey remembers the first time he saw Pete "throwing his shape" on stage: "We were playing before The Rolling Stones at Queen Mary's Hall in Putney. Keith Richards was backstage before they went on, stretching his right arm high above his head. He never did that on stage, although he did play with these little wrist windmills sometimes, but he was just stretching his arm, and we were all standing there, watching, and the next night, there's fucking Townshend, going whoooo! Ha-ha-ha! So thank you, Keith."

For Pete, his windmills came as second nature, especially with a Gibson, but on The Who's 25th anniversary tour in 1989 he played a Fender Strat. For some reason one night he left the tremolo arm sticking out, away from the guitar instead of hovering above the body. As drummer Simon Phillips recalls: "One dramatic windmill motion came to a halt during 'I'm A Man' when Pete noticed that he'd skewered his hand with the tremolo arm. He pulled his hand off it, finished the song and was led off, looking ashen. Mercifully, the puncture had missed all important tendons and bones. The kid's still alright."

Jeff Beck

At around the time of Pete's unfortunate accident, I was fortunate to be present when Jeff Beck, the master of the tremolo arm, was recording "Where Were You?" for his *Guitar Shop* album at The Sol (also known as The Mill) in Cookham, Berkshire, a studio originally built by Gus Dudgeon, then bought by Jimmy Page, and later taken over in 1995 by Chris Rea. Jeff and keyboard player Tony Hymas patiently played take after take of this haunting ballad, which was harmonically unusual in taking as its basis an old Bulgarian scale. One particular note repeatedly caused a problem, and it was required that it was sustained for a very long time. Time after time, a crackle from the amp or a finger noise would intrude and spoil the purity of the sound, which bore an uncanny resemblance to a mixture of panpipes and voices.

After one particularly intrusive *clank* from a tremolo spring, Jeff leapt off his stool and, with arms outstretched, mock-implored the ceiling with a cry of "This has got to sound like the voice of God!" His frustration was understandable: he doesn't just play or pick a note; he creates it. He picks a note with his thumb, fades in the volume pot with his little finger and moves the arm into gentle vibrato. While the note is still decaying, his hand seems to race all over the control area, adjusting tone and volume pots and the pickup selector switch prior to picking the next note. Each note has a different emotional charge.

Another unusual feature of both this melody and his playing technique is the way in which he uses the tremolo arm to actually play the tune. He hits a harmonic, and while it's ringing he bends the arm up and down quickly, accurately following the contours of the melody, ending with his arm almost touching the body – a wonderful effect! When Jeff is playing, his aim is to master every nuance. He is a true innovator.

PLUGGING INTO THE WALL

Francis Rossi

Once the electric guitar became accepted, much of the fear and confusion that surrounded its existence soon began to evaporate. There was, however, a huge section of society who thought that it functioned in isolation. They certainly hadn't thought about amplification. Status Quo may be known today for their wall-to-wall Marshall stacks, but even Francis Rossi was prone to naïvete in his formative days.

"I wanted to be The Everly Brothers with my brother. We made a pact to get a guitar each for Christmas, but then the shitter backed out and got a train set instead," says Francis, who began with an acoustic guitar but wanted to go electric. He bought a pickup that was mercifully covered in plastic, then stripped the cable and fitted a two-pin mains plug. (In those days the UK hadn't yet standardised its safe earthed three-pin plugs.) He plugged it into the wall socket and genuinely expected the guitar to get louder! It didn't of course. "Ah well," he thought, "perhaps it needs time to warm up!" It was only the cover, and the fact that a wire inside was fractured, that saved him from injury. It came as a revelation that you needed an amp. When I told him about other musicians' early experiences, Francis was genuinely surprised to find that he wasn't in the minority.

Jim Cregan

Of his formative years, Jim Cregan says: "I badgered my dad, day and night, for what seemed like years until he took me to the local music shop and began a most embarrassing haggle with the owner over the price of a black-and-turquoise Rosetti Solid Seven with two pickups. Anyone

Jim Cregan (l) with a turquoise Rosetti Solid 7. The occasion was the school variety concert at Poole Grammar School in Dorset. "I was about 14, so it was probably 1960. The name of the group was The Falcons and I played lead since I didn't know enough chords to play rhythm"

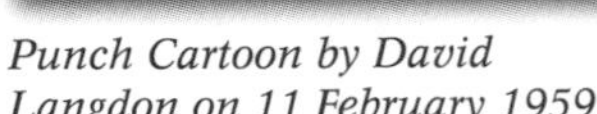

Punch Cartoon by David Langdon on 11 February 1959

could see it was worth £17, but no, my dad wrangled and bluffed until he got it for £11, complete with a powder-blue zip-up plastic case. It was bliss. Taking it to my friend's house on the bus one evening I was sitting upstairs pretty well by myself when some bloke came over and said: 'Is that a guitar in there, mate? 'Yes it is,' I replied, proudly. 'Well, get it out and give us a tune,' he said. 'I can't, it's an electric.' 'Well, don't worry,' he said brightly 'We can plug it in here.' And he reached up and took out one of the light bulbs."

Phil Manzenera

Like every reliable and sympathetic dad should, Phil Manzenera's agreed to take over the payments when his young son received a court order for not paying the instalments on his new Hofner Galaxy. It was then that his dad uttered the immortal words: "Okay, okay, plug it in the wall then and let's hear what it sounds like." Phil says: "I unplugged and exited stage left, explaining that you also needed to buy an amplifier."

Mike Rutherford

Mike Rutherford recalls: "When I was about ten I went to the local music shop in Manchester with my mother – which in itself was very embarrassing – to buy my first electric guitar. I had seen so many cartoons in the newspapers of Mum and Dad in the living room blocking their ears while their son was thrashing his guitar in the same room, obviously making an incredibly loud noise. The drawing always showed a lead running straight from the guitar into the power socket in the wall.

"So, having chosen my Hofner electric guitar, the salesman turned to me and asked 'What amplifier do you want?' I looked at him blankly and said 'I don't want an amplifier (not really knowing what it was anyway). All I want is an electric guitar.' The salesman gently explained to me that an electric guitar obviously needed an amplifier to be heard. Hiding my embarrassment, I carried on, and chose a Selmer Little Giant, which was about two feet by one foot."

Martin Kershaw

When he was 15, at home in Yorkshire, Martin Kershaw had a friend, David, who played accordion and guitar. One day David said "Just watch this, Martin," and proceeded to plug his guitar straight into the mains wall socket. Martin, who

The Selmer Little Giant 5-Watt amplifier

MAINS SOCKET FOLLIES

• Bernie Holland had a friend who sent off for a Rosetti Lucky Seven bass from Bell's Music in Surbiton. As soon as it arrived he fitted a 13-amp plug to the lead and plugged it straight into the wall. The whole moulded pickguard assembly, including pickups and control knobs, began to melt until "it was converted into a sticky omelette of hot plastic".

• Having decided to try out an electric guitar, Mickey Moody asked the music shop assistant if he could plug it in. "Sure," said the assistant, who followed this with a scream of "No!" as Mickey attempted to plug it into the wall.

• Tom McGuinness initially thought that guitars should be plugged straight into the mains socket. His other folly was to put steel strings and a pickup on a Spanish guitar.

• John Fortune worked in a music shop during the 1950s and 1960s, a time of laughable ignorance. "Around Christmas, young boys accompanied by their fathers would come into the store seeking to buy an electric guitar. When we sold one we would include a free quarter-inch jack-to-jack lead (i.e., with one end for the guitar and the other for the amp). They would depart happy. With alarming consistency, Dad would return the next morning requesting a replacement lead since the one he'd been given didn't fit into the wall."

Punch Cartoon by Larry on 29 January 1964

• It was not just guitars that suffered from this kind of stupidity: one day pedal-steel player Pete Willsher heard an incredible sound coming from Selmer's store. A customer had gone there to hear a demonstration of the giant Selmer Goliath two-by-18-inch bass cabinets. On display were two cabinets wired in parallel at the back, with the wires just twisted together. A new salesman who had only been there for two days and was eager to please went around the back, saw the wires and plugged them into the mains safe-block, and then closed the lid, thus switching on mains power directly to the speakers. Obviously, this isn't something for which they were designed. Pete comments: "The noise was like two elephants trumpeting through a mega PA, possibly the loudest noise the street had heard since the war. Everyone froze. The salesman, who was inches from one of the cabinets, went ashen white and just trembled. It shook the entire contents of the shop, glass broke, and it could be heard from Cambridge Circus to Tottenham Court Road. During the minute the noise lasted the grille cloth of one cabinet blew across the room."

thought that the guy was crazy, attempted a rugby tackle to try to stop him, but it was unnecessary.

David had built a complete Elpico valve amplifier into the body of the instrument. He'd taken the back off the guitar and, in the space, had carefully fitted the chassis and speaker which he had removed from the "little green suitcase'. Unfortunately, thanks to a terrible lack of practical vision, the guitar had become virtually unliftable. Martin recalls: "The guy played for a good 60 seconds before being helped into a chair."

Ritchie Blackmore

An original kind of seasonal illumination was in store for everyone at Heston School, where Ritchie Blackmore was a pupil. In preparation for his appearance at the forthcoming Christmas concert, Ritchie assembled a skiffle group called The Two Eyes Junior Coffee Band, which consisted of a dog box (tea chest), a washboard and four guitars. "At one rehearsal I couldn't get the radio to work. Being 12 at the time, I thought I could fix it with no prior knowledge of electronics, but in my frustration to get it working I accidentally plugged the pickup directly into the mains of the school assembly hall. Needless to say, I blew the fuse, burnt out my pickup and fused all the lights in the school. As school was in session, there was basically hell to pay if the masters found out who did this, so we did the honourable thing and ran for it. I don't think they ever found out who fused all the lights."

MUSIC SHOPS

The demand for guitars and their associated equipment grew dramatically in the 1950s. Ivor Mairants reports that it had doubled in 1953, and by 1955 it had risen by 150 per cent of the previous year's figures. When rock 'n' roll arrived in Britain sales began to soar, and by the end of 1956 figures had increased by 500 per cent over those of 1955. Within less than ten years, the musical instrument industry had entered a boom period. With the likes of *Ready, Steady, Go!* and *Top of the Pops* on national TV with images of a new breed of pop musician, by the mid 1960s music shops were having a fight on their hands to stock a whole new range of guitar brands.

Along with Rushworth & Draper's, Hessy's could be described as Liverpool's top music shop in the late 1950s and 1960s, and it helped to equip every major band in the city, including The Beatles. Whereas other stores kept their instruments in glass cases and generally felt that the customer ought to wear a suit, they catered more for the working class and the unemployed – their easy payments were £1 per week. The shop's encouragement to young musicians was not only financial, however: guitar teacher Jimmy Gretty was on hand in store to help out and give lessons. "Before you walked out of the store you could play three chords." As Sara Michaelson (née Hessy, a shop assistant at the age of 17) recalls, in the 1960s Hessy's expanded to the point where all Liverpool bands would come in to buy their equipment and use the shop as a meeting place. "If Brian Epstein couldn't find The Beatles he'd wait at Hessy's and they'd turn up eventually."

During the 1950s and 1960s, music shops attracted aspiring players as never before. Young musicians would visit these places of worship whenever they could in a bid to solve technical mysteries, hear inspirational in-store playing, swap philosophies with others, and drool at the sight of new and seemingly unattainable equipment.

Gerry Rafferty

Gerry Rafferty's account of his local music shop in Scotland is particularly vivid. "In the windows, amidst the displays of cheesy sheet music and sensible pianos, gay castanets and tambourines, there began to appear

SHOP STORIES

- **Mo: "In The Bandbox – my local store in Wolverhampton – a large black and white photograph appeared one day showing a skydiver in mid-freefall. There was a futuristic object (which I now know to be a Fender Jazzmaster) strapped in front of him, and which I had naturally assumed to be some new kind of radio – it looked nothing like any guitar I'd ever seen (and why would he want to take a guitar into a cramped aeroplane anyway?). The caption 'You won't part with yours either' didn't help us, especially since there were no Fender guitars in the shop (nor would there be for the next two years)."**
- John Paul Jones: "I had a secret shrine in Soho. In amongst the clip joints and mucky bookshops there was a record shop with a small window containing a dusty display of about a dozen LPs. One had this picture on the cover of a city gent in a bowler hat posing next to a pink Fender Precision bass. It was the Holy Grail. I could always count on passing this sacred place at least three times in one day. I would stand silently and reverently in front of it, as if it were a beacon in the night."
- **On the school bus every day, Steve Howe would pass a triangle of shops outside King's Cross Station, and one of them was Friedman's Guitar Shop, from where his parents purchased for him a £14 f-hole cello guitar, which sparked his lifelong love affair with arch-tops. His early band, The Syndicats, recorded at Joe Meek's legendary studio in Holloway Road, near Berry's Piano Shop, where Steve spied what he considered to be the superior Burns Jazz guitar.**
- Albert Lee: "I persuaded my parents to sign for a Grazioso which I'd seen in Jennings' shop in Charing Cross Road. I thought it was so cool: it looked a bit like the guitar on the *Chirping Crickets* LP, so that was good enough for me. It cost me £85, second hand, which was outrageous considering that if I'd known better I could have ordered an American guitar"
- **Three days before the music press announced his arrival into the Pink Floyd camp, David Gilmour surprised his Cambridge muso pals (including Tim Renwick) by strolling into the local music shop and buying, with cash, the highly coveted yellow Fender Strat that everyone had been gawping at for weeks.**
- Charlie Watkins: "Accordion sales plummeted when the guitar craze started."

strange bedfellows: the Futurama III electric guitar [a solid-body guitar with a black and white colour scheme and three pickups] and the Gibson Kalamazoo [sunburst acoustic guitar with optional brown canvas carrying bag].

"On Saturdays, my best mate and I would join the growing band of spotty adolescents queuing in an orderly fashion outside the music shop in order to test drive these new and glamorous beasts, and flaunt our mastery of at least four chords in the faces of the less talented oiks impatiently awaiting their turn. Just to annoy them further we'd enquire of the shop assistant whether easy terms might be arranged on the goods in question, and on receipt of the required information we'd have a few more showy runs around the fretboard with the amp cranked up to full volume and depart, smirking, saying we'd think it over. Such was our disposable income, however, that thinking it over – at least in the short term – was our sole option. Similar rites of passage were, we now know, being enacted throughout the country; a generation with one purpose: get guitars and get famous."

Hugh Burns

Hugh Burns and his friends spent their Saturday afternoons searching for the elusive lost chord. "Our pilgrimage to the mecca of Glasgow's music shops unravelled such musical mysteries as 'Is a seventh chord a *barré* chord played at the seventh fret?' (It made sense: after all, there was even a dot on the fret); 'Can anything be played above the tenth fret?'; 'Does G sus (written on sheet music) mean sustained, suspended or, as one drummer suggested, suspect?' (the latter indicating that we had the choice to play or not to play).

"This environment also shed light on the latest technological developments, and eavesdropping customers' enquiries led us to emerge with a greater understanding of this brave new world. We pondered on whether the whole band could get into the echo chamber or if there was only room for the singer. Words from catalogues were mouthed like sacred mantras (and with about as much understanding): Reverb, 15 Watts RMS, Notch Filter, Double Cone Speaker... The sales assistant was like a prophet giving a sermon to an eager congregation. The nonchalant confidence with which he explained such terms with ease indicated that he knew the reply to the question as to how much distortion one could expect from a Selmer Little Giant. 'Don't worry, son, ye'll git ah the distortion ye want, there's nae shortage o' distortion on that amp.' Another happy convert waltzed off into the sunset."

Eric Ford

Some aspiring players took jobs in music shops as a way to improve their knowledge and make contacts. Guitarist Eric Ford heard that Selmer was looking for someone to run the guitar section of its shop on the Charing Cross Road. He successfully applied for the position and built up that side of the business into a very prosperous concern. With American guitars still unavailable, Eric was selling mainly European models – Hofners, Egmonds and Hoffs – and remembers selling an Australian Maton guitar to Judd Procter, supplying all the equipment that John Barry needed for The John Barry Seven, and also that Bert Weedon was a very good customer. Significantly, his tenure in the shop allowed him to meet just about every working guitarist in London, as well as build a reputation and an arsenal of contacts that would serve him well throughout his career. Of course, working in the shop also left his evenings free for gigging.

Joe Brown

Joe Brown bought what he refers to as "the best guitar I ever had" – a Gibson 335 – brand new from Selmer's. "Unfortunately I part-exchanged it for a Les Paul, which I hated, and Roy Wood from Wizzard now has it and won't sell it back to me, the bastard! I can't say I blame him. It's a great guitar, and even back in 1960 it was a far cry from the yard of German plywood that Bert Weedon made a fortune out of!"

Jim Burns

Selmer's was at one time managed by Jimmy Frost, an ex-big band drummer who asked Hawaiian guitarist Jim Burns if he would make an electric guitar, since he knew that Jim had studied carpentry. He made one which was basic and red, and began to make more in the shed in his back garden in Loughton, Essex. He brought them into London by bus, carrying a bundle of twelve or fourteen guitars wrapped in newspaper, and dropped them off at the shop on the Charing Cross Road.

When Jim Burns eventually opened his own music shop near the Charing Cross Road, Pete Willsher worked there, and Hank Marvin used to visit and watch him playing lap steel guitar. "Hank loved the sustain and vibrato of the instrument but felt that it was an unknown quantity – it frightened him." No matter; the Strat came to the rescue. However, Hank was clearly influenced – listen to the Santo and Johnny tune "Sleepwalk" on The Shadows' first LP.

Adrian Lee

Gibson sales representative Dave Roberts became well known on the burgeoning musical instrument retail scene. He was a character Adrian Lee remembers well. "I met Dave some 20 years ago, on the dusty shop floor of Macari's Musical Exchange, otherwise known as the Vox Shop, which originally stood at 102 Charing Cross Road. Dave was always in and out of the music shops in the area in an effort to boost the presence of Gibson guitars, but Dave was different from most of the other reps in that he could really play, and Joe Macari's penchant for buying second-hand banjos would invariably warrant a visit from Dave, who would pluck lightning-fast foot-stomping licks out of some 1922 Ludwig. When it came to fast foot-stomping, bucket-chucking licks from a guitar, you knew exactly where you were with Dave. He would play The Beatles' 'She's a Woman'. Always. Every time. In a foot-stomping, bucket-chucking, finger-licking kind of way.

"I would see Dave at trade fairs all over Europe, and we became good friends. He became very well known as one of Norlin's star demonstrators [the now defunct US music industry giant]. Dave would stun audiences with his flamboyant guitar acrobatics, but especially so when he would tell them, after the obligatory 'She's a Woman', 'I shall now play the guitar with my teeth.' The expectant gathering would await Dave's Jimi-Hendrix-like endeavour with barely concealed excitement. Dave would then whip out his denture plate and commence to play 'She's a Woman' with it. What a pro!"

Andy Fairweather-Low

Through landing a job at his local music shop, Barratts of Manchester (in Cardiff!), Andy Fairweather-Low caught his first sight of a Fender Stratocaster, exchanged his Hofner Verithin for a Gibson 335, and bought his first amp, a Barratts amp, which he hooked up to a single Marshall two-by-twelve-inch cabinet. Being a member of staff had distinct advantages: "I would frequently change guitars: I'd keep paying for the 335, but borrow a Fender Jazzmaster or a Gretsch Country Gentleman. None of these improved my playing for, as my good friend Eric is always telling me 'It's in the hands. It's not in the shorts.'"

Pino Palladino

Also in Cardiff, Pino Palladino talked his parents into buying him an electric guitar from Grimwade's second-hand store in Canton. "It was the most beautiful object I'd ever seen: a black Shaftesbury Les Paul. I can still remember the smell when I opened the case. I soon realised that, although I now possessed the object of my dreams, there was still something missing: an amp! Still, somehow my friend Kevin Hole and I managed to wire it up to his stereo by connecting the wires from the guitar lead to the wires that connected the needle to the arm of his record player. I was hooked. The sound of the Shaftesbury through the stereo was so vibrant and exciting, and I knew from then on that this was it for me."

Gretsch Silver Quimp

This is one of the wonderfully surreal adverts that appeared in the window of One Way Music in Wolverhampton.

Tony Hicks

Tony Hicks was never interested in the players, only the instruments. "You'd get on the Ribble bus from Nelson and travel for an hour to Manchester just to rub your nose against the window of Barratt's. The big occasion was that once a month an American guitar would turn up. It was worth the trip."

In April 1965, The Hollies toured the USA as part of what the media described as "the British Invasion". "In the early days of touring, I discovered the pawn shops. On one occasion CBS were filming us on tour, and they came with us to one of these pawn shops. At one point the proprietor pulled out a brown case containing a Gibson Les Paul Standard. He wanted $80. Being a typical northern lad, only 21, I started haggling. The producer of the film sidled over to me and said 'We'd like to see the sale go through. If the guitar is a bit expensive, we'll buy it for you.' So CBS bought me a Les Paul Standard, on film."

Roger Clarke – One Way Music

Working in a music shop – which can be both demanding and exhausting – is often a test of one's sanity. Possibly as a survival tactic, Roger Clarke of Wolverhampton's still thriving One Way Music has evolved his own unique vocabulary. On a daily basis his simple but friendly greeting is "Perquindis", to which the polite but not-too-formal response might be "Perquindis, indeed." In order to gain access at the rear of the premises it's vital to know both a procedure and a wonderfully surreal two-part password. Bang on the back door. From inside will be heard the challenge "We are not thieves!" If the response from outside is "We fight for Labenius!" then the door opens and you're admitted.

Guitars on display would often feature prominent signs, displaying the historical significance of the instrument, important information such as "As used by John Wayne in the film *Five Go Newt Foncing in Dorset*", or "As used by Robert De Niro in the film *Rumpage – The Revenge Of Lumis*". People would travel from miles around just for the signs. One guitar was advertised as a Gretsch "Silver Quimp".

When demonstrating a piece of equipment, Roger's Unwin-esque abilities sometimes shone through with throwaways such as "Well, if the angle of the 'patrilliance' is wrong, then the 'lapeltris' would be awry." Another impressed but slightly confused customer would make his purchase.

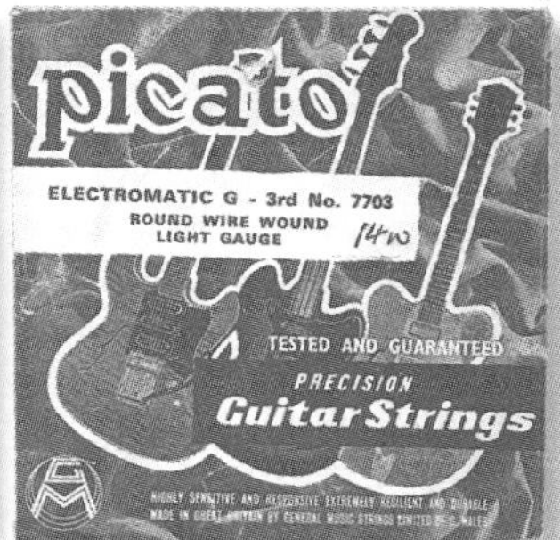

Vintage guitar string packets

STRINGS

Eric Ford

The main problem for British guitarists in the early period of rock 'n' roll was how to recreate the American sound that they heard on the records. Eric Ford, then a member of Lord Rockingham's XI, had managed to secure a Gibson guitar, and by experimenting with an Electron pickup (a British-made version of a DeArmond pickup) and placing it near the bridge he was able to come close. Jack Good was sufficiently pleased, and that was what counted.

However, it was through meeting American singer/guitarist Eddie Cochran that Eric discovered some of the secrets of the elusive American sound. According to Eric, "For a start his strings were so much thinner than ours – he was using a .008 gauge first while ours were nearer .013, and on top of that he had a Bigsby tremolo arm – it was the first we'd seen in this country, and we were all knocked out with the sound that it produced."

Albert Lee

Albert Lee explains further: "About a year before word had got around about the way US players were stringing their axes, Duane Eddy and Eddie Cochran had told of how players would buy a regular set of strings and an extra first or light banjo string, move them over one and throw away the bottom string. This opened up a whole new world to us. Ernie Ball saw this happening in his little music store in Tarzana, California, in the early 1960s and quickly put together the idea for light 'slinky' sets." The beginning of this transition caused Bert Weedon a problem during a 1960s package tour when he was billed alongside Johnny Kidd and The Pirates; he lost his guitar and was forced to borrow Mick Green's. Mick recalls: "My guitar was a 1959 Telecaster with a G banjo third string, and I used to oil the strings to keep them from getting rusty from sweat. I gave the guitar to Bert, who proceeded to go on to do his normal set, and of course he was like a fish out of water because he used a Guild, with heavy-gauge strings and no oil. When he came off the stage, he asked me 'How the hell do you play that guitar?'"

Mick Green in 1962 at the Star Club, Hamburg

George Harrison

George Harrison: "There weren't any light-gauge strings around in the early days. We always had heavy gauge, and by take 20 it was pretty hard on the fingers."

Mark Knopfler

Ed Bicknell (manager of Dire Straits 1977-2001) recalls an event back in 1978: "Not long after I'd met them, Dire Straits supported Talking Heads on a UK tour. One morning Mark Knopfler was changing the strings on his guitar in the lobby of the hotel. Head's keyboardist Jerry Harrison observed this with interest and asked Mark what he was doing. 'Changing my strings. I do it every two or three days,' he replied. At that moment David Byrne joined the conversation, commenting: 'I've *never* changed the strings on my guitar, they're the same ones that were on it when I bought it in a second-hand shop.' He thought about this and added: 'I'd better get some.' The next day David and bass player Tina Weymouth were observed furiously changing the strings on their guitars. In fits of laughter Mark confided to me: 'I've completely stuffed their sound!'"

Mike Jopp

Mike Jopp recalls: "Roger McGuinn of The Byrds went into Ivor Mairants' guitar shop in Rathbone Place and asked for a 12-string set of Rickenbacker strings. All of our faces went totally blank as if to say, 'What's a Rickenbacker?'"

The Tradewinds

Our strings never seemed to 'twang' like Duane Eddy's – our sound was always more of a "thud". We had no idea what the problem was until a friend at school provided the helpful information that Duane's strings were made of gold. I've met many twats in my life – he was possibly the first.

TUNERS

- **In 1911 Henry Wood commissioned a tuning box with bellows. It gave two pitches (the lower pitch was for woodwind, whose pitch would rise during the concert). He would stand by the door with the box and crank the handle. Life is so much easier now – for around £30 one can buy an easy-to-operate and accurate pocket digital tuner which can be placed in line between the guitar and amplifier. Some miniature ones even clip onto the instrument itself. Such devices allow silent tuning between – or even during – songs, providing reassurance to the musician and relief to the audience.**
- But it was not always so: rock tunes are perfect for tuning up the guitar because they tend to be in keys like E, A, D or G, permitting easy checking of the open strings for pitch. Conversely, dance-band tunes are in the keys that saxophones and trumpets love – like F and B flat – which are hopeless keys for tuning the guitar. Martin Kershaw once played in a dance band, and because of these problems he resolved to find a solution. He contacted an electronics boffin, a guy in his fifties from Leeds University, who devised for him a tuner based on the ubiquitous Linear Concorde amplifier. It was two feet square, an all-valve design, it had big dials, and when it was stable it could be used to tune the note E, although it occasionally lied and gave out another note entirely. "It was no better than an electronic tuning fork," says Martin.
  Martin asked the boffin if he could tune it to other notes, but the only possible way was to have a row of them. "It would be the size of a washing machine!"
  It was never a happy device: money was constantly needed to upgrade and replace components. The tuner met its demise one day when someone accidentally dropped a can of Coke down the back of it – a flash and a big puff of smoke signalled its death. From then on it was easier (and cheaper) for Martin to ask the pianist for an E, though not as exciting.
- **Bassist Brian McGhee, who used to work at One Way Music in Wolverhampton, recalls: "One Saturday a guy came in and wanted to see a battery-powered electronic tuner. I showed him the range and then demonstrated one on an acoustic. The guy was impressed, paid £25, and took it home. He brought it back the following Monday and complained that it was no longer working, saying 'I plugged it into the electric guitar and then left it on all night – just to make sure!'"**
- At Snake Ranch Studios one day, guitarist Colin Green, unable to get his guitar perfectly in tune, stared in disbelief at his digital tuner and mumbled quietly "I must have cloth eyes".
- **Affinity once played for a party on a ferry going to the Isle of Wight and back. Unfortunately, every time the ship went into a long turn, the change in motion affected the frequency of the ship's generators, which in turn altered the speed of the Hammond organ's tone wheels. Guitarist Mike Jopp and I found it hard to keep up with the tuning, as songs were constantly changing key at interestingly unforeseen moments.**
- At the start of an orchestral session, double-bass player Chris Laurence needed to tune his instrument. Chris, who was in his early twenties, casually called across the studio to Marie Goossens, a mature lady harpist, "Give me an A please, granny." The MD was furious at this display of disrespectful behaviour and shouted: "How dare you speak to her like that". Chris looked surprised. "But she is my granny" he replied innocently.

CHAPTER 6

THE FIRST BASS GUITAR

IT'S BASS, BUT NOT AS WE KNEW IT

In the early part of the last century, the only articulate instruments available to play the bass part in dance bands and jazz bands were either the tuba or the sousaphone. As fashions and styles of music changed, slowly it became the turn of the upright (or double) bass to provide the foundation. The supremacy of this originally orchestral instrument lasted until the late 1950s, when the bass guitar arrived, seemingly from nowhere, and began to dominate nearly every form of popular music. This was not least because it could match the concert volume of the other instruments in the band. One further refinement in this story occurred in the late 1960s, when the synthesiser made its first appearance on record – as a bass. Of course, the market is now wide open for all basses, each of which has its own strengths and weaknesses. What they have in common, however, is that they all sound wonderful.

As rock 'n' roll became more popular, the demand for an electric instrument increased apace. Brian Odgers recalls that in the mid 1960s, there was panic amongst the UK studio double-bass players who rushed out and bought bass guitars but couldn't play them; the "feel" of the instruments was wrong. Shirley Douglas observes that "The session double-bass players of the day were also quite dismissive of the bass guitar, claiming that it wouldn't last six months! A year later they were all struggling and failing to play one."

In this 1950s advert for Framus, session men were inexplicably called 'recording boys'

Chas McDevitt

In 1958, by a twist of fate, The Chas McDevitt Group replaced US rock 'n' roll star Jerry Lee Lewis on a nationwide tour. (There had been moral indignation when Jerry arrived here with his 13-year-old bride to be). On that same package was a black American vocal group, The Treniers, who had already appeared successfully in films. More significantly, their bass player played a bass guitar. This was the first time that The Chas McDevitt Group had ever seen one, and it prompted them to invest in the only one available to them at the time, a Framus. At first no one in Chas' group had a clue how to play the communal bass, but Shirley Douglas became the bass player by default because she was the only member of the band who could sing and play it at the same time.

Shirley Douglas

Two years after the publication of Bert Weedon's *Play in a Day*, Shirley Douglas also had the smart idea to write a

The Chas McDevitt Group: Shirley with her Framus and Chas with his Grimshaw

BASS

- **Jack Bruce: "The prime objective of the bass is to make everybody else sound better than they actually are."**
- Phil Chen: "Heard and accepted more than they are credited, the unsung heroes 'de bass and de drum' are the most important elements of modern popular music – the heartbeat of life."
- **A friend of John Entwistle's used to hide a Fender Precision under his bed, away from the watchful eye of his girlfriend, but he couldn't keep up the HP payments. Thoughtfully, John took over the payments and became the proud owner of his first Fender bass.**
- "I knew I'd finish up playing bass when I saw Jet Harris's sweater on the first Shads LP, which is still in my collection," says Dave Pegg. "I took up bass guitar when my friend Roger Hill (a great guitarist) and I both auditioned for the guitar spot in super-successful Birmingham pop group The Uglys. Roger was better than me, but Steve Gibbons (the leader), said 'Never mind, Peggy – you can play bass.'"

tutor, but this time for the newly popular electric bass guitar. She then discovered that Jet Harris intended to write one, too, and so the race was on. Jet eventually dropped out, and Shirley went on to publish the highly successful – and influential – *The Easy Guide to Rhythm and Blues for Bass Guitar*. Both John Entwistle and John Paul Jones admit that this book helped them when they started.

Herbie Flowers:

As the bassist in the Geraldo Orchestra, Herbie Flowers travelled back and forth to New York on the *Queen Elizabeth*, enabling him to check out the jazz clubs. On one night in 1960, in New York, Herbie saw a trio featuring guitar, drums and bass guitar, and he was stunned at the power and volume of this instrument. He came home, headed straight for Selmer's on Charing Cross Road in London and bought a blue Fender Jazz bass for £67 on HP and a set of Rotosound black nylon-wound strings for £3. He was lucky – the importing of American goods had just started.

SHIRLEY DOUGLAS'
easy guide to rhythm & blues for
Bass-Guitar
containing
6/-
Shirley Douglas & Chas McDevitt

The Shirley Douglas' Easy Guide To Rhythm And Blues For Bass Guitar

Jet Harris

Jet Harris hung around clubs such as the 2i's in Soho, where he would divide his time between operating the cold drinks machine and jamming with the various musicians who were drawn to this rock 'n' roll mecca. In 1956, jazz drummer Tony Crombie perceived a change in the climate of musical taste and formed Tony Crombie's Rockets, perhaps the UK's first rock 'n' roll band. Two years later, having seen Jet play, Tony invited him to join The Rockets at £18 per week for a 22-week tour backing Wee Willie Harris. Jet was thrilled. "Tony was the guv'nor – he was *the* jazzman for me."

Herbie Flowers in the studio with his blue Fender Jazz bass

Tony Crombie

Tony's band was *loud*, and the volume would easily swamp the double-bass, an instrument that was never designed to cope with such an acoustic onslaught. However, Tony's imagination was fired when he saw the Lionel Hampton Orchestra on a ship to New York, and was struck by the volume and presence of bass guitar player William Mackie. With this in mind, he said to Jet: "Have you seen this new invention? It's a new type of bass, only it's shaped like an electric guitar." Jet reluctantly traded in his beloved double-bass for a Framus Star bass guitar, an instrument that was only just starting be imported and sold by Besson's in Shaftesbury Avenue. He subsequently became one of the first bass guitar players in the UK.

Danny Thompson

While looking for work one day in London's Archer Street, in the spring of 1963, double-bassist Danny Thompson was offered a gig with The Sons Of The Piltdown Men, who were to back Roy Orbison on a package tour with The Beatles and others. However, it meant playing bass guitar, and since he didn't own one he was lent a Vox Precision copy bass and a Vox amp. The Beatles would close the first half of the show, and Roy Orbison the other half – but not for long! He had good fun on the tour but noticed at the end that his left wrist had acquired bad habits. He doesn't touch bass guitar now, and when people ask him why not he answers: "For the same reason I don't play French horn – they're two totally different instruments."

Roy Babbington

In 1961, Roy Babbington was playing sets until 3 a.m. at the Glasgow club The Cell, where he would involve himself in upright bass duets with Jack Bruce, after which Jack would go back to Roy's flat, play chess and wait for the night bus. He then went south to Middlesbrough, where he began to hear older players talking about the bass guitar – how it was lighter, easier to carry, and that you could sit down with it. But he still felt that he was a purist.

Dave Richmond posing for the John Barry Seven with his 1963 Burns Black Bison

Roy Babbington playing his white Fender 6-string bass in concert with Nucleus in 1973

At the end of the 1960s, Roy was resident at the Fiesta, in Stockton-on-Tees, with ex-Seeker Judith Durham. Her parts were written for "Double-bass/Bass Guitar" a previously unseen heading which made Roy panic. He managed to borrow a bass guitar from a friend, an unusual sunburst six-string Fender VI. Although not immediately, he eventually came to enjoy the feel of it, as it combined his knowledge of both upright bass and guitar. When his friend wanted it back, Roy replaced it with a white model from Pan Music in Wardour Street, London.

Playing both double-bass and electric bass caused some problems, and if Roy played bass guitar for only a few weeks he'd lose his upright bass chops, and end up with sore hands and bleeding fingers.

Dave Richmond

Dave Richmond also experienced some physical problems, which in fact led to him changing instruments. "I decided to have some further tuition on the double-bass and went to Eugene Cruft, a retired professor from the Royal Academy of Music. Part of his method was to put a couple of matchboxes between the first and second and the third and fourth fingers of the left hand to stretch the fingers sufficiently to play the lower positions of the double-bass. After my one and only lesson a lump appeared on the back of my hand, and I was unable to play the double-bass properly. That same night I had a job with the Mann-Hugg Blues Brothers at the Ricky Tick Club in Windsor, and so drastic action had to be taken. A friend suggested buying a bass guitar, an instrument which, in the couple of years I had known of its existence, I had looked down upon with much disdain."

SOMEONE HAD TO PLAY BASS

In the enthusiasm of forming a band, there would often be an excess of one instrument. This imbalance was solved during the skiffle period when four guitars would suddenly dwindle to three guitars, as one player was (in his mind) demoted to bass player. Everybody thought that there had to be a bass, although nobody actually knew what it did. The unfortunate player was usually chosen by default: either he knew the fewest number of chords, or he was last to join, or perhaps his personality dictated a desire to stand at the back. (There were occasions when the rest of the band felt that he ought to stand at the back.)

Paul McCartney

Paul McCartney was, he says, lumbered with the bass job in The Beatles. "None of us wanted to be the bass player – we wanted to be up front. In our minds it was nearly always the fat guy in the group who played bass, and he stood at the back. None of us wanted that; we wanted to be up front, singing and looking good, to pull the birds."

The Tradewinds

Meanwhile, back in my village, new members had drifted into our practice sessions to the extent that the little band now featured four guitars. And since I knew the fewest chords, I became the bass player by default. A double-bass was inconceivable. I tried to build a tea-chest bass, but neither it nor I was very good. I also couldn't see the musical validity of random pitch.

Somehow, somewhere, I'd heard the phrase "electric bass guitar". It had a resonance: it sounded longer and more important than just a guitar, and I liked it. Desperate for more information (even though my lack of funds would preclude such a purchase) I scanned the ad pages, but they weren't helpful. For example, I remember one ad for the Hofner bass guitar: "Guitarists, double your income with the Hofner bass guitar. Tuned like a bass, with the third, fourth, fifth and sixth strings of a guitar." Or the Dallas Tuxedo Electro bass guitar: "This instrument is easily played by any guitarist as the tuning is the same as the bottom four strings of the guitar. The instrument can be played with fingers or plectrum." This confusing information led me to believe that to play the bass guitar you merely removed the top two strings of an ordinary guitar, and then in some way amplified it.

It all began to make sense when I caught my first sight of a Fender Precision bass in the movie *Because They're Young*, featuring Duane Eddy. Seeing this awesome instrument proved to be a transcendent moment, but for me to be connected in some way to this world seemed impossibly far away.

MIGRATION

Very few players started out on the bass guitar; most would arrive after having migrated from another instrument, usually guitar, double-bass, drums, piano or, in some cases, trumpet. Real instruments were rare and, even if available, they were prohibitively expensive. A common solution was to remove the top two strings of a guitar and then in some way de-tune and amplify the remaining four.

Presenting the Hofner BASS GUITAR

designed for the professional player

Guitarists—double your income with the Hofner Bass Guitar. Tuned like bass with the third, fourth, fifth and sixth strings of a guitar. Frets ensure accuracy of intonation and enable guitarist to switch to the Electric bass right away. Light and easy to carry, with built-in electronics to give the biggest tone ever.
Adjustable bridge—two pick-ups with tone and volume controls — Craftsman constructed from the finest materials to the high standards synonymous with the name Hofner.

Price complete with rigid dome shaped case, felt lined, 48 gns

Selmer 114 CHARING CROSS ROAD, LONDON, W.C.2

The Hofner bass guitar – this was a confusing advert

The Dallas Tuxedo Electro bass guitar – another confusing advert

Andy Fraser

In Andy Fraser's first major school band, everyone wanted to be the guitarist, the singer, or the drummer. "To stop the arguments I tuned the strings of my Airstream Lucky Three down an octave and I became the bass player," he says.

Roger Glover

Roger Glover's solution was to remove the top two strings from his precious Italian acoustic and buy a 12/6 (62½p) pickup. "I screwed in the pick guard with scant regard for its resale value, and for months we practised using just a radiogram or a tape recorder as an amp."

Alan Jones

Alan Jones was the lead guitarist in his first band, playing a Hofner Colorama. During their gigs and rehearsals it became evident that Harry Fryer, the bass player, couldn't really "hear" the bass-lines as clearly as Alan could, so they swapped roles.

Muff Winwood

Three guitars and drums as a line-up was no good for The Spencer Davis Group, when it formed in 1963, so Muff Winwood began playing bass-lines on his guitar with the bass turned up. During rehearsals at home, all of the guitars went into one amp while the drummer played the arm of the settee. Eventually, Muff used thumb picks to play a Harmony H22 bass with twin f-holes and a single cutaway. For a bass amp, a boffin at school built Muff a box that looked a bit like a drinks cabinet: it had one speaker and was powered by a Leak amplifier.

Graham Gouldman

In 1964, while playing guitar as a member of The Mockingbirds with drummer Kevin Godley, Graham Gouldman started writing his own songs and recording basic vocal and acoustic guitar demos. Several of these became major hits, such as "For Your Love", "Evil-Hearted You" and "Heart Full of Soul" for The Yardbirds, "Look Through Any Window" and "Bus Stop" for The Hollies and "No Milk Today" for Herman's Hermits. He then purchased a two-track Revox tape recorder, on which he could bounce the tracks and make full arrangement demos. Out of necessity he started to play bass. "My friend Bernie Basso (the perfect name for a bass player) lent me his beautiful sunburst Precision bass to use, but unfortunately it got nicked from my car. I did replace, it but the new one was never as good."

John Wetton

John Wetton's first guitar was a cherry-red Hofner Colorama, which he says had an action like a tramline and sounded like contemporary heavy-metal guitars. "There was no tone, only one volume setting (eleven) and the strings were rusted beyond belief. When a vacancy came up in a local group, I applied. The gig was for a bass player. I thought that, maybe after a while as a bassist, I could be promoted to rhythm, and then maybe lead, so I tuned down my little Colorama and off I went. I got the job, I suspect, because no one else turned up for the audition. It must have sounded awful. I couldn't play anything more ambitious than 'Tom Dooley', but I was soon attacking twelve bars and stuff with minor chords in.

"I was then pressured into buying a real bass, a sunburst Framus solid. I suppose I should thank those guys now, but at the time I resented being stuck on the ground floor, as I saw it. My brother had taught me bass-lines on the piano. He is the organist and choirmaster at a church in Bournemouth, and so I had a rudimentary knowledge of melody and harmony, and I have been fascinated by the relationship between melody and bass parts ever since. Ask any singing bassist."

Alan Jones playing a Fender Precision in Rhythm And Greens in 1964. Note the Vox column PA system

Andy Pyle

At the turn of the 1960s, The Shadows were the next big thing to hit Stopsley, near Luton in Bedfordshire. There were consequently around 20

The Rosetti Lucky 7

guitar players at Andy Pyle's school, aided and abetted by three drummers, who took turns using the orchestra's snare drum. The lone bass player expelled himself by spending more time with an Irish showband than at school. "Groups were being formed at an alarming rate in the hope of cashing in on something that even mothers could tolerate," says Andy. "One such group was The Spectres, with lead guitar, three rhythm guitars and drum. Someone had come up with the theory that three rhythm guitars more than compensated for there being no bass.

"The lead guitarist was having none of it. Their first 'engagement' was just a couple of weeks away and the music had to be right or he wouldn't do it. I'd heard the noise they were making and offered to help. I didn't have a bass but I did have £20, which wasn't nearly enough, but drastic action was called for. 'Don't get a Rosetti Lucky Seven' was the sound advice given to me by the school music teacher as I prepared for my trip to London in search of a bargain. I returned with my bargain, a Rosetti Lucky Seven, for which my mother lovingly made a bag out of some floral-patterned curtain material."

Jim Lea

Jim Lea contributed to his first band by strumming his violin, but soon after bought a guitar for £3 from Neil Jackson, a one-time Tradewinds singer. He tried to work through a guitar tutor book, but for him it wasn't the right approach. After "an explosion of frustration" he could suddenly play, and learned the melody to "Perfidia", although he had to re-learn it when he discovered the correct tuning of the guitar. He could get a tune out of anything. Music became an obsession. He turned to bass guitar, seeing it as a way of playing discreetly at the back, but he had a lot of unexpressed anger and therefore his approach became very fast and manic.

Ron Wood

Although Ron Wood has been known as a guitarist at both ends of his career, there was a spell in the mid 1960s when he was exclusively a bass player. "I met Jeff Beck and contacted him when The Birds split up. He had just quit The Yardbirds and suggested I join his band. I was playing Telecaster guitar at the time, but had reached saturation point. We played a few shows and realised that two guitars weren't going to work, so he asked me if I would mind trying bass guitar. I accepted – I loved the challenge."

Pino Palladino

While playing his Ibanez six- and twelve-string double-necked instrument, Pino Palladino and his friend Kevin Hole decided to form a band, but Pino soon found himself changing to the bass. "Our bassist had a Rickenbacker which I used to play at every opportunity. There was something I liked about playing one note at a time. Soon enough, a friend of the band, Jiffy, suggested that I should take up bass guitar. This was the push that I needed. Again, I was lucky in that my parents had faith in my ability and bought me a Fender Precision. At this time I was aged 16 or 17, and decided to get serious about music. Then came the fretless, when my friend Dave Ball sold me his fretless Precision."

John Paul Jones

On his discovery of the bass guitar, John Paul Jones says: "There were two paths which led me to it. The first was my discovery of skiffle. The tea-chest bass was an instantly cheap and easy instrument to make, but proved extremely dull to play. This brought me swiftly to rock 'n' roll. Although I had hated the early country/swing rock of Bill Haley, the straight-eight driving rhythms of Little Richard, Jerry Lee Lewis, Chuck Berry, and The Everly Brothers really excited me. At the time I was playing rock 'n' roll on the piano, and when I heard of a local group forming, I eagerly offered my services. Unfortunately, they consisted of just two guitarists – Shadows fans – who pointed out that The Shadows did not run to a pianist and they needed a drummer and a bass player, so what would I like to play? A quick calculation revealed that drums would be expensive and too cumbersome to get on the bus, whereas a bass guitar was small and light (I didn't know about bass amps then), it only had four strings and therefore was easy to learn – no contest. The next job was to find an instrument. Being 14 at the time, my [pianist] father would have to guarantee hire purchase for the guitar.

"At first he was against it: the bass guitar was a novelty instrument and would be forgotten in two years. He said I should take up the saxophone – I'd never starve. I was not to be swayed, so it was agreed that if I could keep up the payments he would help me with the deposit. By then I had my heart set on a Dallas Tuxedo solid bass guitar. (The two guitarists both had matching snot-green Lucky Sevens, I had some self-respect.) It was in the window of Garland's, of Deptford, at £25, which I could pay off at £l/13/2d [£1.65] per month through my Sunday job as organist at the local church. I took it straight home and somehow plugged it into the family radio. It sounded awful. I then discovered, to my horror, that the high notes did not have that wonderful Marvin liquid sustain, but just sort of went 'clunk'.

"I was desperate. Remember, I was 14 years old and the bass guitar as an instrument was only about ten. Without giving it a great deal of thought, I not unreasonably assumed that the high notes of a bass guitar would sound like the low notes of a regular guitar, hence my desperation when they didn't. It was only when I heard what it should do that I grew to love it.

"Back home I soon realised that the radio didn't cut it. With the help of a friend I found an old TV set, replaced the tube with a twelve-inch speaker and powered it with a 30-watt amplifier. I later moved the speaker into its own box and the amp into a radio case with coloured lights behind the fabric. I had moved into the big time. By now my father realised that I could play, and he was taking me out on gigs to play jazz standards, thinly disguised as foxtrots and quicksteps, on the local weddings/masonic/bar mitzvah circuit. 'Watch my left hand, son' – I would never starve."

DIY

Meanwhile back home, and having been persuaded to become the band's bass player, the solution to my absence of cash was to convert the Egmond Frères acoustic. The wireless magazines and component shops of the late 1950s were crammed with equipment that the post-war military no longer required, and bomber command headsets and tank commanders' throat microphones were easily and cheaply available, and were being used for purposes for which they were never intended. I acquired some Air Ministry headphones which had circular metal plates as diaphragms, and discovered that these headphones would also work as microphones, although the sound quality was rather poor. My knowledge of physics also told me that, if a moving metal plate caused a signal in the coils of the headphones, perhaps a metal guitar string near the pole pieces would do the same. It did! (I didn't know at the time that some years earlier Les Paul had experimentally screwed a telephone headset onto a section of rail track. Featuring just one string – it sounded great.)

My next step was to make a pickup from the innards of this pair of headphones, and I fixed them inside a plastic soap dish, with holes cut for the four pole pieces. After fixing this pickup onto the Egmond Frères acoustic, I removed the top two strings and tuned the remaining four down by an octave. When plugged into the "gram" input of my parents' radio, a huge wooden edifice made by Murphy, the result was interesting, if not exactly musical. It resembled a deep flapping fart with pitch, and playing anything beyond the third fret was a definite challenge. Above all, however, it was a remarkable, and novel, experience to play "here" and yet hear the sound "there" – albeit only six feet away. I was now an electric bass guitarist.

John Entwistle

Amplification at this time was a mystery to John Entwistle, but rumours abounded that it was possible to access the input stage of a Dansette record player. ("Everyone was opening up their record players to find 'the wires'.") Sensing his frustration, his mum kindly bought him a tiny Selmer amplifier for £7/10/- (£7.50).

John Rostill

Another bass player who dabbled in DIY musical technology was John Rostill. His passion was the construction of complex and intricate working models out of Meccano and a

MIDGET BATTERY ELIMINATORS to convert all types battery portables to mains operation, **57/6** each. **2/6** post. Size 3.7 inch x 1.8 inch x 2.5 inch. Smaller than H.T. battery alone. (Please state make and model no.) Brand new and boxed.

ACOS CRYSTAL MIKE INSERTS, 4/11 each. High quality. Can be used for tape recorders, baby alarms, musical instruments, etc. Post 8d. Brand new.

MORSE TAPPERS. Plated contacts, adjustable gaps, heavy duty, good quality. Special price, **3/6** each. Post 9d.

B.S.R. MONARCH 4-SPEED AUTOMATIC CHANGER. Complete with high-fidelity "Turnover Head," capacity of 10 records. Plays 12in., 10in., 7in. intermixed in any order, 78, 45, 33 and 16 r.p.m., for A.C. Mains 100-250 volts. Exclusive Magi-Disc selector gives quietest and quickest change ever. Brand new, **£6.19.6.** Post and packing 5/-.

THROAT MIKES, 1/- each. Post 6d. Can be used for electrifying musical instruments, etc.

25 mfd. x 25 mfd. MIDGET CONDENSERS. Size 1in., **1/3.** Post 4d. Brand new.

JACK PLUGS. Standard type, **1/11** each. Post 4d.

NEON MAINS TESTER/SCREWDRIVER, 4/6 each. Post 6d.

GERMANIUM DIODES, 1/- each, **10/-** dozen. Post 4d.

RECTIFIER/STABILISER. Input voltage 150 v. at 10 m.a. For low consumption battery valves, **6/6.** Post 6d.

TRANSISTORS. Yellow/Green Spot, **6/11.** Post 4d.

TRANSISTORS. R.F. Yellow/Red Spot, **12/11.** Post 4d.

SUB-MINIATURE TRANSISTOR CONDENSERS. 1.6 mfd., 5 mfd., 10 mfd., 16 mfd., 32 mfd., **2/6** each. Post 4d. Brand new.

SURPLUS, NEW AND GUARANTEED VALVES

All tested before Despatch

Cash with Order or Cash on Delivery only

1D5	10/-	12AH7	7/6	DL96	9/6
1R5	7/6	12K7	7/6	DM70	7/11
1S5	7/-	12Q7	7/6	EB91	5/11
1T4	5/6	25A6G	12/11	EBF80	9/11
3D6	4/9	35A5	10/6	ECL80	13/11
5U4G	6/6	35Z3	13/6	EF41	9/6
5Z4G	8/11	35Z4	7/6	EF50	3/6
6B8G	2/11	807 (B)	3/9	EF50(R)	4/11
6C4	4/9	807(USA)	5/6	EL84	9/-
6F1	13/11	954	1/6	EY86	14/6
6F13	12/6	955	3/11	KT33C	9/6
6K7G	2/11	956	2/11	L63	5/11
6K8G	7/6	AZ1	12/6	MU14	8/6
6L6G	5/11	AZ31	12/6	PL82	9/6
6SN7GT	5/9	CY31	12/11	PY80	7/11
6V6GT	6/6	DAF96	9/6	PY81	8/6
6X5GT	6/6	DF96	9/6	PY82	8/6
6V6G	5/11	DK96	9/6	UF41	9/-

Postage and Packing 6d. per valve extra. S.A.E. with all enquiries. Over £3 post free.

All parcels insured against damage in transit for only 6d. extra per order. All uninsured parcels at customers' risk.

SEND 1/- FOR 56-PAGE ILLUSTRATED CATALOGUE

Adverts for crystal mics and throat mics in Practical Wireless, January 1959. They made amplification look so easy

Air Ministry Headphones

variety of electrical and electronic kits, with devices involving the use of batteries, bulbs, and valves. By his early teens John was building simple radios and amplifiers, and once even constructed an electrical mechanical bird-trapping machine (although the birds were always released quickly and unharmed).

Roy Babbington

At first, Roy Babbington played guitar, and he recalls that Eddie Robinson, the bass player in his early band, was a boffin who made his own pickups and amps, and in around 1957 invented the Bosswell bass. It was a real electric bass, possibly the first fretless that one actually wore. It had round-wound piano-wire strings fixed at the head and was tuned at the bridge end with what looked like snare-drum fittings. Roy also enjoyed experimenting, and later began amplifying his own bass by using a throat mic, a loudspeaker (backwards) and a mic which was designed for checking the flow in pipes at ICI ("It registered the gurgle").

Les Hurdle

As a young classical trumpet player, Les Hurdle performed with huge orchestras. "Those trumpets without valves were a bitch, but what did I know? Trills? No problem. Then, via my girlfriend, I heard rock and pop music. Oh no! Her neighbour's son was the drummer in a band which had no bass player. 'Wait a minute, how hard could that be?' I wondered. Playing a trumpet without valves was not easy, but here was a lump of wood with bits of wire across it telling you exactly where to go. I made my own electric bass."

The Travellers in 1962. Les Hurdle (right) is attempting to disown his flugelhorn

John Entwistle

As did John Entwistle. Intrigued by the massive bottom-end sound of Duane Eddy's "Peter Gunn" theme, John was moved to take up the bass but couldn't afford any of the instruments that were available at the time. His answer was to make his first bass from a piece of mahogany and a neck that was copied roughly from a Fender. Unfortunately he had no idea how long it should be, and his design was far too long. His mistake was to copy the fret positions from a short-scale Hofner "violin" bass, which left him with approximately seven inches of fingerboard with no frets at all! He then fitted a Royal pickup to the instrument. It was straight, with no pole pieces, and was the cheaper of the two Royal models. "It resembled a sardine tin," says John.

Pre-dating his Who colleague Pete Townshend' s intentional antics by a few years, John once accidentally left his unique bass guitar lying across the arms of an armchair. With abysmal timing he tripped on a carpet edge, fell on to his instrument, and smashed it to smithereens. Never one to give up, he began assembling a bass from several "acquired" Fenton-Weill components. John became notorious for building his own Frankenstein basses from elements of various Fender Precisions.

Andy Pyle

Andy's first amplifier wasn't in fact an amplifier at all but a wireless. "The school boffin declared that he could modify it to receive a bass guitar signal in place of radio transmissions – it was the same principle. The five-inch speaker wasn't to be a worry, as it was all a 'matched unit'. He did his thing with the electrics while I disguised the walnut veneer cabinet by covering it with blue "contact", a sticky-backed vinyl which can still be found in kitchens throughout the former Eastern Bloc. A blue plastic handle screwed to the top completed the illusion. My guitar lead was three feet of flex, soldered directly into the chassis and fed through one of the many holes in the back of the cabinet.

"It was with this setup that I made my first public appearance in the spring of 1962. I loaded the blue wireless together with the triangular curtain bag concealing the Lucky Seven onto my sister's pushchair and walked the mile and a half to the church hall. With the 'amp' on the floor I was reduced to a half-crouch position due to the shortness of my guitar lead. With it on a chair, my backside blocked the speaker and rendered it inaudible if more than two people were talking at the same time. When the whole band started up I was forced to turn the volume on full. Thus The Spectres made their debut complete with a bass that sounded like three rhythm guitars. It wasn't such a bad idea after all."

Andy Pyle (r) with the Midnites, December 1964

SHOP STORIES

Brian Gregg

While playing double-bass in Les Bennetts' skiffle group Les Hobeaux, Brian Gregg caught his first glimpses of bass guitars in the film *The Girl Can't Help It*, and also with the touring band of Lionel Hampton. He was impressed by the sight of such an instrument in the window of Selmer's, and it was Eric Ford who sold him a Hofner, which was one of the first in the country.

Roger Glover

Selmer's was the place in London to buy a Hofner guitar. When Roger Glover was playing in his early band, The Madisons, matching Hofners became the goal. "Mine was financially inaccessible in the window of a music shop in South Harrow. I'd pass by regularly and gaze at it, all shiny and new and waiting. Standing there for ages, my eager eyes took in every last detail. It wasn't a Fender, but it was within range, I wanted to believe."

Ronnie Lane

Steve Marriott was working at the J60 shop in Manor Park, East London, when both Ronnie Lane and Kenney Jones walked in one day, looking for a bass. Steve once commented: "I think Ronnie had decided that there were too many guitarists around, and that if he was gonna get a gig he'd have to learn bass. They were both suited up like real mods, and I remember them looking pretty cool. I ended up selling Ronnie a bass – a Harmony – at a whacking great discount."

Ron Wood

After quitting The Small Faces in 1969, Steve was replaced on guitar by Ron Wood, who had been a bass player in The Jeff Beck Group. "I stole my first bass guitar from Sound City, Shaftesbury Avenue, London. It was a Fender Jazz bass. After forging the papers that your parents were meant to sign, I went back to the shop five years later, owned up and paid them back – they had to laugh!"

Andy Pyle

Andy Pyle wanted a salmon-pink Fender Precision, like the one Jet Harris played with The Shadows. In the autumn of 1962, one of these beauties appeared in the window of his local music shop. "I'd go out of my way to walk past it. I'd catch the bus that travelled that route just to see it. I dreamed about it. I hadn't the courage to go in and try it, as it was well out of reach both financially and in size. This nonsense continued for nearly two years until, one day, it was gone.

"They were having a clear-out and it had been bought, shop-soiled, by a member of staff – a guitarist. I tracked him down and asked why a guitarist should want a Precision bass. (He played bass as well, of course – don't they all?) I'd been working my way towards this ultimate goal and was currently the owner of a Burns six-string bass, surely a more suitable instrument for a guitarist who plays bass as well. He thought long and hard about it, and eventually offered to swap, provided that I took over his bass job with Johnny and The Rainbows, the kind of outfit you could take your grandmother to see but definitely no one else. I did a number of concerts with this lot, which was a high price to pay for a second-hand, shop-soiled, salmon-pink Fender Precision, but I paid it, and at last it was mine."

John Wetton

Like red guitars, there was something about pink basses that grabbed the attention. John Wetton was another victim to fall head over heels at the sight of one in the window of Don Strike's music shop in Bournemouth. "Don's shop is legendary – ask any indigenous muso. We would all pass through those hallowed portals at some time or another to buy our strings, get gigs and have tuition. Most of all, Saturday was the day to hang there and gawp, and try out stuff we wouldn't be able to pay for.

"It must have been 1962 or 1963 when I was first entranced by the contents of Don Strike's window. I would go for a late evening stroll and surreptitious ciggie through Westbourne Arcade, and I would just stand and admire and lust and fantasise about her every curve, her every contour, her sensuously long neck and her knobs and scratchplate. She was a delicate shade of pink and was one of the most sensational pickups I'd ever seen. I had to have her. I longed to let my fingers stroke and caress her, explore every detail of the immaculate untouched body. One day we would be

John Wetton and his beloved Fender Precision

joined at the socket – my male giving life to her female, and in turn she would give birth to my seminal hopes and dreams. I was twelve years old and she was a six-month-old Futurama, but I was sold. She was sold, too, but not to me."

BASS STRINGS

Catalogue

The April 1957 catalogue and price list for General Music Strings Ltd of Glamorgan (who made Monopole strings) is an impressive document. The contents page lists strings for an unbelievable range of instruments, i.e., violin, viola, violoncello, double bass, mandolin, mandola, mandolincello, Hawaiian guitar, Spanish guitar, plectrum guitar, skiffle guitar, banjo, tenor banjo, ukulele, harp (where the strings are described as being "waterproof"), zither, autoharp, and even the *oud* – but *no* bass guitar strings! It may help to realise that in the UK there were, of course, no bass guitars either at that time.

Bass strings have since changed out of all recognition, from the thuddy flatwounds of the early 1960s to the bright and twangy roundwounds which followed. As a result of the improved tonal response, playing styles have evolved apace, developing techniques such as slapping, tapping, and the use of harmonics.

Colin Hodgkinson

After a year of playing with one set of bass strings, Colin Hodgkinson bought a new set of Fenders for £5. He had just wound on the new G when it broke. "I couldn't believe it. I was so mad that I wrote a really nasty letter to Fender and posted it to California. About three months later I received a letter addressed to me in Peterborough, Canada! On the letter was scrawled the suggestion 'Try England'. My new G had arrived! There were (at least for bass) only flatwounds or those horrible black nylon ones – roundwounds were still a few years away."

John Entwistle

John Entwistle's pioneering solos on The Who's "My Generation" were originally played on a very twangy Danelectro ("Dano"). "The trouble was that the strings were so thin I kept breaking them. At that time we would record during the day and, to finance the sessions, played gigs nearly every night, but inevitably I would break a string. We had just recorded 'My Generation', but Kit Lambert decided we had to record again. None of the music shops had any replacement strings (no string manufacturers made replacement strings thin enough for the Dano basses then), so I had to go down to Marshall's and buy a new Dano bass for £60. I ended up with three new Danelectros, all with busted strings! In the end I busted my last string at the third attempt and there weren't any more in the country. I thought 'Fuck it' and went and bought myself a Fender Jazz bass and a set of La Bella strings, and played the solo with that. But it was a different sound and a simplified, slowed-down version of the solos on previous takes."

In 1966 John was looking for that Danelectro sound again, and his persistence led to a new standard in bass guitar strings. He says: "I tried everybody's strings, but the E and the A just didn't work. It was the same with Rotosound, so to solve the problem I got in touch with James How and told him that his D and G strings were great but the E and A didn't vibrate properly. He told me to take my bass along to Rotosound and have some strings made until they got it right. After a couple of hours we realised that the problem wasn't in the wire winding but in the core of the string: it needed to be thicker and the overall gauges a bit heavier. They sent me away with twelve sets to use. A couple of days later they called and asked if they could put my name to the strings. I told them I didn't mind as long as they kept me supplied with free strings! But then we had to do the same with medium and short-scale strings because I had loads of different basses by then. Those strings, the RS 66 set, were the first that vibrated properly, other than the Danelectros."

CHAPTER 7

INNOVATION

Picture a band with the following line-up: zither, Hawaiian lap steel guitar, drums, and accordion. It's hardly rock 'n' roll, is it? But players of these instruments – James How, Dick Denney, Jim Marshall and Charlie Watkins – were most definitely at the forefront of the development of British rock guitar. Certainly, without the vision of these four pioneers our musical heritage would never have been as colourful – or as loud!

THE PIONEERS

James How

The 1949 film *The Third Man* was filmed mostly in Vienna, a city torn apart by the war. At the end of a long day's shooting, director Carol Reed and actor Orson Welles found themselves in a dark, smoky bistro, where their attention was drawn to a 40-year-old musician playing a zither, just for tips. Reed realised almost immediately that this instrument was the perfect sound for the film. The player, Anton Karas, was persuaded to come to England to compose and record the soundtrack at Shepperton Studios. The music was a great success, and the theme to *The Third Man* sold over 500,000 copies.

One of the people who saw the film and bought the record was the young James How. "I liked the theme music so much that I decided then and there to learn how to play the zither." How had trained initially to be a professional violin and viola player before the war, and was also interested in engineering – an interest he took to its logical conclusion by becoming an apprentice engineer at the Vickers company. War intervened, however, and he joined the RAF for some six years, four of which were spent abroad, where he found it difficult to continue to pursue his musical aspirations. Coming out of the RAF he decided that the only future left to him was in engineering, so he took a job at the Royal Ordnance Factory in Woolwich. Then he saw the film in 1952 and his interest in music was revived. He began those zither lessons.

"The strings for zithers were pretty awful. It was still basically an unknown instrument, and for a time the only way I could get strings was literally to buy old zithers and take the strings from them. I ended up with a collection of some 350, the best of which I've kept. Eventually I despaired, and decided to make my own strings, which so impressed my tutor that I decided to form my own company in 1958."

James How with his favourite Zither

With his knowledge of engineering he built his own string winding machines. As well as zither strings, James began expanding into making strings for virtually every stringed instrument – pianos, violins, double-basses, violas – but it wasn't until 1962 that Rotosound strings made their first appearance. The Shadows were one of the first bands to use the new strings, quickly followed by The Beatles and many more.

James created the roundwound bass string in 1963, but when The Who became customers in 1966 it was bassist

John Entwistle who spotted a problem: he was looking for that Danelectro sound again, and his persistence led to a new standard in bass guitar strings. He says: "I tried everybody's strings, but the E and the A just didn't work. It was the same with Rotosound, so to solve the problem I got in touch with James How and told him that his D and G strings were great but the E and A didn't vibrate properly. He told me to take my bass along to Rotosound and have some strings made until they got it right. After a couple of hours we realised that the problem wasn't in the wire winding but in the core of the string: it needed to be thicker and the overall gauges a bit heavier. They sent me away with twelve sets to use. A couple of days later they called and asked if they could put my name to the strings. I told them I didn't mind as long as they kept me supplied with free strings! As a result of these meetings John became an endorsee, and the standard-gauge bass string was born.

Dick Denney (2nd l) playing guitar at a casual gig with the Skyriders dance band at the Embassy Ballroom in Welling, Kent, in November 1958. His lap steel rests on a Jennings organ amplifier which he had converted for guitar use. This is possibly the earliest appearance of the 'Vox' logo. The amplifier combination would soon evolve into the Vox AC 15

Dick Denney

While James How was starting up string manufacture in Bexleyheath, his wartime friend Dick Denney was starting Vox Amplifiers just down the road in Deptford. Dick was a lap steel guitar player. "In the early days, in big bands, they wouldn't let you use an amplifier – you had to play a big archtop. But with the Hawaiian guitar you had to have an amp and pickup."

From the age of 12 he was always dabbling in electronics and winding coils. "As a keen lap steel guitarist I'd looked a long time for a particular sound which had been eluding me. I'd been building circuits and amplifiers since the age of 14, driven by a curiosity sparked (so to speak) by an early attempt at converting my dad's prized new radio – bought with 3,000 Summit cigarette coupons – into an amplifier for my home-made lap steel. I'd seen the socket on the back of the set marked 'PU', and occasionally connected the instrument, with its pickup derived from a magnetic earpiece, to it. This was only possible when my dad was out, although generally it didn't have any ill effects. But one evening my curiosity ran away with me: the back came off and the screwdriver went in. One accidental short circuit later and the radio was no more. My electronic experiments had begun. First, though, I had to outrun my dad!"

Many years and experiments later, Dick's interest in electronics led him to developing the circuit that became the first Vox amplifier. By the end of January 1958, the 15-watt Denney twin-channel amplifier had been developed to production standard. The styling and presentation weren't that much different from the classic Vox style of later years, and it had the first model number allocated to a Vox amplifier: Amplifier Combination 15 watts (AC15).

The Shadows acquired AC15s in mid 1958, and were very pleased with the sound. As their tour load increased and the gigs became bigger, however, it was evident that this amp wasn't big enough. Dick says: "I remember when The Shadows came back from their first tour of America they piled up their AC15s in my hallway for service." They had tried the Fender Twin amp, but although they were impressed by its volume, it lacked the richness of tone of the AC15. The spontaneous reaction from the group was characteristically direct: why not a twin AC15? It had the sound they wanted – all they needed was more of it. Why not simply use two AC15s apiece?

But using two amplifiers in tandem isn't as straightforward as it might seem. For a start, adjustments in volume level aren't as straightforward – two volume controls must be operated, and in mid performance this can be one too many. Secondly, one of the amps must always be de-earthed to avoid the production of hum when they are connected together. Thirdly, the increase in numbers of units to be transported (from three to six) was deemed excessive. Lastly, amplifiers weren't yet respectable; using three was already a borderline matter, giving rise to observations about excessive noise and limited musical ability. Six would have been written off as unreasonable, bordering on manic. Although in reality the overall production of noise would only have been marginally greater, those in charge of clubs and theatres, who were already alarmed at noise levels and didn't see the need for amplifiers of any kind, would have probably refrained from allowing a group with two amps per player to perform at all.

Dick looked into the matter. His design for the AC15 used EL84 output valves, which he describes as having "the sweetest sound ever." The solution, he reasoned, was to use four of them. With a change in cabinet dimensions and the addition of two twelve-inch speakers, Vox's most successful model was born: the AC30. The Shadows finally took delivery of three AC30s late in 1959. The beat boom had started.

Jim Marshall

Jim Marshall began his engineering career as a toolmaker, largely by teaching himself from books. His semi-professional music career blossomed into obtaining regular work as a drummer, and by 1947 he began to study under Max Abrams, a highly respected drum teacher. Jim was so busy playing and teaching his own pupils that by the early 1950s he had to consider turning professional. He subsequently became successful very quickly as a sought-after professional drummer and drum teacher. At one point he had up to 65 pupils attending his school a week.

From the amount of retail that his drum school was generating, it became obvious that he should open his own shop, which he did in 1960. Many of Jim's pupils became successful with their own bands, and consequently began to bring their guitarists and bass players into the shop. Their demands for guitar products meant that Jim now had to stock guitars and amplification. In addition, Jim soon realised that he could produce his own cabinets to cope with the louder volume levels required, and turned his garage into a workshop, building just two cabinets a week in 1961. Meanwhile, as the shop in Hanwell became more popular, the café across the road expanded to three shop fronts, and became a focal point for contacts and for advertising work – a sort of rock version of Soho's Archer Street.

The guitarists coming into the store demanded an amp that sounded brighter than the Fender amp, and to help Jim achieve this aim he contacted Dudley Craven, an 18-year-old electronics boffin who was then working at EMI in Hayes. To improve upon his wage of £4 per week, Jim offered him £15 per week to start working on the design of a suitable amplifier, along with Jim's right-hand man, electrical technician Ken Bran, who was the builder and repair man. After months of trials they finally settled on a design, and the Marshall sound was born. Dudley, however, vanished to Canada only three years after joining.

The first 50-watt amp was so powerful that it kept blowing speakers in the two-by-twelve-inch cabinets, so Jim had the brilliant idea of constructing a four-by-twelve-inch cabinet, the dimensions for which were the smallest possible for that configuration.

Jim had known Pete Townshend for many years after having played drums in bands with his father, saxophonist Cliff. In 1965, finding himself needing more power on stage, Pete suggested the creation of a 100-watt amplifier. As soon as this was developed, he wanted something bigger: an eight-by-twelve-inch cabinet. Jim complied, and a prototype was built. Within two weeks of the creation of this ludicrous edifice, however, there were so many complaints from the road crew that the idea was dropped. Pete then suggested a division: "Why not two four-by-twelve-inch cabinets?" And so the stack was born. The top half of the stack's cabinet sloped: an idea of Jim's to make it look more 'designed'. One day Ricky West of The Tremeloes asked why the top two speakers sloped. Jim didn't have a proper answer but bluffed: "They throw the sound up over the audience." He went to the back of the room and to his great surprise found that it was true!

When Pete Townshend started smashing things, both Jim and Pete's dad thought that he was bonkers. In reality he was being very subtle, but Pete would never damage his main Rickenbacker – it would be carefully swapped before the end of the show for one that Jim had glued together from a previous smashing. Jim noticed that Pete only damaged the grille cloth, never the speaker cones.

One day drummer Mitch Mitchell, an ex-student, brought Jimi Hendrix into the store. Naturally, Jim thought: "Oh no, not another American wanting a freebie!" But Hendrix, fascinated by the similarity of their names (James Marshall/James Marshall Hendrix), insisted on paying, although he demanded worldwide service; so whilst Vox was huge in the early 1960s, without Marshall we wouldn't have had Hendrix, Cream, The Who, Free, The Yardbirds, and Jeff Beck, and many of the other artists who, with the help of Jim's amplification, defined the sound of British heavy rock in the late 1960s and early 1970s.

Jim Marshall, the drummer

Charlie Watkins

"The late 1950s was one of the most exciting periods in history, never to be repeated," recalls Charlie Watkins, the man behind the Watkins Dominator, the Copicat, and the WEM PA systems which graced the stages of legendary bands throughout the 1960s and 1970s. And for him, the late 1950s signified a time when he would begin to pour his considerable engineering expertise into shaping the sounds of the next decade.

But Charlie had always been an inventor, even at the early age of six years old, when he would stay awake all night, sitting up in bed, trying to figure out how to convert the mechanism of a door lock into a sewing machine. Although in later life he played the accordion to satisfy his musical needs, it was the mechanics of the electric guitar that began to fascinate him, and with his knowledge of electronics he began to design and construct amplifiers. At first, his designs followed familiar patterns, until one day he conceived the cabinet shape (which looked suspiciously like an accordion case) for what would come to be known as 'the Dominator'.

Charlie Watkins, looking happy with his 'WEM'-logo accordion

He made a prototype of the revolutionary triangular cabinet shape, then (perhaps prematurely) invited the opinion of his Homburg-hatted old-school salesman, who, upon seeing the design, exclaimed: "I can't sell that – it's like selling big packets of cornflakes!" In retrospect, Charlie admits: "He was mad. He walked out on me. He was on 10 per cent, silly sod!" The salesman was indeed foolish, since the Dominator went on to sell in excess of 25,000 units before it was discontinued in 1964, and it is now a highly prized and collectible amp.

Charlie called me up some time ago and said: "Come over – I've got something for you." I went to his house in South London where he presented me with a Dominator that he had made specially, using an old chassis he had left over. I was stunned. It was beautiful – the 'last' Dominator. What a kind man.

WEM (Watkins Electric Music) was founded by Charlie in 1963. "We were jealous of the name 'Vox'. It was a big name, but with only three letters, like 'Oxo'. It made sense. I had a friend, a very sharp advertising man, who sat down at his desk and sketched a sign that would be easily visible. He contended that the London Underground sign was a very cleverly designed logo, and used it as a basis. He was also intrigued that W was similar to an upside-down M. This gave him the design. It was punched out in aluminium, and then our designer sprayed it in phosphorous red. It was the guv'nor!"

An exhausted Charlie Watkins in front of his Isle of Wight PA

Another of Charlie's gifts to 1960s guitarists was the totally functional Copicat tape-echo machine, a staple effect of most bands in the period. Towards the end of that swinging decade, Charlie diversified into PA systems. Gigs were getting bigger (e.g., Hyde Park), and the idea of the open-air festival had evolved. His WEM columns and mixers were to be seen everywhere, and he remains proud of his Audiomaster, which was the only serious PA mixer at the time.

Charlie looked exhausted after staying awake for 48 hours putting together the huge PA system for the 1970 Isle of Wight Festival, which featured Jimi Hendrix, Free, and The Who. On top of the PA was a huge parabolic dish, like a satellite dish. The dish idea came about after he drove past Philips Research in Byfleet, Surrey, and saw models of radar dishes in their windows. He thought: "Why shouldn't this idea work for sound?" Inspired, he built a huge dish out of fibreglass on the top floor of his premises and then had to lower it out of the window. Madness! Its speakers reproduced the mid range 1kHz to 4kHz, and it could focus up to five miles away! In those days, the speakers themselves didn't have a very high power rating, and the total output of the huge rig was only about 5kW. The PA was on a hill, and what he didn't bargain for was a prevailing wind of 40mph, which meant that those backstage could hear more clearly than the audience out at the front. People began throwing bottles, and fighting broke out among the road crews on stage. Charlie says: "When the first bottle hits you on the head, you quickly learn what the customer wants."

And as if that wasn't bad enough, at one of these huge gigs he had displayed warning signs which read: "Do not approach the banks of speakers without protective headphones." One afternoon he was climbing the PA truss, fixing and testing the system, and had foolishly forgotten his own headphones. Some idiot, thinking it was funny, suddenly played a Hammond organ very loudly through the speakers, but it was really an act of crass stupidity. The shock was enormous, and poor Charlie was blown off the rig and flung to the ground. Mercifully, he survived to tell the tale.

Although Charlie continues to invent, he will be affectionately remembered by many of the guitarists in this book for the blue-and-white wedge-shaped Watkins Dominator – all 17 watts of it. A true pioneer, today, despite being in his eighties, Charlie has no intention of retiring. "What am I going to do, dig the garden? I like to be innovative – still! I don't like following the general drift. I never want to stand still."

Leo Fender and the Precision Bass

Over in America, Clarence Leo Fender had by 1946 progressed from tinkering with radios and had started to experiment with pickups, amplifiers, and lap-top steel guitars. In 1950, while based in Fullerton, California, this stocky and slightly balding 41-year-old ex-radio repairman launched the Fender Broadcaster electric solid-body guitar with a bolt-on neck. It was incredibly successful, especially among country players. Ironically, the demands for an electric bass guitar came from the guitarists rather than the bassists; at that time many guitar players had to "double" on bass just to make a living, but they couldn't hear it or pitch it properly. To their rescue came the aptly named Precision bass.

Essentially a larger, modified version of the Broadcaster (now renamed the Telecaster for legal reasons), the Precision was tuned the same as a double-bass, but it had frets, was lightweight and, with an amplifier, it was clearly audible. The scale length of an upright double-bass is generally 42 inches (1067mm), whilst that of the electric guitar is 25.5 inches (648mm). A little maths shows that the mid-point between these two measurements is 33.75 inches (857mm), which is so temptingly close to the 34 inches (864mm) which Leo chose for the scale length of the Precision. This idea has never been confirmed, but in the absence of an alternative theory I'll stick with this one – it's the perfect compromise.

In his expedient way, Leo was merely adapting to the market. He didn't predict the future – he was just a genius at getting things right first time. At the time, however, not everyone agreed with him. Indeed, some even went as far as to call the instrument "a vulgar plank".

The Fender Precision bass underwent its final transformation in 1957, and has remained essentially unchanged to this day. In the intervening years, electric basses in general have undergone many modifications: five-string models have appeared with a low B, and there are now even six- and eight-string basses. Ironically, the fretless bass is now in common use, and some modern basses have MIDI capability. Despite these progressions, however, the Precision, along with its younger cousin, the Jazz bass (introduced in 1960), continues to be the most popular electric bass in the world.

The Stratocaster

Not content with his brilliant innovations, Leo Fender further revolutionised the musical instrument business when – in 1954 – he launched the Fender Stratocaster, the guitar which has had the most profound and lasting effect on modern music.

Guitars come and go, but the Stratocaster is always there. Its original design has remained practically unchanged since its launch. Designed by Leo, with assistance from colleague Fred Tavares and country picker Bill Carson, it was first looked upon as a subversive intruder, a curious object that looked as if it had come from outer space. Today, like the Boeing 747, and the Citroen DS, the 'Strat' is hailed as a twentieth-century design icon – the best-selling and most celebrated musical instrument in history. What an achievement from a guy who was not a guitar player himself.

Most people's introduction to this guitar would have been through seeing Buddy Holly cradling a remarkable object on the cover of his LP *The Chirping Crickets*, but by

Buddy Holly and The Crickets' legendary LP cover

the early 1960s the instrument's late arrival on British soil, and Hank Marvin's echo-laden use of his red Strat, led to a massive surge in interest. Everybody wanted a red guitar!

At the time, most electric guitars featured only one or maybe two pickups, but the Strat had three single-coil pickups, strategically positioned to provide maximum variations of tone, which was vital in developing its characteristic sparkling clean sound. It was built with a standard three-way pickup switch for selection of bass, middle or treble sounds. Anchoring the switch between these positions gave access to out-of-phase sounds, and demand for this encouraged Fender to introduce a standard five-way selector in 1977.

The guitar came with a tremolo arm, which screwed into a tension-balanced bridge vibrato unit, enabling the player to bend the pitch of a note or chord and return to (approximately) normal tuning. Other guitars of the era relied on the fitting of specialist tremolo units – such as Bigsbys – as extras. Also, for the first time, the teardrop-shaped jack socket was positioned on the front of the instrument, and there were individual saddles for each string. It was a revelation.

Optimum player comfort was provided by the instrument's curved tailfin appearance, which mirrored some of the Precision bass' design values. In fact, Fender's advertising for the guitar included the boast that the instrument was 'comfort contoured', but there is little doubt that this look was influenced by classic postwar American automobile designs. Although originally only available in a black-and-yellow sunburst finish, towards the end of the 1950s – when custom Strats became available in colours such as Lake Placid blue – the use of standard car paint accentuated the automobile influence. These are among the highest valued Strats in the world.

In 1965, Leo Fender sold his organisation to CBS for $13m but stayed on as a consultant until his resignation in 1970. He later went on to produce the highly successful Music Man guitars. But he was sorely missed at Fender in the 1970s at a time when musicians were noting that good new Strats were thin on the ground, prompting another drop in popularity. However, the mid 1980s witnessed an about-turn when a new regime took over the Fender name and, with renewed commitment and increased production, this has led to manufacturing not only in the USA and Japan, but also in Mexico and Korea. Leo sadly died in 1991.

STRAT TALES

Mark Knopfler

Mark Knopfler remembers when a red Strat first appeared in his local shop. He stared at it for weeks, on his way to and from school. He'd never been so close to one before – only three feet and a sheet of plate glass separated them! "There was an advert for The Shads a few years ago, with little kids – one little kid in spectacles – in a back lane. And that's basically what the whole thing's about, isn't it? Pressing your nose up against shop windows, looking at a real Fender. I know what the Fender catalogue smells like, what the grain of the paper was like, I wanted this thing so badly. That's why my first guitar had to be red – from that, from the Fender, and going and watching a kid in the woodwork class making one, and just picking the body up that he was making, and holding it and being completely consumed by this thing."

Jeff Beck

Jeff Beck has a vivid memory of travelling on a bus with a friend up the Charing Cross Road and shouting "Stop the bus!" when confronted by the overwhelming sight of a bright red Fender Stratocaster in a shop window. "I owe a good deal to Leo Fender. I used to collect Fender catalogues and leave them on the table so people would think I was going to buy a guitar. In fact, I couldn't afford one."

Tony Hicks

Of course, the Strat doesn't suit every guitarist's style, and The Hollies' Tony Hicks was never attracted to Fenders. When flying to Dundee for a TV show in the mid 1960s, The Hollies had to borrow equipment from a support band, whose guitarist had a Fender Stratocaster with strings that were as light a gauge as was possible in those days, plus a tremolo that seemed to be tensioned by only one spring. Tony had such a hard time with the instrument that from that day to this Strats have frightened him to death.

David Gilmour

There are some players, however, who will always be linked with Leo Fender's finest achievement. The Strat has been crucial to the Pink Floyd sound, from the days of *Ummagumma* through to *The Division Bell*. David Gilmour says: "For me, the Strat is the ultimate all-round guitar, but once you've played one for a while it's hard to get used to something like a Les Paul. I use a Strat because I'm comfortable with it and it gives me the sound and feeling I like best. Ever since hearing Hank Marvin I've liked using the tremolo bar, and it has become increasingly common for me to play with it, because it allows me to play one note's vibrato with my finger and then the next one with the tremolo bar. It's a different sort of sound, and I don't plan in advance to use both – I just play it without thinking."

Russ Ballard graduated to a Futurama Grazioso: "It looked like rock'n'roll with switches and a whammy bar. It was my pride and joy. I'd had it for about five days when my band, Norman Eddy and the Imperials, was photographed with Cliff Richard. It really brought me down when he said: 'Wow, one of those imitation Fenders'"

Eric Clapton

Apart from Hank Marvin, arguably the most famous of all Strat users is Eric Clapton, whose Blackie was assembled by him from four different guitars. "I bought about twelve Strats for about $100 each from a shop in Nashville at a time when they were pretty unfashionable. I gave most of them away to friends, but I kept four back. Blackie has a 1957 body, a 1956 neck, a scratchplate from another, and early 1970s pickups from yet another. It was a guitar on which I stamped my own personality, and it was my main one until my Signature model came out. I've played a lot of guitars over the years, but I always go back to the Strat."

Graham Gouldman

"I went with my dad to Stock & Chapman, in Oxford Road, Manchester, and bought my dream guitar: a salmon pink Fender Stratocaster. I had seen The Shadows playing theirs, and I knew that this was the guitar for me. I would sleep with the guitar case open beside my bed – it was the last thing I saw at night and the first thing I looked at in the morning, and... ooh, that smell."

Mick Green

"My earliest recollections of rock 'n' roll in Britain go back to St Mary's Ballroom, Putney, where we used to watch such groups as Cliff Bennett and The Rebel Rousers, Neil Christian and The Crusaders (with Jimmy Page – who later became a good friend – on guitar) and Chris Farlowe and The Thunderbirds with Bobby Taylor on guitar. Bobby was the first guitarist that I saw in this country to play a Fender Stratocaster, well before Hank Marvin. I was unfortunate enough to be on the same show when he got it – I was in a band called Earl Sheridan and The Houseshakers, and we were supporting. I had just got my first electric guitar, a Futurama, which I was quite pleased with until Bobby walked in, slapped the Fender Strat case on the piano, opened it up and took it out. When you're 14 and have never seen anything like the Strat before, it does your brain in! I didn't play one note right for the whole set, waiting for him to come on and play the Strat."

Jeff Beck (extreme right) playing with the Deltones in 1961 at Dowgate Hall in Tonbridge, Kent – an enviable display of Fenders

Dave Pegg

"Hank and The Shads soon became gods to me and I spent all my time in art class at Yardley Grammar School drawing Fender Stratocasters. I'd miss school to go and touch them in Yardley's, Kay Westworth's, Woodroffe's and all the other Birmingham music shops. Sometimes the shop owners would let me play them, but I never dreamed I would ever own one. What a guitar! Never equalled in my book. That I would ever progress from 'Apache' still amazes me."

RADIO LUXEMBOURG

In 1925, eight years after World War I, the first commercial radio station in America was launched, and it wasn't long before forward-thinking businessmen began to plan the introduction of commercial radio in Britain, in competition with the established BBC.

It was on 3 December 1933 that Radio Luxembourg began to transmit on a long-wave frequency from its purpose-built Villa Louvigny studio, and even from its early days it was obvious just how different its programming style was, compared with the serious and staid establishment. It played the pop music of the day, and broadcast to millions of listeners. Unlike American stations, it was wide-ranging in its listener-friendly choice of music, and didn't pigeonhole styles. This was just the kind of formula to fire the public's imagination.

The station was founded by Steven Williams, who had transferred from Radio Paris and taken his portfolio of advertisers with him. Until World War II, few people outside Luxembourg were aware of the country's existence: no one knew where it was, there was no airport, and by train it took seven hours from Paris and five hours from Brussels. For source material, the broadcasts used either gramophone records, or local and touring orchestras passing through the country – although Bush Radio recorded some programmes in London.

Palmolive Soap and Ovaltine made the first fully pre-recorded programmes on the photo-electric track of 17.5mm (half-width) film at Lime Grove studios in Shepherd's Bush. The listeners liked what they heard, and the advertisers liked the kudos it accorded them.

At the outbreak of World War II in 1939, however, the Grand Duchy of Luxembourg was occupied by Germany, and the radio station's powerful transmitter was seized to transmit Nazi propaganda broadcasts to the whole of Europe. After the Allied victory, the station bounced back to life and resumed its normal transmissions in 1946. By the mid 1950s, Radio Luxembourg was transmitting on medium wave, on its now-famous 208-metre wavelength, and started the first ever Top 20 chart show, which was then based solely on the sales of sheet music rather than records. This highly entertaining programming format was a major influence when the BBC later introduced *Pick of the Pops*, the Light Programme's (or Radio One, from September 1967) weekly run-down of the best-selling singles on 247 metres medium wave.

As a medium wave station, Radio Luxembourg was restricted to a bandwidth of 9kHz (or cycles per second, as it was then known). This meant that the audio response could only reach 4.5kHz, and when one considers that the frequency response of CDs stretches to 20kHz it's easy to understand that the lo-fi sound quality of Fab 208 was actually far from fab. Listeners would suffer frustration at the constant fading and phasing, which seemed to permeate at least a couple of verses' worth of each record. (For some reason, it always affected your favourite records the worst!) Nevertheless, most listeners found the compression and fading quite magical, certainly in hindsight, and preferred to listen to the latest hip sounds and put up with audio inadequacies rather than hear Max Bygraves at his most crystal clear.

Jeff Beck says: "Radio Luxembourg was one of these stations that you could just tune into, as if it was coming from the far-flung regions of Africa or something, but it was only in Luxembourg. And it was all muffled and indistinct, and you had to strain your ears so much to hear the guitar."

Deep Purple's Roger Glover was another ardent 208 listener. "Luxembourg was a saviour, beaming in through the static and transporting me away, never to be returned. I was turned on to Barrett Strong, Bobby 'Blue' Bland, Bobby Soxx and The Blue Jeans, James Brown, The Hollywood Argyles, and so on. Only the 'hambones' – the nerds with no taste – liked Craig Douglas or Mark Wynter. Cliff Richard was sort of acceptable but only because of his backing band, The Shadows."

Airtime on Luxembourg could be purchased by record companies to allow their promotion of new artists and releases. Throughout the 1960s, The Beatles made twelve appearances on Luxembourg, the first on 8 October 1962, for which they played at EMI House in London in front of 100 invited teenagers. Record companies, including EMI, would also send their artists to record shows in London, at Hertford Street Studios near Park Lane, and then fly the resulting tapes to Luxembourg for broadcast. Richard Millard, the studio's chief engineer in the early 1960s, recalls recording hundreds of top pop acts, including The Shadows, for this very purpose.

DJ Mike Read, who went on to join BBC Radio One and become a TV personality with his *Pop Quiz* show, spent a year as a Luxembourg broadcaster in 1978. "It only transmitted for the eight hours between 7 p.m. and 3 a.m. This created a problem because, as a DJ, you were left wondering what to do during the rest of the day. It was fatal to go out drinking since you had to read your own news, and enunciate very carefully!" Of course, for "pop pickers" in the 1950s and 1960s, this meant that there was no alternative to the drab and dreary Light Programme until the early evening.

The importance of Radio Luxembourg, especially its role in expanding the awareness of the 1960s pop fan, cannot be overestimated. But it wasn't alone in its cultural mission. Its rival pirate stations – including Radio London and Radio Caroline, which broadcast from ships moored outside UK territorial waters – also helped to change the way in which pop music was received, and the establishment quickly learned of its own weaknesses and the huge market it was alienating. In August 1967, the Marine Offences Act finally outlawed the pirates, and one month later, on 30 September 1967, BBC ('wonderful') Radio One was launched... staffed by a generous supply of ex-pirate DJs.

THE THERMIONIC VALVE

The thermionic valve, or "tube" as it is known in the USA, has been with us since the American Dr Lee de Forest borrowed the idea of the Fleming valve, an English invention that could convert alternating current to direct current (also known as rectifying) and therefore detect radio. He created a device – which he named the Audion tube – by utilising the simple but brilliant idea of adding a bent piece of wire (the grid) between the anode and the cathode. Thus the triode was born, and electronic amplification at last became possible.

Valves have continued to evolve throughout their history, becoming smaller and smaller. An American valve from the 1930s, the 6L6 output pentode, mutated into the English EL34, as used in Marshall amplifiers. It was further refined into the smaller but hotter-running EL84, as used in the Vox and Watkins range of amplifiers. Another logical progression led to one of the finest pieces of valve technology, a generic double triode known in the UK as the ECC83 and in the USA as the 12AX7. The whole package – including the shape of the glass envelope, the location of the pins sticking down and the entire internal structure – was invented by Philips at their laboratories in Holland sometime in 1955. Intended for general audio use, its heater voltage was 6.3 volts. This was no arbitrary figure as it was designed with possible military use in mind, and could be powered by the car batteries of the day.

The ubiquitous ECC83

The ECC83 has been at the heart of audio amplifiers since its inception, and in the 1950s the English company Mullard produced many domestic hi-fi circuit diagrams designed to promote the use of their valves. When it was discovered that the ECC83 produced a lovely warm second harmonic distortion when overdriven, it wasn't long before it became a major component in the construction of specialist guitar amplifiers.

Ultimately, because of the arrival of the semi-conductor and the dramatic proliferation of the transistor, finances and fashion dictated that these valves should evolve no further, although it's interesting to speculate on what they would have become if they had they done so. In recent times – and in response to the occasionally clinical sound of solid-state equipment – a retro movement has emerged, with many mixing desks, effects processors, pre-amps, and amplifers all incorporating valves (especially the ECC83) into their designs.

It must be a thrill for the designers to know that their invention is still in service after 55 years of continuous use, rather like that flying workhorse the Douglas DC3 Dakota. When you next crank up the level on your favourite amplifier, spare a thought for the genius behind the components that helped to create that wonderful sound over half a century ago.

There is a further irony that during the Cold War Russian electronics were still constructed using all-valve technology. This means that had there been any nuclear explosions then communication gear in the East would still function, whereas in the West, with all the transistors burnt out by massive elecro-magnetic pulses, the only equipment still functioning would be old guitar amplifiers, the odd hi-fi, and the mixing desks of several old studios. That would show them.

One final story

The Brookmans Park Transmitting Station in Hertfordshire was built by the BBC in 1929 for regional programmes to be transmitted on medium wave to the Home Counties, London and the South East.

The communications company Marconi of Chelmsford – who, in 1960, manufactured a replacement transmitter for the BBC at Brookmans Park – used a modified Leak TL12 plus hi-fi amplifier (which employed a pair of EL84s in the output) as a pre-amplifier for the audio signal in the modulation amplifier for the transmitter.

So, if you were in South East England listening to the Light Programme, or later Radio One between 1961 and 1978, or even Radio Three until mid-1980, you were effectively listening via a pair of EL84s – valves identical to those used in the output section of a Watkins Dominator.

CHAPTER 8

BRITISH BEAT

In the late 1950s, a new style of music caught the imagination of the record-buying public: the rock instrumental. It was an exciting form, untainted by what some people felt to be the irrelevance of a singer. At first it was an American phenomenon, with artists such as Duane Eddy, Johnny and The Hurricanes, and The Champs producing powerful, rocking sax-and-guitar-based melodies. Over in Britain, the only artists producing music in a similar style were Bert Weedon and John Barry, but this was to change in July 1960, the month that The Shadows' "Apache" was released.

With their dynamic stage presence and choreography, The Shadows had already built up a following as Cliff Richard's backing band, but now – armed with the revolutionary new sound of their red Fender guitars and amplifiers, which were capable of being heard in large theatres for the first time – they were able to tour as an act in their own right. The novel line-up of lead guitar, rhythm guitar, bass guitar and drums was so elegant in its simplicity that it immediately became the template for copycat bands throughout Europe. Everyone featured in this book has probably played "Apache" at some point in their career.

The supremacy of The Shadows – and, incidentally, their easy access to EMI's Abbey Road Studio Two – reigned for three years, until a band called The Beatles arrived on the scene. Both bands took their original influences from the same sources, American rock 'n' roll and skiffle, but while The Shadows evolved to play melodic instrumentals, The Beatles retained the rawness of vocals. However, the vocals of Harry Rodger Webb, who in 1958 sold himself under the guise of Cliff Richard, were of huge significance at the start of the band's career.

After singing at school in Cheshunt, Middlesex, with the five-piece vocal group The Quintones, and subsequently as a member of The Dick Teague Skiffle Group, Cliff teamed up with the latter's drummer, Terry Smart, and guitarist Norman Mitham to form the rock 'n' roll band Harry Webb and The Drifters. Within weeks they were offered a management deal with John Foster, a Teddy boy who spotted this Elvis look-alike and his band at the Five Horseshoes pub in nearby Hoddesdon, and with financial assistance from John's parents they made a demo at the HMV record store in Oxford Street. John says: "I had a great grounding for the music business – I used to work in the sewage industry."

A week's engagement followed at the 2i's in Soho, during which they met guitarist Ian Samwell, who expressed a wish to join the band. He was accepted, and when his latent songwriting talents emerged Cliff's faith was soon to pay off with unexpected dividends. Meanwhile, the demo had attracted the attention of producer Norrie Paramour, the head of A&R at EMI's Columbia label, and after an audition Cliff signed to EMI and left his job at the Atlas Lamps factory in Enfield. Changes to the band were made immediately, when Ian switched to bass and Norman Mitham left. Then came the release of the single that was to revolutionise British rock 'n' roll and hastily instigate the formation of the band that would become The Shadows.

"Move It"

Recorded on 24 July 1958 in three takes at EMI's Abbey Road Studio Two, "Move It" had actually been intended for the B-side of Cliff's first single. Norrie Paramour had chosen the Bobby Helms number "Schoolboy Crush" as the featured side, and the record was issued as such on 29 August 1958, in both seven-inch 45 r.p.m. and ten-inch 78 r.p.m. versions.

It was only after Jack Good raved over "Move It" and insisted that Cliff perform it on his *Oh Boy* TV show, and Radio Luxembourg and other disc jockeys expressed a preference for the B-side, that "Schoolboy Crush" was ignored completely. "Move It" was not the only earth-moving single to have been recorded and issued as an afterthought: classics such as "Rebel Rouser" (Duane Eddy), "Apache" (The Shadows), "Shakin All Over" (Johnny Kidd and The Pirates), "Rock Island Line" (Lonnie Donegan) and even the track that kick-started the whole international rock 'n' roll movement, Bill Haley and His

Comets' "Rock Around The Clock", were all either initially earmarked as B-sides or were created at the tail end of a session, often at the urging of the artist.

The novice composer of "Move It" (which was given its title by John Foster), Ian Samwell, says: "I had written a couple of hymns and poems, but 'Move It' was my first song. It had begun with a 'need' – and after all, necessity is the mother of rock 'n' roll." He describes "Schoolboy Crush" as "a poppy, mushy kind of thing. I thought I'd take a shot at it. I'd been trying to figure out how Chuck Berry did what he did – a lot of his playing involved just two notes at a time. I evolved an intro and a rhythm part which both involved playing only two notes. It's not a strum part; what makes it strong is the drive and rhythm that it provides. The whole song wouldn't have existed without the introduction, and it was the process of working out that introduction that led me to the two notes at the bottom."

Ian wrote "Move It" on top of a Green Line bus going to Cliff's house in Cheshunt, and he played it to him immediately on arrival. "It was essentially one long verse, as in blues. Cliff later lost the lyric, so I rewrote it on the bus on the way to the studio. I then had to rewrite it again, but more legibly, while lying on the floor of the studio." Ian felt that there were too many "ings", so to help Cliff sound more American he actually wrote apostrophes, as in "goin'".

Ernie Shear's intro, a series of descending fourths, is deceptive; generations of guitarists have played it incorrectly. It only makes rhythmical sense if the phrase is started with a quaver rest. The "Move It" session was just an ordinary date for Ernie, and he played a top-of-the-range Hofner with a DeArmond pickup near the bridge, through a Fender amp. The parts were worked out in the session. Ian says: "I was in the studio expecting to play the opening riff, but Norrie said 'Ernie has a much better sound, let him play it,' so I showed him how to do it." Ian settled on rhythm guitar instead, itself a vital part of the song, with fellow Drifter Terry Smart on drums and Cliff wearing (but not playing) an acoustic guitar to help his nerve as he sang. "At the time I felt that, in the rest of the song, Ernie was playing Bill Haley licks, but in retrospect he did a heck of a good job. Also, we felt that we didn't want a stand-up bass player because that wasn't real rock 'n' roll anymore. It was time to move on – electric bass was better, so I was initially very disappointed when Norrie booked Frank Clarke on his enormous acoustic bass. But he was a terrific guy, and he played beautifully, with great energy.

"We spent most of the session recording 'Schoolboy Crush'. The real engineer left, and then, almost as an afterthought, assistant engineer Malcolm Addey stepped in and, being our age, he cracked it. He's as responsible for 'Move It' as anybody else. The unsung hero. What a mix! It still stands up today. Some things are meant to happen, and 'Move It' was one of them. The song was really a clarion call to everybody to 'come on and rock'. Which we did."

It was certainly a huge inspiration for Andy Summers,

Session great Ernie Shear is seen here playing what colleague Dick Abell recognises as a (very expensive) D'Anjelique guitar

Andy Summers with his Framus, at about the time he discovered the intro to 'Move It'

who was then an aspiring 15-year-old guitarist. "A clever dick at my school had figured out how to play the guitar intro to 'Move It', but he wouldn't show it to anybody. By subversive means I became his friend, with the sole purpose of stealing this lick from him. Finally, one afternoon, as the late afternoon sun was penetrating his mother's front room, he showed me the lick. It was a religious moment, during which my heart pounded. I went home and played that lick every possible way I could think of. It was a very simple double stopping in fourths, ending on the E major chord, but to me that lick resonated with glamour, sex and the blues."

The Shadows

While "Move It" was still occupying the singles chart in September 1958, Cliff was signed to appear on a nationwide package tour, headlined by The Kalin Twins, who had recently found fame with their hit "When". With the departure of Norman Mitham, The Drifters were now without a permanent guitarist, but John Foster, who was then only 18 years old, sought to solve the problem by visiting the 2i's, where he hoped to hire Tony Sheridan, the singer/guitarist who would later use The Beatles as his backing band in Germany. Tony was not to be found, but John's eyes turned instead to club regular Hank Marvin.

Not long before they both left school in Newcastle upon Tyne, Hank quit his own band, The Crescent City Skiffle Group, in order to join Bruce Welch's band, The Railroaders. They auditioned for the Saturday morning radio show *Skiffle Club*, but producer Dennis Main Wilson was unimpressed. In 1957, with great determination, Bruce came down from Newcastle to do a recce – he'd heard that Tommy Steele was playing at the 2i's and stayed for a few days, thrilled to be in London. The 2i's – situated at 59 Old Compton Street, the Wardour Street end – had been so named by its original proprietors, the brothers Irani. The neon sign outside described the place as a café, but in truth it was much more than a place which served espresso and hot dogs, especially when the two Australian wrestlers Ray Hunter and Paul Lincoln took over in April 1956. The 2i's reputation grew throughout the year as singers and guitarists attracted custom. Wally Whyton, then of The Vipers, once commented that, by early 1957, the 'café' had become a veritable magnet for music fans, and added that "pulling birds was unbelievable. The place was stacked with them!" As word got around the music industry of the home-grown talent regularly appearing at the 2i's, it became equally stacked with record-company talent scouts and agents. If you were a musician, this was the place to 'hang'. On bass player George Williams' recommendation, The Railroaders travelled to London in April 1958 for a talent competition at the Granada in Edmonton. "We lost – to a jazz band and a Malaysian opera singer," says Bruce. Contacts were made, however, and Bruce and Hank played for a while with Pete Chester's Chesternuts.

When Hank moved to London with Bruce that spring, against strong parental objections, he began to admire and emulate the single-note solo style of players such as American guitarist James Burton, but he couldn't figure out how Burton bent the strings so easily. "Was he some kind of Incredible Hulk figure?" What he didn't know was that Burton used the banjo trick (ie banjo string for first, guitar string for second, and so on, discarding the sixth guitar string). "Now, of course, we can get ultra-light-gauge strings, almost like fuse-wire," says Hank. "But not then."

In an attempt to achieve the American sound he heard on records, Hank bought an Antoria guitar from a shop in Shaftesbury Avenue. "It was very crude, like a plank with a sloping cutaway, and cost £35. It had a rotten action, with a half-inch gap in the middle – like a cheese cutter." Even though it had a *clacky* sound it was a step in the right direction (and can be heard alongside Bruce's white Ernie Grimshaw on Cliff's imaginatively titled debut LP, *Cliff*, recorded live at EMI's Abbey Road Studios in the spring of 1959). For a while, Hank had been using a Selmer amp until he discovered the Vox AC 15 single-speaker amp.

The Guyatone LG 50, similar to the Antoria

Soho was buzzing, certainly in comparison with the Newcastle they had left behind, and Hank and Bruce started hanging out regularly at the 2i's. Skiffle guitarist Les Bennetts would occasionally get a spot on the Cliff Michelmore *Today* TV show, and he would pick up whatever backing musicians he could from the 2i's, including on one occasion Hank and Jet Harris, paying them 30/- each (i.e., £1.50) and saying "Nice doing business with you." The tables were turned when, at their peak, The Shadows were playing the Blackpool Winter Gardens and Les was booked to play with Lonnie Donegan in the adjoining Opera House.

Hank Marvin and Bruce Welch, both aged 16.
5 November 1957, Guy Fawkes' Night, The Railroaders played a steaming gig at Newcastle University. One of Hank's idols, jazz clarinettist, Monty Sunshine, sat in with them. Hank was so happy that he didn't notice how much cider he'd been drinking all evening. He became quite pissed and after the gig recalls "crawling along the floor and holding on to it in case I feel off!"

Bruce Welch was ill, but Les kindly stood in for him for what was his second show of the night. Quite rightly, he anticipated a huge cheque. At the end of the week, Jet Harris said to Les, "Nice doing business with you," and handed him one pound and one ten-bob note (50p)!

Bruce: "In 1958, the casual nature of the music scene was similar to that of the jazz world, with many musicians 'sitting in'. The repertoire consisted of songs such as 'Whole Lotta Shakin'', 'Rock Around the Clock', and skiffle songs such as 'Worried Man'. When we first arrived at the 2i's, we worked as a duo – The Geordie Boys! We used to get 18/- (90p) for four hours' work." It was, of course, on one of these evenings that John Foster bowled in and discovered Cliff's future cohorts. John says: "Hank agreed to do it, as long as he could bring his mate Bruce along to play rhythm [on his American Vega, an acoustic with a huge horseshoe pickup]. I took the guys around to a tailor where Cliff was having a fitting for a lurid pink jacket." They were now in The Drifters, and Hank and Bruce took a Green Line bus from Portland Place to Cheshunt to rehearse with Cliff in the front room of his parents' council house for the new line-up's concert debut at the Victoria Hall in Hanley, Stoke-on-Trent, on 5 October, for which Hank used Bruce's Vega.

Another frequent visitor to the 2i's was bassist Jet Harris, whose big break also came on the October tour, when he was given the chance to play with supporting act The Most Brothers, who featured the legendary producer-to-be Mickie Most. Jet smartly observed two things: that Cliff was not entirely happy with Ian Samwell on bass, and that Cliff and The Drifters were at number 19 in the singles chart. Jet replaced Ian at the end of the tour, and two months later brought Tony Meehan, his pal from The Vipers, to replace Terry Smart, who had quit and joined the merchant navy after realising his limitations. The full line-up of Hank, Bruce, Jet and Tony recorded with Cliff for the first time on "Livin' Lovin' Doll", and debuted together on stage at the Free Trade Hall, Manchester, in January 1959.

Jet continued to use his Framus bass until an unfortunate accident during a panto at the Hull ABC in December 1959. "We'd just finished the show and I leaned the Framus up against the dressing room door. When Tony Meehan opened the door it fell over and the neck broke off. However, the next day, the Fender Precision turned up. I was presented with it on stage, still in its cardboard box. Otherwise I'd have been miming with a tennis racquet."

By July 1959, serious problems regarding the band's use of the name The Drifters had arisen and were preventing the issue of records in the USA, because of the existence of

Jet Harris aged 17 playing modern jazz on double bass

Tony Meehan aged 15 playing down the 2Is Club

an identically named American vocal group. Hank remembers: "For legal reasons, the name 'Drifters' had to go. Jet and I had travelled on our scooters to the Six Bells pub in Ruislip. Although we were prepared for a long discussion, almost immediately Jet said 'What about The Shadows?' The lad was a genius."

Hank realised that, when playing at bigger venues, such the Free Trade Hall, his AC 15 was just not powerful enough. He tried a Fender Twin, but missed the richness of the Vox tone. A suggestion was made to Vox's chief design engineer, Dick Denney: "Why not a twin AC15?" It was difficult to achieve, but late in 1959, The Shadows took delivery of three AC30s. A legend was born.

THE ARRIVAL OF THE STRAT

Earlier that year, after seeing a headstock in a photo of Rick Nelson's band, The Shadows realised that their hero, James Burton, played a Fender. They sent off to California for a catalogue. (At that time the post-war trade embargo with the States had still not yet been lifted: no American guitars were being imported, but an instrument could be privately imported.) Like watching colour TV for the first time, when the catalogue arrived, they stared in amazement at the beautiful shiny instruments on every page. Convinced that James Burton would play the top-of-the-range instrument, being the legend he was, Cliff arranged to import the top-of-the-range Fender: a Stratocaster. This was one of the most fortuitous errors in musical history; months later they would discover that Burton in fact played a Telecaster – with no tremolo arm.

The guitar arrived at a flat shared by Hank, Bruce and Cliff in Marylebone High Street. When they opened the tweed case, saw the crushed-velvet lining, smelled that smell, and saw the pinky-red Strat with birds-eye maple neck, gold-plated hardware, three pickups and a tremolo arm, no one spoke. No one touched it for a while: they just stared at it. The guitar was the most beautiful thing they'd ever seen. Seven years after its creation, this was the first Fender Stratocaster in Britain – an icon.

Hank was so thrilled by his new acquisition that he used to take it to the clubs in Soho and "flash it around". People couldn't believe what they were seeing or hearing. He sounded American, at last. The tremolo arm was perfect for Hank, and he was able to breathe life into a single note. For a while he'd felt that British guitarists "showed a lamentable lack of feeling. If they played a melody, it was simply a series of notes; no feeling, no soul at all."

Bruce now owns that Strat, and has had it restored to its original salmon pink (it was white for a while when Cliff had it) with all of its original parts and capacitors, and it's now worth a fortune. I once played it, and my hand strangely gravitated to A minor, the key of "Apache"! "Between that and Buddy Holly songs," Bruce says, "our entire early career was based on the key of A."

AMERICA TRADE RESTRICTIONS

Essentially, the reason why there were no Fenders and Gibsons, or in fact any American goods available in Britain until 1960, was because of the post-war US trade embargo. This was introduced at the end of World War II with the lease-lend deal, which involved the USA's supply of old warships to Britain. The resulting trade deficit meant that the only way that Britain could stabilise its economy was to restrict the movement of sterling to the USA. It was unfortunate for America, however, that this period should coincide with the emergence of rock 'n' roll, because British retailers had no option but to satisfy demand by importing inferior guitars from other countries. Ben Davis, of Selmer's in London's Charing Cross Road, imported Hofners from Germany, while Rose, Morris & Co imported Tatay guitars from Valencia and cheaper guitars came from Czechoslovakia. An even cheaper guitar, which was manufactured in the USSR, had to be purchased in exchange for razor blades. Eventually, in 1960, the embargo was lifted, opening the floodgates for the re-introduction of famous American guitars. Gibson and Epiphone were imported by Selmer; Fender by Jennings, and Martin, Guild and Harmony by Boosey & Hawkes, all adding to the excitement of the forthcoming 'Swinging Sixties' and its increased demand for guitars.

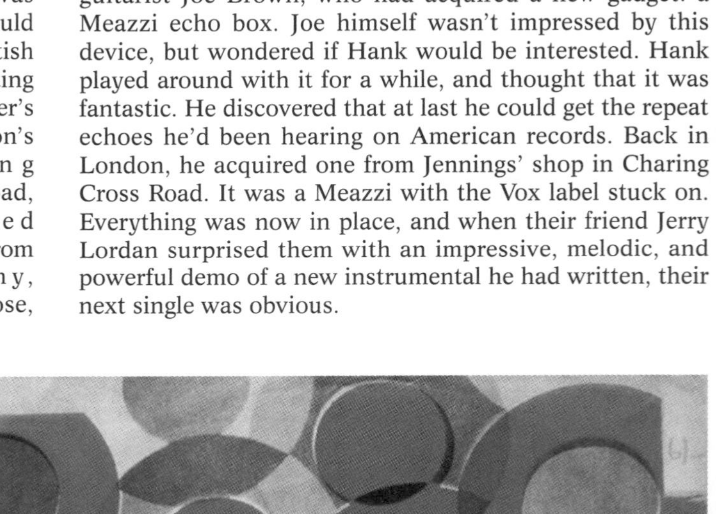

Page 2—MELODY MAKER. July 30, 1960

Melody Maker charts service

Data supplied by over 100 record dealers

TOP TWENTY

1. (2) PLEASE DON'T TEASE .... Cliff Richard. Columbia
2. (1) GOOD TIMIN' .... Jimmy Jones. MGM
3. (3) SHAKIN' ALL OVER .... Johnny Kidd. HMV
4. (5) MAMA/ROBOT MAN .... Connie Francis. MGM
5. (7) WHEN WILL I BE LOVED? Everly Brothers. London
6. (—) MESS OF BLUES .... Elvis Presley. RCA
7. (15) IF SHE SHOULD COME TO YOU Anthony Newley. Decca
8. (4) AIN'T MISBEHAVIN' ...... Tommy Bruce. Columbia
9. (6) JOHNNY COMES MARCHING HOME/MADE YOU Adam Faith. Parlophone
10. (11) ITSY BITSY TEENIE WEENIE YELLOW POLKA DOT BIKINI .... Brian Hyland. London
11. (8) LOOK FOR A STAR .... Garry Mills. Top Rank
12. (13) BECAUSE THEY'RE YOUNG .. Duane Eddy. London
13. (9) WHAT A MOUTH .... Tommy Steele. Decca
14. (10) ANGELA JONES .... Michael Cox. Triumph
15. (—) APACHE .... Shadows. Columbia
16. (12) THREE STEPS TO HEAVEN Eddie Cochran. London
17. (—) HE'LL HAVE TO GO .... Jim Reeves. RCA
18. (20) LOVE IS LIKE A VIOLIN .... Ken Dodd. Decca
19. (—) ANGELA JONES .... Johnny Ferguson. MGM
20. (16) I WANNA GO HOME .... Lonnie Donegan. Pye

JAZZ PARADE

1. (3) SEVEN AGES OF ACKER (LP) .... Acker Bilk. Columbia
2. (1) CHAIRMAN OF THE BOARD (LP) ...... Count Basie. Columbia
3. (8) BEAUTY AND THE BEAT (LP) George Shearing and Peggy Lee. Capitol
4. (7) TIME OUT (LP) .... Dave Brubeck. Fontana
5. (2) BLUES IN ORBIT (LP) .... Duke Ellington. Philips
6. (4) SIDNEY BECHET MEMORIAL ALBUM (LP) .... Fontana
7. (5) BIRTH OF A BAND (LP) .... Quincy Jones. Mercury
8. (6) TUBBY'S GROOVE (LP) .... Tubby Hayes. Tempo
9. (9) KIND OF BLUE (LP) .... Miles Davis. Fontana
10. (—) THE SOUTHERN SCENE (LP) .... Dave Brubeck. Fontana

TOP TEN LPs

1. (1) ELVIS IS BACK .... RCA
2. (2) SOUTH PACIFIC .... Soundtrack. RCA
3. (3) IT'S EVERLY TIME .... Everly Brothers. Warner Bros.
4. (4) ELVIS'S GOLDEN RECORDS, Vol. II .... RCA
5. (6) OKLAHOMA .... Soundtrack. Capitol
6. (5) MARIO LANZA SINGS CARUSO FAVOURITES .... RCA*
7. (7) CAN CAN .... Soundtrack. Capitol
8. (9) THE TWANG'S THE THANG .... Duane Eddy. London
9. (8) LATIN A LA LEE .... Peggy Lee. Capitol
10. (10) MY FAIR LADY .... Original Cast. Philips

* This album also contains a free Caruso LP—"From The Best of Caruso."

Meloday Maker, 30 July 1960. The Shadows enter the charts at number 15 with 'Apache'

ECHO

Jack Good was then producing a TV music programme from Manchester called *Boy Meets Girl*, an edition of which was due to feature Gene Vincent, and The Shadows were invited to attend. Appearing in the resident band was their mate, guitarist Joe Brown, who had acquired a new gadget: a Meazzi echo box. Joe himself wasn't impressed by this device, but wondered if Hank would be interested. Hank played around with it for a while, and thought that it was fantastic. He discovered that at last he could get the repeat echoes he'd been hearing on American records. Back in London, he acquired one from Jennings' shop in Charing Cross Road. It was a Meazzi with the Vox label stuck on. Everything was now in place, and when their friend Jerry Lordan surprised them with an impressive, melodic, and powerful demo of a new instrumental he had written, their next single was obvious.

'Apache' the 45 single

"APACHE": A MAGNIFICENT CONVERGENCE

The nation woke one morning in July 1960 to hear a new and exciting sound on their radios. It was a piece of music by The Shadows called simply "Apache". Things would never be the same again; the old had been replaced overnight by the new. "Apache" entered the *Melody Maker* chart at number 15 on 30 July, although it found its first placing at number 19 in the *Record Mirror* chart of 23 July. The phenomenal success of this record took everyone by surprise as it then climbed even higher up the chart, to finally displace Cliff's "Please Don't Tease" at number one, on 20 August, where it would remain for five weeks (*Record Mirror* chart). There is a question that is often asked in connection with the early 1960s: "Do you remember what you were doing the day that President Kennedy died?" This may perhaps sound like bathos, but for many of the players featured in this book a far more appropriate question would be: "Do you remember what you were doing the first time you heard 'Apache'?" It was a powerful event, and for some, in retrospect, it has become a kind of cathartic experience. For many guitarists, "Apache" was the first tune that they ever learned – sometimes, it must be admitted, on only one string. That didn't matter, however: it was exciting, and so far removed from the music that was then being taught at school.

The original sheet music for 'Apache'

Jerry Lordan

Born in Paddington, Jerry Lordan was subject to a few rudimentary music lessons at grammar school, but he was largely self-taught, and played guitar, ukulele, and piano. He once said: "I always wanted to be in show business, from the age of about 12. I thought I wanted to be a comedian." After his demobilisation from his National Service in the RAF, he did the usual round of auditions and odd jobs, one of which was as a cinema projectionist in Coventry Street.

By now it was 1958, and rock 'n' roll was here to stay. Jerry and his co-projectionist, Tony Mahoney, used to listen to Radio Luxembourg to while away the time between spool changes. Tony brought in his guitar on one evening, but he only knew three chords. Fired up by the banality of some of the songs on the radio, Jerry was sure that he could do better than this, and started to write a tune in his head. "I didn't know anything about music, and I didn't know anything about chords, but I just knew how the tune should go."

His career as a composer and songwriter sprang from this intuitive beginning. Jerry wrote several songs that were covered successfully in the USA, but it was only when he had his own entry in the UK's Top 20 in March 1960, with a song called "Who Could Be Bluer?", that people here took notice. Later that month he was booked to play second top on tour with Cliff and The Shadows. Prior to this, Jerry had continued to compose and had on occasion written music for which he could find no suitable lyrics. "The inspiration for 'Apache' was a real mish-mash of things. I used to play (very badly) second trumpet in a semi-pro jazz band called The Perdido Street Six, while doubling as a bus conductor. The pianist, clarinettist, and I were more interested in modern jazz. One day, the pianist played a few chords. I said 'What are those chords? What are those chords?' He said 'That's C minor and F major.' I said 'How do you do that?'"

Jerry had a love of harmony. Many composers absorb information which will emerge years later in a modified form. Transpose the change of C minor to F major down a minor third and you have A minor to D major, the opening chords of "Apache", the title of which was taken from the Burt Lancaster/Charles Bronson movie of the same name, which was a favourite of Jerry's. "I wanted something noble and dramatic, reflecting the courage and savagery of the Indian – two opposite qualities. The second theme was suggested to me by the Mexican 'De Guello' (which means 'no quarter' or 'forget it') in Dimitri Tiomkin's wonderfully evocative score of *The Alamo*. Somehow the two things got into my mind together – the chords, south-west America, Mexicans, and of course Indians. Don't ask me how it came. I'm not very good at titles, normally. I just called it 'Apache' – that's what it sounded like to me." Although initially delighted when Bert Weedon agreed to record "Apache" for

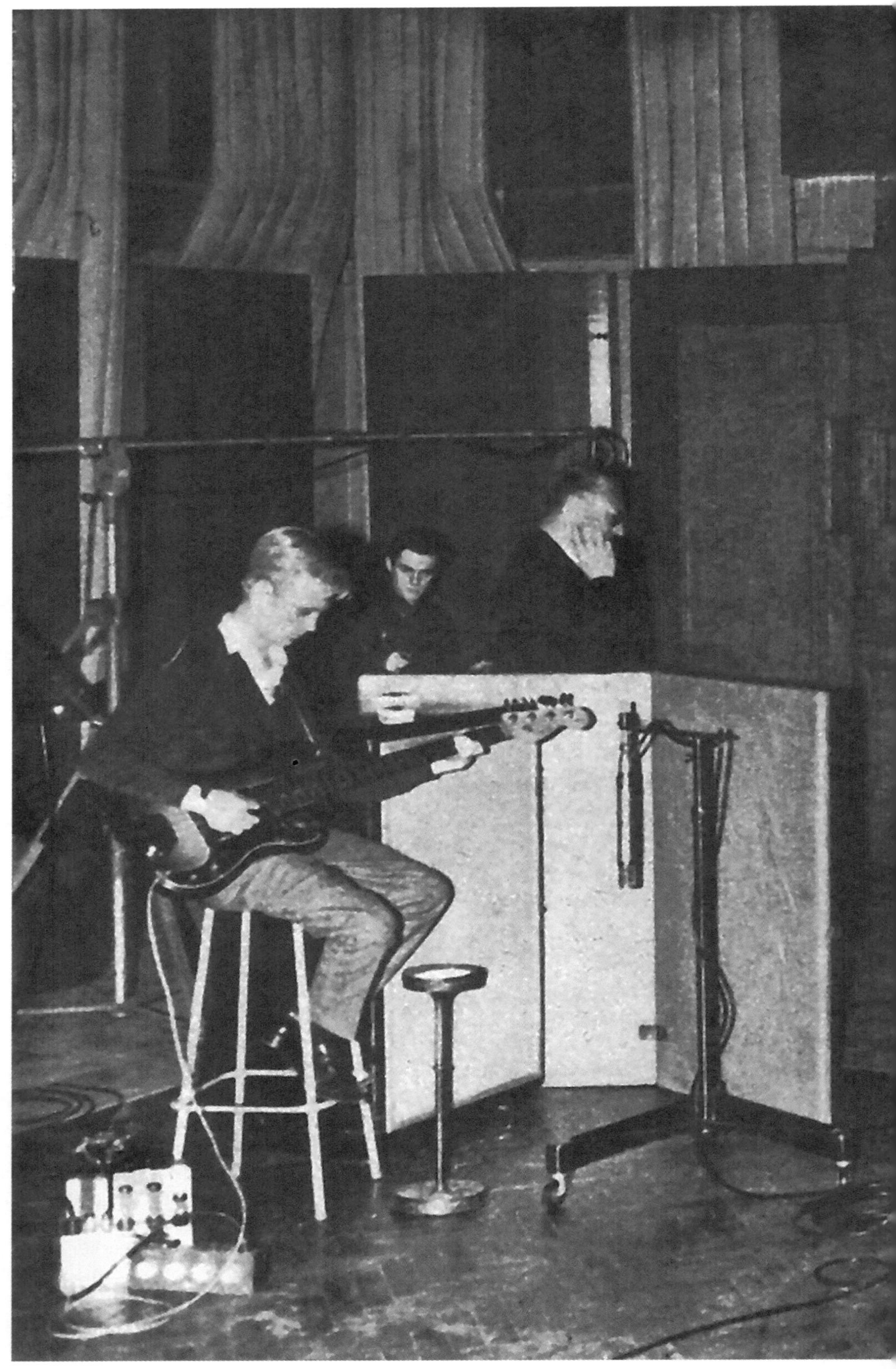

The Shadows, with Cliff Richard on acoustic guitar, recording at Abbey Road Studio Two in 1960. Interestingly no one is wearing headphones. When I asked Jet about this he recalled: "someone said go, and we went." Producer Norrie Paramour looks on. (L-r) Jet, Tony, Norrie, Hank, Bruce, Cliff

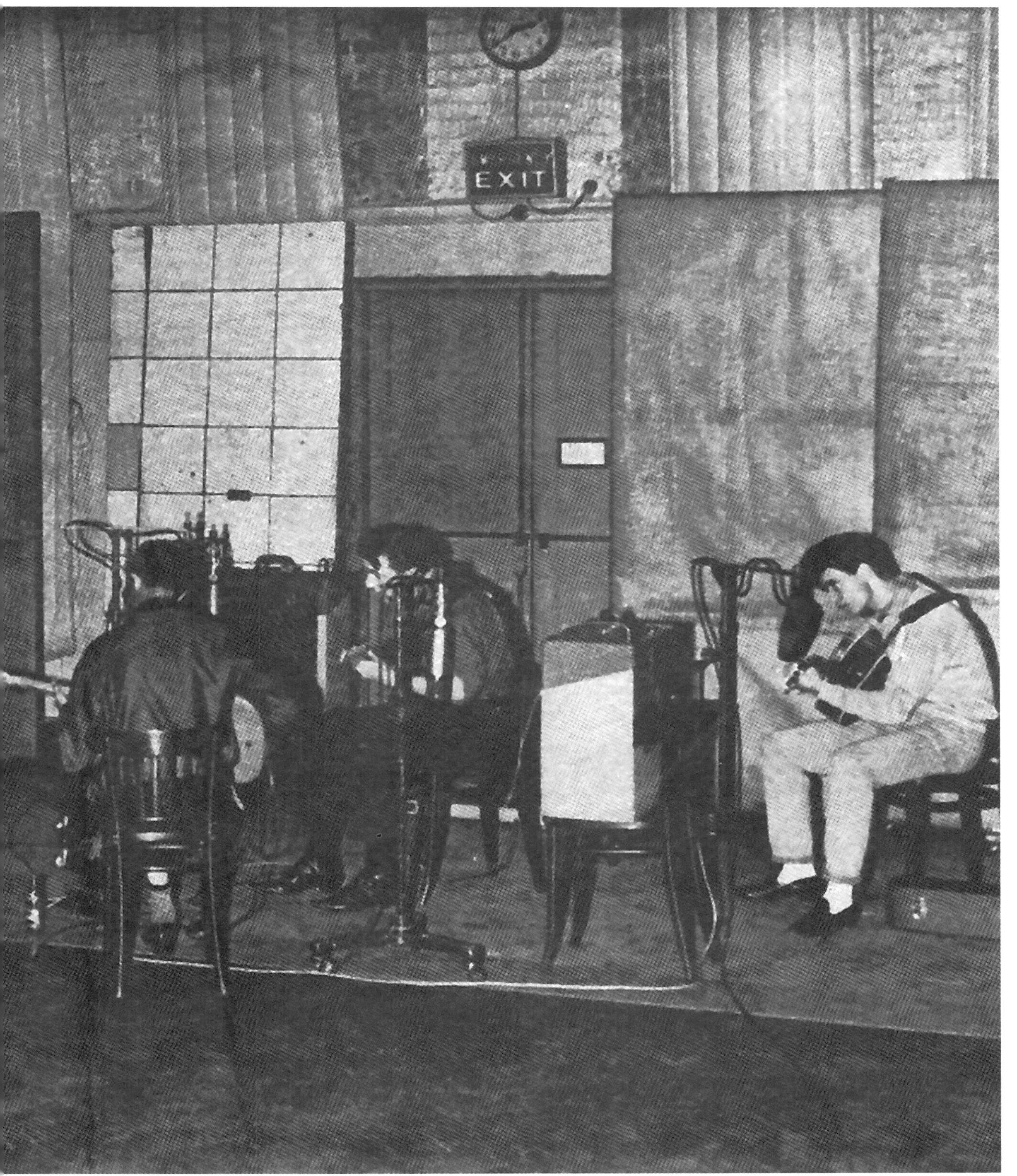
EXIT

inclusion on an album, Jerry was disappointed when he heard the finished result. "It wasn't anything like I'd envisaged."

The 22-night tour with The Shadows began with everyone travelling on the same bus, and Jerry passed the time by writing songs, using his ukulele as accompaniment. The Shadows had been very disappointed that their third single, 'Saturday Dance', hadn't been successful, and during long and friendly chats on the bus Jerry became aware that they were seriously on the lookout for new material. "I was travelling on the London Underground with Jet Harris on the way home to Paddington. I had the ukulele with me and – to this day I don't know why – I hummed and strummed 'Apache'. Jet asked me to play it again, and when I told him that I'd written it he said straight away: 'You've got to play that to Hank and Bruce.' I played it to them on the coach the next day. They went berserk, and were emphatic that they wanted to record it as soon as possible."

There was still one problem: Norrie Paramour wanted the guys to record a version of "The Quartermaster's Stores", which they felt would sound too much like a Johnny and The Hurricanes number. The tour finished, and the band went into EMI's Abbey Road Studio Two for a three-hour session. Both tunes were recorded, with "Apache" completed in only three or four takes, direct to two-track machine. Studio Two was the perfect room in which to record "Apache": it had a comfortable, natural ambience for a small group, as many bands have since found, and just outside the building was one of the best tiled reverb chambers around. Engineer Malcolm Addey knew how to get the best out of the gear, and how to break the rules and push levels to the limit. As a result of this, he was often reprimanded by higher authorities. The control room featured an in-house designed desk and a complement of the best outboard gear of the day, including Fairchild limiters and Pultec equalisers – no wonder "Apache" still sounds great. The composer and the band were thrilled with the way "Apache" turned out, and were convinced that it should be the A-side. Norrie was not initially convinced, but relented after his daughter, having heard both tracks, agreed with the band. It was a wise decision, for in that year's *NME* polls "Apache" was voted the 'Best British Disc of the Year', while The Shadows, as a consequence, were bestowed the honour of being 'The Best British Small Group'.

Hank Marvin

Hank had taken his recently acquired Fender Stratocaster to the session. No one had ever heard a Strat playing a melody before, but the instrument was perfect for his intuitive melodic sense, and the tremolo arm allowed him to impart an urgent quality to some notes and a relaxed Hawaiian-guitar-like effect to others. The uniquely rich and bright sound of a Vox amplifier was the perfect complement to the Fender. Hank also had his Meazzi/Vox tape echo, and for this session the second replay head was switched off to

Jet Harris at Abbey Road on a late-night recording session with The Shadows. Note the Pepe Rush bass cabinet. Tony Meehan is in the background

Bruce Welch recording at Abbey Road on the session that would produce The Shadows' first hit, 'Apache'

create the unusual staggered repeats. An electric guitar had simply never sounded as fresh as this, and it set a precedent. As Joe Brown says: "I'd like to have as many pennies as people who don't even realise they've been influenced by Hank Marvin."

I asked Hank about the melody on the intro, which was quite different from Bert Weedon's version. I suggested that it had a bluesy flattened-fifth feel to it. "The intro was mine," Hank admitted. "We didn't get to hear Bert's version until after ours was released. Jerry hadn't written an intro, or indeed an arrangement – just the tune and basic routine. Is it a flat five or a sharp four? The idea of being flat seems to relate to the blues more than being sharp, doesn't it? For example, my suit is sharp, my wit is sharp, I feel good. Whereas my beer is flat, my tyre is flat, I don't feel good, I got the blues."

Jet Harris

Only four months before the "Apache" session, Jet Harris had replaced his damaged Framus bass with one of the first Fender Precision basses in the country. The warm, punchy sound of the instrument through his massive Pepe Rush enclosure, coupled with his driving style, generated a new and refreshing perspective. For the first time, it seemed that we could actually hear the bass. Jet's bass-lines were innovative, too, with counter melodies, chromatic descensions, and creative passing notes. His jazz background was evident (his heroes were the jazz double-bass players Ray Brown and Oscar Pettiford).

Bruce Welch

For a long time, Bruce had been unhappy with his recorded sound. When he listened to a playback of his rhythm playing on electric guitar, he described it as "a hum, like a tube train going underneath". Earlier, Cliff and The Shadows had all gone to see the film *Loving You*, and what struck them most was the beautiful black Gibson J200 that Elvis was wearing. Cliff immediately acquired a beautiful sunburst Gibson J200, and Bruce asked Cliff if he could borrow it for the "Apache" session. The transformation was incredible: upon hearing the playback, Bruce was thrilled that his sound was now so huge and so clear. "The sound was a fluke," he admits.

Tony Meehan

Tony Meehan's drumming was unusual for its day: crisp, dynamic, original and driving. He knew the rudiments, and used single-stroke rolls to wonderful effect in the main theme of "Apache". Sadly, the miking techniques of the day tended to miss out the bass drum, but the rest of his kit sparkled. At around bar four of the outro, Tony had great fun with cross rhythms by playing continuous dotted crochets on the crown of his ride cymbal. To lend an authentic flavour, they hunted through the vast cupboard under the stairs of Studio Two for something that would sound like an Indian tom-tom. They emerged with a Chinese drum, the kind that you hold in one hand and beat with a mallet with the other. It was perfect. Because there was no provision for overdubs (and Tony couldn't play both at the same time), Cliff held the drum over Tony's kit and played all the way through the track. "He kept great time, too, you know," Jerry later recalled.

Tony: "The evolution of The Shadows' sound was something the four of us put together from our characters, our heads, our souls. Everybody was throwing in ideas with an amazing chemistry between the four of us. The basic sound of The Shadows was that unit: Hank, Jet, Bruce and me. That was where the sound was born, and it never really changed."

CELEBRATION

After the tremendous success of "Apache" the publishers gave a special lunch for The Shadows and Jerry Lordan at Kettner's, a smart restaurant in Soho. There was smoked salmon, champagne, and the finest Burgundy. Everyone was celebrating. Everyone, that is, except Jerry, who was slumped in a chair looking gloomy and dejected. EMI publisher Kay O'Dwyer was concerned, went over to him, and said "Come on, what's the matter, everybody is so happy?" But in the manner of Eeyore – a character out of A.A. Milne's *Winnie The Pooh* – Jerry replied despairingly "Let them enjoy themselves – but me, how am I going to write the next one?" But he did: the majestic "Wonderful Land", which was also recorded by The Shadows, and which was another number one.

Jerry Lordan entertaining Cliff and The Shadows at Kettners restaurant in Soho at a party to celebrate 'Apache' reaching number one

Jerry Lordan died in 1995. At his memorial service in St Martin-in-the-Fields, which was attended by his many friends from the music industry – including Sir George Martin – Bruce Welch paid tribute: "He gave us our first number one, a million seller, and a career that lasted for 35 [now 50] years. Jerry was a man after my own heart. He was a perfectionist, he loved the best things in life, and last but not least he was the sort of man to order the meal to go with the wine." Jerry posthumously received a BMI award for a million performances of "Apache" on US radio. He is missed, but his music lives on, as writer Jon Savage maintains: "'Apache' continues to reverberate, stately and mysterious." Or, as Bruce Welch puts it: "Not bad for a tune without any words."

AN INVITATION TO THE SHADOWS

My fellow Tradewinds and I went to see The Shadows at the local theatre, the Cannock Danilo, at around the time of "Apache". With a bravado that could only be the product of stupidity, we passed a note backstage, which Dave Left recalls as stating that "The Tradewinds would like to meet The Shadows afterwards for drinks." The Shadows were unimpressed.

Hank as guitar tech. To stop rattles he placed paper under four strings of his Strat

GUITAR TALES

For the next couple of years The Shadows could do no wrong. They basked in the glory of hit tunes such as "Man Of Mystery" (the theme of the TV series *Edgar Wallace Mysteries*), "FBI", and the beautiful "Wonderful Land" (also composed by Jerry Lordan). Between tours, in 1961, The Shadows recorded a set of tunes that would become their first LP, the sleeve of which is world famous.

Hank: "When we started to record instrumentals, it seemed fairly obvious to us that strong melodies were important, but not easy to write or find. 'Apache' was a classic. Written by Jerry Lordan, it had a strong and evocative melody yet still fitted into the rock 'n' roll context – our arrangement helped to keep it in there. Most of our instrumentals had strong melodies, and some were in fact film or TV themes, namely 'The Frightened City', 'Man Of Mystery', 'Maroc Seven', 'Rhythm And Greens' (no melody!) and, later, 'Theme from *The Deer Hunter*' ('Cavatina').

"My first experiments with the echo box were relatively simple, first just trying to get the echo that we heard on all the early rock records and then setting it up so that I could play harmony lines with myself, much as Brian May did later on 'Brighton Rock'. Unlike Brian, I was never brave enough to do this live. I also experimented with the different types of echo that the echo box was capable of, and came up with some interesting effects, such as the part on 'Wonderful Land' where I dampened the strings near the bridge and used a very fast multihead echo. Sometimes, on a slow tune, I would use a long, slow echo, but whether fast or slow I would try to get the echo in time with the tempo of the music, even if at times it would sound across the beat."

The Shadows in 1963 with their new Burns guitars. L-r: John Rostill, Hank Marvin, Brian Bennett, and Bruce Welch

In the early days, however, they knew nothing about the mechanics of the guitar and how to service it. (There were no guitar techs!) Hank points out that, because his fifth and sixth strings rattled, he shoved bits of paper underneath at the nut. The problem of pitch, however, proved to be more elusive. Hank had noticed that, when he played at the twelfth fret on the low E-string of his Stratocaster, the guitar sometimes sounded an E flat harmonic, which was confusing and uncomfortable to the ear. At the same time, Bruce Welch had acquired an acute sensitivity to pitch that was, perhaps, a little extreme.

In 1963, in an attempt to solve these problems, Hank approached British guitar designer Jim Burns, and requested a guitar that looked like a Strat and had a similar sound, but had none of the accompanying tuning problems. Jim locked himself away for a while and, after further consultation with Hank (who suggested the "scroll machine-head"), emerged with a fine machine: the "Burns-Marvin" guitar. The Shadows used these guitars throughout the 1960s, and Hank loved them.

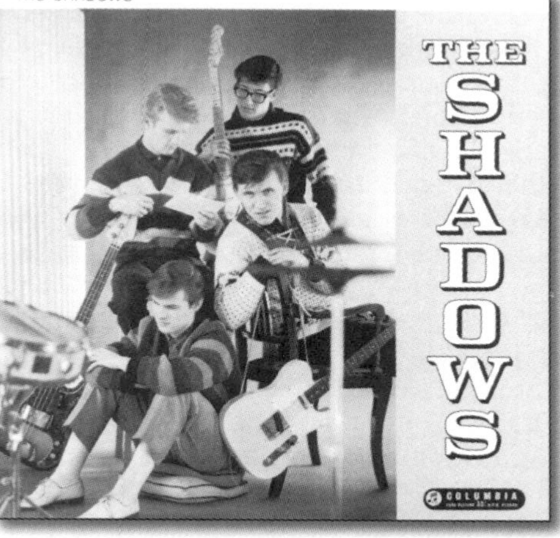

The Shadows' debut LP

On many sessions, including those for the band's eponymous debut album (which went to number one in September 1961 and remained there for six weeks), Bruce used Cliff's Gibson J200 jumbo acoustic guitar. The album featured a beautiful ballad called "Blue Star", the chord sequence of which contains a diminished chord. Bruce had never heard of one of these before, but producer Norrie Paramour patiently showed him where to place his fingers on the neck. Like George Martin, another influential EMI figure, Norrie was a knowledgeable musician, and Bruce even goes as far as to say that "Norrie was like our dad." However, at all sessions they had rigid contracts, and were required to finish three songs in three hours, even if they were crap. There was evidence of the problem: both Hank's solo on "Kon-Tiki" and Jet's bass-line on 'Man of Mystery' could have benefited from a few more takes.

Among the other standards and originals on that landmark first LP was a unique instrumental written by Hank, Bruce and Jet called "Nivram" ("Marvin" spelled backwards). The inspiration for this slightly jazzy piece came from a desire to write something a little in the style of "Swinging Shepherd Blues". Hank unusually played a Gretsch guitar throughout the piece, and the track featured possibly this country's first recorded bass-guitar solo. The famous cover of the LP featured that sunburst Precision and those sweaters. It sets hearts racing for those of us who were there.

DEBUT LP

• *Roger Glover*

Roger Glover recalls: "The Shadows were the band. We gazed at the cover of their first album and salivated over their Fenders nonchalantly strewn about as they lounged around in their curiously out-of-place knitted sweaters. That's how cool they were – they could get away with wearing stuff like that because they had Fenders!"

• Andy Summers on Hank Marvin

"When we saw Cliff and The Shadows perform at the Bournemouth Winter Gardens our tongues were hanging out – real men with real guitars! I went outside during the interval and saw Hank Marvin walking down the street on his own, and I immediately ran after him to get his autograph. He started running, I started running faster after him, and eventually there was no one else, just the two of us running and running and running. Hank seemed scared of me! After half a mile or so he finally gave up, turned around and gave me the autograph. Several years later I was actually sitting with him somewhere and I reflected on this, but didn't have the heart to mention it. But he was a hero then, and he's a hero now. Nobody can play a melody like Hank."

THE LATER YEARS

At the height of The Shadows' success, Jet began to drink too much, and it not only affected his personal life but also began to intrude into the professional world. Bruce Welch, who was perhaps the most affected by Jet's worsening behaviour, says: "It's sad. He was getting so pissed. He was such a good player, and invented all of his own lines. He was smart, too; when recording, he'd wait until the red light was on and then turn up the volume of the bass – that's why the bass was so clear on the early Shadows records."

John Paul Jones adds, in further tribute: "He was great. He wasn't a good technician, but you'd bloody well hear him if he came in on bass. The band would just take off when he started playing. He was a really driving bass player, and that's what made The Shadows."

Brian Bennett

In October 1961, Tony Meehan quit the band in favour of a production career, and he was replaced by Wildcats and Krew-Kats drummer Brian Bennett, who has remained with the band through to the present day. Six months later, Jet also threw in the towel, went solo and signed to Decca with Jack Good as his manager and producer. He recorded two singles, 'Besame Mucho' and 'The Man with the Golden Arm', playing a new six-string Fender Bass VI (tuned like a guitar but an octave lower) at the suggestion of guitarist Big Jim Sullivan. It was a magnificent, huge sound, and after the success of these tracks Jet was always looking around for new material.

Jet Harris

For his next single release, in 1963, he teamed up with fellow Shadows exile Tony, who says: "Composer Jerry Lordan loved the sound of the Fender VI, and had this new melody called 'Diamonds'. We only lived about five minutes from each other, and were always popping in and out of each other's houses. Jerry played 'Diamonds' on the piano, and we agreed that it was ideal for Jet. I arranged 'Diamonds' because Jerry didn't want to know about that side of things; once he'd written a tune, that was it. Anyway, I'd really given up playing drums, but as I was arranging the session I just got drawn into it, and decided to play the drums myself." "Diamonds" (with Jimmy Page on acoustic rhythm guitar) reached number one in February 1963, displacing The Shadows' own "Dance On" in the process. The lead instrument was now a detuned Fender Jaguar. All of this was happening just a few months before Jet was admitted to a clinic suffering from "nervous exhaustion".

Jet's last real chance on bass came in 1968 with The Jeff Beck Group, but he only lasted for two or three rehearsals before being replaced by The Artwoods' Ron Wood. Despite his personal problems, Tony Meehan insists that "Jet was the progenitor of the bass guitar – the daddy of them all."

Brian "Licorice" Locking

Formerly the bass player alongside drummer Brian Bennett in backing groups for Marty Wilde and Vince Taylor, Brian "Licorice" Locking joined The Shadows in April 1962, following Jet's departure. However, as a committed Jehovah's Witness, as Hank Marvin later became, he stayed only until late 1963. "I used various amps in those early days, like the Selmer Truvoice, a square object with one switch on the back and one red light situated, I believe, at the bottom back of the amp. This one hummed as it was switched on, and crackled and banged as your guitar lead plug went into the socket. What a delight it was when I was invited to join The Shadows. They provided me with a lovely Vox bass amp with no trouble at all, and a Fender bass guitar. The rest is history."

In November 1963, Licorice Locking made his final appearance with The Shadows at the London Palladium, and a replacement was thus urgently required. Following a tip-off, the guys first checked out the young bass player in Jet Harris and Tony Meehan's backing group. He sounded fine, but they felt that his image wasn't quite right. Perhaps it was the long cigarette holder? It didn't matter; John Paul Jones had other plans. Then Bruce Welch remembered seeing John Rostill in The Terry Young Band. "He was an immensely talented player, and it showed. It was John, not the drummer, who pinned down the beat in the band. Also, he was a very good-looking, smartly dressed guy who reminded me of Don Everly. He looked the part. He was someone who stuck in my memory."

John Rostill

An audition was arranged. As Bruce recalls: "John came up on a Sunday morning to the Palladium and we played through 'Dance On'. That was it. It really was as simple as that. He couldn't believe it, but we knew that he was a great bass player. Also, I paid John £10 a week to tune my guitars, which he did by playing harmonics. I never questioned his tuning the same way that I did my own." Shortly after recording a TV special, John flew out to the Canary Islands to film *Wonderful Life* with Cliff and The Shadows. Bruce: "The whole ten weeks was a mixture of fun and boredom, I think, to most of us, but to John it was a never-to-be-forgotten experience, as he hadn't yet played a note for The Shadows but found himself in the Canary Islands making a film."

Back in England, John's first single with The Shadows was "The Rise and Fall of Flingel Bunt", which was essentially a jam in the studio. It restored the group to the Top Ten, and was voted 'Best Instrumental Disc' of 1964. Four years later, on 19 December 1968, The Shadows were at the London Palladium. It was the last time that Hank, Bruce, Brian and John would play together – the end of an era.

John then teamed up with Tom Jones and spent the next few years touring the States with him. Touring colleague Jim Sullivan says: "At least with Tom, John didn't have to do The Shadows' steps. It was an essential part of their routine, but John really hated it. If I wanted to wind him up on stage then I'd just start doing the old Shads steps. John would glower and give me a black look, as only Rostill could!

"John never changed his bass strings. Bassists don't need to change their strings as frequently as lead players, and they're much less likely to break strings. Maybe they break them more often these days, with this slap-style playing. Anyway, back in the 1960s it was far less common. John had his strings on for years [Bruce Baxter confirms that John bought the Jazz bass in 1961] – nine or ten years, at least. Then he busted an A string prior to a gig and fitted a new one. But of course new strings 'sing', and that wasn't John's sound, so we spent hours going around music shops in Chicago, looking for an old Jazz bass with its original strings intact. Eventually we found one, and John bought it. He didn't play it, but he took off the A string and fitted it to his own bass. That's the way he was."

During their time in the States, Big Jim and John had the opportunity to meet many of their idols. "We met Elvis Presley several times," says Jim. "It's no secret that he admired Tom's live shows. Presley was getting back to regular live performance himself, and he wanted Tom's rhythm section to join him [including Big Jim and John], which was quite an accolade. Let's face it, by 1972 we were a very tight section. We were both awestruck and incredibly flattered, but we were under contract to Tom, anyway, so it wasn't to be. But what an offer!"

In the early 1970s, John had begun to take songwriting seriously, and had installed a small studio in his house. His demos were received enthusiastically by several artists who covered his songs. More importantly, he had written "Please, Mr Please" with Bruce Welch, and also (alone) "If You Love Me Let Me Know", and 'Let Me Be There' for Olivia Newton-John. These three songs between them sold only about 25,000 copies in the UK. Ironically, during the following year (1974), each one of these songs was destined to become a million-selling smash hit for Olivia Newton-John in the USA.

John couldn't be part of the reformed Shadows in October 1973 because he was still under contract to Tom Jones until the end of the year. Tragically, John wasn't to live to see the enormous success of his songs, nor the incredible popularity of The Shadows' revival. On 26 November 1973, Bruce arrived at John's house to complete work on some songs. He couldn't gain access to John's studio as something was blocking the door. "The door wasn't jammed; it was blocked by John's piano, and John himself was lying at a strange angle, with his bass in his hand. I forced the door open. John was sitting there, with his hands still on the strings of his guitar – he looked as though he was still playing. But he wasn't. He was dead. I went numb. I couldn't believe it." John's death is still a mystery. He had apparently been electrocuted by his guitar.

Alan Jones

One Sunday night in 1973, bassist Alan Jones received a surprise call to deputise for John Rostill in the Tom Jones Band at the London Palladium. It was the tragic day that John had been found dead at his home by Bruce Welch. "I continued to play with Tom Jones, and spent the next three years travelling and working with him all over the world. Big Jim Sullivan was on guitar when I joined – what an excellent player." On returning from his travels with Tom Jones, Alan was offered a gig with The Shadows. "I first did their Twenty Golden Dates tour (in May 1977) to coincide with their *Twenty Golden Greats* album, which topped the charts for six weeks. I've worked for them on and off for about 18 years now, and played on all their hit singles and albums and videos – except when a bass guitarist known as Mo Foster once worked with them on *Top of the Pops*."

Hank Marvin

An incredible 50 years on from "Apache", the record that changed our perspective of the guitar and our appreciation of its potential, Hank Marvin is resident in Perth, Australia, but continues to return to British shores to thrill audiences with his masterful Stratocaster tones. Looking back on his contribution to the instrument, he says: "Over the years I've tried to keep an identifiable sound, style and personality in my playing, but at the same time develop and mature. I liken it to a singer whose voice will mature and improve over the years but is still recognisable. Of course, with age the singer's voice will eventually begin to deteriorate. I hope that is not true of guitarists!

"There are many fine guitarists and other musicians that I enjoy listening to, and I believe that I continue learning and absorbing from all of these influences to a greater or lesser extent. Recently, in Sydney, I had the pleasure of spending some time with Allan Holdsworth and his fellow musicians, who were performing there. He's a lovely man, and a genius. We saw two of their performances, and it was a wonderful musical experience. In the rock field, Eric Johnson is inspiring. Martin Taylor is also a joy to listen to. Now and again, though, I stick on a blast from the past and listen to some early Elvis Presley and those good old Scotty Moore licks, and Gene Vincent with the late Cliff Gallup.

"In 1989 we did two nights at Wembley Stadium with Cliff, and during The Shadows' part of the show we had the 80,000-strong crowd rocking around to 'Flingel Bunt', 'Shadoogie' and 'FBI', and then we slowed the tempo down and played 'The Deer Hunter', which seemed possibly a wrong move in that atmosphere. But it was the right move: a hush fell over the crowd, and it was a most beautiful thing to see the audience gently swaying, and to feel their quiet emotion as they soaked up every note. The sound of my Strat through the still summer air was incredible, almost like a voice. It was probably the most moving guitar-playing experience I've had. The applause was... well, show-stopping. As demonstrated by that and many other experiences, the guitar is my way to reach people's hearts with music. It makes them happy, makes them sad. I will never master it, just sometimes persuade it to my way of playing."

(I should add that In 2010 Cliff Richard and The Shadows completed their sell-out 50th anniversary tour. It was a unique, stunning achievement; no other band has – or could have – achieved this landmark).

THE SHADOWS' WALK

During Jerry Lee Lewis' first visit to Britain, he was supported on tour by The Treniers, a black American rhythm and blues band. Hank and Bruce went to see a show at the Gaumont State Cinema in Kilburn and came away impressed, not only by the excitement of Jerry Lee but also by the tightly choreographed stage act and visually entertaining routines of the band.

A while later, when "Apache" became a hit, they decided that it was time to incorporate some sophisticated movement into their own stage act. At first, inspired by The Treniers, this took the form of just a few simple crossover steps, but ultimately it evolved into a sequence of dramatic synchronised kicks and postures, with all three Fender

THE SHADWALK

- **Roger Glover: "We looked great on stage, our matching red Hofners gleaming in the lights as we turned first one way, then the other in time to the music: The Shadows' Walk."**

Roger Glover and his gleaming red Hofner in 1962

guitars uplifted to enhance certain key moments. Cliff says: "We'd play places where the stage was no more that five feet deep, and we couldn't have the drums set up and stand in front of them and do our little dance steps, so we'd all just stand in a long line."

Now known as 'The Shadows' Walk', this became an established part of the band's act, and was a set of steps that was copied by hundreds of Shadows-inspired bands throughout the country. Jet Harris was the first to experience a problem, however, when The Shadows were playing at the Cavern in Liverpool. Jet had one too many drinks before the show, and in his inebriated state he misjudged part of the walk and fell off the stage into the audience. It was embarrassing, to say the least. Bruce apologised to the audience: "Jet's not too well tonight." Liverpudlians are never slow to respond with a witty remark, and one wag quickly yelled back "That's because he's pissed!"

When Jet departed the band, Licorice Locking amiably fitted in and had no problem with the steps. On a couple of occasions, when Bruce was ill, deps had to be found at short notice. Playing the rhythm parts was fine, but not everyone enjoyed the steps; Les Bennetts was perfectly happy to join in, but Chas McDevitt refused. John Rostill really had a problem, while Alan Jones slotted in with consummate ease.

In the early 1970s, Hank, Bruce and Australian guitarist John Farrar recorded an album of songs that showcased their rich vocal harmonies. I had met John at Abbey Road while playing on a session that he was producing for Olivia Newton-John (*Music Makes My Day*), and it was during this session that he asked me if I'd like to join him and Hank for a few club dates, where the act consisted of their new material and crowd-pleasing Shadows' tunes. It felt right to join in and perform the steps with them – it was fun and it looked good, especially on tunes like "FBI", which featured a dramatic high kick during Hank's solo.

My problems started on day two of a week in Hull. I contracted gastro-enteritis and felt so awful and weak that I was confined to my hotel bed for the next few days. When you're feeling ill what do friends bring you for comfort? Normally it's grapes, books, or magazines. John Farrar very kindly brought me his new ARP Odyssey 2-voice synthesiser for me to try out whilst sitting in bed, and I had an enjoyable afternoon experimenting until – not really knowing what I was doing – I accidentally set up a rough patch which produced a very emphatic farting sound. Needless to say, within seconds I was back in the toilet. It wasn't John's fault. However, there were still the shows to play, which meant playing "FBI" each night, with – oh no – the kick! The front row of the audience that week will never know how close they came to disaster.

"Shakin' All Over"

One of the most significant records of the pre-beat boom era, Johnny Kidd and The Pirates' "Shakin' All Over", leapt to the number one spot on 4 August 1960. It became a British standard, one which would resound at fairgrounds, take up residence on jukeboxes, and define the sound of early 1960s British rock.

Kidd had already released a couple of mediocre singles, produced by Wally Ridley, one of which featured the seasoned touch of Bert Weedon. For the band's next release, a recording session was fixed to take place in EMI Abbey Road Studio Two. Peter Sullivan, who was Ridley's assistant and would later become their producer, suggested that they write the B-side (The A-side was to be "Yes Sir, That's My

Baby") and so, on the night before the session, Johnny Kidd, bassist Brian Gregg and guitarist Alan Caddy sat in Chas McDevitt's club, Freight Train, where it was decided that they would write something collectively. In a dismal, dank cellar, with empty Coke bottles stacked everywhere, they wrote the lyrics and the melody and structure of "Shakin' All Over", without the aid of even a guitar.

Session guitarist Joe Moretti's intro was inspired by Ernie Shear's intro to Cliff's "Move It" and Duane Eddy's "Shazam". Clem Cattini's drum break immediately before Joe's guitar solo was inserted simply because the song was too short. (Some years later, when Clem was playing on a "covers" session, the arranger omitted the drum break from the part, thinking that Clem wouldn't be able to play it!) The bass riff of the song was inspired by Ray Charles's "What'd I Say". The song was recorded in six takes, live, with no overdubs.

In 1959, bassist Brian Gregg asked Pepe Rush, a Cockney-Italian electronics boffin, to build him a large five-feet-high cabinet with sand in the bottom. A 50-watt amp powered its single 18-inch Audiom 90 speaker, but this was later replaced by *two* 18-inch speakers when Brian continually blew the single driver. With this rig he joined Johnny Kidd and The Pirates in January 1960 with guitarist Alan Caddy and drummer Clem Cattini – this line-up was one of the first power trios. This was in no small part due to Brian's fat-sounding riff playing (the majority of his bass-playing peers favoured walking lines), which contributed to The Pirates being arguably the best rock band in Britain during 1960 and 1961. Clem, Brian and Alan later became the nucleus of The Tornados and recorded with Joe Meek the massive hit "Telstar". Johnny, whose real name was Frederick Heath, died in a car crash on 7 October 1966 while on tour near Manchester. In The Pirates, Alan was replaced by Mick Green, whose trademark was his Telecaster sound. Because of his ability to play lead and rhythm parts simultaneously, and so well, some rated him the UK's best guitarist in 1963. His style was an inspiration for later Tele-wielders, such as Wilko Johnson.

THE EARLY SIXTIES

It was an inspirational start to the decade: Duane Eddy released "Shazam", Johnny and The Hurricanes released "Beatnick Fly", the John Barry Seven (featuring Vic Flick on guitar) released "Hit and Miss" (which became the theme tune for *Jukebox Jury*), The Shadows released "Apache", and the Dave Brubeck Quartet released "Take Five". Johnny Kidd and the Pirates released "Shakin' All Over", the Ventures released "Walk Don't Run", and Eddie Cochrane released "Three Steps To Heaven". In addition the live album from the revolutionary satirical revue *Beyond the Fringe* (produced by George Martin) had just become available. There was change in the air and – for young bands – there was new stuff to learn.

Unfortunately the record industry was still obsessed by music that had no meaning at all. In these same years Max Bygraves released "Jingle Bell Rock", Brian Hyland released "Itsy Bitsy Teenie Weenie Yellow Polka Dot Bikini", Paul Anka released "Puppy Love", Ken Dodd released "Love Is Like a Violin", and Nina & Frederick released "Little Donkey". It was against this pointlessness that the new wave of British music emerged.

THE BEATLES

John Lennon

John Lennon was strictly a rock 'n' roller. Throughout his entire 40 years little impressed John unless it was new, exciting, and original. This was never more true than in his teenage period, when most post-war crooners such as Frankie Laine and Johnnie Ray passed him unnoticed, until he first came across one Elvis Aaron Presley. Suddenly, like millions of kids all around the world, he yearned to form a band and play guitar.

His banjo-playing mother, Julia, took a shine to "Heartbreak Hotel" in the summer of 1956, and shortly afterwards she agreed to buy her son his first guitar, a second-hand £10 Eastern European Gallo Champion acoustic which was "guaranteed not to split". However she only managed to send him to two lessons before he complained that they were "too much like hard work". She eventually encouraged him by teaching him simple banjo chords, and he soon gathered like-minded schoolfriends together to form his first band, The Quarry Men, which was named after his Quarry Bank High School in Allerton, Liverpool. Day in and day out, John would sit transfixed by the few rock 'n' roll and skiffle records emanating from his wireless, crudely backing them with his guitar while admiring his stance in the mirror. His Aunt Mimi, with whom he lived at the time, would often have cause to snigger at his show-off antics and mutter the immortal line "The guitar's alright, John, but you'll never make a living with it."

Paul McCartney

Paul McCartney's dad, Jim, played trumpet, and bought one for his 15-year-old son to learn, but Paul had his own revelatory moment: "I realised I couldn't sing with the trumpet, and I wanted to sing as well, so I asked him if he wouldn't mind if I traded it in for a guitar [a Zenith acoustic]." But Paul was left-handed, and this soon became a problem: "I didn't know what you did about that. There were no rule books. Nobody talked about being left-handed. So I tried it right-handed, and I couldn't get any rhythm because it was all the wrong hand doing it. Then I saw a picture of Slim Whitman, and I just noticed – hang on, he's got the guitar on the wrong way around. I found out he was left-handed, so I thought, that's good, you can have it the other way around."

The Quarry Men at New Clubmoor Hall, Broadway, Liverpool, on 23rd November 1957. L-r: Colin Hanton (drums), Paul McCartney (guitar), Len Garry (tea chest), John Lennon (guitar), Eric Griffiths (guitar). Note the PA cabinet on the floor and the light show on the piano

George Harrison

George Harrison used to get on the same bus to go to school, and he and Paul realised that they shared a common interest, the guitar, and quickly became friends. George spent £3/10d (£3-04p) on his very first round-hole acoustic, the neck of which was held to the body by a large bolt, which he experimentally removed. To his dismay, he discovered that he was unable to reassemble the instrument, and it lay in a heap in the wardrobe for the next year.

It was in the same year that the fateful meeting between John and Paul occurred, on 6 July 1957, after a Quarry Men gig. John said in the early 1970s: "We met the first day I did 'Be-Bop-A-Lula' live on stage. After the show, we talked and I saw he had talent. He was playing the guitar backstage, doing 'Twenty Flight Rock' by Eddie Cochran. I turned around to him then on the first meeting, and said 'Do you want to join the group?', and I think he said yes the next day."

Paul: "I kind of went in first of all as lead guitarist, really, because I wasn't bad on guitar, and when I wasn't on stage I was even better. But when I got up on stage, my fingers went all very stiff and then found themselves underneath the strings instead of on top of them, so I vowed that night that that was the end of my career as the lead guitar player."

The Elpico amp: "a small green suitcase"

To Paul's credit, however, it was he who began to fire John's imagination as a guitarist by weaning him off the banjo chords his mother had taught him and showing him all the orthodox guitar chords he knew. By 1958, John and Paul had amassed a considerable vocabulary of chords which would assist in their formative songwriting. They would "sag off" school and art college to spend afternoons with acoustic guitars in the McCartney family's front parlour to rework the rock 'n' roll, doo-wop, and country hits of the day as their own songs. As they gained confidence as guitarists they went beyond basic chord voicings to use invented chord shapes, based on perceived vocal harmonies, and thus set the foundation for their unique sound.

Armed sometime later with his f-hole Hofner President, complete with pick-up, George would wait patiently with Paul outside the home of Mr Dykins, John's stepfather. "When he was safely down the road, on the way to his local pub, we would sneak into the house so that we could all plug our instruments into the back of his radiogram," says George. Eventually, when George had progressed to a Hofner Club 40, the communal amp was Paul's first, an Elpico, which he describes as "looking rather like a small green suitcase". (This was probably because all of the fittings would have been made by a suitcase manufacturer.) Meanwhile, a plastic microphone from a Grundig tape recorder handled the vocals.

If any band's apprenticeship was long and arduous, it was The Beatles'. Few bands of today would even consider playing four 90-minute sets every night for 15 weeks, and yet this was exactly what was expected of The Beatles when they were resident at the Indra and Kaiserkellar clubs on their first visit to the dubious Grosse Freiheit in Hamburg in 1960. Paul describes the episode as "a character-building experience", and it was certainly responsible for helping in their development as musicians. Before Hamburg they were a lively but ragged combo, with a carefree attitude. Afterwards, however, they had matured into players of some discernment who could cover virtually any style with conviction. This was a quality which was to blossom and become evident on their later albums.

Of the solidity of the band, which was honed from this regular playing in the German clubs, John once said that the best of their early music was never recorded. This may have been stretching a point, but a lesson can be learned by today's young bands from The Beatles' early determination to win through. As John said: "When I was a Beatle I thought we were the best fucking group in the whole goddamn world, and believing that is what made us what we were."

Prior to the band's trip to Hamburg, Paul had invested in a Rosetti Solid Seven guitar in Liverpool before they went. "It was a terrible thing. It was really just a good-looking piece of wood. It had a nice paint job, but it was a disastrous, cheap guitar. It fell apart when I got to Hamburg, with the sweat and the damp and the getting knocked around, falling over and stuff. So I turned to the piano."

Hamburg

When The Beatles first hit the Hamburg clubs, Lennon was playing his first electric guitar, a blonde single-pickup Hofner Club 40. During the same trip, John caught a nightclub performance by jazz man Toots Thielemans, who happened to be playing a Rickenbacker. The sight and sound of the guitar, rarely seen in Britain at that point, obviously impressed the Beatle, who bought one virtually on arrival in Hamburg for the band's second marathon gig there in April 1961.

Used with a tweed Fender Deluxe, John's first Capri 325 – a three-quarter scale guitar – was one of only eight made in 1958, and originally sported a hi-lustre blonde finish, with four control knobs, three pick-ups, a gold lucite scratchplate, and a Kaufmann Vibrola tailpiece, which was soon replaced with a Bigsby. In January 1963, the guitar was handed to Jim Burns, who gave it a new black finish. (In February 1964, Rickenbacker honoured The Beatles' first visit to New York by presenting John with a new Jetglo 325, featuring a white double scratchplate and the company's own Accent Vibrato.)

During the early period of their career, when Paul played the role of guitarist/pianist, their bass player was the James Dean look-alike Stuart Sutcliffe. Stuart possessed little skill as a musician, but as a creative soul he was an enormous influence on John Lennon, and it was he who named the band. Paul: "Stu Sutcliffe was a friend of John's. They were at art school together, and Stu had won a painting competition. The prize was £75. We said to him 'That's exactly the price of a Hofner (500/5) bass!' He said it was supposed to be for painting materials, but we persuaded him over a cappuccino."

In 1961 Stuart remained in Hamburg when The Beatles returned to Liverpool, and he quit the band in favour of his blossoming art career and relationship with his girlfriend, Astrid. Paul took over, and the bass he chose and used as his main instrument until around 1966 was the Hofner 500/1, or violin bass: a 1960s icon. "I got my violin bass at the Steinway shop in the centre of Hamburg. I remember going along and there was this bass which was quite cheap. It cost the German mark equivalent of £30 or so. My dad had always hammered into us never to get into debt because we weren't that rich. John and George went easily into debt, and got beautiful guitars: John got a Club 40 and George had a Futurama [actually a Neoton Grazioso] – which was like a Fender copy – and the Gretsches. Then John got the Rickenbacker. They were prepared to use hire purchase credit, but it had been so battered into me not to do that that I wouldn't risk it, so I bought a cheap guitar. And once I bought it I fell in love with it. For a light, dinky little bass it has a very rich sound, and you tend to play a lot faster on one because you feel very mobile when you're not carrying a lot of weight on your shoulder. My five-string Wal [which he used on his 1989–90 world tour] feels like a ton weight in comparison. The violin shape was symmetrical, and so, with me being left-handed, it didn't look quite so stupid as some other guitars did when their cutaways were on the upside."

Short of cash to pay for such luxuries as real bass strings, Paul used a common solution at the time for replacing old or broken ones: "We used to cut strings out of the pianos. All these clubs would wonder what had gone wrong with their pianos! We had these pliers and it was 'Alright lads, quick it's an A – which is the A? – *dong, dong!*', and we'd just nick an A string. You'd be surprised how well they work."

Gerry Rafferty on the Fab Four

"Suddenly this band called The Beatles had begun to be played on the radio, and photographs appeared of these guys with strange haircuts and an intriguing electric/acoustic line-up. Everybody was suddenly converted to this new hybrid of obscure Motown, raw rock 'n' roll and original material, all of which constituted a quantum leap from Cliff and The Shads, Marty Wilde, and Bobby Vee."

Merseybeat

The Beatles had become big news by late 1962, and the term "Merseybeat", which linked all Liverpool bands, including Gerry and The Pacemakers and Billy J. Kramer and The Dakotas, was capturing the attention of London's A&R men. One of the city's top club acts, Latin-American quartet Cass and The Casanovas, disbanded at around this time and re-formed as the rock 'n' roll/R&B trio The Big Three, featuring bassist John Gustafson.

John says: "As our sound developed, so did the direction we wanted to take. It began to take shape as a response to the power we had available. We veered towards the heavier kind of music: R&B, Isley Brothers, Bobby Freeman, Ray Charles and all that. I already loved Little Richard and the other rockers, so all that kind of gelled into one solid direction: that super-powerful R&B rock. And that's the way we kept going until the death of it, really."

John Gustafson of the Big Three in 1960: "this live shot, taken at Liverpool Boxing Statium at a Gene Vincent show (we were 900th on the bill) shows me in full Ricky Nelson stance, clutching a Hoyer semi-acoustic. This was loaned to me by Adrian Barber, the guitarist with the Futurama. The nut had been sawed to accommodate bass strings, and, being a German guitar, the machinehead was inscribed with 'Herr In Frach', which, as we all know, means 'Man In Evening Dress'"

Although a bassist, John's influences included guitarists Cliff Gallup, Scotty Moore, Eddie Cochran, Buddy Holly, and Little Richard, who was revered like a god in Liverpool. John, who later left The Big Three in late 1963 to join The Merseybeats, says: "I got to play on the same bill as Little Richard when he played the Tower Ballroom. What a blast! He is my vocal hero – always will be. Us and The Beatles, we all shared early rock 'n' roll as our influences, then we branched out in our own directions. But I know for a fact that The Big Three were John Lennon's favourite band, and we would swap lyrics and tunes with each other. The Beatles weren't as raw as us, though they did a lot of the same numbers.

"There was a kind of friendly rivalry between us and Lennon and McCartney. Many times I would go to NEMS – Brian Epstein's North End Music Stores – and either Lennon or McCartney would be in there in those little listening booths where the staff would pipe in records. If I was in a booth The Beatles would stick their heads in to see what I was listening to, or try to catch up on these obscure numbers. That's where I first heard 'Hippy Hippy Shake' by Chan Romero. Paul McCartney was having it played to him, and I said 'What's that? I'd like that', and we both bought it on the same day, and there was a kind of race to see who would do it first at the Cavern – but it wasn't really heavy rivalry. Those were really great days, and that feeling between the bands made it even greater."

BREWOOD GRAMMAR SCHOOL MAGAZINE 25

The Uppesurge of ye Mersey Beate

Herken, lordes! Lat me talke in wordes fewe,
And ye poppe musicke scene lat me yow shewe.
Allas! by my faith, a ful pitous thynge
Hath caused men neere and far to synge
"Twyste and Shoute" and muche other droole.
The home of this is inne Liverpoole,
Wher folke do bange and stampe hir feet
Y-dauncinge al to ye Mersey Beate.
These men do pleye ful loude the sax and drumme
And with ferocitee giternes do strumme.
Yonge folke with hir musicke do they arouse,
Synging ye poppe songes in accents Scouse.
By Seint Ronyan! Thise same men do choose
To wear longe hair and sharpley poynted shoes.
To coffee barres anon they go echoon
And sit, and tappe out rhythme with a spoon
Upon hir cuppes filld with Espresso coffee,
Which is, as wel ye know, both weake and frothee.
Allas! O, poppe musicke ! Yea, wikked curse!
The noyse increseth eke with every verse.
The juke-boxe jangleth forth both daye and night
Ye diskkes of hairy yobs with trowsers tyghte,
Ye latest songes from over the Atlantick
Y-songe by nastye types with haircuts frantick,
Performing al this noyse, O, piteous sighte!
With straunge wiggles and shaykes over hir might.
These same beate-groups alle auncient songes do seeke:
Ye hairey Beatles, Dreemers and Searchers eke
Pounde out swich musicke loude with all hir hertes
And with hir recordes they do crashe ye chartes.
O! what cacophonie in yeares hencefoorth,
What straunge musicke shal our singeres bring forth?
Shal it be loude, pardee, shal it be swinginge?
To what row then shal alle our ears be ringinge?

P. WATKINS.

Blending his O-level knowledge of Chaucerian English with the contemporary rise to public awareness of Merseybeat, Tradewinds guitarist Peter Watkins wrote a poem for the Brewood Grammar School magazine in 1963.

BEATLES GUITARS

At the urging of his one-time songwriting partner Elvis Costello, Paul McCartney dragged his Hofner out of retirement for recording and touring. Looking back on the early 1960s, he says: "I think that Hofner were one of the first companies with any decent instruments. My big influence was the bass, but John and George had the guitars and, even though they weren't as good as Fenders or Gibsons, they had a great, distinctive sound."

Although money may have been an issue, one of the reasons that The Beatles preferred not to use Fenders at the early stages of their recording career was to disassociate themselves from The Shadows. In doing so they helped to popularise a comparatively new range of guitars (sales of Rickenbackers and Hofners went through the roof after 1964). However, the Strat was clearly in evidence on *Rubber Soul* (1965) and some later tracks. George later took it to heart as his choice of slide guitar. Another guitar which was vital to The Beatles' sound was the Gibson J160E. On the eve of the band's recording session on 4 September 1962 for their first single, "Love Me Do", John and George strolled into Liverpool's premier music shop, Rushworth and Draper, and bought two identical sunburst models of the jumbo electro-acoustic, fitted with a P90 pickup at the bottom of the fingerboard. The J160E remained John's exclusive acoustic, both on stage and in the studio, until the late 1960s.

For quite different reasons, The Shadows and The Beatles were the two most important British bands of the early 1960s: the former for creating the innovative four-piece line-up and bringing the guitar to the forefront with an original new sound, and the latter for conquering America and delivering the concept that it was possible to write one's own songs and become a world-class commercial success. In both cases, that success continues to this day.

This picture was taken in Abbey Road Studio Two, February 1968. Grouped around the Hammond organ are Paul McCartney, George Martin, George Harrison, and John Lennon. Ringo Starr sits patiently in the drum booth. (Compare this picture with that of the Shadows in 1960 – the room hasn't really changed)

EXIT
TO FIRE EXIT

CHAPTER 9

DO WE REALLY NEED 17 WATTS?

Brewood

Brewood is a quiet village about eight miles north of Wolverhampton. It is built on a hill of pure sea sand brought by a glacier from the shores of the Irish Sea during one of the ice ages. The first inhabitants of Brewood forest were Celts from the shores of the Mediterranean: at that time Britain was still joined to the mainland. The area was later settled by the Romans who built a fort nearby, and one of the main streets – Engleton Lane – was a Roman road. King John even mentions "Breude" in the Domesday book.

This is all impressive stuff, but unfortunately it didn't hold that much fascination for rock 'n' roll-obsessed 15-year-old boys; no matter how hard we tried to pretend otherwise, cycling in convoy around the old pump in the village square did not have the same allure as cruising the strip of a small Californian town in a little deuce coupe. Any crime in the village was swiftly dealt with by a warning from Police Sergeant Left, my friend David's father, as he pedalled fearlessly into the fray armed only with his truncheon and his cycle clips. *American Graffiti* it wasn't! We therefore had to rely totally on our highly developed imaginations to pull us through, especially when it came to giving our earliest public performances.

The very first gig we ever played was at a private barbecue with the assembled musicians on a four-wheel trailer in a farmer's field. The line-up featured three acoustic guitars, military bass drum and snare drum (an old tenor banjo frame with no neck, across which stiff paper was stretched and held on by elastic bands), accordion, my pretend bass guitar, descant recorder and lots of enthusiasm. We were so bad that, while we played, a tractor was hitched to the trailer to tow us to the other side of the field. We no longer had access to electricity. It didn't matter – we had encountered our first critic.

For our first few amplified gigs I would plug the Egmond Frères pretend bass guitar into Richard Hallchurch's Fidelity Argyle two-watt tape recorder with its seven-by-four-inch elliptical speaker. Completing the awesome power of our embryonic backline, Peter Watkins played his black guitar through one of my discarded radios, which drove an unmounted six-inch speaker, sellotaped to a chair. It probably punched out at least three watts. To help Peter achieve that "Duane Eddy" sound, I had built a three-valve tremolo unit from a circuit in *Practical Wireless*. It was too big to fit neatly inside the wooden cabinet of the radio so it just stuck out of the back at right angles. The unit worked fine until one afternoon – at a practice session at rhythm guitarist Roger Swaab's house – when his corgi, Taffy, took an instant dislike to it being on *his* lounge floor and pissed all over it. Somehow I just couldn't face repairing it.

900 PRACTICAL WIRELESS February, 1961

A Tremolo Unit for an Electric Guitar

THIS PIECE OF EQUIPMENT MAY BE USED SEPARATELY OR IN AN AMPLIFIER

By F. C. Judd, A.Inst.E.

Three valve tremolo unit

The Tradewinds

All groups had to have a name. Through a friend we had secured a booking to play at a party in the large concrete shed we knew as Bilbrook Playing Fields Pavilion, and with this gig in sight we became The Peasants, although no one can remember why. As our music matured and moved away from skiffle, a change of name was deemed necessary, and so we became The Sandy Engleton Six, for the simple reason that one guy lived in Sandy Lane and two others lived in Engleton Lane. The name was dreadful, but it soon metamorphosed into something much more euphonious: The Tradewinds.

Our act had now become a blend of mostly American pop songs and mostly English guitar instrumentals, but this didn't prevent programme notes at vicarage fêtes listing us as 'The Tradewinds Trad Band' or even 'The Tradewinds Rhythmic Band'.

We had noticed that Duane Eddy records from the USA

The Peasants circa 1958. L-r: Mo Foster (Egmond Frères pretend bass through Fidelity Argyle tape recorder), Peter Watkins (the 'black' guitar through an old radio whose six inch speaker is sellotaped to the chair on the right), Patrick Davies (snare drum supported by two chairs, military bass drum), Richard Hallchurch (piano, banjo, guitar, toy xylophone, vase of flowers)

sounded very different to records from UK artists, and Peter Watkins felt that it was important to transcribe the strange Texan cowboy whooping sounds that we heard behind the sax solos on tracks such as "Forty Miles of Bad Road": Ben DeMotto even had a credit on Duane's LP sleeve for "rebel yells". But there was a cultural divide here, and I don't think we ever had the nerve to perform these "yells" live – especially to an audience in a small village just outside Wolverhampton. It would have been incomprehensible, and possibly embarrassing. And we didn't have a saxophone to hide behind.

Apart from the innumerable problems of obtaining a safe power supply, outside gigs were especially difficult because a piano was generally unavailable. A neighbour, Mrs Whittaker, had offered to give us a beautiful upright piano, as long as it found a good home. "Yes, of course," we promised, and then proceeded to push it across the village on a wobbly trolley along two miles of bumpy track to an evening gig at a party in a marquee in someone's back garden. By the time we arrived, the poor instrument was damaged, unplayable and hopelessly out of tune. We couldn't return it, but neither could we leave it, and so, with the logic that only 17-year-olds can muster, we dismantled it, burnt the wood and secretly buried the frame. It'll still be there.

The obvious solution to the outdoor problem was an organ. We couldn't possibly afford to buy one, so I set out to build one using a simple one-valve oscillator, some filter circuits and a keyboard rescued from a piano in a nearby demolished chapel. I tried to convince the band that it made a pretty authentic representation of the tenor saxophone and Hammond organ sounds that appeared on records by Johnny and The Hurricanes. They were unimpressed. Someone enquired: "Do you think a kazoo might sound better?"

Like most young bands, especially in the early 1960s, finding transport was a constant struggle. On one Saturday afternoon we played at what I assume was a youth club or some kind of party, and Bernard Watkins (Peter's father, and our manager) arranged for his neighbour, Mr Evans, to drive our equipment and certain band members to the venue. "Mr Evans was probably about 30 years old, if that," Peter remembers. "He had recently set up a security business with a friend, and it was this friend who stole the show. Arriving in a car straight from the set of *The Untouchables*, and in a full uniform of peaked cap, braiding, and epaulettes, he took the whole occasion as seriously as a delivery of gold bullion, and stood guard while we performed."

The gigs we played mostly took place at a set of small interconnecting villages in Staffordshire, the journeys to which involved driving along many narrow country roads with no street lighting. "The show had to go on whatever the weather," says Roger Swaab. "On one evening, in the days of real smog, I remember someone literally having to walk in front of the procession of vehicles with a torch to guide us to the Promised Land. Looking back, this was rather a pointless exercise, since he could see no more out of the car than in it. In fact, the main result of this supreme effort of endurance was to wear out the legs and transform the hoar-frost-covered individual into a character from *The Snow Queen*.

"I was always amazed when we finally arrived at our destination, obviously late, to find so many other people who had endured the same conditions to get there. At least we were getting paid – albeit modestly – for our efforts. I cannot, even now, believe that it was anything to do with us. It must have been the challenge of beating nature that drove the audience to turn up."

Steve Winwood, who was only eight years old at the time, playing guitar with the Ron Atkinson band in Birmingham, 1956. His father, Laurie Winwood, was on tenor sax, whilst his older brother Muff Winwood was on second guitar

The Tradewinds invitation cards

Muff and Steve Winwood

Laurie Winwood played sax and ran a band that specialised in Dixieland but played at weddings, bar mitzvahs and similar social functions. Most dance bands couldn't support even one guitarist, but unusually Laurie brought in two: his sons Muff and Steve. In the middle of the set, the boys, along with the drummer, would play a rock 'n' roll interlude, but they were also into New Orleans jazz and used to frequent a small record shop in Birmingham that specialised in jazz and blues. Going around the clubs while playing as the Muff-Woody Jazz Band, they spotted folk singer Spencer Davis and were thrilled to hear him performing a Big Bill Broonzy blues number. Obviously, here was a singer of like mind. They already knew drummer Pete York, who was interested in jazz, and the evolution of the Spencer Davis Group in 1963 seemed but a formality.

Richard Brunton

When Richard Brunton formed his R&B group The Epidemics in Newcastle upon Tyne, the audiences at their first few gigs were treated to a mix of guitar, bass, contact-

GIGGING

- **One-time Johnny Kidd and The Pirates drummer Clem Cattini recalls: "At some Pirates gigs, Jimmy Page, in the support band, would be watching us attentively observing every detail."**
- Richard Thompson: "After a while I realised there was a trick to carrying a Selmer Selectatone and a HofnerV3 on a bus. Our first gig broke our spirit. We did an opening spot at a school dance and, being severely under-amplified, we couldn't rise above the background chat, whistles and abuse. We disbanded."
- **Martin Taylor: "I embarked on a musical career which was only briefly halted when, on a gig at a local working man's club, the guitar neck came away from the body with an almighty bang during the 'Spot Waltz'. The club secretary, thinking I was doing a Pete Townshend impression, came over to me and whispered in my ear 'We'll have none of that in here, lad!'"**
- Colin Green would skive off from school with his dinner money and travel to London to play in the coffee bars, where he was discovered. (He was very surprised when he got paid – he thought you just played for fun!)
- **Despite Jim Mullen's enormous reputation for working within the R&B genre, he dispels the myth that this was how he began. "My roots were always jazz, from about the age of 16. I grew up in the Bridgetown area of Glasgow, and my first instrument was double-bass – like Jack Bruce. I knew him really well in those days, and around 1960 when I was starting, my biggest influences were the jazz musicians in the town."**
- When he was a member of The Hi-Rs, bassist Brian Odgers played in working men's clubs, where musicians were paid according to their needs i.e., £7, £9 or £11, depending on their marital status and on the number of children they had. I thought this was a sophisticated approach.

miked piano and vocals, all hot-wired through the twin channels of their awesome red-and-gold-fleck rig. He describes the result as "a sound both hard to imagine and difficult to forget". The Epidemics soon upgraded to a Selmer Zodiac twin 50-watt combo amp in mock-croc covering. This delightful device featured a push-button selector tone and magic-eye vibrato indicator.

Richard: "Towards the end of a late club set at one of the notorious Bailey's night spots, my normally reliable Selmer Zodiac went critical. Since it didn't seem to affect the amplifier's performance, I can be forgiven for not noticing that the power stage had caught fire and was emanating plumes of green paraffin smoke behind me. The bass player smelled it first and, whirling around to alert me, the headstock of his bass caught the crash cymbal, and as I turned towards the conflagration, I watched the edge of the cymbal topple and slice neatly through the mains supply. It produced a bang, a flash, and screams of alarm from the punters and plunged the club into darkness. It also saved the Selmer."

It was a very busy period for bands in the Newcastle area, and Richard describes Saturday trading in second-hand equipment as "vigorous". On one occasion they purchased a Shure Unidyne III mic, which was "hotly debated at around £30, but is still in regular use". They also bought a pair of Philips four-by-ten-inch PA columns from a band that had folded. "We collected them from the drummer's mum in Wallsend," says Richard. "She helped us prise the cabinets – grey, with torn grille fabric – out of an upstairs wardrobe. And, at her insistence, we accepted four glistening turquoise glitter jackets as part of the deal."

Mickey Moody

One of Mickey Moody's early bands played their first gig in a local village hall which had no power points. Ingeniously, they plugged all of their gear into the light sockets and played in the dark. To overcome this problem at later gigs, they organised their own light show. A bulb was fixed into a large metal biscuit tin with a coloured gelatine front, and one of these constructions was placed at either side of the stage and moved up and down by friends, who also flashed them on and off with light switches.

"We were only going out for £15 a night," says Mickey. I'd be down on my knees with a Telecaster, doing a Jeff Beck bit, heavy fuzzbox and that, and Paul came on with his bamboo stick with a sock on the end, which he'd soaked in paraffin beforehand. I got up off the floor with the guitar, rushed over, got a cigarette lighter out of my pocket, set fire to it and it went up. *Whum!* Imagine how that went down in 1966, when everyone else was trying to copy Geno Washington stuff with terrible sax players. Nobody ever clapped. The audience seemed frozen with fear. Still, we were ahead of our time. Jimi Hendrix may have set fire to his guitar at Monterey in 1967, but it was us that set fire to one of my dad's old socks at Thornaby-on-Tees in 1966."

Jeff Beck

Jeff Beck's first public performance was in 1958, when he was 14. "I played in Carshalton Park and couldn't find a bass player, so this art student came along. He still had his duffel coat on, and he didn't have a bass, he had a cello! It looked ridiculous: he was six feet three inches and he played this cello like an upright bass. I said: 'Put it on a chair, put it on a chair...' We got through half a number before we folded up and couldn't remember the rest of it, and we got off the stage." Three years later, Pirates' bassist Brian Gregg was about to play a gig and needed a guitarist. He placed an advert in *Melody Maker* and met the guy who answered it at the station: a gangly silhouette at the end of the platform. He had a fine drawing of himself on his guitar case. He played the gig with Brian and was brilliant. This may well have been Jeff Beck's first professional booking.

Tony Hicks

After leaving school, Tony Hicks became an apprentice electrician, playing at weekends with a band called The Dolphins. "Bobby Elliott joined on drums, and with bass player Bernie Calvert and Ricky Shaw on vocals we'd play gigs all over the Manchester area for £15 a night. It was just so exciting getting on a stage."

Paul Day

At school in the 1960s, Paul Day's band, The Downtowns, could not afford the Vox AC30s with two-by-twelve-inch speakers that they longed for, but Paul convinced himself that, from a distance, his Vox AC10s, with their two-by-ten-inch speakers, looked to the audience just like AC30s. On one night at the Pavilion Theatre, Teignmouth, the band's guitarists were using their AC10s while the two vocal mics and bass guitar all went through one 15-watt Watkins pick-a-bass amp. To Paul's amazement and indignation, they were asked to turn the volume down! (Paul also noticed that people were wary of red guitar leads: "They thought you must be louder.")

Paul Day (r) – from a distance

David Gilmour

Well known in Cambridge for his skills as a floating guitarist in local bands, David Gilmour's first proper group was the R&B outfit Jokers Wild. November 1965 saw them and a band then known as The Pink Floyd Sound performing at a birthday party in their home town. Sharing the bill was an unknown singer called Paul Simon, who was backed by David's band on songs such as "Johnny B. Goode". The night also witnessed the shape of things to come when Syd Barrett, Roger Waters, Nick Mason and Rick Wright were joined by David for an end-of-party R&B romp – the first of several joint appearances.

Based on the Continent throughout the famous summer of 1967, David and two of his fellow Jokers, bassist Ricky Wills and drummer Willie Wilson, formed a new power trio: Bullitt. "We spent most of our time rehashing early Jimi Hendrix songs to crowds of strange French people," remembers David. By the time David returned to the UK, The Pink Floyd had become the darlings of London's underground scene, with their free-form, jazz-inspired psychedelic workouts, such as "Interstellar Overdrive", which often lasted an hour and was based around one riff or chord. Syd Barrett was a Telecaster player, like David, who relied heavily on his bottleneck and echo to achieve his unusual and unworldly blend of guitar effects, while the other band members fought to keep up the *audio-verité* momentum.

Tom McGuinness

Tom McGuinness was desperate to play R&B and meet players who liked the same music and musicians. In his search for a suitable gig, he rang a promising advert that he saw in *Melody Maker.* He chatted to the guy about musicians that they liked, and all seemed okay until his final question: "What do *you* play?" "Trombone." (This in itself should have been a warning to Tom.) The audition took place at the Station Hotel, Richmond, where The Rolling Stones played. As Tom reached the doorway, he momentarily froze when he heard the music of Dave Hunt's Confederate Jazz Band, the line-up of which was three trombones, piano, bass and drums. They were trying to make the transition to R&B. During a discussion to find at least one tune in common, they settled on "Kansas City". Tom asked: "What key shall we play this?" "E flat," was the answer. (To Tom this meant playing at the eleventh fret.) During the jam, Tom played Jimmy Reed boogie style, while the rest of the band played in jazz mode. Afterwards, Dave said to Tom: "Sounds great!"

In the audience was Tom's girlfriend, Jennifer Dolan, and during a break she introduced her friend from art college, a keen young guitarist called Eric Clapton. Tom invited Eric to join his own new band, The Roosters, and they started rehearsing in a back room of a pub in New Malden. The advantage of this room was that they rehearsed

Eric Clapton (l) gigging with Tom McGuinness' R&B Band the Roosters

on alternate nights with another band, whose gear they used without permission. Found out one night, they helped the other band to carry their gear out in embarrassment.

Andy Fraser

Andy Fraser's early playing activities took him across London to play with an all-black blues band in Willesden and a Jamaican reggae band in the East End. "All the guys were much older than me, and the club didn't open until 11 p.m. I was obviously the odd man out – this 13-year-old white kid who could play the bass!"

Gerry Rafferty

Much of the reputation of Gerry Rafferty's band The A-Beats rested on their innate grasp of the chord changes in a wide swathe of Beatles material – at last they were in demand! Gerry: "In time I soldiered on with a succession of local outfits, ending up with The Maverix, Paisley's premier exponents of beat, who had also recruited Joe Egan, something of a local hero. He earned himself the timeless accolade of 'Mr Pretty Flamingo' on the basis of a spirited rendition of the Manfred Mann biggie at venues throughout the length and breadth of our fair borough."

This angelic creature on drums would soon metamorphose into Snail's Pace Slim, the fabled guitarist of the Hamsters

Roger Glover

The Madisons, Roger Glover's early band, debuted at his school's Christmas show. Roger: "Bert Weedon, whose son Geoff attended the school, graced us all with his presence on the first night, and we must have sounded very distorted because after the show he tactfully suggested that we borrow his amplifier for the next two nights. It was a brand new Selmer, with a leather name tag bearing Bert's name, and it had wheels! Very posh. And clean. I didn't get to use it though – the more important instruments had that privilege. I was only the bass player; but at least I had the battered Watkins Westminster to myself. Despite that, I don't think it sounded much better."

Ray Russell

From his early days, Ray Russell liked both rock and jazz, and while still only 12 years old he sat in at the legendary 2i's club in Old Compton Street, Soho, and noticed that everyone seemed to be taller than he was. He formed a band at school with his friend George Bean, the son of woodwork teacher Mr Bean. Since George looked great, and the girls fancied him, it seemed natural that he became the lead singer of the band, who – with tongue firmly in cheek – christened themselves George Bean and The Runners. Ray played lead guitar on his new Burns Vista-Sonic, the bass player had a Fenton-Weill, and the rhythm guitarist (who really wanted to play lead but wasn't as good as Ray) played a white Fender Strat. Bass and rhythm were both plugged into one Watkins Dominator.

Snail's Pace Slim

"The riff to 'Sunshine of Your Love' was our inspiration, and so the Magic Inkwell Retaliation was born," recalls Snail's Pace Slim, who was then a drummer. "It died, a few gigs later, on account of us being crap. The rhythm player switched to bass, and with me on drums we recruited a Keith Emerson-style organist. No knives in the keyboard, though – his mum would've had kittens. We learned The Nice's repertoire, and even some of the first ELP album. Honestly.

(it refers to Keith Emerson's live show, where he would stick knives in the keyboard of his Hammond organ)

"After drumming for some time, I got tired of lugging tons of gear and having a sweaty bum all the way through gigs – every drummer I knew had got piles and I didn't fancy that – so I thought I'd switch to guitar, get up front of the stage and be a *real* Flash Harry. Easy. Walk in, plonk combo down and plug in. I had to start singing as well, 'cause frontmen are such a pain and I couldn't be bothered with all their bollocks. So now I play lead guitar and sing for a living – I suppose that must make me an egomaniac and a narcissist. But that's okay, I'm great and everybody loves me for it."

Colin Hodgkinson

By 1962, almost every club gig was geared to dancing, which meant that The Dynatones, Colin Hodgkinson's band, had to compile their repertoire accordingly. "We all played covers. Nobody wrote anything, and the only way to be really hip was to play something by Duane Eddy like 'Rebel Rouser'. All the bands touring at that time, however, weren't in the least big time. We frequently opened for groups like Mike Berry and The Outlaws, Neil Christian and The Crusaders (with a fantastic young guitarist called Jimmy Page!), and everyone was very friendly and approachable – it was a great feeling." The Dynatones, incidentally, became local heroes after playing at the Embassy in Peterborough on the same bill as The Beatles!

Colin Hodgkinson (left) with The Dynatones and their luxury Vox AC10

Ron Wood

On forming their first group, The Birds, Ron Wood and his school pals rehearsed and finally set up a weekend residency at their local community centre in West Drayton, calling it the Nest Club. "We pushed our equipment [a Bird amp for two guitars and vocals, plus a Fenton-Weill amp for bass] in a huge home-made wheelbarrow to and from the gig," says Ron. "We built a following, and soon our manager had us working the length and breadth of England, seven nights a week, packing and unpacking our equipment and all piling into the back of a van."

Bruce Baxter and John Rostill

Bruce Baxter recollects that he and John Rostill used to read *Melody Maker* avidly. They replied to an ad which read: "Wanted. Young rocking musicians." Deciding that the description fitted, "I wrote this letter going on about how wonderful we were, and fortunately I included in the letter

John Rostill (2nd left) with the Terry Young Five at Butlins in July 1961. His guitar-playing flatmate, Bruce Baxter, is on the right

the fact that we had these matching guitars. Not to mention the matching uniforms: blue corduroy drape jackets with gold backcloth, drainpipe trousers and black suede winkle-pickers! Really tasteless. Before we went, we had our hair done the same, too: a DA at the back and a huge quiff called a half-roll at the front. Bloody hell! Still, we must have looked the part." The audition was successful, and they became members of Terry Young and The Youngsters, a band that metamorphosed into The Terry Young Five.

In the summer of 1963, John parted company with Terry Young and joined The Interns, although for a while John took a job as a clerical assistant in a ladies' lingerie shop! John's parents gave him £100 for his 21st birthday, and he used the money to buy an old ambulance to carry The Interns and their equipment around the country. To fit in with the medical image, The Interns wore surgeons' outfits on stage.

Ron Wood (second right) with The Birds

Gary Moore

In Belfast, gigging was never made easy for Gary Moore, who in 1965, at the age of 13, was playing in local clubs. "In those days it was a dangerous place: you would come out of the club and there would be a gang waiting for you, demanding 'Have you got any odds?' (i.e., spare change), and whether you gave them some money or not they'd hit you anyway. Sometimes, my bus fare gone, I'd have to walk home while they took the bus with my money, and then they'd be waiting for me halfway home. It was a nightmare. The bands would always be sabotaging each other with stupid pranks, like pulling the speaker leads out so that the transformer would go up in flames."

School was no better, although there was one good teacher, Mr Clements, who encouraged Gary to play along with various folk songs, but he was unusual. "Some of the teachers really hated me, and one of them used to threaten to report me to the council, because I was doing gigs under age."

Bernie Holland

Unusually for such a delicate instrument, the ukulele got Bernie Holland out of trouble. "I took the ukulele to school and it saved me from many a beating up. It was like those clubs where the Mafia come storming in and smash the place up while the band seems to be sacrosanct, the unwritten rule being 'Don't shoot the piano player.' The ukulele was a very useful tool of survival." (Imagine, however, an alternative stand-off: the leather-clad gang is walking menacingly towards you, but you fearlessly pull out the ukulele, give them a dose of "When I'm Cleaning Windows" and watch them scatter.)

A REAL BASS

In the window of local Wolverhampton music shop the Band Box there appeared one day a second-hand bass guitar. It had a long neck, one real pickup, two knobs, a single cutaway like a Les Paul, and adorning the headstock – for some unexplained reason – was the silver emblem from a Remington typewriter. I had to have it. It was a Dallas Tuxedo, and after withdrawing my entire GPO account savings of £16 it was mine.

Not only did the instrument sound wonderful played through my parents' Murphy radio but it looked great too. It was the first solid-bodied instrument in the village, and I was the first to attach the shoulder strap to the body itself (a dressing-gown cord attached to the headstock had been the previous method).

John Paul Jones, a fellow Tuxedo player, says: "I had convinced myself and my friends that the Dallas Tuxedo was in every way equal to a Fender, and superior in terms of price; but deep down I knew that I would never be a real bass player, like the people in the pictures of Shirley Douglas' *Teach Yourself Bass Guitar* book, until I owned a Fender Precision."

On my Tuxedo, I attempted to recreate the warm sound that Jet Harris always had on record. Not knowing that it was a combination of his style and technique, the strings, his Fender Precision and amplifier, the valve mic, the mixing desk, the valve compressor, the EQ, the engineer, the producer, and the sophistication of Abbey Road Studio Two, I decided it was *the plectrum* that was the crucial factor, and cut one out of stiff green felt. One piece was too floppy, but two stuck together had the required stiffness. Unfortunately it sounded like shit, and after one song the bass had acquired a new look as it became covered in thousands of minute electrostatically attracted green hairs, which took days to remove.

AMPS AND CABS

Amplification was now becoming an issue, as I couldn't take the family radio on gigs. However, a solution was to be found in the pages of my bible, *Practical Wireless*: a design for a hi-fi bass reflex cabinet. I persuaded my dad to help with the carpentry, and together we built a huge hernia-inducing wardrobe-like object with one twelve-inch speaker. It was covered in black star-speckled fablon, with gold-mesh fabric protecting the speaker front. And for the first time, my on-stage bass sound approximated the earthy rumbling that emanated from jukeboxes. We were rockin'.

Joe Brown

Joe Brown began his professional career as a guitarist in the 1950s, when bass guitars were a new phenomenon in Britain and dedicated bass amps and speaker cabinets were non-existent. Everyone made their own. "All sorts of boffins appeared from nowhere

Murphy 188 Radio and Dallas Tuxedo bass guitar, reunited after all these years

September/October, 1959 PRACTICAL WIRELESS 461

A Twin Speaker BASS Reflex Cabinet

Practical Wireless – *the Bass Reflex Cabinet*

I built this amplifier to drive the reflex cabinet but was confused by the output rating of '10/14 watts' – was this an option?

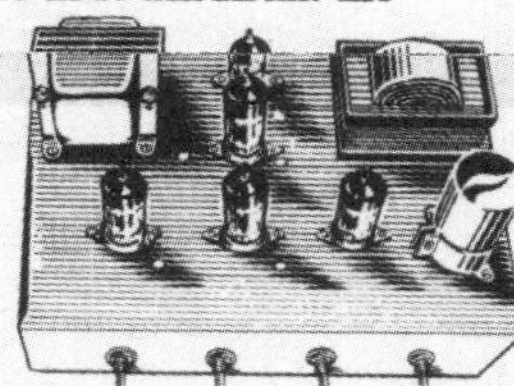

with various theories. Some said 'the bigger the better'; some said 'it depends on the shape'; others commented on the 'air displacement behind the speakers'; but no one really knew. Our version turned out to be five feet tall by three feet wide by two feet deep, housing two twelve-inch speakers, and it had a screw every two inches in the back panel. We had also taken the precaution of relying on the air displacement theory and stuffed the back with thousands of pieces of rolled-up newspaper.

"We were on our way back from a gig at the Star Club in Hamburg to do a show in Purley, probably at the Orchid Ballroom. Apart from our allowed duty-free, the drummer had stashed a couple of bottles of whisky in his traps case. When we got to Customs, the officer's eye went straight to the bass cabinet, which he could hardly miss – it was like a bloody coffin. 'What's in that?" he asked. 'Two twelve-inch speakers,' I replied. 'Right,' he said, 'let's have the back off.' Nearly 100 screws later, off came the back. When they saw the rolled up bits of paper, they thought they'd struck gold. They flattened every single piece out, and when they found nothing they had to squash them all up and put them back again. By the time the last screw went back we were two hours late for the gig. But we still had the whisky!"

Licorice Locking

When Licorice Locking met Marty Wilde on Jack Good's *Oh Boy* show he was playing double-bass with Vince Taylor and The Playboys, along with Tony Sheridan on guitar and Brian Bennett on drums. But when he was invited to join The Wildcats with Big Jim Sullivan, Brian Bennett and Tony Belcher on guitar, Licorice started to play a Framus electric bass. It was suggested that he meet Marty's father, who had made an amplifier.

Licorice: "What an amp! The cabinet was at least four feet tall, a massive square thing that I believe resembled a very large rabbit hutch, with wire mesh at the top and a square opening at the bottom. The amplifier itself was detachable and separate. But there was always trouble with

AMP TALES

- **Brendan McCormack's valve sound relied on an old radio, which was three feet tall and weighed in at around 60lb. This soon led to the exotic Watkins ten-watt Combo amp in black-and-white Rexene with gold stars, one ten-inch speaker and a built-in tremolo unit "Even the neighbours knew this was class."**
- Joe Brown: "Every time anyone came up with a new guitar or amp we were on it like a shot. I remember a fist-fight breaking out over who was going to plug into the tremolo channel of our new Vox AC30. Eventually, we wired everyone up to one jack plug and plugged the lot in. It sounded bloody awful, but it was different."
- **Tony Hicks: "My only amplification was the radiogram at home. Fortunately, my favourite record at the time was 'Peggy Sue', by Buddy Holly, and the guitar on the record sounded just like mine through the radiogram: 'woof, woof woof!' So I thought: 'This is it, I've got a guitar sound here.'"**
- In 1962 the crocodile-skin-covered Selmer Truvoice Concord Eight amplifier sported a small plate on the back which read:

> This amplifier has an undistorted output of ___ watts. If distortion occurs, reduce the volume setting accordingly.

Guitarist Martin Sage, then at school and playing with his band The Strollers, recalls: "The wattage rating was left blank, so I suppose you filled in whatever you wanted!"

Marty Wilde and the Wild Cats recording a radio broadcast (L-r: Licorice Locking, Marty Wilde, Brian Bennett, and Big Jim Sullivan)

this thing. Practically each night I was trying to find the fault of a wire or connection coming off, and fixing it so as to be ready for the next performance. Strangely enough, it was used with the Framus bass on Marty's recordings of 'Sea Of Love' and 'Bad Boy', and also when we were Eddie Cochran's backing group on his British tour. How on earth did we manage in those days? To get to gigs we all travelled in a Bedford Dormobile with Brian Bennett driving. My amp slid perfectly down the middle of the van, and we just piled everything else on top. The amp served for good ballast for the Dormobile, I'm sure. If the gigs were in London we travelled by tube!" In fact, the cabinet was the first home-made amp that Joe Brown ever saw on the road.

Jet Harris

Needing an amplifier, Jet Harris responded to an advert from Foote's in *Melody Maker:* 'New 30w amp with extensive negative feedback, six valves, two inputs. Separate 15-inch speaker in specially designed cabinet. Sand-filled baffle giving clear undistorted power over the whole range. Very attractive contemporary design. 89 guineas.' Jet describes what was quite possibly the first purpose-designed bass amp in the UK as being "red, four feet high, three feet wide, three feet deep, and so heavy that it took four of us to carry it." Unfortunately, his revolutionary new instrument had other problems: amplification was in its infancy, and earthing was a concept of the future. "If my nose touched the microphone I got an electrical shock off the metal scratchplate."

Richard Brunton

Richard Brunton's first amp – apart from his Pam home radio – was a Stroud chassis which he bought through *Exchange & Mart* ("the valves glowed when a chord was struck"). This amp drove two Fane speakers in a plywood case covered in red-and-gold-fleck fablon. He gigged with this setup for eight months, until he could afford a Futurama "piggy-back" bass amp and a Hofner Verithin with a genuine Bigsby tremolo arm. Richard also confesses to using a £4/17/6d (£4-87p) tape recorder as both fuzzbox and echo, and building an "Electric Twit": a single-string slide guitar of his own design which he described as "hideous!"

Jim Cregan

"Why were amplifiers were so expensive?" asks Jim Cregan. "£85 for a Vox AC30 was completely out of the range of a schoolboy with a Saturday morning job at Dewhurst's, the family butcher, and an early morning paper round – my weekly earnings totalled 25/6 [about £1.25]. Still, there were the summer holidays, and I worked all through mine until I could afford a Linear Concorde Amp and a twelve-inch Goodmans speaker, but I had to make the cabinet myself. Working from a principle that I'd learned from the family radio, I made an enclosure about half the size of a small car, covered it in pale blue quilted fablon, and finished the corners and edges with gold trim. It was magnificent, and could easily have been used as a second home for the vertically challenged. Unfortunately, it fell off the roof rack of a Ford Anglia one day outside Ruislip Manor tube station and disintegrated, so the whole band had to play through a Watkins Dominator."

John Rostill

Fender basses were still pretty scarce in the early 1960s, but John Rostill found a Jazz bass in Lou Davies' shop which had been brought in by an American serviceman. A quick trade and some dodgy signatures on HP forms and it was his. Then, in 1962, the group needed another amp. Already heavily in debt, John decided that it would be cheaper to build his own amp and speaker cabinet, basing it on the design of a Fender "piggy-back" model. The project got under way in a small bedsit.

Bruce Baxter: "We lived in this hole in Swiss Cottage and played one or two gigs a week, occasionally paying the rent. We bought enough tea to last until the next weekend, and if there was any money left we ate and smoked. There was a gas fire with a meter, and if we ran out of money for that we stayed in bed to keep warm. It was a nightmare. I had my bed and my wardrobe and a little path over to the sink to wash and make the tea and the rest of the place was full of John's bits of wood and stuff. But his cabinet was an impressive piece of work." John used this equipment both with Terry Young and the Bournemouth-based band The Interns. When he eventually joined The Shadows, The Interns bought the amp, a Leak, and John stored the speaker cabinet in the large shed at his mother's house.

The speaker cabinet that John Rostill built

John Gustafson

For a brief period in Liverpool, when the Cavern's popularity was at its height, The Big Three were rivalling The Beatles in the local talent stakes and were even taken on by manager Brian Epstein. However, before they could begin to compete any further (and score the hit "Some Other Guy", which would fund John Gustafson's transition from a Framus to a Fender), some technical enhancements were needed, as John explains: "We needed extra amplification to make up for the lack of the other guitar; we thought we should beef up the bass department, 'cause you couldn't really buy commercial bass amps at the time. We had Selmer Truvoices and that kind of thing – you know, £30 15-watt amps. Adrian Barber, our original guitarist, made these speakers for The Big Three; he made one for himself and one for me. His was a slightly thinner version of mine: his had two twelve-inch speakers in it, and he powered it with a 30-watt amp he had. He built them in a basement in Canning Street underneath a flat he was living in. Mine was a big fat thing with one 18-inch speaker. He bought the speakers from Goodmans and made the cabinet out of one-inch chipboard, and he bought handles and wheels and put it all together.

"Now, later on, when Adrian left The Big Three, he sold his own rig to Paul McCartney for use as a bass amp. Adrian experimented with all kinds of stuff – sheets of foam, polystyrene, whatever – to try to stop the vibrations, and he did quite well for someone who'd never built anything like that before. These were probably the first stacks, and they worked very well. I'd never seen anything that big. We'd seen a couple of bands from London with cube-shaped speaker enclosures, but nothing like this – these were twice the size. My cabinet was a reflex cabinet. Adrian had built a baffle inside to deflect the sound out through a hole in another part of the speaker cabinet. It was quite advanced, really, for those days. I used a 50-watt amp, but I can't remember the name – it did the trick, though. That amp, together with the speakers, caused a lot of problems in the Cavern at the lunchtime sessions, with this heavy bass noise reverberating up through the floors of the offices above. People were forever barging in to complain."

Hugh Burns

The innovations of Hugh Burns and his young colleagues were typical of the day. These included mounting a speaker on a record turntable to emulate the sound of a Leslie. A Clavoline Univibe keyboard was built into a chest of drawers (top drawer, of course), complete with a Watkins Copicat echo in the lower drawer ("We were never sure if he was going to play the keyboard or serve drinks!"). Hugh: "My mother made several 'custom' speaker cabinets to

Promotional shot for the Big Three at the time of their hit 'Some Other Guy'

make it look like we had more equipment and fill up the stage. Many people who booked us were impressed by how much equipment we had. Little did they know there was nothing in the cabinets." Hugh's band also dreamed up a method of doubling its output by soldering two cables to one jack plug, and used bird-cage holders in the absence of real microphone stands.

Francis Rossi

They were not alone: in 1962, prior to his second gig as a member of The Spectres, Francis Rossi realised that he had no stand for the tape-recorder mic that he'd been using for vocals, but he really wanted to be able to sing and play at the same time. Guitarist and schoolfriend John Rushden suggested the stand from his parents' bird cage. They unhitched the poor bird and taped the mic onto the end of what looked like a tall brass question mark. This must have been a unique sight – imagine: the whole band plugged into one AC30 with Francis singing upwards into a bird-cage stand. So that's how he developed that trademark Quo stance!

Francis Rossi, playing with the Spectres at Butlins. (Note the PA mixer on the floor in front of the bass drum)

Roger Glover

For Roger Glover, amplification was a constant problem. "I resolved to rectify it by building my own speaker cabinet and buying a cheap amplifier from one of those mysterious electrical shops in Tottenham Court Road. To me, as long as it was called an amplifier it was okay. I didn't realise that there were differences; I thought I was being very clever not paying through the nose for an expensive Selmer or a Vox from a proper shop." I was hopelessly naïve when it came to electronics and relied heavily on Tony, who always managed to sound as if he knew what he was talking about. We infuriated his parents on many an occasion, sawing and gluing together pieces of wood in his living room, wiring up these contraptions, plugging in the instrument and then scratching our heads in consternation, wondering either why it didn't sound too good or didn't sound at all. We built

Roger Glover playing bass with Episode 6 in 1967

several units over the years, and gradually got better at it, but apart from the last set of cabinets – which I used through the latter years of Episode Six, and even had them when I joined Deep Purple – most of them were not very good.

"I remember one of the more ambitious designs. It was going to hold a large array of eight-inch speakers, and so a cabinet was called for that had a very large front surface, but no depth whatsoever to compensate for that. We tried really hard, this being something like our third or fourth effort, and bought the finest quality chipboard, glued it really well before driving in the screws (I can still feel the sore muscles), and, having bought the best speakers we could afford (Goodmans), we reckoned that we had done well. The idea of using eight-inch speakers for a bass guitar was a bold plan, based on the rather fanciful theory that the lack of size was compensated for by the sheer quantity, and we were convinced – or rather Tony had convinced me – that it would work brilliantly. In the event, it didn't: its debut was at the Railway Hotel in Wealdstone, a legendary gig, and the sound that it produced was so pathetic that the rest of the band didn't even laugh at us; they just turned away and ignored us. To say the least, it was embarrassing. Back to the drawing board."

WIRELESS

I began to tire of standing on guitar leads while playing with the band. It would be another 25 years before luxuries like the Samson wireless guitar transmitter system became commonplace and within financial reach of the semi-pro musician. However, with more than a little help from *Practical Wireless*, I managed to devise a transmitter for my new bass: a simple two-transistor circuit built into a plastic toffee case. The aerial went inside my trousers and down my leg, and it transmitted illegally on medium wave at about 200 metres – quite near the frequency used by Radio Luxembourg, on 208 metres. Unfortunately, it had a range of only about three feet before severe distortion set in, and so was hardly a sophisticated and reliable lead replacement. My hopes of casually wandering into the audience while still playing were dashed. It was back to cables and tripping over.

Top: Practical Householder. It contained very good post-war DIY advice on items such as 'Building a Refrigerator', or 'Chromium Plating at Home'. Bottom: 1956 Practical Householder article: 'Chromium Plating at Home'. A&E would have to be notified

February, 1956 THE PRACTICAL HOUSEHOLDER 343

CHROMIUM Plating at Home

How to Replate Those Fittings

By M. P. DAVIES

Wireless Guitar – a transmitter idea

THE WATKINS DOMINATOR

As pupils of Brewood Grammar School, we all theoretically had careers ahead of us in teaching, physics, farming, and architecture – not music, we thought; that was just a hobby.

By 1959 my friends and I had accumulated some small amplifiers (little Selmers and converted radiograms), each rated between 2 and 5 watts output. This "wall of sound" was fine at first for our intimate circuit of young farmers' parties, village fêtes and school dances. However, in an attempt to make the band look more impressive, and indeed more audible, we discussed purchasing a bigger amplifier. The ultimate choice of amplifier was the Vox AC30, but given our restricted finances and aspirations, this particular option was inconceivable.

In the trade papers of the day adverts began appearing for an impressive-looking 17-watt amplifier: the blue-and-white, two-by-ten-inch, wedge-shaped Watkins Dominator, with four inputs. This seemed to be the perfect choice, as between us we could just about afford the requisite £38/10/- (£38.50). But there were problems: four of the guys in the band thought it was wonderful, and that we should buy it immediately, whilst the other three were a bit cautious and thought that the powerful output might be excessive to our needs. Anticipating the possibility that we might cause a room to empty, one guy said: "Do we *really* need 17 Watts? – do you think it might frighten the audience?" But, after some deliberation, we did buy the Dominator, and within weeks this fine amplifier was proudly on display at gigs, wobbling precariously on its three new gold-sprayed coffee-table legs, with all four inputs in use.

Oh, the innocence of it all. Twenty years later, while playing a stadium tour in the USA with Jeff Beck, my bass rig alone was rated at a mighty 1,500 watts. It generated a stiff breeze.

COFFEE-TABLE LEGS

The late Fifties and early Sixties were periods of burgeoning DIY Magazines like *Practical Householder* which featured articles such as 'Building a Refrigerator' and 'Chromium Plating at Home', and furniture of the day looked very spindly. In desperation to throw off the old and to embrace the contemporary, there was a mania to fit screw-in coffee-table legs to anything that stood still, as demonstrated in an advert for Brianco Legs, which boldly stated: 'Convert your spare wood into elegant tables with these easy-to-fix legs.' In our case we converted all of our stage equipment – including the Watkins Dominator – into elegant wobbling amplifiers.

SATURDAY SCENE

I dreaded compulsory football at school; the muddy game seemed to be a complete waste of 90 minutes. I discovered that, if I elected myself to be a full back, I could spend most of the game pretending to be a television cameraman, viewing the proceedings from a distance through my rolled-

The Watkins

DOMINATOR

17 WATT TREMOLO AMPLIFIER

A top quality instrument designed for the professional who needs the best. The "Dominator" embodies all the tried and trusted features of the earlier models with detailed improvements made possible by the continuing research of "Watkins" designers.
Natural quality of tone to suit the most discerning player. Generous valve line-up and circuit efficiency ensure ample volume and some to spare for all occasions together with the brilliant and sparkling attack associated with "Watkins" Amplifiers.
Twin 12,000 line 10″ speakers drive in a cabinet geometrically angled to give maximum sound projection and directional treble impact.
Comprehensive control panel is flush mounted for safety in transport and features: Four inputs. Two volume controls. Two tone controls. Tremolo Speed control. Tremolo Depth control. Jewelled pilot light.
Tremolo is operative on two of the four inputs and is flash-controlled for on/off by foot switch on wander lead.
Tremolo speed and depth controls provide "Full Compass" tremolo pulse combinations.
Acoustically designed luxury cabinet, presented in two-tone leather cloth with gilt trim completes the striking and exclusive appearance.

PRICE £38 - 10 - 0

(Heavy quality waterproof cover 27/6.)

A.C. Mains 200-250V.

66 OFFLEY ROAD · LONDON · S.W.9 · *Telephone RELiance 6568/9*

The Watkins Dominator

up hands and avoiding the danger like a fearless war correspondent. I became an expert at tracking shots, and even managed primitive vision mixing on close-ups, from one eye to the other, just before the ball (or another player) hit me on the head.

As the popularity of rock 'n' roll increased, so too did the feeling of competitiveness among us instrument-playing school pupils. While other boys were testing their athletic prowess and playing team sports on cold and muddy fields, the guitarists were sensibly indoors holding occasional Chet Atkins competitions. In this bizarre ascension to manhood, the challenge was to play the whole of a tune called "Windy and Warm" in the finger-picking style of Chet Atkins, and in the key of C minor (involving a constant *barré*), without faltering. There was always a cheer when someone managed it. Years later I discovered that Chet played the song using a capo, so that the much less physically demanding A minor shape could be used

The Tradewinds rehearsing in early 1960 with full back-line.
L-r: Patrick Davies (a truly bizarre drum kit), Roger Swaab (Framus: 'The Little Guitar With The Big Tone'/Selmer 'Little Giant'), Mo Foster (Dallas Tuxedo/Murphy 188 Radio), Peter Watkins (Hofner Congress/'Invicta' PA Speaker). We were rockin'!

DOMINATOR TALES

- John Etheridge owned a Watkins Dominator which rattled so badly his dad took out the amplifier section and made a cabinet for it on coffee-table legs.
- **Roger Glover: "I used to dream of owning my own Watkins Dominator, with its angled baffles, but by the time I could afford it I didn't want it any more – I'd moved on. But I'd love one now."**
- Mel Galley: "My friends and I formed The Staccatos when 'Telstar' was the big single of the day. We found a guy called George Foster who had a Clavioline and a Watkins Dominator with four inputs. Everyone could plug into that, so he got the job."
- **Chris Spedding: "There was a bass player in our neighbourhood who wasn't as good as ours, but he owned a Watkins Dominator, a much bigger amp than my Westminster, so we asked him to join our band! So The Vulcans ended up louder, but with not such a good bass player."**
- Sometime in 2000 I had a call from Charlie Watkins: "Come over – I've got something for you." He had found an original chassis, and built a new cabinet – I was very happy to receive the "last Dominator". What a wonderful gesture. What a gent.

The anniversary Dominator

- **News just in: a limited edition, brown and gold, hand-wired 50th anniversary Dominator will soon be on the market.**

(but *we* had muscles on our index fingers).

To keep up further, I often tape-recorded shows from the BBC Light Programme, Radio Luxembourg, BBC TV and ITV – anything that featured our favourite artists performing their new material live in advance of their record release. If we were quick enough, we could learn this new song and play it at a local dance before the records came out. It seemed to be an achievement at the time, although it was probably only a motivation for us to learn new stuff. Like Paul McCartney watching Buddy Holly, we watched everybody for clues. We saw The Beatles singing "Till There Was You" on the Royal Variety Show, and at the end of George Harrison's solo he played what to us looked like an unusual chord shape. Rummaging through the chord books, we decided that it was a B13th flat ninth, whatever that meant. It probably wasn't, but all of our knowledge was gleaned empirically, and we soon had quite a repertoire.

My keenness for tape-recording radio programmes paid off amongst my social crowd. Our village was too small to support a youth club, but occasionally various local organisations such as the Young Farmers or Young Conservatives would coalesce for a social evening.

One such event took place at the Jubilee Hall, in the centre of the village. Some twit had devised the idea of a "Jukebox Jury" evening, during which we would reproduce the popular TV show on stage in a minimal form. The "set" consisted of four stackable chairs, one office desk plus chair, one hand-held microphone and The Tradewinds' Watkins Dominator, borrowed for a PA. In order to imbue some semblance of "newness" in the music on offer, I'd volunteered to record as many recent releases as possible from Radio Luxembourg on my home-made tape recorder. In my enthusiasm, however, I'd forgotten that Luxembourg, whilst it may have played some of the better and newer music of the day, had the habit of fading to radio static, distant Morse code and, occasionally, even silence. A consequence of this was that, while almost no one in the audience really gave a shit what the poor panel thought about the songs, it was bizarre to witness the allocation of a "hit" or a "miss" to a piece of music that had virtually degenerated into phasing hiss! David Jacobs (the presenter of the original TV show) would have been baffled.

THE GAUMONT CINEMA

The Tradewinds graduated to their first gig in a proper theatre: the Gaumont Cinema in Wolverhampton. Every Saturday morning, the Gaumont supported a "teenage show", with dancing to records on the stage, a feature film and a half-hour spot from a local band. It was a measure of our success that we played at one of these shows. As we set up our gear backstage, I became aware of that unique, but slightly foetid, smell that all old theatres have, and the thrill of standing next to the massive folded horn speaker enclosure booming behind the screen.

Wolverhampton Gaumont Teenage Show.
The Tradewinds featured in May 1961.

The Tradewinds in frontier pose 1961. L-r: Richard Hallchurch, Peter Gallen, David Left, Patrick Davies, Roger Swaab, Mo Foster, and Peter Watkins. The Dominator is just visible balancing on its three coffee table legs

Richard Hallchurch

An unspoken democracy within the group allowed everyone a "feature" if they so wished. Richard Hallchurch, who played piano and guitar, had chosen to play the swing ballad "Whispering" on his Hawaiian guitar, an instrument that is notoriously difficult to pitch accurately. And, with immaculate timing his home-built amplifier chose this particular morning to become unreliable.

Richard was an enthusiastic musician and a dedicated constructor of his own equipment. This dedication, however, was tempered by a reluctance on his part to use conventional construction methods. His choice of support for internal components was to use less-than-state-of-the-art items such as flat, wooden lollipop sticks or sellotape. During this performance, there were surprise intermittent silences from his amplifier. Since Richard's left hand had to hold the heavy steel slide firmly in contact with the strings, only his right hand was free to administer the blow required to regenerate life in the amp behind him. This dramatic gesture necessitated a rotation of his body, which in turn wrenched his left hand from its original position. The consequence being that this normally bouncy melody evolved into a sequence of bizarre, truncated yodels as power randomly returned in response to Richard's hammering. The audience was impressed.

Peter Gallen and David Left

Other members of the band had their own problems. Unusually, we had two singers, Peter Gallen and David Left. Peter was the archetypal rock star; he would rush on stage, wiggle his hips and, even though no one could hear him sing, the girls would scream. David, although he sang with gusto, wasn't really built for this job; he would walk on stage, trying very hard to be Cliff Richard, but would be met by a less-than-complimentary response from the front row: "Hello, Porky!" With remarkable scholarly detail, he kept minutes of every gig, and would write them up afterwards in a big red book.

Roger Swaab

Roger Swaab, on rhythm guitar, looked good and played well. He had recently fitted a pickup to his f-hole guitar, but the spindle of the solitary volume pot stuck out too far from the scratch plate. In an attempt to rectify this, he had over-enthusiastically hack-sawed the offending spindle in such a way that the solitary knob now only stayed in place as long as he didn't touch it. Consequently, he spent a considerable proportion of the gig searching the stage for a volume knob that had been inadvertently sent spiralling away after a particularly emphatic downstroke.

Peter Watkins

Peter Watkins had by now grown into a fine lead guitarist, hampered only by the substantial deficiencies of his f-hole Hofner Congress. This particular morning he also had another problem, thanks to his tape echo machine. It was a revolutionary device, thoughtfully constructed by local Wolverhampton boffin Jeff Pocock from the innards of an old Fidelity Argyle tape recorder and with additional replay heads glued to a flat aluminium plate. (Jeff and Richard shared similar design philosophies.) Unfortunately for Peter, we hadn't yet heard of splicing tape, so the tape loops were joined with Sellotape. The net effect was that, without warning, the loop would weld itself to the record head, and a guitar solo which would one moment be splendidly shimmering with alpine valleys of echo would suddenly sound as if it were being played in a cupboard.

Patrick Davies

Perhaps a throwback to a distant memory of trad jazz, it was felt that a drum solo was *de rigueur*, and if the drummer was incapable of playing one then too bad. A drum solo from Patrick Davies was always a challenge. In theory it was twelve bars long, and everybody aimed at a point where they thought it would end, but it was always a trap. Confusion reigned. All of the instruments would re-enter with confidence but then collide in a terrible road accident which slowly sorted itself out over the next few seconds. Another of Patrick's tricks was to emerge from a turnaround with his bass drum and snare reversed. One never knew where the downbeat was. Perhaps he was pioneering reggae?

My own problems were different again. As soon as the huge theatre curtains parted (proper showbiz) to expose the faces of several hundred excitable teenage critics, my lower lip began to tremble uncontrollably. It felt like my face was one vast twitch.

At an earlier practice session, it had been decided that some simple visual cues would make the act flow more smoothly and look generally more professional. Instead of a count-in to a particular tune, it was arranged that I would effectively become a conductor by raising and then rapidly lowering the neck of the bass to signal the start of the piece. All eyes would be on me. The technician in charge of the stage lights at the Gaumont was not blessed with the greatest insight, and he seemed to have a formidable difficulty in following the very simple lighting plan we had given him. For reasons that only he will ever know, he chose the moment a fraction of a second ahead of my dramatic conducting gesture to black out the entire stage. All eyes couldn't find me.

Panicking wildly, the best I could manage to salvage the cue was to yell a rather feeble "now!" Simultaneously, I trod on my lead and pulled out the jack plug. The audience was baffled by this chaotic, unlit, bassless intro. So were we. I wanted the world to end. We were paid three guineas for the performance, and to our utter disbelief were booked to appear again in three months' time.

Hugh Hopper with his Burns Bison Bass at the Beehive, Canterbury, in 1965

Hugh Hopper

In Canterbury, around 1965, Hugh Hopper and his brother formed The Wilde Flowers, a band that included, at different periods Kevin Ayers and Robert Wyatt (later of Soft Machine), along with Dave and Richard Sinclair, Richard Coughlan and Pye Hastings (who became Caravan). One of their first (and last) steady gigs was in between the Children's Film Foundation movies at their local ABC Cinema's Saturday morning flicks, dodging the hurled choc-ices. Hugh: "Drummer Coughlan had to sneak out of work for 20 minutes to play three or four numbers, stuff like the Small Faces' 'Whatcha Gonna Do about It?' with Robert Wyatt doing his Steve Marriott impression. Instead of cash, we got six months' complimentary tickets for the Sunday night horror movie show. As a further doubtful bonus we were roped into promoting the Dave Clark Five film *Catch Us If You Can* by driving around Canterbury in a Mini-Moke. I think it's safe to say that none of us could actually stand Dave Clark, or his Five, but it did get our pictures in the local paper. Like all semi-pro bands, our hopes were higher than the number of gigs we actually got to play. By a factor of several thousands, probably."

Bernie Holland

In the 1960s, Bernie Holland joined The Fantons, a Shadows copy band whose uniform was red sparkly jackets. His first experience on stage with them was following the main film at his local ABC's Saturday Morning Minors' Matinee. ("We pestered the manager for a spot and played for nothing.")

Mike Hurst

The young and talented Mike Hurst also earned a prestigious cinema gig in 1958, after performing at the Met in Edgware Road on numerous kids' shows. "I was spotted by the official Elvis Fan Club secretary and then given the dubious honour of singing 'Jailhouse Rock' at the movie's premiere at the Odeon, Leicester Square – in the foyer! It was a source of great embarrassment, but great fun," he recalls. "My first experience of band playing came in 1960, when I did a Saturday afternoon rock show at the Shepherd's Bush Theatre. I couldn't believe the volume – no stage monitors – as I sang 'Baby I Don't Care'. Boy, but I loved it!"

Brian Odgers

With puberty and rock 'n' roll converging, these were dangerous times. Every Saturday morning, in the cafeteria of the Portsmouth branch of Selfridges, a small band called The Hi-Fis would play for the customers. Brian Odgers was enchanted and fascinated, and he went every week to see them. Eventually, he plucked up the courage to meet them and ended up joining the band. He felt he needed a stage-name: "Mel Hayes" was cut out on a piece of white paper and stuck on his Club 60! The Hi-Fis were another band to play at their local Gaumont cinema on Saturdays, with guitar, bass and sax microphone all plugged into the same Selmer Truvoice!

Ray Russell

"On Saturdays the Holloway Road Odeon would hold teenage mornings and, after the films had been shown, the resident skiffle band would invite people onstage to play. I was only twelve at the time so my dad took me down with my ukulele.

Ray Russell's first gig on ukulele at the Odeon Holloway

"I probably contributed very little, but I did play a Lonnie Donegan song – I think it was 'Rock Island Line' – with some words that I had made up as I couldn't understand them all on the record. I can't remember the name of the band, but it must have been a hoot!

"My dad really helped me, and as time goes on I appreciate it more."

TRENTHAM GARDENS

My dad had begun working as a manager for the Goodyear Tyre and Rubber Company in Wolverhampton, and in 1962 he arranged a booking for The Tradewinds to play at the Families' Day in Trentham Gardens, a large recreational park near Stoke-on-Trent. We were asked to play two shows – one in the afternoon and one in the evening – both from the massive central ballroom.

We had no PA of our own and – as usual – had to rely on what each theatre or venue had already installed. We were always at the mercy of microphones that looked like they ought to be suspended in wooden frames from four pieces of elastic, and huge dusty corporate amplifiers with large glowing valves behind grilles.

After much arguing with municipal jobsworths, we obtained permission to use the in-house PA. No one showed us how to use it, and it never occurred to us to check where the speakers were, but we finally got it to work and balanced the vocals with the band (Watkins Dominator and home-built amps, all on coffee-table legs). We finished the afternoon set with a raucous version of Eddie Cochran's "C'mon Everybody", congratulated ourselves on playing well and, as it was still sunny, went for a walk in the park.

After a few minutes, Patrick suddenly said to Roger: "Look up that pole." Every 100 yards or so there was a large Tannoy horn mounted high above our heads to relay messages from a central source. It took us a while to realise it, but the central source in question was in fact our on-stage vocal mic. This meant that the entire park had been treated to the whole of our afternoon set, without the benefit of any backing instruments at all, just Peter and David's singing bursting from these Tannoys. We were so embarrassed; it must have sounded dreadful – like karaoke without the backing tapes.

We couldn't face performing the evening set with the same arrangement, and so our only alternative was to plug the vocal mic into a spare input of the lead guitarist's tape echo. This may have made the rest of the park a safer place for music lovers, but on stage it had the bizarre effect of making the vocals sound as if they were underwater.

Neil Jackson

When our singers, Peter and David, left school and therefore the band, we had to cast wider to find a good replacement. A local lad, Neil Jackson, arrived at my house one afternoon for an audition and, bizarrely, sang just one song: "Wimoweh". "That's great," we said.

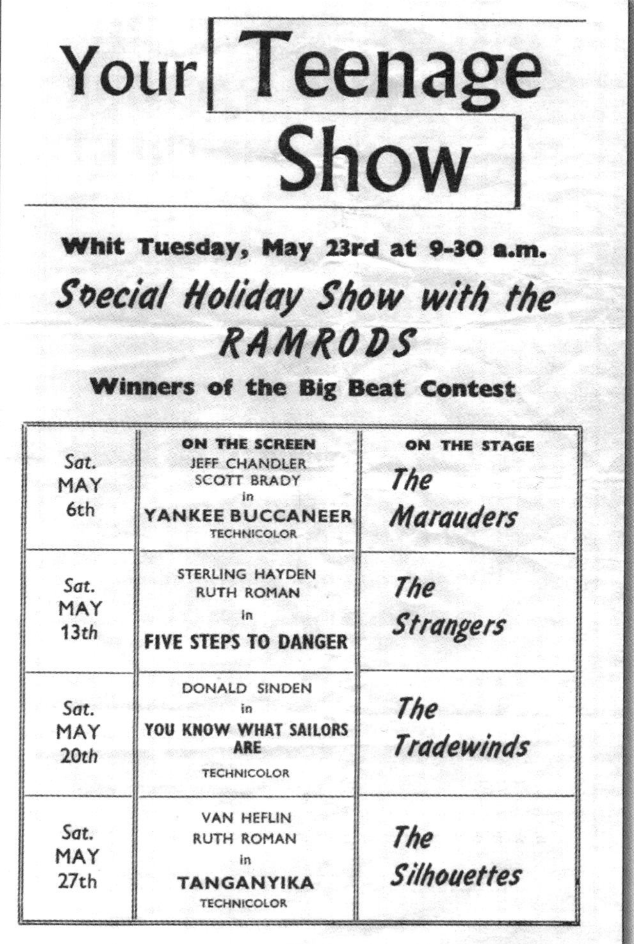

Your Teenage Show

Whit Tuesday, May 23rd at 9-30 a.m.

Special Holiday Show with the RAMRODS

Winners of the Big Beat Contest

	ON THE SCREEN	ON THE STAGE
Sat. MAY 6th	JEFF CHANDLER SCOTT BRADY in YANKEE BUCCANEER TECHNICOLOR	The Marauders
Sat. MAY 13th	STERLING HAYDEN RUTH ROMAN in FIVE STEPS TO DANGER	The Strangers
Sat. MAY 20th	DONALD SINDEN in YOU KNOW WHAT SAILORS ARE TECHNICOLOR	The Tradewinds
Sat. MAY 27th	VAN HEFLIN RUTH ROMAN in TANGANYIKA TECHNICOLOR	The Silhouettes

Your Teenage Show

Our first proper gig together was a resounding success, the audience chanting "We want Neil," as he left the stage. Our second gig at the Wolverhampton Gaumont Teenage Show was, however, more of a challenge. The poor chap became terribly nervous, and during his first song, "How Do You Do It?", his throat totally dried, his tongue stuck, and he completely lost control of his voice, causing a considerable yodel to appear on the second word, "do". Although by now in a state of numbing panic, he dutifully struggled through two more songs, "Blue Suede Shoes" and "Please Don't Touch", both seemingly pitched higher than his normal key. As the last chord of the final song faded, Neil thanked the audience and made a professional exit from the huge stage. There was no applause, just the faint hum of indifferent conversation; it was as if he had just sung "Please Don't Clap". Suddenly a solitary voice wafted down from the back of the stalls, shouting in an impenetrable Midlands accent: "It's about toyim yo fooked off!" Our fans were clearly fickle.

The Tradewinds survived and continued to play at many local gigs, including the Milano coffee bar, a newly fashionable teenage gathering place in Wolverhampton. The basement was so small that our amplifiers had to be placed on part of the long, continuous wooden wall seat, and I noticed that, whenever I hit a low G on the third fret of the E string, girls sitting 20 feet away on the same seat would move their bottoms, squirm a bit, and knowingly smile at me. I had discovered resonance.

TWIST AND SHUDDER

The late 1950s and early 1960s were years of immense change, in many ways. At most functions where there was dancing, the waltz and the foxtrot still reigned supreme over emerging forms such as the jive or the twist. But older dance crazes just made no sense. What on earth is the hokey-cokey? And why did people seem to enjoy taking part in this bewildering ritual? It was beyond me. It was *so* embarrassing.

Some pop songs of the day referred to things called "Dancing Shoes" and "Blue Suede Shoes". What *were* these items? I wore the same sensible black leather shoes everywhere and didn't feel the need for such specialised footwear.

The Waltz

At our sixth-form dances the main entertainment was provided by John Carrier and his band, a local quartet consisting of tenor sax, accordion, drums and piano, but with no bass. Everyone was relieved when The Tradewinds came on for a half-hour interval spot. In the weeks before the dance, our PE teacher, Walter Wragg, bravely volunteered to teach us all how to waltz, but without the aid of girls from the convent down the road. It was hopeless. To this day I can still only waltz in a straight line until I hit the wall and have to regroup. I think it's safe to generalise that most musicians from this period are terrible dancers, partly because they hated it, but mainly because they would be on stage every Saturday night and never got the chance to try. Or maybe that's *why* they were on stage?

(Later at university I was so relieved to discover that waltzes, foxtrots, etc were no longer important. And it was also the first time that I'd seen couples dance apart from each other, and express themselves – often in an unintentionally funny way.)

At the end of one dance we were about to leave when Rick spotted some uneaten cakes and jellies, which he proceeded to cram into the large pockets of his raincoat. There was an inevitability to what happed next: he was shoved against a wall. I will *never* forget the sound.

The Twist

The twist is a strange dance: it is far from elegant, and far from sexy. But it swept around the world very quickly, and it is immense fun to watch any party scene in any film from that period.

For a musician there is nothing more rewarding than watching over a hundred people performing this particular abomination under the delusion that they are cool. On a good night our stomachs hurt from stifled laughter.

"Roight, will the people who've been eliminated from the twist competition please go roight down the far end." This instruction, boomed out in a strong Wolverhampton accent, meant that we only had to play in this style for about another fifteen minutes. Relief.

Tony Ashton

Pianist Tony Ashton (who later played with The John Barry Seven, and Ashton, Gardner and Dyke) was fired from The Stereophonic Sound of The Blackpool Echolettes because his image was too beatnick. But he then passed the audition – at the age of only fifteen – to be resident pianist (mainly because he owned a piano) at the Picador Club in Blackpool, which was in fact a sort of corrugated shed. One night he got up to dance. The front page of the following morning's Blackpool Evening Gazette shouted to the world:

Blackpool's First Twist Victim!

Tony Ashton, of 83 St Leonards Road, Marton, Blackpool, was gaily twisting to Chubby Checker's No 1 hit record "Let's Twist Again" when suddenly "ouch!" – Tony was writhing in agony on the floor of the Picador Club. He was rushed to hospital, where it was discovered that he had dislocated his patella.

Can The Twist Kill?

A leading surgeon reports on page nine.

CHAPTER 10

ADULTHOOD

At our village grammar school in Brewood there was no music department, or indeed music education of any kind. Our band – the Tradewinds – was *it*, although we only ever played for fun, and the occasional bonus of gig money whilst our abilities gradually improved. We were not rebels – that would be laughable – but it was generally accepted that our music was a passing fad, and that the path we would individually take would be the conventional one of exams, university, and – one hoped – a career in a chosen discipline. That was how it was then. Music as a job was neither undesirable nor forbidden: it was *inconceivable.* Even if I had wanted to study music, the bass guitar was not perceived to be a legitimate instrument at that time, and consequently there were no dedicated music colleges like there are now.

Falmer House, the University of Sussex in 1964

In June 1964 we sat our A-levels, and as the summer progressed we gradually went our separate ways. So it was that in September 1964 I travelled down to the University of Sussex to study for a degree in physics and maths. For me this university was a lucky choice: it was founded in 1960 – one of the then 'new universities' – and was set in parkland near the village of Falmer, halfway between Brighton and Lewes. It was vibrant, colourful, and far more exciting than the places I was leaving behind.

BRIGHTON

When leaving home and going to university most students would take things like books or tennis racquets with them. Perhaps prophetically I took with me to Sussex my red Futurama guitar (I had decided that the Dallas Tuxedo bass should stay at home) and a large grey tape recorder that my dad and I had built. It weighed a ton. (Later, using borrowed microphones – and the toffee-tin mixer – I made several recordings of the university bands such as The Jazz Trio and The Baskervilles on this wonderful machine. Some of these recordings have survived and have since been released on CD on the Angel Air Records label.)

I desperately needed to connect with whatever music scene there might be and at first I tried the folk club, but I hated the earnest "finger-in-one-ear" approach, and the interminable sing-along choruses. The songs seemed to me to be too hearty, and harmonically shallow. It was not for me.

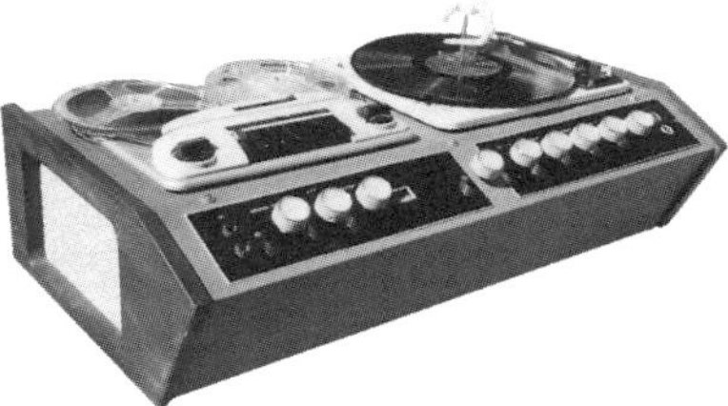

The 'Northpond Mobile' tape recorder combo (built by my dad and me circa 1962)

Reslo Ribbon Mic

The University of Sussex Jazz Quartet

The bass guitar as I knew it then, however, didn't seem to be going anywhere, and the time felt right for a change. This feeling was compounded by my discovery of a double-bass in the music room of Falmer House, which at that time was the centre of all social activities on the campus. I loved it, and tried to play this wonderful monster for a while with some new friends – pianist Derek Smith, alto saxophonist Tony Bradford, and drummer Jake Haskell: the University of Sussex Jazz Quartet. But it was physically hard, and with no one to show me any sensible fingering, and not having enough time anyway, I eventually gave it up.

University of Sussex Jazz Quartet rehearsing in the Junior Common Room. L-r: Jake Haskell, Derek Smith, Tony Bradford, Mo Foster

The Baskervilles

Bass was my instrument, but a quick look around revealed that there was in fact no need for a bass guitarist anyway, since the university's pop band, The Baskervilles, already had one in the shape of John Carter, who was very good, and could sing. Kris Johnson and Brian Davis took care of the guitars. I then made a significant discovery that they did, however, need a drummer, since the existing player, Grant Serpell, was retiring from the band to study for his final chemistry exams.

Some years earlier I had dabbled with drums at home, my early hero being Joe Morello, the drummer in Dave Brubeck's quartet. "Take Five" was the big hit of the day, and Joe's intricate 5/4 pattern intrigued me to the point where I had learned to play it, using a pair of small copper aerial rods for sticks with two cushions, a chair and the floor for a kit. I was fascinated by the way you could make all four limbs work together, and yet independently of each other. (Ironically, it would be two years before I could play anything in 4/4: I just couldn't seem to lose that extra beat!)

Pragmatic as ever, I suggested that if the group could organise a drum kit for me, I would learn to play it. A small loan was arranged – to be repaid by gig money – and I became the proud owner of a basic white-pearl Premier kit (fantasising that it was a match for Joe's silver-sparkle Ludwig kit), and the debating chamber soon rang to the sound of snare drum rudiments.

It was fun to be back in a band, playing at dances and balls, some of which were at other universities like York, Norwich, and Southampton, and it also helped to pay for the Indian meals. Lectures were fitted in somewhere, although it is just possible that I may have had to cancel a few of them.

At the time I didn't really own up to how powerful the pull of music was to me, but my unacknowledged education was indeed derived from the incredible number of major bands alongside which we played at these dances, artists such as Cream, Georgie Fame and The Blue Flames, The Who, Graham Bond Organisation, The Zombies, Jimi Hendrix (can you imagine dancing to Hendrix?), The Moody Blues, Pink Floyd, Steampacket with Rod Stewart, Long John Baldry, Julie Driscoll, and Brian Auger.

At the Christmas Ball we supported Georgie Fame and The Blue Flames. During the afternoon soundcheck their diminutive drummer came over to our stage to ask if he

UNIVERSITY OF YORK

Annual Ball

ARTISTES APPEARING

Humphrey Lyttleton
Marquee: 10-0—11-30 p.m., 12-30—2-0 a.m.

Joe Harriott Quintet
Cellars: 11-30 p.m.—1-0 a.m., 3-0—4-0 a.m.

Marrianne Faithfull
Marquee: 11-30 p.m.—12-0 midnight.

The Baskervilles (University of Sussex Beat Group)
Marquee: 9-30—10-0 p.m., 2-30—3-0 a.m., 3-30—4-0 a.m., 4-30—5-30 a.m.

The Spinners
Cellars: 2-0—2-30 a.m.
Courtyard: 5-30—6-0 a.m.

The Nightingales
Courtyard: 10-30—11-30 p.m., 2-0—3-0 a.m., 4-0—5-0 a.m.

University of Sussex Jazz Trio
Cellars: 10-0—11-0 p.m., 4-0—5-0 a.m.

The Buffet in the Dining Hall will open at 11-0 p.m.

There will be Cabaret in the Dining Hall at 1-30 a.m. and 3-30 a.m.

University of York Annual Ball

sixth session
sixth session
sixth session
sixth session
sixth session
sixth session
SATURDAY 8 OCT FALMER HOUSE 8-30-12-30
THE CREAM (WITH ERIC CLAPTON GINGER BAKER AND JACK BRUCE) TONY JACKSON
sixth session
AND THE VIBRATIONS. PAUL STEWART. RUSSELL'S CLUMP. BARS. LATE TRANSPORT
OVER 18s ONLY. STUDENTS CARDS. 6BOB

Cream Poster for a dance at the University of Sussex

could borrow my large tom-tom as he had left his in London. No problem. Six months later I was amazed when I heard that this same drummer – Mitch Mitchell – had joined The Jimi Hendrix Experience.

Vocalist Andy Brentnall recalls another occasion: "The Baskervilles were setting up in the junior common room of Falmer House for our spot at the Summer Ball. Our dear leader, rhythm guitarist Brian Davis, had managed to mislay his plectrum, and no other spare was available. I mentioned that there was a folk singer/guitarist on the bill, consigned to a smaller coffee area for his performance. I was delegated to seek out this performer to request a plectrum, and found him also setting up for his spot. After initial reluctance, and with the promise that it would be returned, he duly handed over a spare plectrum. Sadly the plectrum was never handed back as the performer had left the building by the time we finished our (triumphant!) set. Who was the folksinger short of one plectrum and playing second fiddle to The Baskervilles? Er, Paul Simon!"

The Baskervilles also had a regular gig – the Sunday Hop – which was staged every week in the junior common room. It was a fun night out, and a joy to play. My joy was always tempered, however, by the realisation that I still hadn't written the physics essay that was due to be handed in the following morning. Oh shit.

The Baskervilles supporting Georgie Fame at a dance in the Refectory at Falmer House. L-r: Andy Brentnall, Kris Johnson, Mo Foster, Brian Davis, John Carter

The University of Sussex Jazz Trio

One sunny day during my first term I was walking through the quadrangle of Falmer House when I was surprised to hear the ambient sound of piano, double-bass and drums echoing across the courtyard. I could hear the most amazing chords (13ths, and 7 flat 10ths) with gorgeous clashing semitones. These chords generated quite new emotions in me, feelings that were impossible to experience from the simple triadic harmony I'd been used to. Like the characters in an old gravy advert, I followed the sound to the junior common room and, in my innocence, I made the daft assumption that these musicians were, in some way, hired to entertain the students (it was the sixties, after all – anything was possible). During a break I introduced myself, and was stunned to find out that it was second-year students themselves who were playing – the University Jazz Trio. I'd never heard anything like this before: the sheer swing and the quality of their improvisation was so exciting that I knew I wanted to join in and be part of this experience in some way. I then ruined everything by saying something as mindless as "Do you make it up as you go along?" At least I didn't ask the bass player what strings he used.

The Sunday Hop

Some months after my debut as a drummer with The Baskervilles, the drum stool of the University Jazz Trio became vacant when Grant Serpell graduated. Pianist Lynton Naiff (who was studying mathematics), and double-bassist John Morton 'Nick' Nicholas (who was studying physics and philosophy) asked me if I would like to join. Of course I said yes. I was amazed and excited, and immediately set about learning how to play with brushes: drummer Ed Thigpen of The Oscar Peterson Trio was my new hero.

Physics Versus Drums

In the coffee-bar breaks between lectures my tutorial-group friends would talk knowledgeably and passionately about the theories of Erwin Schrödinger, Werner Heisenberg, Wolfgang Pauli, Paul Dirac, Nils Bohr, Richard Feynman, Albert Einstein, and many others. I could join in to an extent, but my head was somewhere else: I slowly realised that all I really wanted to discuss were the different techniques and polyrhythmic approaches of drummers like Tony Williams, Joe Morello, Ed Thigpen, and Buddy Rich – and perhaps the unbelievable bass-playing of Ray Brown and Ron Carter. I also needed advice on stick-sizes.

The University of Sussex Jazz Trio playing on a live TV show from Keele University in 1966. L-r: Lynton Naiff, Nick Nicholas, Mo Foster

Brian Auger

At one all-night ball, organist Brian Auger (who had been a fine jazz pianist, and with Julie Driscoll would enter the pop singles chart in 1968 with Bob Dylan's "This Wheel's on Fire") spotted our jazz trio, came over, and said the fatal words: "Mind if I sit in, man?" This was exciting. A musician from the real world wanted to play with *us*. We decided to play a simple twelve-bar blues. Brian counted us in –"1,2... 1,2,3,4" – at such a fast tempo that my initial joy transformed instantly into fear, the like of which I had never known before. The bars flew past in a blur. Within 30 seconds I was soaked in sweat and my right arm became one single taut muscle, rigidly locked in a right angle. In my desperate attempts to keep time on the ride cymbal I must have resembled one of those weird crabs that has one very large claw. As if this wasn't embarrassing enough, after what felt like half an hour (but was probably only five minutes) Brian yelled "fours!" – the swapping of four-bar improvised solos. He was great. I, on the other hand, was tragic. All I could do was stare into the middle distance with the expression of an idiot while keeping time with the ride cymbal and hi-hat. Forget the bass drum and snare. The humiliation wasn't over yet. As the final chord dissolved into polite applause, Brian got up to go back to his own seat. He looked over at me – this miserable, soaking, breathless heap of aching muscles – and said: "Nice."

The Jazz Trio – which drew its repertoire mainly from jazz standards – could, with ease, become a rhythm section for soloists and, in this respect, we played with artists such as vocalist/percussionist Bobby Breen, tenor saxist Art Theman, and vocalist Jeanne Lambe. On one occasion we were invited to play a gig at Swansea University with flautist Harold McNair. Nick, the bass player, drove us in his old estate car for the long seven-hour journey from Brighton, during which I was wedged in at the back between the drums and underneath the double-bass, with the spike inches from my nose. The cramped position played havoc with my digestive system, so much so that Nick later said to me accusingly: "You were farting all the way and there was only a pint of air between us."

I became fascinated by harmony. There is a beautiful section at the end of a track called "Gone, Gone, Gone" on Miles Davis' *Porgy And Bess* LP where Gil Evans has voiced the reeds and brass in such a way that it makes the spine tingle. The whole section lasts 24 seconds. I was so intoxicated by it that I wanted to hear it over and over again, so I made a tape loop. Unfortunately, 24 seconds running at 7.5 inches per second means 15 feet of tape. It looked ridiculous, and ran all around my room, supported by books, lamps, shoes, cups, and packets of biscuits. But it sounded wonderful.

Just as modern jazz was becoming more accessible, rock music was beginning to mature. Miles Davis' *My Funny Valentine* was released in the same year as The Beatles' *Hard Day's Night* and, although their worlds at first seemed so divorced, I loved and learned from both of them. (Aged 18, keyboard player Rod Argent saw no musical boundaries: "At a party I put on a Bartok LP and was amazed when everybody left the room.")

I continued to play drums in both bands, and began to enjoy jazz concerts given by visiting artists such as Tubby Hayes, Johnny Scott, and the New Jazz Orchestra. One night we were privileged to be entertained by legendary jazz drummer Phil Seaman. During a break, Ernest Cockram – a drummer friend of mine – accidentally bumped into him in a corridor, and used this chance encounter to glean wisdom from his idol. "Excuse me, Mr Seaman," he enquired nervously, "but have you got any tips for young drummers?" Without breaking his step, or dropping the cigarette that was stuck to his lower lip, Phil responded gruffly: "Yeah, man, don't wank."

Barry Morgan

Like The Baskervilles, the Jazz Trio would occasionally appear as a support act. One evening, after we had played our half-hour set, The Johnny Scott Quintet still hadn't arrived. To cover for them, and hoping that the audience wouldn't notice, we played the same set again. The quintet, who had got stuck on the way down from London, suddenly burst through the doors of the debating chamber, and drummer Barry Morgan rushed over to me: "Can I use your kit to save time? I'll just use my own snare." How thrilling! a drummer from the "real" world would be playing *my* kit!

All, however, was not well. Premier stands and fittings of the day were neither as strong nor as reliable as they are today, but, owing to my relatively light playing technique, this wasn't normally a problem. Barry was, of course, a much more powerful and exciting player, and on this night he really began to enjoy himself. His enjoyment, however, was not to last: I first spotted trouble when I saw that his ride cymbal was suddenly two feet lower than it should have been. A while later, the snare drum sank from view... and then it was the turn of the toms to rotate to an impossible playing angle.

Whilst the kit was rearranging itself, Barry had to keep playing with one hand while the other attempted repairs, and it was in this unrewarding and bizarre fashion that he played most of the gig. I wanted to run away. Ten years later I recorded with Barry on a session in London. He was very amused to be reminded of the event.

THE SUMMER OF LOVE

After leaving university I spent the summer methodically avoiding any decision about the future, and shared a dingy but cheap flat in Brighton for six weeks with five other friends. It's a common belief, held by many journalists and historians, that 1967 was the Summer of Love. Looking back, I think that anyone who was actually there experienced it in his or her own very different way. It wasn't all kaftans and beads, even though the local newspaper – the *Evening Argus* – proclaimed in an hysterical headline: "Students were caught last night smoking joss-sticks down at the Arches". Oh, the naïvety. Can you imagine that journalist applying for a job on the *Haight-Ashbury Gazette*?

Desperate to avoid the usual holiday jobs (deck-chair attendant, pool attendant, beach scavenger, etc) I sought a residency for the Jazz Trio. We had a call from the Blue Dolphin, a recently opened nightclub in Shoreham, just along the coast from Brighton. On the first night we were treated to a superb three-course meal, after which we played to a club that was strangely devoid of customers for the entire evening. At midnight, the owner made us a deal: "I'll tell you what, how about £15?" The following week our meal wasn't quite as elaborate, consisting of only two courses, and after again performing to an empty room there was another deal: "I'll tell you what, how about £12?" This bizarre behaviour continued weekly, with our meal incrementally dwindling to beans on toast in parallel with a correspondingly reduced fee. On what was supposed to be our very last gig we hadn't even entered the building when the proprietor met us, keen to offer us his final deal: "I'll tell you what, fuck off!" It was very good training for the future.

LONDON

Meanwhile, London was calling. The move to London from Brighton necessitated a search for somewhere very cheap to live. At first I shared a double bed-sit in Earl's Court with Martin Kennard, an old university friend. It was winter, there was ice on the *inside* of the windows, and a one-bar electric heater (which was strangely angled towards the ceiling) was all we had to heat the room. When the shilling in the meter ran out – as it often did – we just stayed in our beds.

The early morning was a special challenge and I would watch with amazement as Martin disappeared back into his bed after his alarm clock had sounded. There would then follow a series of extremely bizarre convulsions inside the blanket which were only resolved when – in the manner of a butterfly escaping from a chrysalis – he would spring from his bed, fully dressed in a suit and tie, ready for work. It was a cabaret I looked forward to every time.

Whilst working as a research assistant at a laboratory in Stratford, in the East End of London, I tried to get a gig on drums – *any* gig. After scouring the advert pages of *Melody Maker* I was invited to play with a quintet at the Gatehouse pub in Highgate. Double-bass player Dave Holland – who was soon to be invited to the USA by Miles Davis – sat in. This was theoretically very exciting, but as a result of not having played for weeks I was both technically inadequate, and terrified: it wasn't fun. And although I didn't realise it, this would be the last time I would play drums.

I began to explore Soho and soon discovered Ronnie Scott's jazz club at 39 Gerrard Street (which was later called the "Old Place" when the "New Place" sprang up at 47 Frith Street). It was a strange, dingy basement that came alive as soon as John McLaughlin, or John Surman, or Frank Ricotti, or Ray Russell started playing. I used to make one vodka and coke last for four hours.

Ice

Meanwhile, Lynton Naiff and Grant Serpell (together with singer Glyn James and bassist John Carter from a later university band called Russell's Clump) had been trying to make it in London with a new band called Ice, and had had a radio hit with a song called "Ice Man". In November 1967 I received an urgent telegram requesting me to dep for John Carter on a broadcast for Ice at the BBC Piccadilly Studios. I did a bit of practice and used my old Dallas Tuxedo bass. It was the night before this recording that I helped to carry a Hammond organ up a spiral staircase and ruined my back – this was a problem that would plague me for the next few years.

I was still living in the flat in Earl's Court, and in order to be at Stratford by 8.30 a.m. I had to get up inordinately early, catch the District Line tube to Liverpool Street, then change to the Central Line for the rest of the journey. I was always late to bed, and so I would often fall asleep on the tube and wake up somewhere in deepest Essex. Annoyed, I would cross to the other platform to come back, fall asleep again, and wake up – even more annoyed – back in central London. It was getting ridiculous. This pendulum-like motion was happening so often that I eventually gave in and just arrived for work at the crack of noon. My employers were baffled.

I wasn't really happy, working amongst the high-vacuum equipment, and would clean up at the end of the day by pouring a few drops of (incredibly expensive) liquid nitrogen on the floor: a beautiful expanding circle of the furiously bubbling liquid would slowly but inexorably push all of the dust out of the way and deposit it underneath the lab furniture – my services were not cheap. More interestingly, I built a laser drive unit (these were indeed pioneering days) that actually went on display at the Physics Exhibition in the Great Hall at Alexandra Palace from 11–14 March 1968, and to everyone's genuine amazement – especially mine – I actually got it to function properly on the last day of the show.

By early 1968 Ice had disbanded but, still keen to pursue a career in music, Lynton and Grant invited me to revert to bass guitar permanently in a proposed new jazz-influenced rock band. It sounded like heaven, and I agreed immediately. We held auditions for a guitarist and were delighted to find ex-Tridents guitarist Mike Jopp who had both jazz and blues chops. More importantly he also had his own amplifier and a car! We also held auditions for singers but finally realised that the only serious contender for the job was Linda Hoyle, a qualified English teacher, whom we had met earlier through a friend at university, and who had sung with The Jazz Trio. Linda's voice was steeped in jazz – her main influences were Billie Holiday and Bessie Smith – and with her looks and sense of humour she fitted in perfectly. DJ Anne Nightingale would later proclaim with authority that Linda Hoyle was "the girl most likely to succeed in 1970". We called ourselves Affinity, after the title of an Oscar Peterson LP.

Just before I quit my job my employers were even more baffled when I told them I had 'flu and then suddenly appeared in an episode of the TV soap *Crossroads* (we had trekked up to Birmingham to appear in a nightclub scene backing singer Benny Wilmott, played by Deke Arlon – it was to be our first gig!).

THE BUNGALOW

All five musicians spent the summer of 1968 "getting it together" – writing and rehearsing – in a rented bungalow that Nick Nicholas had originally found at 169 Wilson Avenue, near Brighton racecourse. With a loan guaranteed by John Jopp – Mike Jopp's father – the band bought some Impact amplifiers (I was 23, and thrilled to be playing for the first time in my life through an amplifier that I hadn't built myself), a Hammond M102 organ, a Gibson EB0 bass guitar, some microphones and, eventually, a grey Ford Transit van. It was strange to be back on bass guitar. I'd missed out on four years of change and evolution in both playing styles and equipment, and it took a while to catch up. With a tinge of sadness I sold my Premier drums to pay the rent.

ROADIES

The roadie – or road manager – is a relatively recent invention made necessary by the sheer quantity and size of equipment on the road these days. They are a special breed. But there is also a contradiction in that whilst a good roadie must be intelligent, resourceful, reliable, hard-working, and musical, he/she has to be completely bonkers to want to be one, and put up with the insanities, the sleepless nights, the hard work, and the low pay often associated with touring.

We simply couldn't afford the luxury of a roadie, and the very idea of a road crew remained a concept of the future. I once made the terrible mistake of admitting to the others that I could solder, and from that day on I was put in charge of leads and plugs. This often meant crawling around the stage fixing things at the last minute and then jumping up as the show started, hoping that the audience wouldn't notice the dirty patches on my hands and knees. Also, the proper flight case had yet to be invented, and two-handled canvas leads bag used by Affinity had a sad, faded, khaki, ex-military look to it. No one ever knew either its origin or its original purpose. Perhaps it had once carried tennis racquets into battle?

RONNIE SCOTT'S

Through a friend we secured a broadcast on BBC radio's *Jazz Club*, and we travelled up to London to record our part for the programme at BBC Maida Vale studios on 28 August 1968. Humphrey Lyttleton was the presenter. When it was later transmitted I was able to make a tape recording from my B & O FM radio. (Several of those tracks have subsequently been released on Angel Air Records.)

At the end of the sixties an exciting new hybrid music form, jazz-rock, was evolving. Musicians such as Miles Davis, Brian Auger, Jimi Hendrix , and bands such as Blood, Sweat, and Tears, Cream, Chicago, Lifetime, and Colosseum were all experimenting with the blending of jazz improvisation and the power of rock rhythms. This liberating and exciting approach suited Affinity perfectly since it would separate the band from other contemporary outfits such as Yes, Genesis, Led Zeppelin, Family, and Humble Pie.

We had heard through the trade papers that Ronnie Scott was looking for jazz-rock artists with a view to management. I took our tape to the club (or should I say building site?; number 47 Frith Street was at that time in the midst of total reconstruction) and gave it to Ronnie's partner, Pete King, personally. He had a listen and offered us a try-out booking in the new "upstairs" part of the club. This new space had stunning contoured foam seating designed by artist Roger Dean who would go on to design the famous LP covers for the band Yes.

(NB: if you stand on the steps at Ronnie's in Frith Street and look left you will see a blue plaque for Mozart, who lived and composed there. If you look to the right you will see a blue plaque for John Logie Baird who, on 26 January 1926, demonstrated the first television there and broadcast from the roof. All that in just one Soho street!)

As a result of hearing our tape – and seeing us play upstairs – Ronnie agreed to manage the band and to book us into his club. Affinity's first ever London gig took place on 5 October 1968 at the Revolution Club in Bruton Place, just off Berkeley Square. The second was on 12 October 1968 at Ronnie Scott's Upstairs.

It was at Ronnie's that I would receive another musical education: watching world-class players such as Stan Getz, Gary Burton, Elvin Jones, Charles Mingus, Steve Swallow, Roland Kirk, Miles Davis, Keith Jarrett, Les McCann, Larry Coryell, the young Stanley Clarke playing a Gibson bass, the young Billy Cobham playing a *small* kit, and Jack de Johnette (one afternoon I observed him methodically practising 16th-pattern rock rhythms – this was just a few months before he played on Miles Davis' *Bitches Brew*). We may not have been earning much at this point but we did get to see these incredible artists for free – every night.

Affinity

Singers in rock bands were unfairly treated in the late sixties: whilst the power of backline amplifiers for guitar, bass guitar, and keyboards was increasing in increments of 100 watts, vocal PA amplifiers and mixers were still in their infancy – and the stage monitor had yet to be invented.

Linda Hoyle was often unable to hear herself sing above the racket made by the band; so much so that by the end of 1968, having strained her voice night after night for some months, she was eventually forced to have an operation on her vocal chords to remove what were then known as "singer's nodes". For several weeks following this operation she was not allowed to sing or even talk, a condition she found very difficult – especially when members of the band wound her up!

The four players in the band still had to make a living, however, and we determined to continue working as a four-piece during this period. Most bands would have been unable to perform at all without their lead singer but after a couple of hastily convened rehearsals we were able to convert our existing repertoire into an all-instrumental set focusing on a novel mixture of jazz, pop, funk, and blues.

In January 1969 Affinity had been booked to play a month at the club, supporting the legendary American tenor sax player Stan Getz and his quartet, with Jack de Johnette on drums, Miroslav Vitous on bass, and Stanley Cowell on piano. Also on the bill was the British comedy band The Scaffold featuring Roger McGough, Mike McGear, and John Gorham. It was a bizarre – and bold – mixture.

Every night we would play the first set in the downstairs main room, and then struggle – with all of our gear – up two long flights of stairs to play two more sets in the upstairs discotheque room. It was hard work. Sometimes other musicians would join us: one jam session featured Tubby Hayes on tenor sax, and another Jack de Johnette on melodica. That was fun. What wasn't fun was when Stan Getz tried to push Lynton off the organ stool and then began randomly bashing the keys whilst yelling "freedom". We just kept playing.

Jazz-rock was still in its infancy and we were naturally cautious in such auspicious surroundings. But after an occasionally miserable response from the audience to an opening set, it was very satisfying to hear Ronnie Scott walk up to the mic, thank the band and launch into his act:

In January 1969 Ronnie Scott's Jazz Club in Frith Street had just re-opened after extensive building work

"Thank you very much, ladies and gentlemen, for The Affinity. You've been a wonderful audience, and we're particularly impressed by the way some of you have been controlling yourselves. Now, in just a few moments, we'd like to bring on to the bandstand Stan Getz and his quartet, and we'd also like to remind you that we're open until three o'clock in the morning, and that you can eat and drink up until then... and we very much hope that you do... for Chrissake."

(There is a recording of this announcement at the end of the track "Day in the Life" on the Affinity CD *1969 Live Instrumentals* – Angel Air SJPCD135.)

Ronnie was scathing about indifference: "What have you been drinking? Concrete? It's like working in Madame Tussaud's. Why don't you all hold hands and try to contact the living? It's the first time I've seen dead people smoke." He had an inimitable, laconic delivery as he stood in the half-light, casually leaning against a pillar, the microphone close to his lips: "You should have been here last night – *somebody* should have been here last night. We even had the bouncers chucking them in. The band was playing 'Tea for One'. It was two hours before we found out the cashier was dead. Someone phoned up and asked 'What time does the show start?' I said 'What time can you get here?' I should have stayed in bed – there were more people there. Don't go away sir, we get worse."

His nightly observations on club cuisine were the best: "The food here is great. A bit expensive. I think it's cheaper to eat the money. We never get complaints about the food. A few people throwing up from time to time, but no complaints. After all, three million flies can't be wrong. Our food is untouched by human hand – the chef's a gorilla. Our assistant chef is wonderful. He's unique – pygmies come all the way from Africa just to dip their arrows in his soup. But how can anyone fuck up cornflakes? Even the mice eat next door. He's half black, half Japanese – and every seventh of December he attacks Pearl Bailey."

Our month at the club was a success – with great reviews – and the band grew in confidence, but a fire ravaged the new building in 1969 occurring, as Ronnie was heard to drily announce, almost a year before it was scheduled. Unfortunately it wasn't funny for us since the overnight fire – probably caused by a discarded cigarette – had started upstairs where we had left all of our gear set up. Everything was ruined, charred, and wet. The keys on the Hammond organ had melted and curled upwards which made them look like part of a Salvador Dali painting. And – *of course* – we were not insured.

Affinity: the load-in at Ronnie's, 1970

We had lined up a festival gig at Plumpton racecourse in Sussex, but now – with no gear – it would be impossible to play, and we would have to cancel our appearance at this important event. Amazingly, in the midst of our despair, the band Soft Machine (who often played in the club) came to our rescue, and very kindly offered to lend us all of their equipment for the day. I got to use Hugh Hopper's Marshall stack. Thanks guys. What a treat.

On one occasion, when I was between flats, Ronnie Scott and his partner Pete King very kindly allowed me to stay in the club overnight – for just a week. I slept in the little changing room behind the downstairs bar. At about 3.30 a.m., when Ronnie had stopped wandering around the main room practising scales on his tenor sax, the club would go quiet. At about 4 a.m. I discovered that it was possible to sneak into the adjacent kitchen where there were huge cauldrons of spaghetti sauce, which had cooled and solidified. I was hungry, and realised that by employing an old Eskimo trick it was possible to make a hole in the surface, scoop out the food, and then smooth over the evidence.

DISCOTHEQUE CIRCUIT

Affinity also made a living by playing the then-thriving London discotheque circuit: clubs such as the Revolution, Blaises, the Speakeasy, and the Pheasantry (where, at one time, both Eric Clapton and poster designer Martin Sharp lived in the apartments above).

We hoped that the drink-sodden hoorays in the audience wouldn't notice that we had converted our repertoire into an all-instrumental set. Bizarrely, this turned to our advantage one night at the Revolution Club, situated in Bruton Place just off Berkeley Square. We had just finished playing an instrumental version of The Zombies' hit "She's Not There", featuring long guitar and Hammond organ solos from Mike and Lynton, when suddenly a very young Stevie Wonder emerged from the audience, eager to sit in.

There was a ripple of enthusiasm from the monied throng who still had more than two brain cells firing. It transpired that Stevie, too, had damaged his throat, but fortuitously he did have with him his famous chromatic harmonica. After a quick discussion we agreed to play "She's Not There" again. The next ten minutes were joyous as Stevie wailed through chorus after chorus, improvising beautifully in his inimitable way over the changes of the song. I didn't want the moment to end, and as is often the case for an event as special as this there was no tape recorder present, nor was there a camera.

We rehearsed for a while in artist Roger Dean's flat on the fourth floor of Egerton Court, opposite South Kensington tube station. We had to place the Hammond organ in a small lift (it only just fitted), close the rickety sliding metal doors and then run up the steps and call the lift. Because I had seriously hurt my back some months earlier, at gigs we had to find a fourth man to help with the load-in and load-out of all our gear, including the organ. At the end of a long and exhausting night's playing at the Pheasantry discotheque in the Kings Road, one helper, instead of lifting powerfully, just seemed to drape his hand limply over one handle. From the unfocused and baffled look on his face he'd entered a dimension unavailable to us. He spoke: "My mind is red." Oh, fucking great.

Within a few weeks we were re-united with Linda (who had by then fully recovered), we improved our PA system, and we continued our career with renewed enthusiasm. Playing at the Revolution Club one night was the American soul act Charlie and Inez Foxx, who asked if they could use our mic stands. This was not a problem, but unfortunately they weren't to know that we could only afford the cheapest ones on the market, made from the lightest aluminium. Poor Charlie burst onto the stage and, in the manner of Rod Stewart, grabbed one of our stands with the intention of impressively shaking it at the ceiling, but because it was far lighter than he could possibly have anticipated the whole thing left his hand and flew upwards, causing much consternation in his band as they waited for it to return to earth.

Everyone played at the Marquee Club in Wardour Street, Soho, and during this vibrant period the Holy Grail was to be the top of the bill and on a percentage of the door. After playing countless gigs there we finally achieved this exalted position, but unfortunately, on the night in question, there were four major events on in town, and during the actual gig it felt as if there were more of us on stage than in the audience. It was one of our worst nights: before expenses, we earned £0/13/8d (about 75p) between us – even our support band earned £15.

JACKET

I needed a jacket. One day, whilst strolling along The Cut – a popular street-market near Waterloo – I spotted a beautiful leather jacket that looked exactly like the one Bob Dylan was wearing on the cover of his LP *The Freewheelin' Bob Dylan*. It looked cool. Even better, it was a bargain.

The problems started a week later when I attempted to wear the item, and I accidentally pushed a finger through the leather. It was obviously a flaw, I reasoned, and perhaps that's why it was so cheap? It was no problem: I unpicked the lining a little, and glued a small piece of tea-towel behind the hole – invisible mending.

In time, however, so many holes began appearing in the jacket that it seemed to have been constructed entirely of flaws. What was amazing was that it had held it together in the first place.

I gave up my repairs when I noticed that the inside of the jacket didn't look like leather anymore, just hundreds of bits of glued-on tea-towel. The whole garment was now stiff, and the simple act of reaching out to shake someone's hand required planning because of the creaking involved. It was not cool. I even began to feel sorry for the original cow.

NIGHT WATCHMAN

I was always hard-up, so to make a little more money (£5 a night) I became the night watchman at the Revolution Club. At the end of Affinity's gig there I would change from my "stage" outfit into more comfortable clothes (probably not that much different), and stay on in the club from 3 a.m. to 9 a.m. It was part of their fire regulations. The unique

Affinity in The Aviary at London Zoo. I'm wearing the leather jacket/tea-towel combination

benefit to me was that I was able to play records all night on the massive club hi-fi system. It was a weird sensation in such a vast, empty room to be able to wade through racks of vinyl LPs, checking out loads of the new bands such as Creedence Clearwater Revival ("Bad Moon Rising") and Jefferson Airplane ("White Rabbit"), and to play them very loudly. It was yet another university.

After one of my bizarre all-nighters I wandered up to the club office one morning and was most surprised to meet the secretary, Judy Dyble, who had been the original vocalist for Fairport Convention. It was great to chat to another human being. But there was a downside to these nights: I felt a little shaky walking home at 9 a.m. through Mayfair. But that £5 would buy a curry!

WORK

Affinity recorded a critically acclaimed first album for the new Vertigo label. Live work was plentiful: there was a thriving discotheque and club scene in London, the college circuit paid well, there were European and Scandinavian tours (which didn't pay well!), festivals, the occasional TV show (*Colour Me Pop* – the predecessor of *The Old Grey Whistle Test* – and *Sez Les*, comedian Les Dawson's own show), Radio One sessions, and even the occasional jingle session (Linda, Mike, and I recorded an advert for Shredded Wheat: "There are two men in my life..."). Things were looking good. The band was able to buy the ultimate instrument, the "split" Hammond B3 – supported on two massive steel pillars – that had once belonged to Brian Auger. We became a very powerful unit.

CHAPTER 11

THE FIRST GIGS

AUDITIONS

Roy Babbington

Melody Maker's classified advertisement section was always the place to seek out auditions for bands. Roy Babbington saw two ads: one in London (he felt that they'd be too good!) and one in Aberdeen (the soft option), and so, at age 17, he travelled to Aberdeen with his double-bass to join The Leslie Thorp Orchestra, which was both great training and an important experience in sight-reading, especially when one considers the range of music which the orchestra performed in an average week: Sunday – concert evening; Monday – rock 'n' roll (when Roy doubled on guitar for songs such as Cliff's "Move It"); Tuesday – night off; Wednesday – Penguin Night (strict tempo); Thursday – Old Time Night; Friday/Saturday – dance music (augmented band).

Roy Babbington at the Aberdeen Beach Ballroom in 1959. His guitar had an unusual supporting device: a saxophone harness

Tim Renwick

Tim Renwick remembers hungrily scanning the back pages of the *Melody Maker* for vacant jobs. "I spotted one for Sounds Incorporated, then a highly respected group who backed a lot of visiting American artists and supported The Beatles at Shea Stadium. They were managed by Brian Epstein, and the auditions were at his Saville Theatre in the West End. I turned up paralysed with nerves and sat in the stalls watching Sounds Inc going through their paces. A stranger appeared and asked if I was the trombonist. Yes, there had been a mix-up and they actually wanted a brass player. I was given 10/- (50p)expenses and off I went."

Some years later Tim fell victim to his own goodwill and instrumental versatility when – in 1982 – he toured with Mike Oldfield. "I went for an audition for a last-minute replacement guitarist for a world tour due to begin in five days' time. I rushed out and bought Mike Oldfield's latest LP, *Five Miles Out*, which I enjoyed immensely. Because of its complex nature (many time signature changes, unison riffs and key changes), I wrote the whole of this new album out in chord chart form on manuscript with relevant parts written in notation. This alone – I should have realised – got me the job; they were pretty desperate and I was obviously dead keen to do it right. Well, I made the mistake of telling Mike that I also played the recorder. Fatal! I spent the following year touring the world with sopranino, descant, and treble recorders stuffed into every available pocket or orifice available in order to accommodate Mike's requirements. Along with playing mandolin *and* bass, this was one of the most demanding jobs I've ever had."

Tony Hicks

One lad who was keen to air his pubescent vocal skills in search of talent-scout recognition was Tony Hicks, who says: "Seemingly hundreds of guitars, plus tea-chest bass

Tony Hicks (centre) is just one of the three hundred guitarists in Les Skifflettes. The tea-chest bass is a work of art

and washboard, coalesced into our group, Les Skifflettes. We passed the audition for the *Carroll Levis Discoveries* talent show in London and bought a half-bottle of sherry to celebrate on the train." Les Skifflettes first played a radio version of the show at the Playhouse Theatre on the Embankment and then returned for a TV presentation at the Hackney Empire, which was then home of the *Oh Boy* show. Later, when Tony was back at school: "I couldn't understand why I wasn't getting all these calls from record companies – I thought this was most strange."

Ray Russell

Ray's very first TV appearance, at the age of only twelve, was on the *Carroll Levis* talent show. Accompanying himself on the guitar, Ray sang the Paul Anka song "I Love You Baby", but during the summing up he fell asleep on a sofa and had to be nudged awake!

At the age of 14, Ray auditioned for Eric Delaney's band wearing his new Cuban boots with built-up heels. There were three wooden steps down to the rehearsal room and, carrying his guitar in one hand and amp in the other, he stumbled on the second step and felt a crunch on the third: one Cuban heel had come off and the solitary exposed nail was now embedded in the wooden step. He couldn't move. Too embarrassed to say anything, but noticing a wall socket nearby, he set up his amp by the stairs and began the audition in a bold and dramatic posture with each foot on a different step. It was quite a while before the band said: "Why don't you come over here?" He failed.

One day, Ray read in *Melody Maker* that guitarist Vic Flick was about to leave The John Barry Seven to concentrate on session work, so he took the day off work to go to audition as his replacement in a huge cinema in Archway, North London, and arrived early to check out the opposition. Miraculously, no other guitarists arrived. For some daft administrative reason they couldn't get into the building, and so, rather than waste the morning, the tenor sax player volunteered to crawl into the pay kiosk at the front so that he could plug Ray's amp into a socket. Shoppers and passers-by were then baffled to hear Ray playing his Burns Vibra-Sonic through his Burns Orbit III amp in the entrance lobby of their local cinema.

A lot of music parts were spread out, and Ray seemed to sail through these charts without a problem. The band were so impressed by his reading ability that they asked him, without any deliberation whatsoever, to join immediately – he was still only 15 years old. Ray had become a permanent member of the band when, four months later, they had to learn some new material. It was a moment of truth: Ray couldn't read the new parts at all! A week before his audition, Ray had bought every record that John Barry had made and played them over and over on his Dansette Minor record player until he knew every note. Ray had to own up, but bass player Dave Richmond kindly helped him to learn all about "the dots". He wasn't fired this time.

Steve Marriott

Steve Marriott's first public appearance was at Jaywick Sands, near Clacton, Essex, in June 1958. While he was staying in a holiday bungalow with his family, he entered "Uncle Ken's Talent Competition for Children". With his newly acquired guitar, he sang and played Gershwin's "Summertime" and won first prize. Clearly on a roll, he entered the same competition a year later and won again, this time singing Tommy Steele's "Little White Bull" (a song which featured Judd Procter playing the guitar on the original record!).

THE

UNCLE KEN SHOW

JAYWICK SANDS

This is to certify that

was adjudged the

WINNER of the TALENT COMPETITION

held on

Signed

The Uncle Ken Show – Steve Marriott, 1958

In 1988, Steve said: "I started playing guitar by accident or rather through necessity. Mum and Dad almost forced me into acting, and I certainly didn't feel that I had any say in the matter. I did a few things, like *Oliver!* (he sang a Buddy Holly number at his audition) and some TV and film parts, but I began to resent it after a while. I hated a lot of the other kids, 'cause they all came from snobby, well-to-do backgrounds and had pots of money behind 'em, unlike me."

Rick Parfitt

Another future rock star to show precocious talent was Status Quo's Rick Parfitt. At the tender age of 11, in 1959, he took a recording test at the Decca Studios in West Hampstead, singing and playing the song "Baby Face". A&R man Marcel Stellman was looking for an excuse to get rid of this young performer, and said to his mum, with great tact: "He's good, but bring him back when his breathing is better." What did this mean? Thereafter, Rick would practice the song thus: "Baby face [intake of breath] you've got the cutest little [intake of breath] baby face..."

Alan Jones

A talent contest at a venue in Camberwell was advertised in the local newspaper and Alan Jones – who then played lead guitar on a Hofner Colorama – couldn't resist it. He enjoyed the night out, but of course he'd failed to complete his homework and the French master took him to the headmaster the next day for a severe reprimand. But it was worth it.

Jim Lea

In February 1966, after only about three gigs with The Axemen, Jim Lea responded to an audition for The In-Betweens and took along his Framus bass in a polythene bag. A week later he was accepted, along with singer Noddy Holder, and was suddenly in a top professional band. Chas Chandler, Jimi Hendrix's manager, discovered the band playing in London at Rasputin's Club and soon became their manager and producer. He told Jim: "You're like Hendrix on the bass." A few years earlier, Sapphires singer Tony Jenkins saw "a bass twice as big as Jim, and steam coming off the strings." Frustratingly, however, the recording techniques of the day couldn't handle Jim's dynamic sound and range, and he constantly felt that his music was never as good as it had sounded in his head.

Steve Marriott having a great time on the beach at Jaywick Sands, Clacton, in 1958

Rick Parfitt, encouraged by his mum and dwarfed by his Martin Colette

Bernie Holland

Bernie Holland secured an audition in London with Bluesology, Long John Baldry's backing band, which later became The John Baldry Show. "My dad drove me up to Studio 51 near Leicester Square, where a chap called Reg Dwight was checking out guitarists and Hammond organ players. There were three parts to the audition: firstly, just jamming on a blues; secondly, you could choose any tune you liked and play it for them; then you had to sight-read a chart that was mostly chord symbols. The strange thing was that, while I was playing this chart, Reg kept stopping me until he found out that I was reading it correctly and that there were in fact some wrong chords written down." Reg later explained why he was holding the audition: he was about to leave Bluesology, change his name, and start a solo career as Elton John.

Andy Fraser

One day in 1967, John Mayall called Alexis Korner in a panic, urgently in need of a bass player. Alexis recommended Andy Fraser (still only 15), who passed the audition and, with the first gig in Guildford, became a member of The Bluesbreakers. "I still had freshly pressed bell-bottoms," laughs Andy. "I may have looked odd, but I could play! With the first week's wages I was instructed by John Mayall to buy a new bass and stereo system. It was a great time, and we toured all over Europe."

Noel Redding

Perhaps one of the most significant instrumental transitions was made by Noel Redding, after an audition with The New Animals. "I saw this advert for a guitarist. I went along, played a few things with drummer Barry Jenkins, then after the audition Chas Chandler came in and asked me if I could play bass. I said that I couldn't, so then he asked me if I'd like to give it a try. I said okay, and Chas brought his Gibson in for me to play. He then asked: 'Would you mind playing with this guy?' Thus, in September 1966, I met James Marshall Hendrix and suddenly became a bassist."

Noel Redding, guitarist, in Germany, 1965

Ritchie Blackmore

Ritchie Blackmore passed an audition with Screaming Lord Sutch and things were looking up. He would be making £30 a week backing a man who came out of a coffin.

Noel Redding (r), six-string bassist with Jimi Hendrix

Ritchie Blackmore in Hamburg

Alan Murphy

Several years spent playing on the tough East End pub circuit prepared Alan Murphy for his future as a busy touring musician. "It was really amateur stuff – four or five nights a week for about £2 a night! The game then was to answer small ads in the *Melody Maker*, so everyone in the band would answer little ads for Free-style bands – they were our favourites, Free and Deep Purple and that kind of stuff. I finally answered an ad for a band named Mahatma Kane Jeeves, and to my surprise I actually got the gig. In those days I was untogether; I had no gear, I just had my little (home-made) guitar. They had to supply the amp and all that, but out of about 20 or 30 guitar players they chose me. We went off to Germany every so often, toured England up and down – terrible little gigs, really. We did this for about two and a half years, until they could no longer afford to keep us going, so then they started to push the band out to work with other people."

Alan Murphy at the Bottom Line, New York City, on 24th March 1978

The Beatles

Interestingly, on 27 November 1962, The Beatles made one of their first BBC radio appearances on *The Talent Spot* for a fee of £75. Producer Brian Willey, now vice-chairman of BASCA (British Academy of Songwriters, Composers, and Authors) made a note at the time which read: "They're rough, but they entertained me." Paul McCartney comments: "In early days of talent-spotting contests, we kept being beaten by this woman who played the spoons. This little old lady wiped the floor with us every time, so we decided to knock talent contests on the head."

TOURING

- **Ron Wood: "They don't make gig wagons like they used to."**
- Jeff Beck had to cancel a London show after he injured his back during a burst of guitar histrionics at an earlier appearance in Manchester. Later, his manager explained to me on the phone that, at one dramatic point in the act, "Jeff threw a shape." Unfortunately, it was a bad line and I thought he said "Jeff threw a sheep." This would certainly have explained the back injury.
- **When The Beatles appeared at the Olympia in Paris in January 1963 their amplifiers failed three times. In an issue of *Beat Instrumental*, the late Beatles roadie, Mal Evans, commented: "I've never seen anything like the electric wiring they had at the back of that theatre. It amazed me that we didn't all go up in smoke in the first five minutes." On their first US tour, in February 1964, their revolving stage broke down at the Washington concert. As the audience was all around the stage it had to revolve, or half of the crowd would have only seen the backs of the boys. Mal made a lengthy appearance on stage, pushing the rostrum around manually to the cheers of the crowd.**
- Tom McGuinness remembers touring America with Manfred Mann on a package show with, amongst other artists, the duo Peter and Gordon. One particular show, in December 1964 at the Clearwater Football Ground, Florida, stands out in Tom's memory: "The screaming audience was in the stands while the little stage was on the other side of the ground. The PA was two four-by-ten-inch Vox columns, as if we were a cabaret act. We carried our own amps onto the stage, and there were no monitors at all. The logistics of the tour were absolutely awful. We travelled massive distances, from Montreal to Florida and back up to Toronto, and so on. We got home owing thousands of dollars to lots of people with Italian-sounding names." Even though Manfred Mann had further hits in the USA, they never returned.
- **Richard Thompson: "All gigs in those days seemed to be on boats going up the Thames with disastrous AC power I don't remember being in a band with a PA system until Fairport Convention in about 1967; before that all vocals went through the guitar amp. When I left Fairport [in 1971], I did forget my blue guitar lead. If they read this, I'd really like it back."**
- In the seventies there were no videos. We had to watch the TV show *Monty Python* live in the dressing rooms. As a consequence gigs all over the country ran half an hour late.

ACCOMMODATION

Accommodation in the early days of rock touring was not what it later became. The words "four-star hotel" at no time appeared in a musician's vocabulary, unless of course he possessed a particularly fertile imagination. This was a time when a good night's sleep normally meant getting a little more leg room in the back of the band's van, or at best a local hostel. Small hotels in Great Britain were very different in the 1950s and 1960s, and the cheapest places to stay for any travelling musician or actor were known as "digs". These were generally so appalling, and offered so few amenities, that a whole mythology sprang up around them. The humour quickly followed. The landladies who ran these small guest-houses seemed to have fitted especially squeaky floorboards so that they could easily detect illegal late-night visitors. Hot water for a bath was only available at specified times – and you sometimes had to book in advance. But the real masterpiece of frustration was the timing of breakfast – often strictly between 6 a.m. and 7 a.m. If you missed it, you didn't eat. How many musicians or actors were awake between 6 a.m. and 7 a.m.?

Cliff Richard

Cliff Richard: "We would often sleep on the bus, and we were too ashamed to say we couldn't afford a hotel, so if someone said 'Where are you staying?' we'd say, 'We're staying at the Bedford', which was the name of the bus, and everyone would think that was the name of the hotel."

Sailor

When the group Sailor first toured Britain, their accommodation always seemed to be stuck at the level of the dingy guest-house, but they promised themselves that, if they ever made it, they would stay at the best hotels. Several tours later, and enjoying the success of their first hit, "Glass of Champagne", their dream came true. After a sell-out concert in Scarborough, the band returned in style to the four-star Grand Hotel for a comfortable night. Keyboard player Phil Pickett went over to the night porter and asked politely: "In the morning could I have a wake-up call at 8.30 a.m., a cup of tea, and a *Guardian* please?" The man looked up and, with incomprehensible indifference, replied: "Well *you* can fuck off for a start!" *Fawlty Towers* rules!

DIGS

- On the speed with which a landlady could take offence: "She had a mouth like a cat's bum."
- **At breakfast, the portion of honey on the plate was exceptionally small. This prompted drummer Rod Quinn to observe: "I see you keep a bee."**
- His portion of cornflakes in the bowl was equally small, prompting him to enquire: "Did you trip?"
- **"The walls were so thin you could hear people changing their mind." (Karen Bates)**
- "I got into my room, opened the window, and there was a seagull outside throwing bread in."
- **"I went to see the landlady to complain about the ceiling. She asked "What is the problem?" I said "Can I have one?"**
- "I plugged in my electric razor and the streetlights went dim."
- **"I wouldn't say my room was damp but there was a jetty at the end of the bed."**
- "I opened the curtains and the room became dimmer."

Dave Pegg

When Dave Pegg played guitar with Ray Everett's Blueshounds, they toured the country in a red Bedford van and a VW Beetle. "If we couldn't find people to put us up we'd usually sleep in these vehicles, on top of the Hammond with the condensation dripping onto your face. The van was the comfier. It wasn't easy."

Affinity

Stuck in Portsmouth one night we found an old seaman's hotel. We were both exhausted and desperate, and were shown to the one free bedroom, which contained seven beds and four massive wardrobes. It was impossible to see the floor, and to reach the door you had to sort of hover across the room. "Yes, we'll take it", we said.

Sid Phillips

One band tried a unique approach to the problems of where to stay after the gig: drummer Simon Phillips describes the unique method that his father – bandleader Sid Phillips – used to avoid staying in digs.

"The band preferred to camp in tents rather than check into dodgy B & Bs which, in the fifties, were pretty gruesome. Even my dad joined them – my mum had bought an ex-army bell tent – and after the gig they would find a quiet spot somewhere nearby and pitch the tent. In those days this was not normally a problem.

"One night it was very foggy after the show. The trombonist and bass player drove for a while, but eventually they gave up and pulled over onto what they thought was a grassy knoll. They managed to get the tent up and went to sleep.

"They woke up in the morning to the bizarre sound of cars circling. They looked out of the tent – the fog had cleared by now – and, to their dismay, they discovered that they had pitched camp on a roundabout."

ON THE ROAD

As the 1950s came to an end, the demands of young audiences forced a change in the concept of the live show or package tour. Previously, the hit rock 'n' roll groups of the day would feature in variety bills alongside comedians, acrobats and magicians, booked into unsuitable venues by old-fashioned agents who were clearly still living in the days of the music hall. However, a number of new entrepreneurs, such as Arthur Howes and Danny Betesh, emerged towards the end of the decade to give the kids what they wanted: no-nonsense live rock 'n' roll, interrupted only by a star linkman, who was often a well-known TV personality or disc jockey. The choice of venues also changed and, whereas theatre chains had become complacent with their one-time monopoly in live entertainment, the new agents began to develop a network of provincial ABC, Gaumont, Granada and Odeon cinemas, with capacities of up to 2,500 people, for nationwide tours. Until the evolution of the indoor arena and the stadium show many years later, the cinema circuit remained the ultimate choice for agents booking top-flight artists.

Bruce Welch

In 1958, British theatres were still experiencing the tail end of variety, and acts requiring electricity were unknown. When The Drifters played the Met in Edgware Road, Bruce Welch played through a little Selmer amp, but since there were no mains sockets or plug boards he had to run a 200-foot cable to a socket in the dressing room. Even worse, the Chiswick Empire still had DC mains (i.e., direct current, as opposed to the modern standard alternating current, or AC). "You could blow yourself up," says Bruce. "You got hold of a microphone and it stuck to your hand! We used to plug into light sockets. And with regard to light shows, in those days we had a choice: they were either on or off!" It must also be noted that, in those days, only the vocals were fed into the PA. The audience only heard what was coming off the stage, which could have been as simple as three small amps and one drum kit.

Cliff Richard and The Shadows (then The Drifters) at the Finsbury Park Empire. None of the amplifiers onstage – all rated at 15 watts - are mic'd into the PA. Laurie Jay, depping that night on drums for Tony Meehan, recalls: "We had to follow a dog act!"

Cliff Richard

Cliff remembers: "We didn't have any mixing desks, so the boys would just set up their amps pointing up towards the balcony and we'd look at the hall and go '1,000 seats, um...', set the volume on number five, and that was our mix. Everyone on the right-hand side of the hall heard Hank, everyone on the left heard Bruce and no one heard me in the middle because the mic always belonged to the hall, and you know what they're like; they're really just PAs for speaking into. Those mics were no darn good at all. So, as good as we could have been, we must have sounded like a joke, really, because it was all so primitive, I'm afraid."

Vic Flick

In addition to sessions, Vic Flick was still playing live gigs, which in the early 1960s, he says, was a character-building experience. "The venues were often dangerous, with curtains falling, electrical systems installed at around the time of Adam and Eve, and stages with holes in them. We even had an electrician commit suicide while we were rehearsing on stage.

"When I see the extreme safety measures and standards enforced today in theatres with the use of electricity, I cringe inwardly at the practices that went on in the early 1960s. Most of the plugs were made of a brittle bakelite substance which left many a live wire exposed and often meant that the pins weren't supported or, in some instances, separated. Many flopping pin tops became arc-welded together. There were two-pin sockets, large 15-amp round-pin sockets, industrial sockets, modern flat-pin sockets. Whichever socket a theatre had, it was a sure bet that the plug for the amps didn't fit. On some tours we dispensed with the plugs and just twisted the wires together. The Christmas tree of wires was then stuck in the socket holes backstage, dutifully jammed in with Bryant & May safety matches."

The Shadows

The Shadows, as they became, played mostly theatres rather than ballrooms, with one exception: the Lyceum, in The Strand. It had a rotating stage, with the dance band on one side and Cliff and The Shadows on the other. As the dance band finished, the stage began to rotate, and The Shads started the moody sliding-semitone rock 'n' roll intro to "Baby I Don't Care". As they came into view, a hail of missiles greeted them (we guessed that they were meant for Cliff), along with a barrage of eggs and coins, one of which split Tony Meehan's cymbal. The stage kept rotating until they were back where they started, and they fled the theatre. They went on to play in a Glasgow theatre where Saturday night was fatal for comedians. One poor guy had the job of fending off the audience for the ten minutes while The Shadows set up behind the curtain. The racket was so extreme that he dropped his act and just walked up and down for ten minutes.

Mike Hurst – The Springfields

The first electric gig that The Springfields played was at the Blackpool Winter Gardens in 1963. Guitarist Mike Hurst remembers: "We started the rehearsal in the afternoon, and after the first number the promoter, impresario Harold Fielding, strutted forward and said: 'That'll have to go.' 'What?' I said. 'The amplifier,' he replied. 'It makes the act look clumsy.' Dusty [Springfield] snapped: 'It's staying. It's part of the act.' A female voice cried out from the stalls: 'Don't let her speak to you like that, Harold!' It was Harold's wife. Before I could say anything, Dusty yelled: 'And you can tell that stupid bitch to mind her own business!' Harold went puce and shouted: 'You'll never work in one of my theatres again!' We didn't."

The Springfields. Mike Hurst's guitar featured a bewildering array of controls for an acoustic. Presumably each of the knobs was allocated specific control of the lights, curtains, temperature, kettle, etc

Eddie Cochran

When Marty Wilde and The Wildcats toured with American singer/guitarist Eddie Cochran, Jim Sullivan was astounded at what a boozer he was. Bourbon was Cochran's favourite. At a Liverpool Empire show, as the safety curtain went up, the house PA mic stand dutifully rose hydraulically from the stage. The guys had carefully arranged things so that the stand would rise between Eddie and his guitar, so that he could stand up and be supported by it! On that sad day when Eddie's car crashed, by a remarkable twist of fate Jim had changed his plans and travelled in a different car.

Relaxing backstage. L-r Licorice Locking, Eddie Cochran, Brian Bennett, Big Jim Sullivan

Gary Moore

Even though he was to break free of the restraints of the education system and form the successful Irish band Skid Row with Phil Lynott in the late 1960s, it would still be some time before Gary Moore would enjoy a comfortable existence. On Skid Row's first tour, in Scandinavia, they slept on the WEM PA cabinets in the back of a three-ton truck. Freezing and unwashed, they turned up at their record company reception in Stockholm looking like tramps. But the music (the forerunner to Thin Lizzy's) was scorching stuff.

Affinity

Affinity also toured Scandinavia, and I have a painful memory of our Ford Transit being stranded in central Sweden at 2 a.m. one night in December. We couldn't find a motel, we had a puncture, it was 15° below zero, and the wheel nuts had frozen to the spindles. I remember wishing that it was next week.

When we eventually did find a place to stay I couldn't help noticing that every truck driver in the park had left his engine running all night to avoid any problems with starting in the morning. The Swedes know how to cope with low temperatures.

After a successful two weeks' stint at the Gyllene Cirkeln club, in Stockholm, Affinity wearily drove across Sweden to Goteborg to catch the ferry home. During what was supposed to be an uneventful 36-hour crossing of the North Sea, lead singer Linda (whose full name is Linda Gay Hoyle) managed to lose her bag, which contained all of our wages for the gig. Morale plummeted. Mercifully, a few hours later the bag and its contents were handed in, and we were summoned over the ship's tannoy with the immortal announcement (in an accent reminiscent of the Muppets' Swedish Chef) "Can a member of Miss Gayhole's party please report to the purser?"

Tim Renwick

In Tim Renwick's early touring days, he would trek gypsy-like across the country for ridiculous fees which, he says, were so minuscule that they just about covered his expenses. For Tim, though, it was satisfying enough to have engagements in the book. "Memories of many trips to Wales come to mind, with Wages of Sin amongst others. Every time, we would break down either on the way there or the way back. It was as inevitable as, say, getting lost on every trip to Birmingham: another constant! On one particular doomed expedition we had digs at a local pub. We duly arrived and dumped our motley bags at this local hostelry and departed for the gig. We returned at 12.30 a.m. to find the doors firmly locked. After rousing the owner of this fine old establishment, we were told to 'bugger off' as it was after midnight. We spent the night in the group van, collected our things in the morning and duly broke down on our return journey to London. Oh, the glamour!"

Tim Renwick (second left) grooving with his band The Wages of Sin (nice scarf, Tim)

Keith Richards

Of course, if you happened to be one of the top bands with a string of hit singles things tended to be a little different, especially when touring America. When The Rolling Stones were on their May 1965 tour over there they stayed in some of the best hotels around. It was in one of these that Keith Richards woke up and wrote the main riff for "(I Can't Get No) Satisfaction", complete with the Gibson Maestro fuzzbox he had recently bought. He turned on a tape machine by his bed, played one chorus and fell asleep. On tape was 30 seconds of the riff, the sound of a dropped pick and a falling guitar (*clang!*), followed by 45 minutes of snoring!

Tony Hicks

For many years the UK was still without a comprehensive highway system, so being on the road usually involved many miles stuck behind a truck travelling at 25mph with an environmentally unfriendly exhaust system. Add this to the problem of the cramped confines of band vehicles and one begins to appreciate just how much musicians had to endure on the road. Tony Hicks: "We'd tell Graham Nash that there was no room in the van for another amp, plus it was too much bother. He was happy, and would just strum away."

Gerry Rafferty

Gerry Rafferty: "With The Maverix, Joe Egan and I tasted our first experience of schlepping around Scotland in a Transit, in company with a motley collection of lunatics and depressives, playing every conceivable kind of gig – more often for the experience than the money. The things you do when you're young."

Andy Pyle

As well as being the bass player, Andy Pyle became the driver of his band's old ambulance, which, he says, had the driver's cab mercifully separate from the back. "On arrival at a gig, opening the back doors was like taking the lid off a dustbin full of rubbish that'd been smouldering for two days."

Steve Marriott

Being crafty Eastenders, The Small Faces were no strangers to a little ducking and diving on the road, although even they were surprised on one occasion. In an interview with John Hellier, editor of the band's fanzine *The Darlings of Wapping Wharf Launderette*, Steve Marriott once said: "In Manchester, we did the Twisted Wheel [R&B club]. That was our first gig on the trip. Some bastard lent our Black Maria van out for an hour and came back with a load of leather coats in the back – he'd done a job when we were playing! Me and Ronnie Lane and Kenney Jones all got a leather coat out of it."

WORD GAMES

A common ploy to while away the long hours on the road is the word game. It can be almost anything.

- I once drove from London to Penzance with Mike d'Abo. On this particular trip the challenge was to think of very famous people with very silly names, and then imagine what they had said to achieve that name. Mike was the clear winner, with "Ethelred the Unready" who, upon being informed that his courtiers were now ready to take him to Westminster Abbey for his coronation, said: "What, now?" And Iain Pattinson – in his book *Lyttleton's Britain* – wittily pointed out that Ethelred The Unready had also launched an unsuccessful range of torch batteries (see Ever Ready).
- **A variation in the game would involve trying to guess the childhood name of a famous person whose middle name enhanced their status. Thus Isambard "Kingdom" Brunel would have worked his way up from Isambard "Housebrick" Brunel, presumably via "Loft Conversion", "Patio", "Cul-de-Sac", and "City Centre". It *was* a long journey.**
- Based on an advert for a "frying pan/radio" that I had seen in an old copy of *Practical Wireless*, Lynton Naiff and I spent hours thinking of pointless combinations. The winner was a "cigarette lighter/wardrobe".

Affinity

Despite – or perhaps because of – the lack of comfort, long journeys are a breeding ground for humour. In around Christmas 1969, Affinity played a concert in Swansea. It was freezing after the gig as we set off back to London, and we mentally prepared ourselves for a long and tedious journey. On the edge of town the whole electrical system of our Ford Transit suddenly stopped working, but mercifully the diesel engine kept on running. We had no lights or heat. We also had no credit-cards or money, and so couldn't afford to stay in a hotel for the night. After some agonising deliberation we decided to attempt the journey by following the lights of other trucks, and hid like highwaymen in a succession of lay-bys off the A4 (this was before the construction of the M4). I wouldn't wish the experience on anyone – it was insane! Linda Hoyle and I were in the front seat, with Mike Jopp driving, and the others were on the back seat in the kind of coma that is brought on when you recognise how awful the journey is going to be – it's better not to think about it. We tried to cheer ourselves up with fantasies about the cab of the lorry in front, with its log fire, plaster flying ducks, well-sprung sofas, and endless hot soup. After one long silence, Mike suddenly noticed the solitary twinkling red warning light on the dash board, rubbed his hands near it, and started to sing the Nat King Cole hit: "Chestnuts roasting on an open fire..." Perfect. The laughter kept our spirits up for miles.

Muff Winwood

Muff Winwood recalls that club gigs were generally a lot quieter in the 1960s than they are today. This meant that in the front three rows were people who really wanted to listen, while behind them were the dancers and at the back were the chat-ups. "At many gigs, now, conversation is impossible because of the excessive volume. It would seem that modern bands and sound engineers have lost the plot when it comes to creating an atmosphere that is conducive to socialising. An outcome is that, at some clubs or raves, there are now quieter 'chill-out zones'."

Mo and Ralph

I experienced a version of this when I played a small gig at the Mean Fiddler in London. At the soundcheck the front-of-house engineer, clearly unused to music with any dynamics, and resenting our requests for sophisticated monitoring, spoke to drummer Ralph Salmins and me through the monitors: "You guys are all pansies." Remembering a quote from Groucho Marx, I corrected him: "That's *Mr* Pansies to you." He treated us with great respect after this.

Graham Gouldman

Years before Bernard Manning became a national star, through his appearances on TV's *The Comedians*, he was the owner of Manchester's Embassy Club, which featured regular appearances from local bands, one of which was Graham Gouldman's band The Whirlwinds. Graham: "Bernard was one of the first people to give us a break. Our dressing-room toilet facilities consisted of a small hole in the floor. Bernard kindly gave us a demonstration of how to use it. All I will say is that he had a very good aim." He adds: "Our manager used to go to Italy every year and bring back the latest hits. We did lots of continental songs, as well as the UK hits of the day. We used to finish our act with 'Alexander's Ragtime Band'. It used to go down a storm, but eventually I got fed up with schlepping round working men's clubs and playing cabaret-style music. I quit, taking two members of

Graham Gouldman (3rd left) loses all credibility with The Whirlwinds

The Whirlwinds with me and nicking the drummer, Kevin Godley, from another Manchester band, The Sabres. We became The Mockingbirds. Kevin and I had played together before, when we and Kev's best pal, Lol Creme, would set up two guitars and a drum kit in Kev's dad's warehouse and play Ravel's 'Bolero' for two hours solid!"

Affinity

With Affinity I toured the UK, Europe, and Scandinavia and recorded an LP and two singles. We were playing a lot, but we never seemed to have any money. What little we earned was always ploughed back to improve and repair our equipment. Consequently, the sense of theatre and sartorial extravagance that is all part of showbiz was not very much in evidence. Just before going on stage at a club somewhere in Sheffield we were stopped by an incredulous promoter who asked: "Aren't you going to get changed?" Our reply was rather pitiful: "We *have* changed." Something obviously had to be done. A friend of mine, Angie, was a seamstress in television wardrobe, and she agreed to make a long patchwork waistcoat for me – inspired by Keith Emerson's – out of hundreds of small pieces of different-coloured leather. Her sewing may have been flawless, but with hindsight my design was hideous. One night, after we'd played at a Newcastle University dance, someone stole this waistcoat from our dressing room. I didn't bother to report the missing item; it was a merciful release. Somewhere in Newcastle is a thief with absolutely no taste whatsoever.

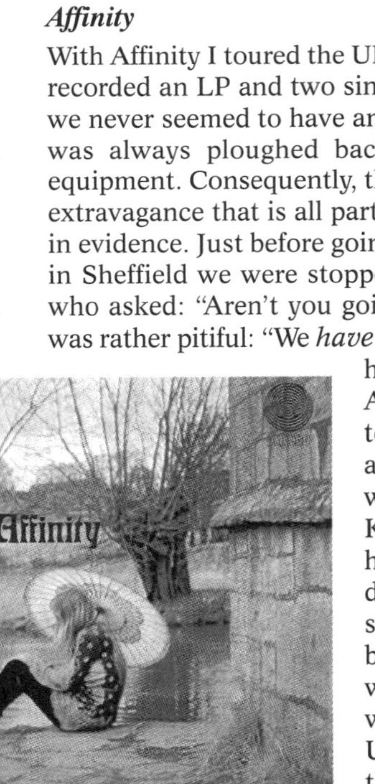

The Affinity LP on the Vertigo label

The Jeff Beck Band in Japan 1980

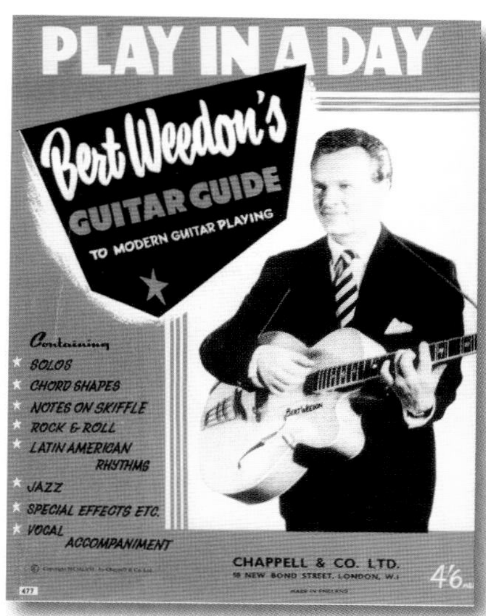
PLAY IN A DAY
Bert Weedon's
GUITAR GUIDE
TO MODERN GUITAR PLAYING
Containing
SOLOS
CHORD SHAPES
NOTES ON SKIFFLE
ROCK & ROLL
LATIN AMERICAN RHYTHMS
JAZZ
SPECIAL EFFECTS ETC.
VOCAL ACCOMPANIMENT
CHAPPELL & CO. LTD.
50 NEW BOND STREET, LONDON, W.1
4/6

SHIRLEY DOUGLAS'
easy guide to rhythm & blues for
Bass-Guitar
containing
BASS PATTERNS & RIFFS
12 BAR BLUES etc.
EXERCISES & SCALES
EASY FINGERING CHARTS
DIAGRAMS
CHORD SYMBOLS
EXAMPLES of :-
BOOGIE BASS
WALKIN' BASS
ROCKASHAKE etc.
PHOTOS of :-
CLIFF RICHARD & THE SHADOWS
EMILE FORD & THE CHECKMATES
JOHN BARRY 7
TRENIERS
JOHNNY KIDD
6/-
COMPILED & EDITED BY
Shirley Douglas
&
Chas McDevitt
© Copyright 1960 by
BEATNIK MUSIC
SOUTHERN MUSIC PUBLISHING CO. LTD.

The MEL BAY
MODERN
GUITAR
METHOD
INTERNATIONALLY ACCLAIMED
Grades
1
2
3
4
5
6
7
PUBLISHED BY MILLS MUSIC LTD., BY ARRANGEMENT WITH MEL BAY, KIRKWOOD, MISSOURI 63122

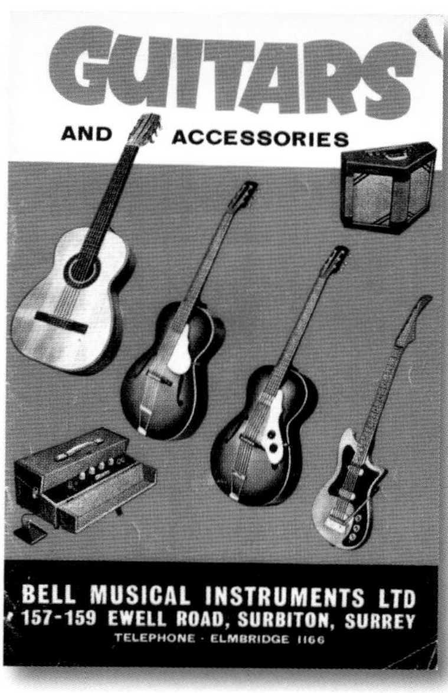
GUITARS
AND ACCESSORIES
BELL MUSICAL INSTRUMENTS LTD
157-159 EWELL ROAD, SURBITON, SURREY
TELEPHONE · ELMBRIDGE 1166

ELECTRIC
BASS LINES
NO. 2
WRITTEN BY
CAROL KAYE
AND
DAN MARK
ALL ROCK STYLES
BASS DUETS AND EXERCISES
HOW TO SIGHT-READ BOOGALOO
FAMOUS RECORDED BASS LINES
GWYN PUBLISHING COMPANY
P.O. Box 5900
Sherman Oaks, Calif. 91413

ray brown's
BASS METHOD
VOLUME I, NUMBER I

NONE GENUINE WITHOUT THIS TRADE MARK
N·M·S·CO.
GUITAR
B or 2nd
STEEL
N740
ONE
Black Diamond
String
TESTED AND WARRANTED
MANUFACTURED BY THE
National Musical String Co.
NEW BRUNSWICK, N. J. 08903, U.S.A.

ELECTRIC
Hawaiian Guitar 1st
No. 611
Cathedral
String
British Music & Tennis Strings Ltd, London
MADE IN ENGLAND

Electric Spanish Guitar
B or 2nd—Plain
Gibson
MONA-STEEL
STRINGS
Hand Made
TONE-POWER-DURABILITY
NON-TARNISHING
GIBSON INC., KALAMAZOO, MICH.

No. 766 D or 4th
GRETSCH
Chet Atkins
RHYTHM 'N BLUES
GUITAR STRINGS
For Electric Spanish Guitar
Special for Rhythm 'N Blues
Perfect for Easy Pickin'

THE
Ivor Mairants
TESTED & GUARANTEED
De Luxe
BRONZE TAPE WOUND
STRINGS
FOR THE
PLECTRUM GUITAR
ELECTRIC or ACOUSTIC
AS USED AND RECOMMENDED BY
IVOR MAIRANTS
BOOSEY & HAWKES LTD
SOLE DISTRIBUTORS

MEDIUM
1st
No. 561
B
Made in England

monopole
string guitar
B - 2nd

MADE IN GREAT BRITAIN BY
GENERAL MUSIC STRINGS LIMITED

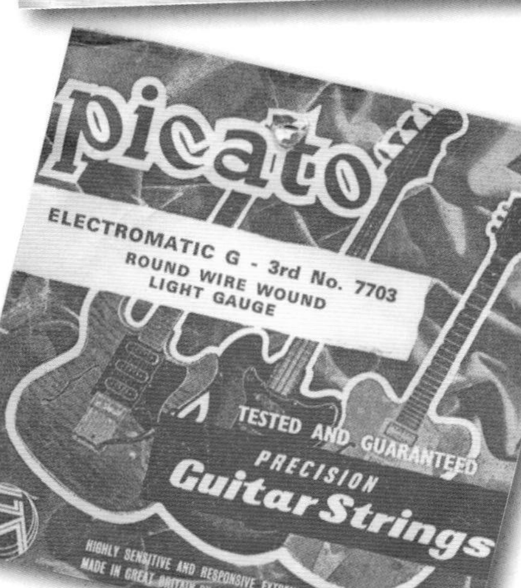
picato
ELECTROMATIC G - 3rd No. 7703
ROUND WIRE WOUND
LIGHT GAUGE
TESTED AND GUARANTEED
PRECISION
Guitar Strings
HIGHLY SENSITIVE AND RESPONSIVE EXTREMELY RESILIENT AND DURABLE
MADE IN GREAT BRITAIN BY GENERAL MUSIC STRINGS LIMITED

'SWING KING'
Plectrum Guitar
Nylon Flatwound
LIGHT GAUGE
ROTOSOUND
music strings

SOUND CITY
perfection in strings
ELECTRIC GUITAR
EXTRA LIGHT GAUGE
High Carbon Steel
2nd
No.4002
.013

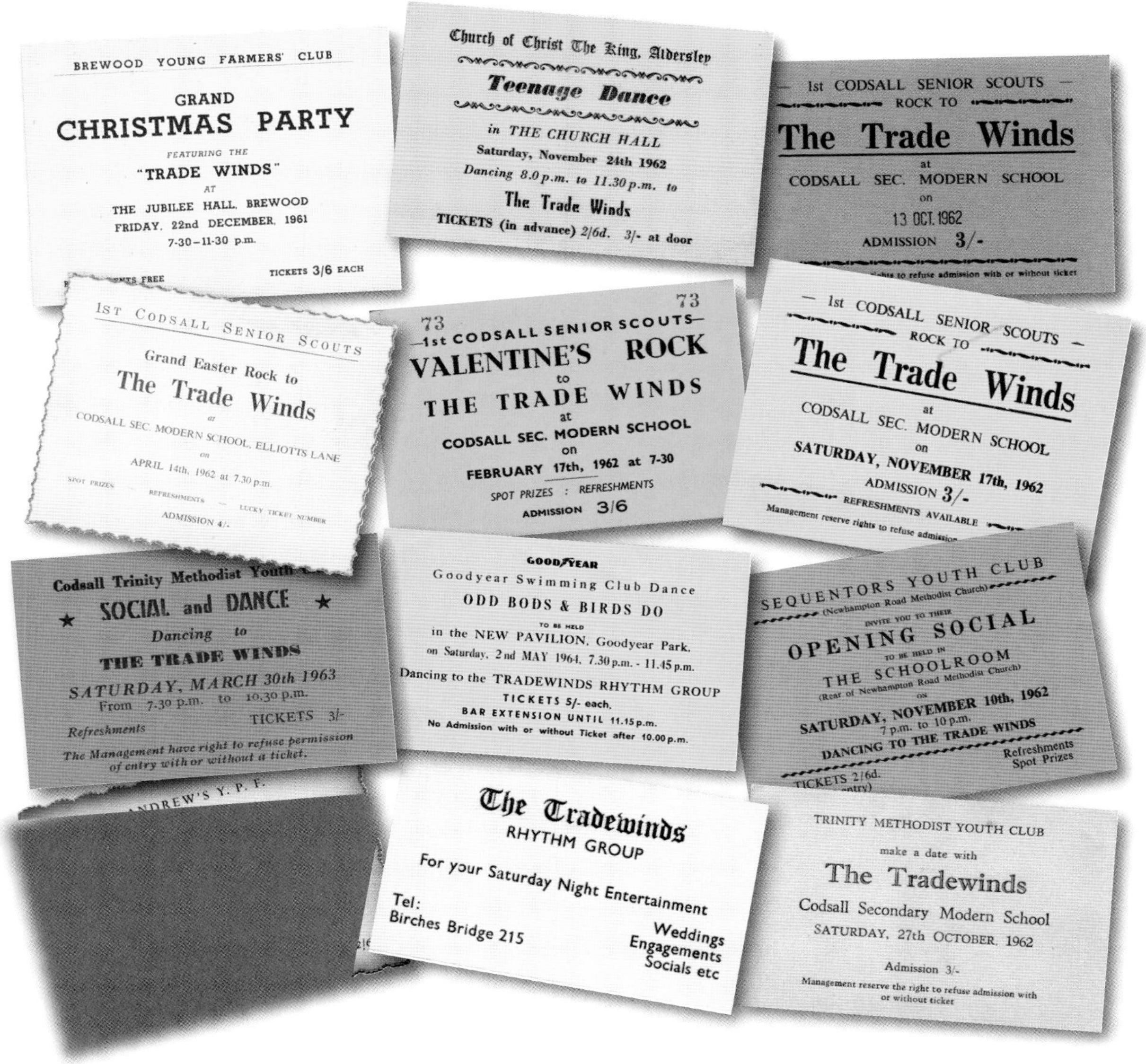

BREWOOD YOUNG FARMERS' CLUB

GRAND
CHRISTMAS PARTY
FEATURING THE
"TRADE WINDS"
AT
THE JUBILEE HALL, BREWOOD
FRIDAY, 22nd DECEMBER, 1961
7-30–11-30 p.m.

TICKETS 3/6 EACH

Church of Christ The King, Aldersley

Teenage Dance
in THE CHURCH HALL
Saturday, November 24th 1962
Dancing 8.0 p.m. to 11.30 p.m. to
The Trade Winds
TICKETS (in advance) 2/6d. 3/- at door

— 1st CODSALL SENIOR SCOUTS —
ROCK TO
The Trade Winds
at
CODSALL SEC. MODERN SCHOOL
on
13 OCT. 1962
ADMISSION 3/-

1ST CODSALL SENIOR SCOUTS

Grand Easter Rock to
The Trade Winds
at
CODSALL SEC. MODERN SCHOOL, ELLIOTTS LANE
on
APRIL 14th, 1962 at 7.30 p.m.
SPOT PRIZES — REFRESHMENTS — LUCKY TICKET NUMBER
ADMISSION 4/-

---

73 73
—1st CODSALL SENIOR SCOUTS—
VALENTINE'S ROCK
to
THE TRADE WINDS
at
CODSALL SEC. MODERN SCHOOL
on
FEBRUARY 17th, 1962 at 7-30
SPOT PRIZES : REFRESHMENTS
ADMISSION 3/6

— 1st CODSALL SENIOR SCOUTS —
ROCK TO
The Trade Winds
at
CODSALL SEC. MODERN SCHOOL
on
SATURDAY, NOVEMBER 17th, 1962
ADMISSION 3/-
REFRESHMENTS AVAILABLE
Management reserve rights to refuse admission

Codsall Trinity Methodist Youth

★ SOCIAL and DANCE ★
Dancing to
THE TRADE WINDS
SATURDAY, MARCH 30th 1963
From 7-30 p.m. to 10.30 p.m.
Refreshments TICKETS 3/-
The Management have right to refuse permission of entry with or without a ticket.

GOODYEAR
Goodyear Swimming Club Dance
ODD BODS & BIRDS DO
TO BE HELD
in the NEW PAVILION, Goodyear Park,
on Saturday, 2nd MAY 1964, 7.30 p.m. - 11.45 p.m.
Dancing to the TRADEWINDS RHYTHM GROUP
TICKETS 5/- each,
BAR EXTENSION UNTIL 11.15 p.m.
No Admission with or without Ticket after 10.00 p.m.

SEQUENTORS YOUTH CLUB
(Newhampton Road Methodist Church)
INVITE YOU TO THEIR
OPENING SOCIAL
TO BE HELD IN
THE SCHOOLROOM
(Rear of Newhampton Road Methodist Church)
ON
SATURDAY, NOVEMBER 10th, 1962
7 p.m. to 10 p.m.
DANCING TO THE TRADE WINDS
Refreshments
Spot Prizes
TICKETS 2/6d.

ANDREW'S Y.P.F.

The Tradewinds
RHYTHM GROUP
For your Saturday Night Entertainment
Tel:
Birches Bridge 215

Weddings
Engagements
Socials etc

TRINITY METHODIST YOUTH CLUB
make a date with
The Tradewinds
Codsall Secondary Modern School
SATURDAY, 27th OCTOBER, 1962
Admission 3/-
Management reserve the right to refuse admission with or without ticket

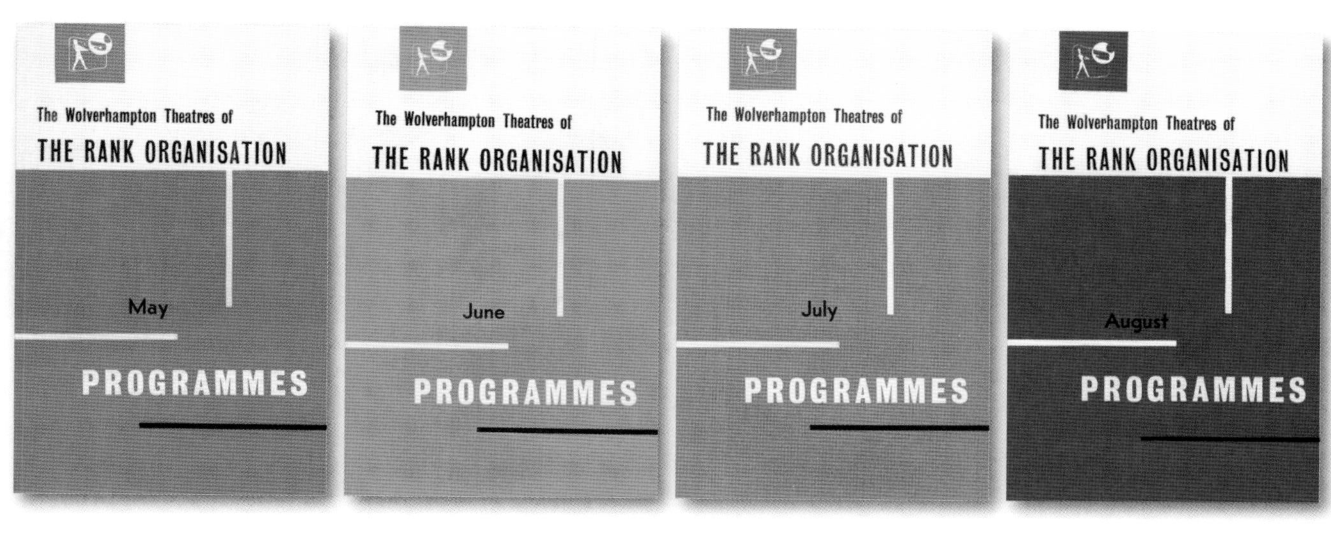

Women's Lib

In 1969 the world was changing, and womens' liberation was making its mark – except, it would seem, at London University's Imperial College, where we were booked to play at a dance supporting Gentle Giant. Before the gig we wandered into a students' union bar and were suddenly greeted by a strange, communal, repetitive whooping sound, like a flotilla of destroyers. It took us a couple of seconds to realise that Linda and Mike Jopp's girlfriend, Mary, were the only girls in this strangely anachronistic male-only bar. We instantly filed from the room, but Linda, who was the last to leave, turned at the door, slowly surveyed the room, and loudly yelled "Wankers!" It was the only response possible. The room went very quiet.

Unbelievably, this was Affinity's publicity shot for a while. L-r: Grant Serpell, Mike Jopp, Linda Hoyle, Lynton Naiff and Mo Foster (wearing 'that' waistcoat)

Steve Marriott

Sheffield was especially responsive to The Small Faces' early professional gigs, and few were more excited by the band than club owner Peter Stringfellow. Steve Marriott: "The Mojo Club was the biggest club we'd played. It was a great club, it really was. It was like *Ready, Steady, Go!* Very much a mod club. I think we only did the one gig at the Mojo Club, until we had a hit record, and then it was all over. It wasn't very long after, just a couple of months, that we hit. We were *their* band – it was like they'd discovered us, so they went crazy when we went back. They used to go fucking berserk whenever we played there. We used to play two sets a night for a couple of nights, something like that. The mods there were great, but there were also people like Stringfellow who were very good at seeing a trend and merchandising it. Obviously, he saw what was going to happen. He saw this whole mod thing in London and saw it fringing around where he was and knew it would be big."

Steve relied on his charm with the fairer sex to bag his first Marshall rig, in particular a lady (not a fish) called Wanda. "She had a very well-to-do family, sort of country family type. I don't know if she had the readies or not herself, but she signed the HP agreement for me, God bless her, which allowed me to get a Marshall. Either a 50-watt or a 100-watt Marshall – the old ones with the big cooker knobs, black and white. It was massive for those days. We were loud, notoriously loud – if you can't play, play loud."

Affinity

On 22 August 1970, we were on the same bill as Steve Marriott's new band, Humble Pie, at Fyens Forum in Odense, Denmark. They were great, and I was particularly impressed by the richness of their Hammond organ, which was achieved by placing the Leslie cabinet in an unused backstage room and then miking it into the PA – it sounded wonderful. Some hours after the gig, our roadie Chris and I were standing outside a club in the town having just realised we couldn't afford to get in. Up bowled Steve Marriott, along with Peter Frampton. We chatted for a while and, when Steve discovered our plight, without hesitation he slipped us ten kroner each, the price of admission. What a nice man.

Poster for Affinity at Fyens Forum in Denmark

Dave Pegg

Semi-pro club band The Crawdaddies featured Dave Pegg in their line-up. Dave remembers playing an all-nighter at Birmingham's Marquee Club, using two Vox AC30s between four members. "The Yardbirds were headlining and Jeff trashed his AC30 (I love Jeff Beck!). Things were starting to happen for me, and I quickly developed a reputation around the Midlands as a reasonable blues guitarist with a drink problem! I couldn't stay working in insurance, as I was now gigging six nights a week and only getting four hours' sleep a night but still doing my proper office job in the day. One of them had to go. My insurance exam results confirmed that I was probably going to be better off as a musician. Ironically, when I became a pro, the Royal Exchange would no longer insure my gear."

Clem Clempson

Clem Clempson's band Bakerloo were devotees of the blues and, in 1968, with nowhere in Birmingham to play or hear such music, they started their own club, Henry's Blues House (named after a dog), and booked acts such as Jethro Tull for £40. The regular drummer lived in fear of guest appearances by a certain local muso. Clem: "After John Bonham sat in, the Premier drums would be spread all across Birmingham."

Allan Holdsworth

The original name of the band that Allan Holdsworth formed with drummer Gary Husband was False Alarm, because each time they thought they had a gig it would be cancelled! They were also victims of the dreaded "pay to play" scam which proliferated among many pub and club venues. Allan: "One such place was a pub in South London, where we did a gig for £50 and ended up giving the guy who had the small PA in the pub £50. Nice one! We then chose the name IOU. Another gig we played, one of our first, was in Covent Garden. We had played a couple of tunes, and during the third or fourth number the manager, assuming that we were still rehearsing, tapped me on the shoulder and yelled in my ear: 'Don't you know the people are in?' We were amazed, and so was he." Some years before this, Allan's experimental band, Igginbottom, paid a fleeting visit to London to play a season at Ronnie Scott's club. Apart from bass guitar and drums, the band featured two guitars, but there was a twist: Allan and his partner would play different chord shapes, the effect of which was a stunning, rich, composite chord that could not possibly be played by only one player.

Clem Clempson in the TV Studio

Colin Green

One of the best acts on the club scene in the 1960s was Georgie Fame and The Blue Flames. The band was originally Colin Green's Beat Boys, a name which evolved into The Blue Flames when they became solely associated with Billy Fury. The link was to end abruptly, however, when impresario Larry Parnes unceremoniously sacked the band for encouraging the star to sing too much jazz and blues. At the time of the split with Fury, Colin Green sometimes played alongside occasional guest John McLaughlin. Colin says: "We went out on our own. The piano player at the time was Clive Powell, who had taken the name Georgie Fame, and the rest is mystery!" No one has ever confessed to the origin of The Blue Flames' name, although a myth has been perpetuated in some quarters that it refers to that strange hue produced when a particularly gaseous fart is lit. During the period when the band had a residency at the Flamingo Club, in Soho, they were greatly influenced by American artists Ray Charles and Jimmy Smith. So much so, in fact, that Georgie persuaded his management to fork out for a Hammond organ. The hits followed, many of which, such as "Yeh Yeh", were arranged by Colin.

Ray Russell

Another guitarist who worked on the road with Georgie was Ray Russell, who stepped in to replace the departing John McLaughlin. On one UK tour, Georgie had organised a double front line – two of every instrument except the rhythm section – to achieve a big sound. Unfortunately, only one of everybody returned to London, while the rest remained up north somewhere, either boozed up, in jail, or both.

Ray then left Georgie's band and toured Europe with Cat Stevens. At the Mecca Ballroom, in Glasgow, there was a rotating stage which had just been made electric (it was previously operated with a winch), but the old boy who controlled it was confused by his three shiny new buttons. Cat had instructed him to rotate the stage so that, as the dance band went out of view, the stage would stop, Cat would leap on from the wings, the stage would carry on rotating and then stop for the gig. On the night, however, the guy became muddled. The stage kept rotating, and then stopped suddenly, with the dance band in full view again. Unfortunately, they'd started relaxing, and so while Cat's band were still pounding out the intro to "Love My Dog" and entertaining a brick wall the 4,000-strong audience had a fine view of the dance band in partial undress with their feet up!

Ray also teamed up with Graham Bond in the infamous Graham Bond Organisation. They once played at Eel Pie Island, a venue which has gone down in British rock history as legendary, if only for the early appearances there by The Who and The Yardbirds. Ray, however, described it as "a dump, like a pub with a hall at the back." Yet again with The Graham Bond Organisation, Ray once played opposite Soft Machine at Brigitte Bardot's villa in the South of France. Because of Graham's impatience with the time it took the Hammond organ to start up, the whole gig ran a semitone flat.

Affinity

Affinity was promised a week's work at Le Bilboquet, a nightclub in Paris where each side of the little stage had a different voltage (110v and 220v), followed by another week at Le Chatam, a similar club in the coastal resort of Le Touquet. It was an exciting prospect. In Paris we played well and went down a storm until the management asked us to play "Le Popcorn", a new dance craze. We tried, but our soul wasn't really into this piece of musical tinsel: we wanted to play chorus after chorus of steaming, Hammond-organ-driven jazz-funk. After two days we were fired. They wanted "Le Popcorn", not music. It was ridiculous, and in our annoyance we exacted our pathetic revenge by locking the toilet door from the inside by using a long piece of string. On the last night, as I sat in despair on the stairway up from the basement club, a beautiful girl walked past me on her way out, pausing only to stroke my hair (which was at that time a large red afro). Momentarily my spirits rose. "I just 'ad to touch eet," she said, and vanished up to the street.

Our next step wasn't a problem. After all, we had a gig lined up in Le Touquet. But the awful truth became evident on our first night there: the gangsters who ran the place quietly explained to us that, unless we arrived an hour before the show started each night, sat around the club buying drinks, invited friends, and generally made the place look more full, they wouldn't pay us (an early version of "pay to play"!). We had no choice. Even worse, at the end of the week they still didn't pay us!

The local *huissier de justice* was useless, and besides we had no money to pay him. With frayed egos and empty wallets, we paused only to shout abuse at the club owners in our exceedingly bad French ("your skunk is in the diversion", "my grandmother is on fire", and "have you a water buffalo? Mine has just split") before limping off in our grey Ford Transit in the direction of Paris. We were all exhausted from the insanities of the last week, especially our driver, Grant Serpell. On the outskirts of the capital we approached a complicated roundabout. In a country where one drove on the wrong side of the road, Grant was suddenly seized with confusion and yelled to all the snoring heaps in the back "Which way do I go?" We weren't helpful. Confused further by the stream of conflicting suggestions from the back seat, Grant took the only option available to him, and proceeded to plough headlong across the local ornate, council-funded flower beds that were planted in the central island. It was different!

After a long search for somewhere to stay we spent that night sleeping on the floor of an office in an embassy in Avenue Foch – which just about sums up how we felt. I do remember that we were near the Arc de Triomphe, but I had no idea whose embassy it was, as I was, by then, too exhausted to care.

Colin Hodgkinson

Depending on a band's line-up, the physical challenges of carrying gear to and from a gig could be extremely demanding, and still are. Colin Hodgkinson: "It was always hard work lifting Hammond organs up the fire escapes of clubs [which were always situated on the fifth floor]. It seemed that such wonderful things as roadies [or technicians] still hadn't been invented! But those days were a lot of fun. I wouldn't have missed them for anything!" Noel Redding's first trip abroad was to Germany in 1964, where his band The Burnettes played in clubs in Cologne, Frankfurt and Wuppertal for a month at a time. "Our gigs were from 7 p.m. to 1 a.m. during the week. On Saturdays, we'd do a 2.30 to 5 p.m. matinee, and then 7 p.m. to 2 a.m. We used to buy uppers from the 'lady' in the gents toilet – my first exposure to drugs!"

Brendan McCormack

A similar schedule was followed in 1964 by Brendan McCormack, who played at the infamous Star Club in Hamburg. "We did two hours on and one off in twelve-hour shifts [4 p.m.–4 a.m.]. This helped us to develop a solid rhythmic style, which was the core of the 'Mersey Sound' of that time. I also remember the Star Club as having the first house PA system to use reverb, and this, coupled with decent Sennheiser mics, made things seem very exotic."

Andy Pyle

Andy Pyle left his job in 1966 and moved to Manchester, thinking it was the place to be. "I got a very small room in the attic of a very big house full of students and musicians. One day, Victor Brox came to the door looking for a bass player. I followed him to a room above a pub in Salford, which contained a selection of drunks, petty criminals and junkies, known collectively as The Blues Train. They greeted me with a series of grunts and carried on playing music I'd never heard before. I didn't smoke or drink, and the closest I'd been to a mind-bending experience was listening to Radio Luxembourg. My hair was very short and my bass was pink. I stayed with them as long as I could, loved every minute, and discovered the blues."

Jim Rodford

By 1967, as pop music became more progressive, groups became bands, and ironically even today the London Symphony Orchestra calls itself 'The Band'. In the space of the next five to ten years, rock 'n' roll touring had become highly sophisticated, with massive backlines and PA equipment, huge entourages and excessive rider requirements built into contracts. On one particular North American gig, on an Argent tour, an incident brought home to Jim Rodford just how far they had progressed from extremely humble beginnings. "I was on stage in the arena, chatting to the crew before the soundcheck, when I picked up the sound of an extremely heated, bellowing argument going on backstage. Somebody was really getting a roasting. When I enquired what was going on, I was told the catering lady had failed to cut the lemons in the correct shape, and was being bawled out by our tour manager. It was at that moment I thought: 'Have we really come very far, when that sort of non-musical detail had become so important?'"

THE END OF THE BAND

Lynton and I had started to write for a second album for Affinity, and the band was lined up for an American tour but in January 1971 – in the middle of a tour of Sweden – Linda announced that she'd had enough and had decided to leave the business. It was a sad, but inevitable, decision: the band had worked hard for two and a half years and yet had little to show for it. The fun had gone. The remaining contracted gigs were honoured and the guys went their separate ways.

Affinity: Wednesday 10 February 1971, the Last Gig

It was an emotional evening when Affinity made its professional exit at the Bournemouth Winter Gardens. After two and a half years of slogging around the circuit and getting nowhere we had decided to pack it in. The whole band played extremely well that night and as the final tumultuous chord died away, and we filed sweatily off-stage, we could hear from our dressing room that the distant crowd wouldn't let us go, and were noisily demanding more!

Having calmed down for a couple of minutes, we stood up in anticipation of returning to the stage to play a final encore, but Linda, sadly overcome by the enormity of the occasion, began throwing up into a bucket and was clearly not fit to sing again. We filed back on-stage to rapturous applause – there was much relief in the audience that we had come back at all – and it became obvious that an explanation for Linda's absence was required. For whatever reason, it fell on me to make the announcement, but unfortunately I had nothing planned, except that I knew that I couldn't say that she was being sick in a bucket.

Through tears, I managed to thank the crowd for being such a supportive audience on this, our last gig, and then apologised, busking furiously: "I'm so sorry, but Linda can't come back on for this, our final song, but I'm afraid... er... she has... er... the shits!" I couldn't believe what I'd just said, but with this aphorism still ringing in everyone's ears we played one last tune before the band came to an end and I was on my own. A new career beckoned... but probably not as an announcer.

CHAPTER 12

OBSERVATIONS

The language of the musician is rich in imagery and self-deprecation. It can be surrealistic, sardonic, creative, and pessimistic, but above all it is very funny.

Some of this humour goes way back to music hall and vaudeville. Wherever possible I've tried to credit the person who first gave me these wonderfully irreverent lines, and I apologise to those authors who are unknown to me and who are therefore uncredited.

SOME OBSERVATIONS:

... on philosophy:

"The older I get, the better I was."
(Recalled by percussionist Jim Lawless)

... future work:

"Oh man, the phone hasn't started ringing."
(Pianist Stan Tracy)

... the rhythmic ability of an unnamed bass player:

"He has the timing of an indoor sundial."
(Drummer Clem Cattini)

... the achievements of another musician:

"If I was as good as he is, I'd have to practice more."
(Jim Lawless)

... dressing:

"Remember, it's shirt, pullover, guitar, *not* guitar, shirt, pullover." (Ray Fenwick)

... influences:

Herbie Flowers' bass influences numbered Ray Brown, Leroy Vinnegar, and Scott La Faro, of whose talents he says: "You could listen to them, dance to them, shag by them, but not necessarily play like them."
(Herbie Flowers)

... interpretation:

Danny Thompson once played such an unfortunate choice of bass note that Tubby Hayes complained: "It was so bad it hurt my eyes."

... classical music:

Danny Thompson hated his school, where they had a Jesuit disciplinarian mentality. "I was always getting whacked," he says. "They told me I would never understand Mozart. They didn't tell me that Mozart was really a raver!"

... drummers:

"So many drummers, so little time."
(Guitarist Bernie Holland)

... pomposity:

"He was a legend in his own lunchtime." (Everyone)

... The reduction to size of an idiotic, large Havana cigar-smoking client:

"You remind me of that famous film star – you know, Lassie, having a shit." (Clem Cattini)

... a musician who trips in the studio, falls, and drags everything with him:

"He had all the panache of a collapsing greenhouse."
(Simon Nicol, recalled by Dave Mattacks)

... polite but firm indifference:

"I'm sorry, but I think you're confusing me with someone who gives a fuck." (Pianist Bill Worrall)

... subtlety:

"How long have you been playing roughly?"
(Recalled by trombone player Derek Wadsworth)

... dimness:

Female singer, who can't hear herself: "Can't you play with more dynamics?"
Drummer: "I'm playing as loud as I can!"
(Recalled by Laurence Canty)

... endurance:

TV interviewer: "Have you been playing the xylophone all your life?"
Patrick Moore: "No, not yet."

... warm-ups:

After single-handedly launching the twist craze with his hit "Let's Twist Again", Chubby Checker came to make a record in London and was rehearsing and attempting to limber up before the session started. All sorts of strange squawks and noises started coming from the vocal booth in a most uninhibited way. Frank Clarke, who was playing bass on this session, was heard to pronounce to the whole studio: "I don't know what that bloody awful noise is, but if it flies over my way I'm going to shoot it!"
(Recalled by Bryan Daly)

... a long career:

"If I'd known pop music was going to be as important as this 30 years ago, I'd have played better."
(Drummer Clem Cattini who played on 42 number one records. His session nickname at the time was 'Thunderfoot')

... a short career:

Due to a confusion over times, and although it wasn't his fault, Clem Cattini arrived an hour and a half late for an orchestral session for Tony Hatch at Pye Studio One. The orchestra had already routined the first track, but as Clem couldn't read music at the time – certainly not the first piece, which was in 9/8 time – he soon realised that it was time to go, and packed up his drums. As he walked up the stairs, he turned to address the orchestra: "I've been slung out of better bands than yours!"

... bluffing:

On another occasion, early in his career, Clem played the part perfectly but genuinely hadn't noticed that his music was upside down. As Clem himself said: "Drummers are all bluff and porterage!"

... reinterpreting the 1960s:

Timothy Leary advocated that we "turn on, tune in and drop out." The studio player's equivalent is: "turn up, tune up, drop in." (Ray Russell)

... a cure for a hangover:

"Take the juice of two bottles of bourbon..."
(Jazz guitarist Eddie Condon, recalled by John Altman)

... oblivion:

When asked if he would like an "Elephant Beer", tenor sax player Al Cohn replied: "No thanks, man, I drink to forget." (Recalled by John Altman)

... reality:

Conductor Harry Rabinowitz interrupted and admonished a cellist who was talking to a lady violinist on a session: "She may be prettier than me, but I'll do more for your career – just look at me – thank you."
(Recalled by Mitch Dalton)

... reviews:

'It had some wonderful moments, and some dreadfully tedious quarters of an hour.' (Review of Wagner)

... bullshit:

"I understand that his music is far better than it sounds." (Recalled by Derek Wadsworth)

... self mockery:

"I'm waiting for the offer to flood in."

... chords:

Some chords have exotic names. For example, C7-5 can be pronounced C seven with a flattened fifth, and C7+5 can be pronounced C seven with a raised fifth. Doodling between takes on a session at Snake Ranch studio, Colin Green stumbled onto a particularly unusual chord. Intrigued, I asked him what it was. He looked first at his hand and then looked up at me quizzically and said: "I think it's a C seven with a raised eyebrow."

... perfect pitch:

"It is the ability to throw a banjo twenty yards such that it lands in a toilet bowl without touching the sides." (Recalled by Mark Meggido)
There is an alternative:
"It is the ability to throw a banjo twenty yards such that it lands in a skip (dumpster in USA), and hits an accordion."

... surrealism:

"I'd give my right arm to be a session player."
(Ray Russell)

... definition of a session musician:

"Half man, half invoice book." (Ray Russell)

... subtlety (yet again):
"Marvellous isn't the word for it." (Guitarist Wes McGee at Snake Ranch studio on a take that was crumbling)

... respect:
"I'll thank you to keep a civil tongue up my arse."

... domestic bliss:
"One word from me and she does what she likes." (Ray Russell)

... obsequiousness:
"I'm on first-name terms with Cliff – he calls me 'Clem' and I call him 'Sir'." (Clem Cattini, spoken on tour many years before Cliff Richard was knighted.)

... ironic compliment 1:
"If you can do it, anyone can do it." (Drummer Graham Jarvis to keyboard player Adrian Lee)

... ironic compliment 2:
"There are words in what you say." (Adrian Lee)

... ironic compliment 3:
"I don't care what people say – I *know* you're a complete arsehole." (Keyboard player Tommy Eyre)

...ironic compliment 4:
"Coming from you, that means nothing." (Ringo Starr's throwaway response to a compliment from Gyles Brandreth on *The One Show*)

... credulity:
"Trust me – I'm a bass player."

... imagery:
"He looked like a fox staring out of a bear's arse." (Producer Gus Dudgeon recalling a description of engineer John Timperly with his bushy black beard and intense, deep-set eyes. According to Keith Grant this observation was originally credited to IBC engineer Allen Stagg)

... survival:
"You need to keep the plates spinning." (Percussionist Ray Cooper)

... justification:
"I only went wrong to make you look good."

... touring:
"You know you've been away from home too long when the kids call you 'Uncle Dad' and the dog growls and bares its teeth." (Producer Chris Neil)

... sinking ship:
"Women and musicians first!" (Musicians are natural cowards)

... absurdity:
On a session there was a prolonged, messy and noisy crash of falling percussion. In the manner of a primary school teacher the producer admonished the room through the talkback: "If I find out who that was..." (This phrase has since been turned around to encompass almost any goof, such as an overhanging note, by any unfortunate musician)

... end of a long tour:
"The first thing I'm going to do when I get home is take the wife's knickers off – they're killing me.' (Drummer Graham Jarvis at Heathrow Airport after a long flight from Australia)

... strings 1:
In a novel response to the timeless (and very boring) question "What strings do you use?" bass guitarist Steve Stroud sententiously replied: "I try to use all four of them!"

... strings 2:
The bass player of The Jesus and Mary Chain was asked why his instrument only had two strings. "In case one of them breaks," he replied with incredulity. (recalled by Guy Pratt)

... things you don't hear very often:
"Is that the banjo player's Porsche outside?" (Recalled by guitarist Paul Keogh)

... old-school management optimism :
"Stick with me, boys, and you'll fart through silk."

... nicknames:
Whilst on tour with The Everly Brothers, drummer Graham Jarvis noticed that Phil, the gaunt one, smoked cigarettes almost continuously, whereas Don, the chubbier of the two, quite enjoyed a drink. With his love of wordplay Graham created the most perfect names for them: "Smoke Everly" and "Drink Everly". He was a genius.

... moving to a very expensive new house:
"It's not home, but I call it much." (Ray Russell)

... ironic farewells:
"... and don't forget, if you're ever passing, I want you to know that all of the staff here will be very pleased." (Senior engineer Peter Vince, saying goodbye to me on camera at the end of an interview for a proposed live television music programme at Abbey Road studios)

... confidence:

On a recording session composer John Barry asked first-call mandolin player Hugo Dalton if his part was okay. "Yes, yes," Hugo replied. "Don't worry, John, I know what you should have written!" John Barry was speechless, and the session continued.
(Recalled by Vic Flick)

... disbelief:

Bandleader: "you're flat!"
Trumpet player: "who told you?"

... options:

"Look, do you want it good, or by Thursday?" (Composer/drummer Brian Bennett – very frustrated – responding to a stupidly impatient client)

... tropical healthcare:

In 1979 guitarist Richard Brunton was at Air Studios in Montserrat as part of a team recording an album with Gerry Rafferty. Richie had to see the local doctor, and almost daily he would regale us with fresh tales of his visits. The doctor's opening phrase "Of course, out here in the Tropics...", spoken in a soft Scottish accent, was always the prelude to the lowering of medical expectation.

... pragmatism:

Patrick Moraz was auditioning for the recently vacated keyboard role in the band Yes. When asked if he was vegetarian he pragmatically replied, "If necessary."

... wit (yet again):

"I'm now semi-required." (An older viola player's witty view of his present work status.)

... being cruel, but fair 1:

"He suffers from a charisma bypass." (Colin Green)

... being cruel, but fair 2:

"He suffers from a case of mistaken nonentity."

... low budget:

"No expense was spent."

... success:

When guitarist Mickey Moody graduated to playing in a soul band his dad was most impressed: "You've made it now son, playing with trumpets."

... the session scene:

"We had the best of it. If only we knew at the time that we had the best of it". (John Altman)

... modesty:

At short notice guitarist Mitch Dalton was booked by producer Peter Van Hooke to play with Herbie Hancock and Wayne Shorter for the TV programme *Live from Abbey Road*. "In such esteemed company I'd set myself the limited goal of not being sent home" (Mitch Dalton)

... good advice:

"What a client often needs is a damned good listening to." (Recalled by Sarah Morgan)

... gentleman:

"Someone who knows how to play the accordion, but doesn't." (Al Cohn's definition of a gentleman. For accordion you could substitute banjo, bagpipes, or many other instruments, depending on your culture and sensitivity. I would include in the list the ability to sing opera)

... freedom:

"We never play anything the same way once." (Shelly Manne's definition of jazz musicians)

... childhood:

"Of all the friends I've ever had, he was the first." (Peter Watkins)

... naming of bands:

Rock group Deep Purple took its name from the favourite song of guitarist Richie Blackmore's granny. How the whole course of rock music would have changed if her favourite song had been something like "How Much Is That Doggie in the Window".

... embarrassing response:

The audient gave us a round of applau.

... malapropisms:

"She was pussy in my hands." (Designer Rick Dewing, recalled by Mike Forster)

... mixed metaphor 1:

"Ah well, it's all water under a duck." (Tonia Davall)

... mixed metaphor 2:

"You can see the carrot at the end of the tunnel."

... cocktails:

1969: on the jazz club menu was a "Ronnie Scott's Special": champagne, Tia Maria, brandy, and a cherry. This was followed by the instruction: "not to be drunk on an empty head!"

... solos:

Saxophonist John Coltrane was widely respected for his seemingly unlimited invention when soloing – his sheets of sound. But it did give him a problem, and he once confided to Miles Davis that he didn't know how to end a solo. In his gruff voice Miles replied: "It's simple – you take the horn out of your mouth."

... drugs:

On one occasion in a London pub Keith Moon turned to Tony Meehan and said: "My dear chap, have you any substances of the upward variety?" (Recalled by Tony Meehan)

... musicals:

"Normally I hate musicals. But tonight was no exception." (character Brett Craig on *Kath and Kim* TV show)

... awards:

"This award will take pride of place in my attic."

... irony 1:

"Nobody has ever erected a statue to a critic." (Sibelius)

... irony 2:

"The only way to make a million pounds running a jazz club is to start off with two million." (Ronnie Scott)

... fear:

Gary Husband was attacking the piano at Ronnie's with incredible muscularity and frightening energy. Composer George Fenton turned to me and said: "I'm glad I don't live below him when he's composing."

... truth:

"It's not the principle, it's the money." (Ralph Salmins)

... tour humour:

Drummer Stuart Elliott was crossing Frankfurt Airport on tour with the Jack Bruce Band. They spotted a magazine in the racks that simply displayed a large picture of a hedgehog. Suggestions for the main title were: "Practical Hedgehog", "Which Hedgehog?", "Ideal Hedgehog", "Homes and Hedgehogs", etc. I love the fantasy – it's what keeps you going.

... surreal:

Friday Night Is Music Night was a BBC radio programme broadcast from the Hippodrome, Golders Green with a live audience. It won an award for 'the best lights on radio'.

... returning home:

"I'm back, and I'm proud." (A reinterpretation of *The Commitments*, by Ray Russell)

... pragmatism:

During the musical *Animal Farm* trumpeter Howard Evans coined the immortal phrase "Done the show, now eat the cast."

... arrangers:

"It beats me how he does it – I can't arrange a vase of flowers." (Ronnie Scott on the brilliance of Tubby Hayes' arrangements)

...trying to do business at MIDEM, the large music industry trade fair, which is held each year in Cannes, France:

"Excuse me, I've just stepped in the music industry." (Producer Chris Neil)

... music industry:

"These are the slings and arrows one must endure to make an outrageous fortune." (Dan Loggins)

... allergies:

Nurse: Are you allergic to anything?"
Friend: "Yeah, bullets!"
(Simon Phillips' friend after being shot)

... rock cred:

While producing an album for Debbie Bonham (younger sister of John Bonham) at Masterock studios I was rummaging through my bag in the control room. Perhaps a bit too loudly, I suddenly said: "Oh no, my library books are overdue." (Mo)

... ballet:

"We used to ask (percussionist) Ray Cooper to play extra "takes" just so that we could watch him playing tambourine." (Bill Tansely)

... after total confusion during a collapsed 'take':

"Is anyone hurt?" (Ray Cooper)

... the ironic call in the studio:

"Oh Mo, you're wanted on the toilet." (Chris Neil)

... dreadful English:

The Ship pub in Wardour Street – meeting-point for many musicians – used to have a sign behind the bar, which read: "Our food is prepared by diploma-holding caterers." What did they do – cook with one hand?

... the future:

"Sax player Iain Ballamy said to his mum: 'When I grow up I'm going to be a jazz musician.' She said, 'Don't be silly, you can't do both.'" (Guitarist Billy Jenkins)

... careers:

"He worked his way up from nothing, to a state of

extreme poverty." (Spike Milligan)

... *desperation:*
"The Scaffold would reform at the drop of a cheque." (Poet Roger McGough)

... *being silly:*
"Yes, I met Earth, Wind & Fire: I passed Earth and Fire on the way in, and then passed Wind on the way out."

... *on the past:*
"It's funnier now than it was then." (Andy Pyle)

... *on promotion:*
"After thirty years at the studio he was catapulted to the role of tea-boy." (via Woody Allen)

... *on praise:*
"I really like what some of you guys are trying to do." (Jay Stapley)

... *not understanding endless instructions on a session:*
"I think I'm going out of your head!"
(Recalled by Ray Russell)

... *writing your name in the snow with the "yellow biro":*
"Essentially a male pursuit. If your name is long then you may need to drink more pints. Special points are awarded for crossing the 't's and dotting the 'i's. Women can, of course, join in as long as their surname is 'Whoosh'."
(Singer Dave Parton of the Cyril Dagworth Players)

... *Guitar Acquisition Syndrome – GAS:*
Q. What's the correct number of guitars?
A. One more than you already own.
(Walter Becker, via Malcolm McDonald)

DUMMY LYRICS

When a songwriter has the music, but not the final lyrics he sometimes uses a 'dummy lyric' just to get started. A dummy lyric is a temporary lyric (often silly, even nonsensical) that allows the writer to outline a song's lyrical structure. These are some of my favourites:

FINAL SONG	DUMMY LYRIC
• 'Yesterday' (Paul McCartney)	'Scrambled Eggs'
• 'Don't Sleep In The Subway' (Tony Hatch/Jackie Trent)	'Don't Shit In The Custard'
• 'Aaahh Freak Out'	'Aaahh Fuck Off'

(Nile Rodgers/Bernard Edwards; written in anger after they had been refused entry to Club 54)

BRUSHES WITH THE LAW

The Jazz Police

A constable from the Jazz Police stops a musician, hands him a chord chart, and says: "I'm afraid I'm going to have to ask you to blow over these changes."

Ronnie Asprey

Sax player Ronnie Asprey was struggling to drive down Park Lane in the evening rush-hour. In frustration he chanced an illegal move by changing to the dedicated bus lane. Within seconds he was – inevitably – totally blocked in between two buses. A policeman, who happened to be standing on the pavement nearby, ambled over to Ronnie's car and motioned for the passenger window to be lowered. Employing standard-issue police irony he enquired: "Is this a bus, sir?" Throwing caution to the wind, Ronnie swiftly replied: "You're new on traffic aren't you?" (Recalled by Cliff Hall)

Bonzo Dog Doo-Dah Band

In 1969 the Bonzos were touring America along with every other British band. Kicking their heels in a New York hotel, the guys decided to drive to Detroit and "see a bit of the countryside". After hours and hours of driving they eventually had to pull up at a toll-booth just outside Buffalo, NY.

A highway patrolman – bristling with weaponry – ordered them to pull into a nearby parking area, and demanded to know who they were, and where they were going. They attempted to explain that that they were a band, but he challenged this assertion, because he could see that they had no equipment with them (the van had gone ahead, and an inflatable elephant evidently didn't count). He also expressed disbelief at the amount of money ($2,000) they were to be paid by the Grandee Ballroom, the next gig.

It was when the patrolman had difficulty reading the name "Bonzo Dog Doo-Dah Band" that Vivian Stanshall – who had been asked by everybody to just keep quiet – began to get restless.

The patrolman then demanded to know if they had any "pot", or "shit", or other illegal substances. "No," they all cried. Had they got any guns or knives? "No." "Okay, what do you use for self-protection?" Unable to contain himself any longer Vivian Stanshall lurched into view and bellowed "Good manners!" in his fruitiest English voice. (Recalled by Neil Innes. Neil tells me that there is a longer version of this story with more detail about such things as Larry's trousers being made from Holiday Inn towels but... another time.)

Andy Fairweather-Low

"It was 1976: we had just played a great gig at Essex University. The band hung around for a few drinks until we were eventually kicked out. The van had left, so it was up to me to drive the car.

"When I saw a police car in the rear-view mirror I panicked and asked if anyone had any chewing gum, and I remember thinking that because of my breath I must keep a substantial air gap between me and the policeman. And I must be polite.

"Is this your car, sir?" asked the man.

("Yes," said my brain.)

"Yes, please," said my mouth.

"A policeman drove our car back to the police station. I have to say that I am not proud of this moment, and I have learnt my lesson: I do not drink and drive"

Bergerac

Ray Russell recalls: "In the eighties I was asked by my friend George Fenton to help with the arranging and composing of the many episodes of the TV series *Bergerac*. In the beginning, we were on a tight deadline of one show a week with oodles of music to compose. George is a true artist, sometimes slipping into a world of true imagination with no bounds. This meant that between us, the music was often not created until the last minute.

"Any music arrangement needs a copyist who dutifully copies from the score to all the separate parts for the band. The late Andre Gersh was the copyist who became a faithful servant of the show and he would never complain about staying up all night to finish his work so that it would be ready at the BBC studio on the morning of the session.

"Either George or I would arrange to meet Andre at the Polish War Memorial on the A40 near Uxbridge – a convenient place for both of us (this was before the advent of mobile phones so it was difficult to change any plans). Tirelessly Andre would wait by the Memorial in the middle of the night waiting for one of us to deliver a few crumbs of creation in the form of a music cue.

"This became a regular event but unfortunately for Andre our deliveries got later and later, and he had to wait longer and longer. It became evident that someone had complained about a strange man in a mackintosh spending over an hour every night in the shadow of this minor monolith when the police duly drove by and asked Andre what he was doing. His statement that 'he was waiting for a man to deliver some music' did not impress the policeman, who arrested him for loitering. Luckily he protested his innocence, and on further explanation he was let off.

"Bergerac ran for over ten years, and writing with George in those days will always hold great memories for me."

Mike d'Abo

Passing through the metal detector at New York's La Guardia airport prior to boarding, Mike was stopped by a security policeman who poked him in the groin with a stick.

Security: "What's that, buddy?"

Mike: "They're my private parts."

Security: "Kinda big ain't it?"

Mike got on the plane feeling ten feet tall. He even told the story at the gig that night.

The Long Walk Home

I'd been to a party in South Kensington. In my uninhibited, drunken haze it seemed to be a good idea to walk home to Wimbledon – a long way. It was about 2 a.m., and I remember trudging miles in search of a bridge to cross the river. I chanced upon a huge empty warehouse, and being in a relaxed but inquisitive frame of mind I couldn't resist investigating. To my surprise the door opened easily. The total emptiness of this vast space had transformed it into a perfect, cavernous echo chamber – I was in my element. I tried an experimental mouth/finger pop: it sounded wonderful. A handclap: the reverb trail seemed to take forever. After a while I progressed to various combinations of yodels, whistles and raspberries until the whole building was resonating with a barrage of ludicrous noises. It was a perfect moment. After about ten minutes I turned to leave and spotted the policeman who had been watching my entire performance. It took a lot of explaining.

CREATIVE SONG TITLES

It's an endless source of amusement for me when composers come up with an innovative title for a piece of instrumental music. Here are a few of my favourites, plus a couple of eccentric "country" titles:

"Trouble over at Bridgewater" (Steve Gray – who lived in the West Country)

"Let's Face the Dhansak and Muse" (Max Brittain)

"Once, Twice, Three Times I've Asked You" (Roger Clarke)

"I Only Have Eyes for You, But You Should See What I've Got for Your Sister" (Derek Wadsworth)

"Outside It May Be Raining, But in My Heart It's Pissing Down"

"Accepting Suites From Strangers" (Django Bates)

"My Sweet Inflatable You" (Spike Milligan)

"Give Peas a Chance" (Alan Hawkshaw)

"My Karma Just Ran over Your Dogma"

"I'm Sick and Tired of Waking up Tired and Sick" (Ronnie Scott)

"The Smoker You Drink, the Player You Get" (Joe Walsh)

"The Importance of Being Invoiced"

"If I Had to Do It All over Again, I'd Do It All over You"

"Rebel Without a Causeway"

"The Lady Is a Trampolinist" (Spike Milligan)

"I Love You So Much, I Can't Shit"

"What Is This Thing Called, Love?" (You can do this trick on any song title that ends with "love". e.g., "There Is No Grater, Love" or "I'm Not in, Love".)

"Parisienne Safeways" (Sorry, Gary)

"I'll Never Get over You, So Get up and Make the Tea Yourself"

"I Feel So Bad Now That You've Gone, It Feels Like You're Still Here"

"How Can I Miss You, When You Won't Even Go Away?"

"Never Pat a Burning Dog" (Ronnie Scott LP title)

"Who Wants To Be a Moules Marinière?"

"Beget the Baguette"

"Deep in the Heart of Telford"

"Lawrence of Suburbia"

"I'm Leaving on the 3.42 p.m. Train to Georgia, Calling at Alabama, Last Four Coaches Only"

"Please Don't Talk About Me One Eye's Gone" (Derek Wadsworth)

"When a Man Writes an Invoice"

"We Are the Champignons"

THEATRES AND CLUBS

Idiot MC 1

In Britain the name Pontin's is synonymous with a chain of holiday camps. One evening, at a camp near Christchurch on the south coast, the chief "Bluecoat" was taken suddenly ill and was unable to make his usual announcement to the crowd in the main ballroom. At very short notice the task was handed to a novice "Bluecoat" who was so terrified of the idea that he refused to speak at all unless the whole speech was written down for him to read.

With his hands visibly shaking he walked in front of Ted Hiscock and his Band, the resident orchestra, and up to the microphone. He cleared his throat and nervously read out the list of performers: "Good evening, ladies and gentlemen. Tonight we have for you an international cabaret, featuring dancing girls, singers, acrobats, and jugglers."

He expanded a little more on the night's entertainment and concluded with the immortal line: "And finally, for your dancing pleasure, we have Ted, his cock, and his Band." (Recalled by drummer Paul Beavis)

Idiot MC 2

Lulu, a well-loved pop singer with many chart hits, was in the wings, waiting to go onstage at Batley, a prestigious northern nightclub. Announcer: "It has come to the

ANNOUNCEMENTS

- "There comes a time in everyone's life, and that time is now." (Ronnie Rampant [Peter Watkins] at Goodyear Pavilion, Wolverhampton)
- **Spoken in a wonderfully phony Californian accent: "Good evening everybody, it's wonderful to be, you know, not so long ago, and it's been very lucky for me, thank you." (Neil Innes at the Venue with RMS in 1982)**
- "I've suffered for my music, now it's your turn." (Neil Innes at the Venue with RMS in 1982)
- **"They're looking for the band plectrum": a covering response for Ray, Simon, and Mo for being late onstage to accompany Neil. (Neil Innes at the Venue with RMS in 1982)**
- "Would you please welcome a good friend of ours, and one of the finest guitarists in his price bracket." (Mo introducing Gary Moore at "Vibes from the Vines" charity concert)
- **"I can't remember when I enjoyed myself." (Cliff Richard)**
- "I'd rather play with these guys than the best musicians in town." (Duane Eddy on tour with The Everly Brothers)
- **"I'm thinking of forming a Jet Harris tribute band." (Jet Harris at Bruce Welch's "Shadowmania")**
- "It's been a pleasure trying to play with you." (Bruce Welch at "Shadowmania")
- **"It's all gone wrong today: I've just spent twenty minutes combing my hair – and I've left it upstairs." (Jet – again)**
- "I've played with some drummers in my time – and this guy is one of them." (Phil Collins on tour, jokingly introducing Chester Thompson)
- **"This next song was a big hit for us in some parts of the world. You may have heard of it – if you were in some parts of the world." (Hank Marvin)**
- Every so often a really great song comes along, but until it does I'll do one of his." (Cliff Richard, invariably nodding towards Hank Marvin)
- **"I know this next song is one of your favourites – I just hope it's one of mine." (Rick Hallchurch)**

attention of the committee that some members, and even some female members, have been seen urinating in the drive outside the club late at night. This is clearly upsetting for the locals and it's not good for the club image. So ladies and gentlemen please, from now on, no more urinating in the drive. Here's Lulu."

Idiot MC 3

In 1972 Graham Gouldman, Kevin Godley, Lol Creme, and Eric Stewart finally coalesced to form the superb band 10cc. At an early gig at the Ironopolis club in Middlesbrough, the MC, who lived on a planet of his own, tapped the mic, blew across it, and then brought them on: "Well, ladies and gentlemen, here's a new group, not my cup of tea, but here they are, put your hands together please for 'EYEOCK'." In his tragic way, this is what he thought the name "10CC" sounded like.

Spike Milligan

Judd Procter once appeared as the lone accompanist on the show *An Evening with Spike Milligan* on London Weekend Television. During the show, Spike introduced him to the audience, saying: "Ladies and gentlemen, would you please welcome Judd Procter on guitar. [Applause.] He's written over 200 songs. They're all crap."

REQUESTS

At a function, a request from the audience for the band to play a particular piece of music is rarely straightforward – there's always a surprise, which is usually because the person who made that request is either incredibly stupid, drunk, or both. The bandleader needs to exhibit considerable tact in his reply:

- "Do you play requests?"
  "Certainly, what would you like to hear?"
  "Oh, anything".
- "Can you play something that you all know?"
- "Can you play 'Far Away'?"
  "Yes"
  "Well, would you mind playing over there?"
- "Do you know (a particular song title)?"
  "I'm sorry we don't know that one"
  "Well, can you play it anyway?"
- "Can you play something out of the charts?"
  "Certainly, sir, here's a song that's been out of the charts for 36 years!"
  (A brilliant response from Clem Cattini with The Tornados)
- "We don't normally do requests – unless we're asked."
  (Hank Marvin)
- Bert Ambrose and his orchestra were playing at a smart London hotel. An elegant woman passed to the band leader a request written on a piece of paper which was then wrapped around a £1 note. He wrote on the paper: "We don't do requests", and returned it to her, this time wrapped around a £5 note. That is style.
- A scrap of paper was passed onstage: "Please can you play 'Jolly Be Good' for Shaun, please?" This was unusual in that it was not written on a beer mat and compared favourably with a request we once received for The Beatles' song 'Hey June'. (Peter Watkins)

RADIO REQUESTS

- Heard on Radio Rowley Regis, a short-lived pirate station in the Black Country (the Midlands): "Can you play a request for my girlfriend – it's a smashing song by The Commodores called 'Three Parts a Woman'." (Recalled by studio engineer Simon Bishop)
- "Can you play Holst's 'Planet of the Apes Suite'?" (A radio request heard by drummer Dave Mattacks)

HECKLERS

When a member of the audience – who is usually quite drunk – decides that his opinion is more important than anybody else's, the band leader has to employ a set of tactics designed to deflect those opinions:

- "Don't move, sir – I want to forget you just like you are." (Ronnie Scott)
- "Oh, it's you, sir – I didn't recognise you in men's clothes." (Ronnie Scott)
- "I'd ask you to keep your mouth shut, sir, but I know it would ruin your sex life." (Ronnie Scott)
- "That's a nice tie, sir. Do you not have a mirror at home?" (Sandi Toksvig)
- "When I want your opinion, sir, I'll give it to you."
- "I see that your tailor has a sense of humour."
- "That's an interesting suit you have on, sir. Somewhere in South London there's a Ford Cortina without any seat covers." (Recalled by Linda Hoyle)
- One night, between sets, I watched Ronnie Scott patiently argue with a really boring heckler. Leaning against a supporting pillar he stood in the half-light with the microphone intimately close to his lips. His adversary eventually became insufferable to a point where Ronnie could take no more and, in his inimitable laconic delivery, he emphatically dismissed the guest: "Why should I talk to you when I could talk to my own prick?" End of conversation.

Ronnie Scott

There has to be a special section here for the late tenor sax player and club owner Ronnie Scott: his stand-up humour was legendary, his delivery unique, and his timing perfect. He once claimed that he could stop a runaway horse simply by putting money on it. I heard "the jokes" countless times whilst working in the club, but it didn't matter: he was still able to make me laugh every time. I miss him. He was special.

"I love this club – it reminds me of home – it's filthy and full of strangers. Last night vandals broke in and redecorated it."

He was sometimes a little abusive about his staff:

"Our soundman, Martin, is the greatest soundman in the country. In the city – useless. No, I'm only kidding about Martin. He does a wonderful job. Badly."

He sometimes picked on the waitresses:

"Mary used to be an air hostess – for the Wright Brothers."

"I asked her if she liked Dickens. She said 'I don't know, I've never been to one.'"

"Wonderful waitresses here at the club. Roy tells me there are eight. I've only seen three, but... oh, one of our waitresses is moving, a very rare sight. That's Rosy. Hello Rosy. Sorry about last night. Where are you working next week? That's Rosy, she comes from Scunthorpe. Very nice town, very quiet, very peaceful. I spent a wonderful fortnight there one Sunday. When we got there it was closed. If more than three people stand together they think it's a riot. It's the kind of town where you plug your electric shaver in and the street-lights go dim. You wake up in the morning and you can hear the birds... coughing. They even fly upside down since there's nothing worth shitting on. I asked a cab driver to take me to where the action was – he took me to watch two guys fishing in the canal without a permit. But it's great. Jesus Christ was almost born in Scunthorpe, but they couldn't find three wise men – or a virgin."

The doorman:

"Then there's Henry. You can't miss Henry. He weighs 32 stone. His shadow weighs more than I do. He's two sizes smaller than Asia."

Occasionally he was just abusive:

"To put it kindly, she's plain. She's so plain she gets obscene phone calls from a man who reverses the charges – and she accepts. Her mother had to tie a pork chop around her neck before the dog would play with her."

"When I was young we were very poor and my mother used to shop at the war surplus stores. Let me tell you it wasn't much fun for a nine-year-old Jewish kid from the East End to have to go to school dressed in a Japanese admiral's uniform."

"It's a great pleasure to introduce a young man who has just finished cabaret in the north, and he's now here to finish it in the south."

"We had Miles Davis in the club last week, he was very kind. He took me to one side.... and left me there"

"Tony Crombie is deputising tonight for our regular drummer, Jackie Dougan, who has unfortunately been taken suddenly drunk."

"If you've enjoyed yourself half as much as we have then we've enjoyed ourselves twice as much as you have."

"Thank you. You've made a happy man very old. Meanwhile, why don't you all get pissed?"

Ronnie Scott died in December 1996. I was one of the thousand people braving the cold at his funeral – he was missed.

CHAPTER 13

THE RED LIGHT DISTRICT

At the end of January 1971, lead vocalist Linda Hoyle and Hammond organist Lynton Naiff, having both given a month's notice, quit Affinity – the band they had been with for two and a half years – to go their separate ways. It was an amicable split.

ENGAGEMENTS WANTED

9d. per word

Minimum 3/-

A ABLE accordionist. — 876 4542.

A ABLE pianist. — 876 4542.

ALL SAXOPHONES, clarinet, flute, PA, gigs, residency. — 01-907 3112.

A YOUNG lead alto/clar experience theatre, ballroom, seeks top class work. — 021-444 4583.

BASS/DRUMMER (both sing), require work with pro group, anything considered, must have work. — Tel Southend 44376 or 526315.

BASS GUITAR, experienced. gigs. — 574 4967.

BASS GUITAR/vocalist doubling tenor saxophone/clarinet, with girl guitar vocalist, solo/harmony singing. — 01 274 3624.

BASS GUITAR. Guitar, vocals. Experienced. — 542 2389.

BASS GTR., gigs, — Gerrards Cross 85050.

BASS-GUITARIST, ex-name group, wishes to join established Family / Colosseum / Traffic type group. — 946 4542.

BASS GUITARIST vocalist. — Phone 527 4653.

BASS GUITAR. musician. — 574 4967.

BASS. (Ken. — Daytime). — 226 0570.

CAPABLE HAMMOND organist, own instrument, read, busk, with or without drummer/vocalist, seeks worthwhile summer season, replies answered. — Box 75.

DEDICATED BLUES/jazz guitarist seeks ambitious group. Has transport. — Orpington 32773.

DEDICATED DRUMMER / Vocals, good gear / image, etc — 552 8443.

DRUMMER, ABLE, experienced gigs, residency. — 570 7362.

DRUMMER — all styles — gigs/sessions/residency. — London / Surrey. — Downland (71) 52131.

DRUMMER A1 experienced etc. (28), works for money. — 607 2347 (evenings), 387-7030 Ext. 556, (day). Des Lawn. Also, seeks summer season

The Melody Maker advert that changed my life

With Affinity I had spent almost three years playing high-energy jazz-rock. When Linda and Lynton left the band, Mike, Grant, and I made the decision, after some discussion, to keep the name Affinity going, and to try to continue as a performing and recording entity. It was not an easy task, since finding replacements for Linda and Lynton – both of whom were superb musicians – was necessarily a challenge.

Affinity had first met Vivienne McAuliffe at Exeter University whilst playing one of our last gigs with the original line-up. She had been lead vocalist with the college band, Principal Edwards Magic Theatre (c'mon, it was the sixties!)

Back in London the band held a set of tortuous auditions but it soon became clear that Vivienne – with her crystal-clear voice and outgoing personality – was the only possible choice to replace Linda. She became one of the lads.

At about this time ex-Tornados keyboard player Dave Watts answered an advert in *Melody Maker* and brought with him not only his own Hammond organ but also an impish sense of humour. Within minutes he slotted into the band banter and, as soon as he played, the guys knew he was the right man. (Six months later – as we travelled down the M1 after a gig, and without any warning – Dave broke the silence and, in his South London accent made this surprising claim: "I bet you £5 that I can do 50 farts in 5 minutes." It was the kind of challenge that needed to be tested. To our incredulity he won the bet! What amazed me was how he had kept that talent a secret – I'd have told everybody within the first week.)

Unlike Linda – whose voice was jazz-tinged – Vivienne's voice was higher-pitched and more folky – in the style of Sonja Kristina of Curved Air.

The band initially adapted some of their older material, but they mainly set out to write and rehearse new songs with Vivienne in mind: Mike spent some time composing and refining material with songwriter B.A. Robertson whilst I wrote with Vivienne herself.

There was soon enough material for a whole new set and UK college gigs and club dates soon followed. But sadly, as quickly as the musicians had come together, there were problems, and the band – crippled by debt and lack of direction – eventually fragmented. Affinity had ended.

It was 1971; I was without work, and panicking. Should I go back to science? Computing perhaps? (I'd done a course at university). Music? My problem was that I knew almost no one in the music industry (which is quite distinct from "music"). In desperation I put an advert in *Melody Maker*, the usual kind of thing: "Engagements Wanted – Bass Player, Ex-Name Group, etc", but I could only afford for it to be in for one week. It was answered by Chris Demetriou, the producer for ex-Manfred Mann singer Mike d'Abo, who was looking for new musicians. It still amazes me that the only week he chose to look at the adverts, mine was the only one he called! The next day – along with the wonderful drummer Henry Spinetti – I auditioned for Mike at a small rehearsal room in Mayfair. And that was the start of our friendship.

In the early seventies the new genre of singer/songwriter was epitomised by performers such as Elton John, Joni Mitchell, and Jackson Brown, and it was clear that Mike fitted into that world. We played a few gigs, and began work on an album at Trident Studios (where Affinity had previously recorded). It was a lovely challenge for me to have to invent melodic bass parts over Mike's sophisticated chord changes.

At about this time I also felt that it was important – and long overdue – to learn to read music, and forced myself to attend Saturday morning rehearsals of the National Youth Jazz Orchestra (NYJO) at the Cockpit Theatre. I was ten years older than most of the other players, and whilst my reading did improve a little, I still found the experience to be acutely embarrassing.

Dave Watts introduced us to American R&B singer Geno Washington, who had been stationed in England with the US air force. We eventually toured the UK with Geno and his Ram Jam Band, where I discovered how to play soul, rhythm & blues, and funk for the first time. It was a fun band. I also discovered how Geno held on to his musicians – by always owing them £5.

At the invitation of cornetist Marc Charig, I had the privilege of jamming at the 100 Club in Oxford Street with South African musicians such as saxophonist Dudu Pukwana, trumpeter Mongezi Feza, and drummer Louis Moholo. It was a night of African jazz-rock. It was joyous. Music is a delightful unifier of culture and class. As trombonist Derek Wadsworth said: "The world of the musician is the most egalitarian society there is."

THE RED LIGHT DISTRICT – "GOOD LUCK, STUDIO"

Slowly these connections began to make sense because towards the end of that year I got a surprise call from Polydor Records for what was to be my first recording session – for singer Barry Ryan, produced by Wayne Bickerton at Lansdowne Studios in London. I didn't find out until much later that their original choice of bass player – Rod Demick – couldn't make the date, and I am forever indebted to this man without whose absence I may not have had a studio career.

I knew nothing about sessions or how they worked, and I thought it would be a good idea to familiarise myself with a few technical terms – signs, codas, repeats, etc – and I spent the evening prior to the session trying to digest a copy of the Associated Board's *Rudiments and Theory of Music*. It was just like the night before a driving test. I took with me my Fender Jazz bass, a Fender Twin amp that I'd borrowed from Affinity's Mike Jopp, a flask of coffee and some sandwiches.

I couldn't possibly have met a friendlier bunch of musicians on my first date: drummer Clem Cattini, guitarist Ray Fenwick, pianist Mike Moran, and percussionist Ray Cooper (I'd never played with a percussionist before – especially someone as brilliant as Ray). They thought that the flask and sandwiches were a bit odd, but soon put me at ease with their daft humour and, to my great relief, they seemed to enjoy my playing. Fortunately, I was given only a chord chart – I couldn't really read a dot yet.

I remember thinking: "I've come home." It was as if I had spent the whole of my life waiting to meet those people, in that building. And, as a remarkable bonus, I discovered that I could earn in a three-hour session the same amount that I used to earn in a week with the band. Hmm.

Since that fateful day, a vast chunk of my professional life has been involved with working in and around recording studios, both as a player and a producer, working with many of the musicians who were key players in the three decades of studio supremacy. I am privileged that many of these exceptional artists are now my friends.

BASS PRACTICER

It was at around this time that I built a device designed to help me learn to play the bass guitar with my fingers, and not just a pick. The "bass-practicer" consisted of a six-inch piece of wood, one string, one tuning peg, and a jack plug casing for a bridge, held in place by two nails. It fitted perfectly in the huge pocket of my ex-Swedish army officer's coat and as I rhythmically plucked the solitary string it definitely helped me to develop hard calluses on my fingertips. I had to be careful, though, since the repetitive motion of my hand inside my coat could easily have been misinterpreted.

The Bass Practicer

THE SESSION SCENE

Session musicians were a strange bunch. Very few of them began their career in music with the intention of becoming a studio player; it was just something that happened along the way. Between the 1950s and 1970s, the number of rhythm section players who did all the work in Britain was very small, maybe two or three hundred guys at the most and only four women, who all happened to be keyboard players. Everybody tended to know everybody else. This world wasn't as closed as it may have seemed to those trying to get in, but it was selective. If a new musician appeared on the scene with something special – whether it was a sound, a feel, a sight-reading ability, a new technique, or just pure musicality – then he or she would be welcomed in.

A sense of humour was a prerequisite to survive the long hours and to fend off the stream of wind-ups and ironic jibes that were part of the job. It was hard work but great fun. ("Laughter occurs when people are comfortable with one another, when they feel open and free" – a quote from an article in *New Scientist* by Mahadev Apte, a cultural anthropologist at Duke University in Durham, North Carolina.)

There was no accepted route into studio work, just as there was no A-level in session playing. Rather, it was the music colleges, dance bands, brass bands, rock and jazz groups that were the most likely starting points, and many musicians who studied their instrument legitimately have stated that they learned most of what they now know at gigs and in nightclubs. It was certainly good enough for Miles Davis, who eschewed the Juilliard College of Music for the jazz clubs of Harlem and 42nd Street, New York City.

Sessions were well paid, and in the golden years there were plenty of them, mostly taking place in studios all over central London. The trade-off was that the session musician was expected to play anything that was required of him. This meant that he had to have a good working knowledge of almost every musical style of the previous 30 years or more, he had to be a fluent sight-reader and had to be able to improvise a part from a chord chart while instantly and consistently sounding great.

These are, of course, massive demands, and some guys couldn't handle it at all. They suffered from acute "red-light disease" – they fell to pieces as soon as the tape was rolling. Others couldn't stand the music itself, and got out as soon as they could to avoid offending their ears any further. Those who stayed the course were rewarded, not just financially but also with the joy of playing with a huge variety of great players. As a bass player playing three or even four separate sessions in one day, during that day it was sometimes possible to play with three or four different drummers. It was exciting, challenging, and always a wonderful source of new jokes.

One extra facet of playing with a four- or five-piece rhythm section together in the studio was that, between takes, impromptu jamming would sometimes occur. Like a private jazz gig, it was a time for risk-taking and experimentation, and this informal playing became a useful safety valve if the main music wasn't particularly demanding. In time, many of the same faces would be present on every session, giving rise to the spontaneous evolution of small "teams" of players. Jimmy Page and John Paul Jones met in this way, and went on to form Led Zeppelin; Alan Parker, Herbie Flowers and Barry Morgan coalesced into Blue Mink; Tristan Fry, Steve Gray, Herbie Flowers and Kevin Peake conceived Sky; and as a result of playing together on countless sessions, Ray Russell, Simon Phillips and I formed RMS, starting work on our album at Trident Studios in Soho in the downtime of another project on which we had all been working.

As well as the music, the players had to respond to the producer, the artist, and the engineer. On a really bad day, if the music was terrible, the producer was clueless, the artist was a pompous oaf and the engineer hadn't slept the night before, the players would pull together and try to play their best, although the result was often less than exciting.

On some sessions, during the first two or three takes of a piece of music, the various players would experiment with the part. Different tempi would be tried and riffs added, and these embellishments would invariably improve upon the original arrangement.

One of the responsibilities of a producer is to know when a take is the definitive take. For example, take four might be great but have a terrible mistake in it, while take six might be technically perfect but have begun to lose its freshness. A good producer would probably choose take five, or patch up take four. A duff producer would be on take ten and still not be happy. Here the conspiracy would begin with looks and glances. The musicians would assemble as usual in the control room to listen to the playback of the last recording. Some would be slumped in chairs, some leaning on the mixing desk, while others stared through the window at the empty studio. As the music filled the room one by one we would start tapping our feet, swaying to the rhythm and enthusiastically murmuring "That's the one," until eventually – and incredibly – the producer would believe us. We would have known it was on tape half an hour ago, while he would never know.

Conversely, a creative and articulate producer, a talented artist and beautiful music would inspire the musicians to gel and to play the written line with feeling, and generate novel riffs and ideas from a chord chart. If the sound in the room was just right, the engineer had taken the trouble to put inspirational reverb in the cans and the musicians were the best, then a "take in one" was possible.

Everyone would be reading, but also listening with great intensity to everyone else; the track would "breathe" and have a vibrant quality. Many famous records sound as good as they do precisely because the musicians playing together on that day generated something quite special between them. In later years, these session players began quite rightly to be credited on album sleeves – a recognition that had been long overdue. As engineer and studio industry legend Adrian Kerridge recalls: "They were perfectionists at their craft and played their hearts out."

SMOKING

Recent years have seen a massive improvement in the environmental health provisions of many studios. Like major corporations, recording and broadcasting studios have imposed blanket bans on smoking anywhere on their premises. Back in the 1960s, however, this was far from the norm. Judd Procter's main recollections of the period are

Judd Procter – the fastest left hand in the business – at Decca Studio Two

not only that musicians all dressed smartly, often in suits and ties, but also that everyone smoked. Adrian Kerridge began engineering at IBC in 1955 and moved to Lansdowne in 1959 with Joe Meek. He remembers control rooms of the day as being "small, very smoky and overheated (everything was valves), with nicotine on every surface. And everyone worked long hours."

Ernie Shear

In his native Scotland, Ernie Shear had played ukulele before progressing to guitar. He came to London, studied, and took lessons from Ivor Mairants prior to joining a succession of big bands led by Lou Stone and Joe Loss. With these bands he played a Gibson 400, while his first amp was a Vortexion. Slowly, he entered the session scene and got to know other players, such as Bert Weedon and Vic Flick. Judd Procter also remembers that, at one time, Ernie and his brother had a double act called Shear Nonsense!

Bryan Daly

At the same time that Bryan Daly began to teach guitar at the Ivor Mairants Music School, he was also making his first inroads into a life as a recording musician. The early 1960s marked the beginning of a period when guitar players were in great demand. No longer were they the last to be hired and the first to be fired, and Bryan remembers that those who persevered for the love of it were now getting a return for their dedication. "There were now changes taking place at a furious pace. I started working in music in so many different ways, such as playing in the orchestra for *West Side Story*, which was a sensational musical with a really superb score. I was teaching, playing television shows, broadcasting, and was just starting to do some studio work. I played on the first BBC *6.5 Special* with Pete Murray as the presenter, and I came to meet Jack Good, who became a producer in his own right with his legendary rock 'n' roll productions, on which I also played. Through Jack I became involved with his artists' recordings. He always insisted on having his 'own men' to play on these sessions, for artists such as Billy Fury, Joe Brown and Gene Vincent. I'll always remember Eddie Cochran, and we were all much saddened by his death."

Bryan, who in the 1980s diversified as a TV presenter and also wrote the hit theme song for the children's

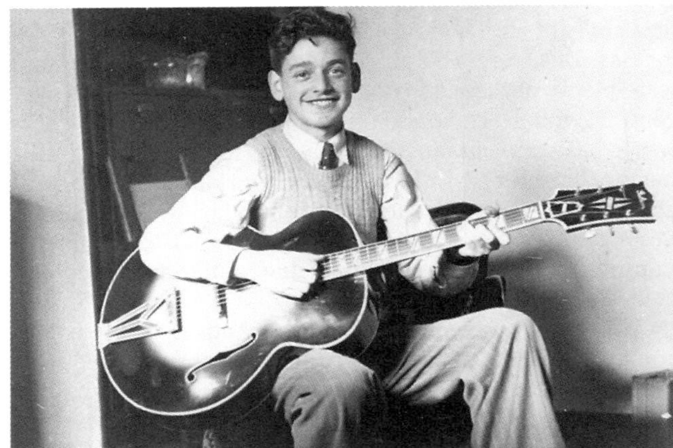

15-year-old Glasgow guitarist Ernie Shear 'gate-crashed' a rehearsal of Oscar Rabin's band at the Playhouse – and kept the job

Bryan Daly and Eric Ford on the 6-5 Special backing up Eddie Cochran

programme *Postman Pat*, adds: "We started making recordings day and night, and it had developed into a business of great potency, especially for the London musicians, who were highly regarded. Stars were born. Some burned out like a Roman candle, but others stayed the test of time and their work is still being played. Records, both singles and albums, started to sell by the million. When The Beatles came along, in one year they produced more revenue than British Steel. The artists on whose records we worked became a "Who's Who" of the record business from that period. Many of the contributions from the session musicians became part of the success of particular recordings. Some of the well-known groups would use session musicians to make their recordings for them, and if they were hits they would mime to the recordings for television shows. Later, this practice was stopped. One group, Blue Mink, was very different and was actually formed by session players realising the potential of their own playing."

Eric Ford, with Ronnie Verrall on drums

Eric Ford

The list of session credits amassed by guitarist Eric Ford from the late 1950s until his death in 1994 appears to be virtually endless. Hits by The Allisons, P.J. Proby, Eden Kane, Craig Douglas, Edison Lighthouse, Love Affair, The Fortunes, Frank Ifield, Kathy Kirby, Chris Farlowe, The New Vaudeville Band, Tom Jones, David Bowie, Hot Chocolate, and a multitude of Mickie Most productions form just a small part of his great contribution to pop music. Percussionist Stan Barratt once said: "Eric was so adaptable – that's why he got all the work," and arranger Ray Davies observes: "It would be easier to find out which records he wasn't on." Less obvious, however was his background influence on the growing popularity of the guitar in the 1950s.

Of the colossal workload both enjoyed and tolerated by session musicians, Eric comments: "In the recording studio, a typical day would start at 10 a.m., and our first session would run through until 1 p.m. We would rehearse around four titles for the first half an hour; the engineer would get a balance and we would do a couple of takes of each. There would be another session from 2.30 p.m. until 5.30 p.m., and then another evening one from 7 p.m. until 10 p.m. If the pressure was really on we would work well past midnight and into the early hours."

As one of only a handful of competent guitarists in London, Eric soon found himself summoned to appear on BBC TV's *6.5 Special*, deputising for regular Frantic Five member Terry Walsh, and also augmenting the band when a fluent reader was needed. The real turning point came in August 1958 when two guys marched into Selmer's where Eric was working and asked him if he would be interested in a 13-week series on ABC TV (the UK independent forerunner of Rediffusion and, in London, Thames TV). Full-time rehearsals would be needed, however and the job

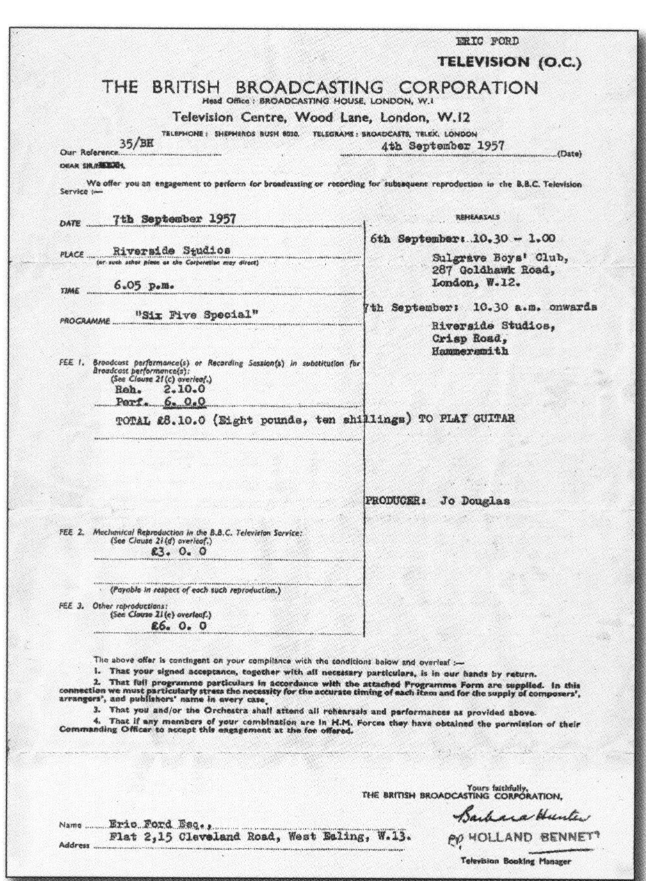
ERIC FORD

TELEVISION (O.C.)

THE BRITISH BROADCASTING CORPORATION

Head Office: BROADCASTING HOUSE, LONDON, W.1

Television Centre, Wood Lane, London, W.12

TELEPHONE: SHEPHERDS BUSH 8030. TELEGRAMS: BROADCASTS, TELEX, LONDON

Our Reference 35/BH — 4th September 1957 (Date)

DEAR SIR,

We offer you an engagement to perform for broadcasting or recording for subsequent reproduction in the B.B.C. Television Service:—

DATE 7th September 1957

PLACE Riverside Studios (or such other place as the Corporation may direct)

TIME 6.05 p.m.

PROGRAMME "Six Five Special"

REHEARSALS

6th September: 10.30 – 1.00
Sulgrave Boys' Club,
287 Goldhawk Road,
London, W.12.

7th September: 10.30 a.m. onwards
Riverside Studios,
Crisp Road,
Hammersmith

FEE 1. Broadcast performance(s) or Recording Session(s) in substitution for Broadcast performance(s):
(See Clause 21(c) overleaf.)
Reh. 2.10.0
Perf. 6. 0.0
TOTAL £8.10.0 (Eight pounds, ten shillings) TO PLAY GUITAR

PRODUCER: Jo Douglas

FEE 2. Mechanical Reproduction in the B.B.C. Television Service:
(See Clause 21(d) overleaf.)
£3. 0. 0
(Payable in respect of each such reproduction.)

FEE 3. Other reproductions:
(See Clause 21(e) overleaf.)
£6. 0. 0

The above offer is contingent on your compliance with the conditions below and overleaf:—

1. That your signed acceptance, together with all necessary particulars, is in our hands by return.
2. That full programme particulars in accordance with the attached Programme Form are supplied. In this connection we must particularly stress the necessity for the accurate timing of each item and for the supply of composers', arrangers', and publishers' name in every case.
3. That you and/or the Orchestra shall attend all rehearsals and performances as provided above.
4. That if any members of your combination are in H.M. Forces they have obtained the permission of their Commanding Officer to accept this engagement at the fee offered.

Yours faithfully,
THE BRITISH BROADCASTING CORPORATION,
Barbara Hunter
pp HOLLAND BENNETT
Television Booking Manager

Name Eric Ford Esq.,
Address Flat 2,15 Cleveland Road, West Ealing, W.13.

Eric Ford's contract for the BBC TV show 6-5 Special on 7 Sept 1957 at the shop would have to go. The guys were Jack Good and Harry Robinson, and the show was to be called *Oh Boy* (ABC had craftily poached Jack Good away from *6.5 Special*.) Wisely, Eric took the plunge and became a founder member of the house band, Lord Rockingham's XI.

In the early 1960s, Eric pursued a career in broadcasting and appeared regularly on BBC Light programmes, such as *Saturday Club* and *Easy Beat* as a member of Arthur Greenslade's G-Men, and the lunchtime show *Go Man Go* featuring the David Ede Band with 'the grooving guitar of Don Sanford' and 'Rocking' Rex Morris on saxes. Eric teamed up with drummer Dougie Wright, bassist Alan Weighell, and Big Jim Sullivan to form the rhythm section, which backed solo artists on Rediffusion's *Ready Steady Go*. However after the rival *Top of the Pops* was launched in January 1964, Eric returned to the BBC and joined Johnny Pearson's *Top of the Pops* orchestra – a job which lasted through until 1981.

Vic Flick

During his time with The John Barry Seven, Vic Flick soon found his distinctive sound in demand for studio dates beyond those he did as part of Barry's group. He assisted in the hit-making processes of Henry Mancini, Burt Bacharach, Adam Faith, Diana Ross, Tom Jones, Herman's

Vic Flick in the studio

Vic Flick's legendary amplifier: the Fender Vibrolux

Hermits and Tony Hatch, for whose original 1964 *Crossroads* TV theme he recorded the melody on his Vox electric twelve-string, with Bryan Daly on rhythm guitar.

"Versatility in the studio was essential," says Vic, "so I always carried a Stratocaster, a Les Paul, a Martin D-28 acoustic, an Ibanez gut-string, a twelve-string Epiphone and a banjo in case of emergencies. The original guitar for the Bond sessions was a big, blonde f-hole Clifford Essex acoustic with a De Armond pickup, with which I used my usual Fender Vibrolux amp and an assortment of archaic pedals. [Studio boss and engineer] Adrian Kerridge always wanted my Vibrolux amp due to its major role in British pop history, having featured on so many early 1960s films and records. He wanted to build a glass box on a wall in Lansdowne Studios to preserve the amp for posterity.

"For many years there was so much work that three and even four sessions a day was normal, day in and day out, every week. Record companies expected as many as five or six songs be cut in a single three-hour session, and then you would head to another studio to repeat the process."

One of the big hits of the late 1960s to be recorded in Decca Studio Two with Vic on guitar was Tom Jones' "Delilah" (1968). Vic remembers: "As happened in those days, things were left to the last minute, and Peter Sullivan, the producer, asked Tom to come over and sing the first couple of lines of the chorus with the guitar. With his mouth two inches from my ear he bellowed out those hallowed words. I walked round in circles for two weeks with my eyes crossed after that."

Brian Odgers

With his bass guitar knowledge, Brian 'Badger' Odgers moved into the session scene and became one of the most prolific musicians, sometimes playing on as many as 30 sessions in a week. In 1972, he was first on the studio scene to have a fretless Fender Precision. I recently told Badger the story of how, in 1976, I was called to a session at

Brian Odgers in the studio

Olympic One (the big room) for Andrew Lloyd Webber. I opened the large studio door, peeked in, and was surprised to find no one there. Panic! Was this the wrong day? No, it was okay. Andrew explained to me that they had been recording tracks for an album, which would eventually become known as *Evita*. He said: "We already have a bass on these tracks but we're not sure about it. Do you think you could improve on it?" This was embarrassing, because I knew it was Badger on the tape, but I had to play something, so quite randomly I selected about half the album to play on. Brian didn't mind. We were both paid, after all. It's a bit demoralising, but it happens all the time now – the price of indecision.

Chris Rae

To his utmost surprise and pleasure, Chris Rae enjoyed an all-expenses-paid holiday when he was booked at a special fee for 18 sessions at the now-defunct Manor Studios in Oxfordshire. Whereas Badger was absent from some of the *Evita* tracks because of my arrival, Chris was missing from his session tapes because he was down the pub!

"The producer had also booked Martin and Philip Kershaw (sons of Eric Kershaw, the author of the tutor *Dance Band Chords for the Guitar*) to play on the tracks. Martin is an excellent player with a fabulous technique, who could tend to be busy; Philip was roaring about; and I was again thrashing the guts out of my wah-wah pedal. When I listened to the 'take' it sounded like a guitar war! I quietly spoke to the producer (who had sandbag shoes on to keep himself on the ground because of the large amounts of illegal substances that he tended to consume). I said: 'As it's so busy, why not put the guitars on one at a time so that we could all knit in with one another?' He said: 'Good idea,' and promptly suggested it to the band, asking who wanted to go first. Being young and keen, Philip said he would go first, and it was at this point I started my all-expenses-paid holiday and drove out to a particular country pub where, after a few hours of drinking, I would fall in love with the landlady.

"Being extremely worse for wear by the end of the day, the Manor would send a car for me so I could have dinner with the other musicians. I think it was only on the last day that they realised I hadn't played a note. I think they felt more guilty than I did. Anyway, they asked me to play guitar on one number. I think I just played on the middle eight, and I bet they lost that in the mix!"

Colin Green

Although technically primitive in the 1960s, the studio looked and felt wonderful to a young guy like Colin Green, who hadn't seen anything like it before. "The nice thing I recall is that you were paid in cash at the door as you walked in (£6 per session). That system went on for some years. EMI was the last company to do it when the accountant got mugged!"

Colin Green in the studio

SESSION RATES

Terry Walsh remembers that the standard rate for a three-hour session in 1955 was £4/10/- (£4.50), while a TV session was £6. Jim Sullivan says that in 1960 the gramophone rate was £7, and it was Jim who introduced the idea of porterage for bringing several guitars. The session rate rose in the mid 1960s to £9, and was £12 when I started in 1971. The basic Musicians' Union rate is now approximately £150.

JARGON

Session players acquired their own rhyming slang – for example:

Desperates:	Desperate Dans Cans (Headphones)
Norwegians:	Norwegian Fjords Chords
Belgians:	Belgian Congos Bongos
Chinese Dentist:	Tooth-Hurty Two-thirty (2.30)
Spanish Archer:	El Bow (Elbow) Fired

HEADPHONES

This kind of code can go horribly awry if you're not comfortable with it. One novice lady singer wanted to pass a message to the engineer that her vocals were too loud in her headphones: "Will you ask the mechanic for less vocal in the tins?" She also threatened him with "Spanish Elbow".

Some cans have a plug-in lead, which occasionally falls out if one little screw is missing. The change in sound would normally be obvious to the wearer, but after a long day in the studio it's possible for the musician to cease to be aware of the headphones at all. This effect was demonstrated on one memorable occasion when the whole band broke from a long and exhausting session at Lansdowne to go to the nearby pub for a well-earned pint. One musician, oblivious of the fact that he was still wearing his headphones, strode into the bar looking a bit like a confused World War II fighter pilot. Exhibiting great control, not one of his friends told him, and they chatted happily away for the next half an hour.

Saxophonist Ronnie Asprey, who played with Colin Hodgkinson in Back Door, used to bring two tenor cases to sessions, one for his sax and the other for a row of Newcastle Brown beers. While setting up the foldback on a session at Advision Studio one day, the engineer asked Ronnie: "How are your cans?" Ronnie, who was enjoying a pre-session drink, stared at the evidence on display and replied: "Well, at the moment there's one down and I'm halfway through a second."

TEN TO TEN

Drummers seem to have a rhythmic language of their own to communicate with other musicians and producers when describing drum patterns. For example, in jazz a triplet-feel ride cymbal pattern sounds like "ten to ten"; in seventies disco the opening and closing of the hi-hat was referred to as a "pea soup"; on sessions, simple snare and tom-tom fills would be "flats in Dagenham" or "duck-billed platypus", or even "disc gone platinum"; more complicated fills involving tom-toms might be indicated as "catching the taxi home" or "popadom, popadom, rogan gosh", the last word being the crash cymbal. Another fill with emphasis on the crash is "wobbly tits" (thank you, Jason), and a fill which starts with a long press roll, goes round many toms and ends with a crash is "I reeeeeally hope – the gigs get better and better and better – and we all make lots of cash" (thank you, Graham). But my favourite, for its simplicity, is "Kate Bush". These, of course, are all improvements on Reg Presley's "dubba, dubba, dubba, cha" from the legendary "Troggs' Tapes".

Bob Dylan

Speaking of Reg, he was once sitting in a London studio, strumming on a twelve-string guitar, when he was chanced upon by Bob Dylan, who had been recording in another studio in the same building. In a gesture of friendliness, Bob asked in his nasal East Coast accent: "How long have you been playing the guitar, man?" In a strong Andover accent, Reg replied: "All fucking day, mate."

PEDALS

On recording sessions you were paid a session fee, porterage for transport expenses, an overdub fee if you recorded on top of your own performance and a doubling fee when required to play more than one instrument (e.g., guitar and mandolin).

In the 1970s, when effects pedals such as fuzz, phaser, wah-wah, and envelope filter began to proliferate, we discovered that by using one it could be treated as a double, because it created a new sound. Have you ever wondered why 1970s records had so many effects on them? Answer: the guitarists received an additional 25 per cent of the session fee and were getting rich! I was determined to join in, and had a pedal built for me which had nothing in it: a "DFA" pedal. On a few occasions I actually got paid for switching on a box whose only effect was to convince some idiot producer that he was getting value for money.

On a session a violinist objected that guitarist Paul Keogh could charge a doubling fee merely by switching on a pedal. Paul's reply was simple and pragmatic: "Get a pedal."

In the early seventies I became aware of a wonderful new, rich, fat, sustaining bass sound made by the Moog synthesiser. Artists such as Stevie Wonder and The Beach

Boys used it to great effect and – because at that time I couldn't play keyboard – I was determined to try to emulate it on bass guitar. The only pedal that came anywhere near it was the Mu-Tron envelope follower which I used a lot, but it was never as good as the real thing. Nowadays – with a programmable midi-interface – amp-modelling, synth sounds, effects, and octaves are all instantly available at the press of a foot switch.

Ten years before, effects pedals were in their infancy, with generally only the wah-wah and fuzzbox available. A hit in the summer of 1964, Dave Berry's "The Crying Game" was notable for its distinctive guitar sound, which, contrary to popular belief, was not created with a wah-wah but the older DeArmond foot pedal. Eric Ford explains: "When you moved the pedal to the left it made the tone more bassy and to the right more toppy but we discovered that if you moved it quickly from left to right and back again you got that sort of weeping sound. Jim Sullivan did the lead on that one and I played the rhythm guitar. I liked the sound so much that I used it again on Donovan's 'Sunshine Superman' when I was doing the lead part."

Vic Flick

During a broadcast session in the mid 1960s at the BBC's studios in Piccadilly, Vic Flick, having been alerted by the instructions on the music chart in front of him to use distortion, brought out of his bag a new foot pedal. At the appropriate moment in the song, Vic purposefully stomped his foot to the floor and switched on one of the very first fuzzboxes in London – an event. The producer, who was not schooled in these new sounds, erupted from the control room: "What is that noise?" "Distortion," said Vic, innocently. "I will not have distortion on the BBC!" raged the producer, supported by the might of BBC engineering ignorance.

Terry Walsh

Not all producers were as narrow-minded. Terry Walsh remembers: "If I did an ad-lib solo, the producer would say to me: 'Too nice. Can you rough it up a bit?' I'd spent hundreds of pounds on an amp that didn't distort, and then had to buy a pedal that did!"

Eric Clapton

When it came to overdriven guitar sounds in the mid 1960s, there were few people to touch Eric Clapton, who was earning a reputation for his high-volume playing, even in the studios where guitarists would normally be recorded at extremely tame levels. Engineer Keith Grant, the owner of Olympic Sound Studios in Barnes, in southwest London, recalls his first experience of the guitar legend. "He was in studio one, playing through a circle of Marshall stacks, with him standing in the middle. The studio was so well soundproofed that it was impossible to even hear Boeing 747s roaring overhead on their descent to nearby Heathrow Airport. On this day, Clapton's guitar playing could be heard in the Red Lion pub 100 yards away on the other side of the road."

Gus Dudgeon

Producer Gus Dudgeon was another to be confronted by Eric's colossal sound, when he engineered John Mayall's famous *Blues Breakers* album in Decca Studio Two in 1966. He set up the studio in the normal way, with screens and booths ready for the various instruments, and Clapton was first to arrive, asking: "Where do you want my amp?" Gus pointed at an area between a couple of screens, to which Eric said: "I don't want to be quiet, like on Yardbirds sessions. I want to let rip." So he set up where he wanted to.

Through the glass dividing the studio from the control room, Gus could hear an incredible wailing sound as Eric checked his gear and started practising. Gus suggested to producer Mike Vernon that he should talk to Eric about the problems of such volume, but Eric was adamant.

As Gus put up various faders during the session he could hear guitar leaking onto everything, it was so loud. Mike and Gus reasoned that the only way to solve this was to do a take, and then gauge Eric's response to a playback. They recorded the first title, called the guys into the control room, and rolled the tape. Gus says: "Eric loved it and he grinned from ear to ear. He took on the rules and broke them."

DISCO

When modern disco started in the 1970s there were no proper drum machines, sequencers or computers to take the pain out of playing endless repetitive music. That four-to-the-bar bass drum was actually played for those ten or fifteen minutes. On the Trident Studio sessions, the tempo was invariably 120 beats per minute, and after a whole day of it the musicians couldn't help but walk to the pub at 120 footsteps per minute.

The rhythm section got a shock on one session when we noticed that the part was a fairly complicated eight-bar-long riff with repeat brackets round it. This wouldn't normally have been a problem, but on this occasion there was an instruction to repeat the eight bars 80 times! That's a lot of counting. Of course, it was impossible. For the first few minutes everyone was out of view, counting and concentrating, behind their music stands. At around the 50th repeat, doubts crept in, and eyes began to rise over the tops of the stands like submarine periscopes. Eyes can say a lot. These eyes were saying, "Help! where the fuck are we?"

Les Hurdle

Bassist Les Hurdle had already been on the session scene for some years when he began to earn a reputation for being one of the top disco players. He was on many a session in Munich which, in the mid to late seventies, became the capital of European disco. "I was there on the day that disco and tendonitis for bass players was invented! That darn octave line... Oh well, it paid for a few very nice vacations, but it did end a career, a marriage and a way of life. Funny how people always misunderstood disco. With the right rhythm section it actually swung, but it meant really being in time – not easy for some.

"One early misty morning, I was called to a jingle session. What a thrill – more octaves. The arranger, Graham, was obviously going to rewrite disco with jazzy chords and bass-lines that swung like lead balloons. The piece didn't work, but as usual it was the musos' fault. Dragging our butts into the control room, the producer shouted at us. I asked if I might change the part, but he didn't like that so I played the line. The producer dragged us back into the box and complained: 'It sounds terrible'. He wanted the track, and especially the bass part, to sound like some damn German guy, and held up a Donna Summer record. I asked who the German guy was. He said: 'Les Hurdle'. Shocked, I said, 'You're looking at him. Same bass, same fingers, your piece of wire to the desk.' One more take and it was the end of the session. I never saw either the producer or Graham, the arranger, again.

"I ran around the world doing the disco thing. Great fun, good friends, and Jim Beam. Off to Paris one wet day, the flight left London late, but the 'disco team' would surely be on the gig. I got to the studio, wet, cold, hungry, where there was no 'disco team' but a huge orchestra. 'Sorry,' I said to deaf ears. 'The weather, you know.' Oh well, tough it out. Rule Britannia and all that. Plug in, tune up, and don't open the music. Be brave, you're a pro. I was convincing myself. Anyway you invented disco, how hard can it be? The French conductor snorted at me and, baton held up, he counted. I flipped the page over to show them. Oh shit. What the hell is Me-5 and La diminished? Tonic sol-fah is like Nashville numbers or 'H' in Germany: great if you know them, but it's sure embarrassing if you don't!"

(I was aware that the German "H" translates as "B" in English notation. Seeking clarification I later asked a German musician friend of mine what 'H' stood for. His reply – "horseshit" – was interesting, if not illuminating – Mo.)

CARTAGE

Roadies were the lifeblood of the session musician. They specialised in moving guitars, basses, amps and drums from session to session, all over town, sometimes working for several musicians at once. In LA and New York they had dedicated "cartage" companies. In London in the seventies we had... Terry. This one guy did *everything*!

London Transport poster: The Musician (1930)

Terry Jones

Terry Jones began working for the percussion rental company Doc Hunt in the early 1970s, when he roadied for drummers and percussionists such as Clem Cattini, Ray Cooper, Tristan Fry, Ronnie Verrell, and Frank Ricotti. In time, and under pressure from other players, he eventually began to deliver instruments to studios for the whole rhythm section. People didn't think he'd last five minutes – in fact he continued for 14 years. It was a tough job, picking up the gear from one studio for four or more separate guys and delivering it to four or more quite separate studios, all between 1 p.m. and 2 p.m. The job – if indeed it still existed in the same form – would now be impossible, since London has become far too crowded. He started with a little green Bedford van and slowly worked up to a much larger Volkswagen LT35. One day he was delivering Graham Jarvis' drums to Odyssey Studios. He had been told to drop the kit in studio one, but should have been directed to the much smaller studio two. Nevertheless, he opened the door and his dog, Jasper, a border collie, shot through excitedly to be faced with a large orchestral session in mid-take. Jasper was happily running around the violins when Terry, embarrassed and anxious, tried to quietly call his dog back. The tape exits: if you lift the faders for the first violins and listen carefully during a quiet string passage, you can just hear: "Jasper... Jasper..."

Licorice Locking

If Terry had been on the scene in 1959 he might have saved Licorice Locking from an embarrassing incident featuring a borrowed amp and the perils of negotiating the London Underground. "The Wildcats were due to do a recording one particular night, and I distinctly remember asking the other bassist on our tour of one-night stands, Vince Cooze, if I could borrow his amplifier for the session at Philips Studios, Edgware Road," recalls Licorice. "Although his amplifier was also a home-made one, it was considerably better than my own. 'Yes,' he said, 'but at the moment it's at the left luggage department at King's Cross Station.' That meant I would not only have to cart this thing on the tube from King's Cross to Edgware Road, but also change at Leicester Square.

"So there I was, sweat, blood, and tears all rolled into one, carrying this dinosaur of a home-made amplifier on the tube. Everything was alright so far, and I finally managed to get it on the tube. 'Where can I put it,' I asked myself, 'so as not to hinder people getting on and off?' Eventually I got to Leicester Square. Crowds got off, so I picked up the amplifier and carried it just an inch or two from the ground, walking with practically tip-toe steps up the flight of stairs and through long corridors, stopping at various points for a brief rest. At last, the escalator came into view. Deftly, and with considerable difficulty and brute strength, I manoeuvred the amp onto the escalator and decided to lay the amp down and sit on it until I reached the top. The amp was on its side with most of it jutting out over the steps. So up we went, with me thinking: 'So far, so good. The last part of my journey to Edgware Road should be a doddle.'

"As I approached the top I stood up and turned around to lift the amp up, but it was too late! The amp tipped over and, before I could grab hold of it, it cartwheeled and bounced all the way down to the bottom, with pieces of wood and valves flying in all directions. Men, women and children were jumping on all sides. I just stood there, petrified, my face as white as a sheet until officials came and stopped the escalator from moving. I went sheepishly down and when I got to the bottom, what was left? Simply put: just firewood. So I collected this pile of wood and bits of metal with the speaker on top and walked to the top. An official said I could leave it next to his office, which I promptly did.

"I finally arrived at the recording studios without the amp. All I had to plug into was a small guitar amp and just hoped I didn't smash the speaker out of that one. I believe the recording was Marty Wilde's 'My Heart and I', which I have never heard from that day to this. That same night we were travelling to Scotland to do a gig at Caird Hall, Dundee. When I got there I explained the bad news to Vince Cooze. He just couldn't believe it. But all credit to Vince, he took it very well, and we shared another amp between us for the rest of the tour."

The Shadows (then The Drifters) at Abbey Road during the recording of Cliff's live album. L-r Norrie Paramour, Cliff Richard, Jet Harris, Tony Meehan, Hank Marvin, and Bruce Welch

ABBEY ROAD

Some studios have a pedigree, but none more so than EMI's famous Abbey Road, the world's first purpose-built studio. The Shadows spent 22 years recording at Abbey Road from 1958 to 1980. "It feels like home. We grew up here," says Bruce Welch. But when he first arrived on the recording scene, Bruce thought that Abbey Road resembled a hospital, with orderlies in white coats. In the early days of British rock 'n' roll, there was in fact a hierarchy of "coats" at the studio: white coats were worn by the technical staff; brown coats were the studio assistants, who moved equipment around and set up chairs; and blue coats were worn by those who cleared up.

There were aspirations to move up this ladder, but the real dream was to have no coat at all – to be a recording engineer, like Martin Benge who started at Abbey Road as a trainee and worked his way up to his position of managing director of the EMI group of studios, which also included the Townhouse and Olympic. Martin: "The desks at that time had only eight channels, so it was a challenge to record a live 40-piece band plus vocals, but if you asked the white coat politely he could organise another four channels. The EQ was minimal, only bass and treble, but we had great acoustics and great valve mics. We had a box called an RSI27, which Paul McCartney liked. It only worked at one frequency, 2.8kHz, and gave an edgy sound to vocals."

When bass guitars first appeared, the amplifiers brought in by the players were mostly terrible and unusable. To improve the sound, the studio engineers would set up a large green speaker, which was probably borrowed from the echo chamber. When The Beatles first recorded in Studio Two, Paul's Vox T-60 60-watt bass amp (with one 12-inch and one 15-inch speaker) was replaced for early sessions with a Tannoy speaker, powered by a Quad or Leak amp.

If there was one aspect that separated Abbey Road from other studios, it was its sometimes obstructive bureaucracy. Bruce Welch: "In February 1959, we recorded Cliff's debut album live in Studio Two in front of an invited audience of enthusiastic fans. Unfortunately, Cliff had laryngitis, but EMI went ahead anyway because they didn't want to cancel the catering!"

Studio Two has a special magic for me simply because of the enormous number of wonderful records that have been recorded in that space: records by The Beatles, The Temperance Seven, Peter Sellers, The Shadows, of course, and so many more. In 1995, Paul McCartney, George Harrison and Ringo Starr returned to Abbey Road for the first time in 25 years, during the mixing of The Beatles' *Anthology* albums, and upon entering Studio Two they headed like kids in a toy shop straight for a favourite old haunt: the sound props cupboard under the stairs, the home of ancient wind machines and strange percussion, as used especially on "Yellow Submarine".

THE DREADED DOTS

I first played in Studio Two on 8 September 1973 as part of a nine-strong rhythm section within a largish orchestra. Working under the American MD, composer David Rose, were Alan Parker and Colin Green on guitars, Harold Fisher on drums, and Arthur Watts on double-bass – all studio legends. I was out of my depth. Although I'd been struggling to teach myself to read music for a while, most of the sessions that I'd played to date merely required me to create bass-lines from a chord chart. It was to be a day of serious bluffing, and by listening carefully to the drums and the guitar and by examining the shape of the written bass-line I was able to cope... just. That is, until halfway through the second session, when David suddenly silenced the whole orchestra and said: "Mr bass guitar player, would you play bars 65 to 85 for me, please?" The whole orchestra turned to look at me. This was the kind of moment that only happens in nightmares. I focused very intensely on the part, tried to ignore the damp patches that were appearing under my armpits, and played what I thought the part *ought* to be. His kind response to my bold attempt was a gently spoken kind of reluctant acceptance: "Well, it's not what I've written, but it'll do." I felt weak. And I felt relief, but I was annoyed that I'd cheated on the exam and passed.

Abbey Road Studio Two, viewed from the rhythm section of the David Rose Session, 1973

This madness had to stop, and I seriously started learning to read with the aid of books by bass guitar legend Carol Kaye (who has since become a good friend), and double bass legend Ray Brown. I'm so glad I did as it enabled me to not only read music, but to be able to write it as well – a vital tool for a composer.

CHORD CHARTS

Session chord parts were often copied so hastily on old Xerox machines that the left-hand margin was omitted. The actual chords – or music – would have been fine, but the information on the left could be bewildering.

What should have looked like this:

INTRO
VERSE
CHORUS
MIDDLE EIGHT
SOLO
CODA

Often looked like this:

NTRO
ERSE
HORUS
IDDLE EIGHT
OLO
ODA

It even became normal to discuss "erses", "horuses" and "iddle eights", but especially "olos" and "odas".

Joe Moretti

In the 1960s, Joe Moretti became a victim of the record playlist at the BBC. He played lead guitar for Nero and The Gladiators on the track "In the Hall of the Mountain King", which was banned by the BBC on the grounds that it was disrespectful to Grieg. He moved to another band, Vince Taylor and The Playboys, because "they had edging to their jackets, which were also sharper than the Roman costumes!" Joe played the guitar solo on their single "Brand New Cadillac". Although played incessantly on all of the jukeboxes it, too, was banned by the BBC, this time because it mentioned the brand name Cadillac!

"A session guitarist must have all-round ability, because the work is so tremendously varied," he told Chris Hayes in his *Melody Maker* interview. "He must be a good, fast, and accurate reader and have plenty of courage, because he will often walk into something beyond his ken which he's never come across before."

Even the most knowledgeable sight-reading musicians can occasionally be foiled by complex charts and scores. Around 1965, Joe Moretti was faced with one of his biggest challenges when he played on what he describes as "one of the weirdest sessions ever" in Decca's large Studio One. A huge session, coordinated by Dick Rowe, producer Peter Sullivan, and MD Mike Leander, it called for 25 guitar players on electrics, cellos, jumbos and twelve-strings.

Front row, left to right: Bernie Taylor, Bob Rogers, Jimmy Page, Joe Moretti

Back row, left to right: Ernie Shear, Cedric West

Front row, left to right: Don Sanford, Alan Parker, Judd Procter, Roland Harker, Eric Ford, Big Jim Sullivan

Middle Row, left to right: Bryan Daly, Cliff Devereux, Sid Del Monte, Dick Abell, George Kish, Bernie Taylor, Bob Rogers, Jimmy Page, Joe Moretti

Back row, left to right: Ernie Shear, Cedric West, Ike Isaacs, Denny Wright, John McLaughlin

Left row, bottom to top: Bryan Daly, Cliff Devereux, Sid Del Monte, Dick Abel, George Kish, Bernie Taylor, Bob Rogers, Jimmy Page, Joe Moretti

Centre row, bottom to top: Don Sandford, Alan Parker, Judd Procter, Roland Harker, Eric Ford, Big Jim Sullivan

Top centre, (upright bass): Pete McGurk

Top right, bass guitars, left to right: Alan Weighell, Dave Perkins, (and two unknowns)

On the right, with his beige 'Klempt' amp, is John Paul Jones. (The others are unknown)

Oh, and six grand pianos!

These remarkable photographs, taken in the mid-sixties by Decca studio engineer Bill Price, graphically depict the aura of confusion on the sessions described by Joe Moretti: everyone looks totally baffled.
I'm indebted to Judd Procter, John Paul Jones, Herbie Flowers, Ray Davis, and Paul Day for their help in identification. Paul spotted that amongst the many makes of amplifier in use those visible are Burns (Orbit), Ampeg, Fender, Gibson, Selmer, Grampian, and Wallace. Amongst the incredible array of arch-tops and semi-solids there are – surprisingly – only a couple of Fenders. Jimmy Page is playing a Danelectro Standard

Joe found himself playing alongside the likes of Judd Procter, Jimmy Page, Ernie Shear, Dick Abell, Roland Harker, Big Jim Sullivan, John McLaughlin, Eric Ford and Cedric West, plus John Paul Jones on one of the basses. The guitars were split into three desks, like violins: first, lead; second, rhythm; and third, bits and pieces of everything. The musician configuration was as follows: 25 guitars, two six-string bass guitars, four four-string bass guitars, six grand pianos, two upright basses, one French horn, one trombone, one flute, two drummers, and one percussionist.

Joe: "We were to record the 'Poet and Peasant Overture' as the A-side of a single. The B-side was to be 'Capriccio Italien' by Tchaikovsky, but both were hideously difficult to read and play. 'Poet and Peasant' is a rather complex orchestral work, and we were expected to grasp both titles in a three-hour session with no rehearsal time.

Joe Moretti and his Guild Stratford

"When we sat down to play there was mass evacuation from the first desk, so we now had two brave men sitting at the first desk, and 23 musical cowards huddled around desks two and three. The engineers didn't have enough inputs, so we doubled up on mics and amps, looking like octopuses. The MD forced me – and some others losers – from the cowards and herded us back to desk one. He counted us in. Wow! What came out was unbelievable!

"Guys were in the wrong key, in the wrong bar, on the wrong beat, on the wrong page. I was one of the better ones and played two bars right out of the first page. We went in to hear a playback and heard three pianos, the horn, drums and about two and a half guitars. I thought: 'How can you mix that lot?' (During a playback, Judd Procter recalls hearing Dick Rowe confide: 'I told you it wouldn't work!')

"Eventually, we finished up recording the work in pieces, four- to eight-bar sections at a time. I think about three guys managed to play the thing correctly. The following week I went back to Decca and we overdubbed more bass guitars, more guitars, and even put a couple of mandolins on top. Months later, when I asked about this session, I was told that the tape had been consigned to the bin. What a shame. If there was a copy available today, with this story it would go straight to number one!" (Gus Dudgeon informs me that the tape does still exist – unheard.)

Alan Parker

In the era when the Mecca Palais bands reigned supreme – the sixties – Alan Parker made a point of getting to know the guitarists in the various bands of Joe Loss, Ken Mackintosh and Johnny Howard, so that he'd get the call if a dep was required. When this did happen, it was a nightmare. The pad (or score) would be about six inches thick, and – this being the period of The Shadows, The Ventures, and Duane Eddy – 75 per cent of it would be written guitar solos – a true ordeal ("Number twelve – two, three, four...").

Chris Rae and Jeff Crampton

On a massive film session with a 60-piece orchestra, Chris Rae and Jeff Crampton were in the acoustic booth, both on acoustic guitars. Jeff was worrying about the finger-style part they had in the key of C flat. Chris, however, was not fazed by the apparent complexity, and told his partner: "Look, Jeff, they'll probably never even hear us with all that going on." Chris takes up the story: "As we were short on time, the MD said we would put one down to see how it sounded to picture [gulps]. How many flats in C flat? Why could it not be written B major? Two, three, four...

"We had to count through about a 130 bars' rest, with some of them in 5/4, some in 7/8. That was hard enough, but just as we agreed we were in the right place, the orchestra reached a huge *crescendo* that was a cross between John Williams and Stravinsky. 'Great,' I thought, 'they'll never hear us.' And then it happened. The whole orchestra was suddenly tacet (silent); that left just Jeff and me roasting with the part, hitting duff notes and dead strings. Jeff screamed: 'Oh no, they've all bloody stopped', not realising that it was actually being recorded. Needless to say, we did another take or maybe two, and it was alright in the end." The score on that occasion was: readers 3, bluffers 1.

CIRCUS

Jeff Crampton

One of Chris' more unusual gigs was as the guitarist in a circus band. "Jeff Crampton found he was allergic to dogs and cats. It was to our amusement when we found out that his girlfriend was a poodle clipper who had to keep a separate change of clothes in an airtight bag when they went out together. Jeff had been seeing an expensive hypnotist to cure him of his allergies, and he told me the treatment was so successful that he could now stroke dogs and cats without getting an asthma attack.

"At twelve noon on a summer Saturday I had a telephone call from a very distraught Jeff. He begged me to do a show that afternoon at 2.30 and he said he would pay me anything! He said his eyes and nose were streaming, and that he had difficulty breathing. It was then that I found out the gig was in a circus. I said to Jeff: 'But you said the hypnotist cured you.' Jeff replied with a little difficulty in breathing, saying: 'He did me for dogs and cats, but he didn't do me for horses and elephants.' That started my circus career as I took the gig over. The bass player wore a dinner suit and Wellington boots. We had to walk through a pile of elephants' dung and then up a ladder to the bandstand that was halfway up the tent, on dodgy scaffolding. It was very hard to get a dep."

Peter Van Hooke

In 1971 Peter Van Hooke made the decision to focus more on his drumming. Pete: "I went to an agent with the intention of getting a job on the boats – the cruise-liners. He said he had nothing available at present, although he did have a circus, but I would need to be there in four days. I said yes. It was my first professional gig. I was to be paid £25 a week – playing for a travelling circus in South Africa called Continental Circus Berlin.

"I met the lion-tamer, Mario, on the plane. His predecessor had been attacked by the lions after he had gone into the cage slightly drunk, whilst wearing a new leopard skin outfit (lions and tigers don't like leopards – lunch!!).

"The three-piece band consisted of a 50-year-old trumpeter who was AWOL from the Rhodesian air force, and a 45-year-old Afrikaner organist called Joyce who fell madly in love with the lion tamer. The music was circus music and we played on top of one of the buses.

"Mario and I shared a cabin. After a few months I couldn't understand why there was always a smell there. We washed ourselves, we washed our clothes – everything was clean. It was only when I opened the seat – which was part of the bed – that I discovered where Mario was keeping the meat for the tigers.

"But I loved it! I was free and playing music... It lasted for a year."

Joe Brown

Few musicians lasted long in the session world if they relied solely on bluff tactics. For some, like Joe Brown, their bluffing skills became an art form. He says: "You ask Eric Ford and Bryan Daly about my reading ability! They were a couple of the session kings, and, although we're good pals now, they must have hated me when I started. I couldn't play the stuff, but I'm a good bluffer and a great one for clicking away on the dampened string and coming in when I know where I am. Mostly I used to get booked to play the hairy bits, and one way or another I did an awful lot of session work."

Ray Russell

Ray Russell would sometimes play alongside guitarist Joe Moretti, and on one big orchestral "direct to two-track" session Joe suddenly stopped playing. Ray, quite baffled, leaned over and whispered: "Why did you stop?" Joe replied conspiratorially: "When the strings come in, they can't hear us anymore!" In his earlier days, Ray had a regular jazz gig at the Café des Artistes. When he was learning the chord changes of standards, he always knew that he'd made a mistake when the tenor sax player, George Khan, poured a pint of beer over his head. "I reckon it was about two pints a night. Perhaps this was how beer shampoo was invented. It didn't last too long though. Aversion therapy works!"

Les Bennetts and Ike Isaacs

Les Bennetts and fellow guitarist Ike Isaacs once played a session for The Ted Heath Band, where part one was written out but part two was a chord chart. Les chose to follow the chords. While both musicians were checking out the parts, the pianist/MD asked Les to play the lead, and whispered to him, knowing that he couldn't read, "Just play what you feel." He played a storming solo. Ike, thinking that Les had sight-read an incredible part, said: "I couldn't have done that!"

Les Hurdle

Les Hurdle started out on trumpet, and so when he switched to bass guitar his reading on bass clef was not too hot. On one session he worked as one of a "click-and-boom" duo alongside Frank Clarke, who was known for his strong, loud sound on upright bass. At one point Frank leaned over to Les and, with his cigarette holder still in his mouth, said: "You don't know what you're fucking doing do you? Oh well, boy, earn while you learn!"

Joe Brown trying very hard to relax in the ATV canteen – Thank Your Lucky Stars, 1960

The very dapper Frank Clarke in the studio

Frank Clarke

Clem Cattini remembers a session with Frank Clarke when, every time the band came to a tacet (short break), the guitarist overshot by a couple of notes, while everyone else stopped perfectly. Annoyed, Frank kept his cool, looked over the screens and started chatting casually to the guitarist.

Frank: "Nice guitar, son."

Guitarist: "Thank you."

Frank: "It's a Gibson, isn't it?"

Guitarist: "Yes."

Frank: "Are those pegs gold plated?"

Guitarist: "Yes."

Frank: (Pause) "It hasn't got disc brakes, has it?" (This guitarist, unnamed to protect the guilty, eventually went on to become a record producer.)

Terry Walsh

Terry Walsh told me a tale of an unnamed guitarist who suffered terrible nerves if his part said "solo": "He'd cross it out and write 'tacet'! He used to always sit at the back, until one day the conductor said: 'Will you come down here at the front where I can hear you?' Two weeks later the guy had a nervous breakdown!" There is a variation on this story. During a session, every time the music came to a short break, another unnamed guitarist would play a brief but roaring solo. The MD, baffled, stopped the session and asked him: "Why do you keep playing through the *tacet*?" The guitarist, suddenly embarrassed, apologised and said: "Sorry, I thought you meant *take it!*"

Frank Clarke

For years, producers would hire "click-and-boom" duos: bass guitar, with pick and full treble, and double-bass playing in unison. In his busiest period, double-bassist Frank Clarke played 20 sessions a week (70–80 hours), but after 20 years he was forced to admit: "It can drive you potty. There is no glamour – you just get on with it. I used to get annoyed when at five to one someone still couldn't play their part. That's when I'd shout at them."

For a while Frank played bass guitar, and of the heavy amplification he says: "I started life as a bass player and ended it as a coalman!" He remembers his early session days with Marty Wilde and others as being "a time of enormous fun", but observes that, eventually "the magic and the fun went; it became too calculated, too serious."

Frank may have been a jazzer at heart, but he was most definitely a champion of rock 'n' roll. To a guitarist, who was moaning about playing rock 'n' roll, he offered the advice: "If you can't play it don't knock it."

Terry Walsh playing his 1938 Gibson L5 on a broadcast with The Steve Race Quintet in 1956. Frank Clarke is on the double bass

WAKE UP

Between the seventies and eighties the demands of constant session work were causing me considerable sleep loss and I would sometimes have great difficulty waking up in the morning. I finally owned up to the problem after I had fallen asleep for several hours on my hands and knees with my arse in the air and my outstretched hand resting comfortably on the alarm clock that I had earlier turned off. I clearly needed to do something about this, and eventually resorted to depending on four separate alarm clocks, each in large metal biscuit tins. Bizarrely, in anticipation of this awful noise, I once got fully washed and dressed and ready to load the car when I noticed that it was it was only 4 a.m. and was still dark outside!

But for me, session work was, and still is, a joy. Whilst it may have been occasionally terrifying, or at its worst boring, it was always challenging, both musically or socially. Over a period of four decades I have had the privilege of recording with many of the best musicians, producers and engineers in town. But even though I was thrilled to intimately experience their fine humour and sheer musicianship, the one thing that enamoured me most with sessions was the discovery that I didn't actually have to be at work until 10 a.m. (unless I was crazy enough to get up for what used to be known as the greedy hour: an 8 a.m.-to-9 a.m. jingle).

CHAPTER 14

THE WIND-UP

The session world is notorious for some of the cleverest practical jokes and creative wind-ups ever played. And as Olympic Studios engineer David Hamilton-Smith observed: "This was a period when there was time to have some fun."

Clive Hicks

The scene: Chappell's Studios, just off Bond Street. It was near the end of a session, and there was just enough time to play one more title, which featured Clive Hicks on solo acoustic guitar, accompanied by a small string section – but it had to be recorded in one take. The engineer needed a quick soundcheck of the acoustic by itself, and in an attempt to cut through the mayhem of between-take orchestral doodling he pleaded to all of the musicians in the studio through the talkback: "Can I hear the guitar without the strings, please?" Hidden from sight in his isolation booth, and speaking in a tone of voice that suggested that this was perhaps not a very good idea, Clive drily replied: "Well you can, but it'll take about five minutes and all you'll get is a sort of scratching sound."

Ray Russell

Ray Russell was booked to play guitar on a big orchestral session at CTS Studios in Wembley. While the engineers were setting up mics and headphones for the 80 or so musicians present, the MD carefully ran through the many problems he anticipated in the great pile of scores next to him. Finally, when he felt he had covered every point, he looked around the room and enquired: "Right, are there any questions?" Ray Russell raised a hand and tentatively asked: "Er, do you think one should pet on the first date?" Before the MD could answer, the silence was punctured by loud guffaws and shrieks from the entire orchestra.

Porky Byford

In the early 1970s, a bass guitar player called Porky Byford slowly appeared on the session scene. This musician, from "up north", was a virtuoso. He had a great sound, was a flawless sight-reader and an excellent time-keeper and

Clive Hicks playing through a Watkins Dominator alongside The Squadronaires with Ronnie Aldrich at The Palace Ballroom in Douglas, Isle of Man, 1962

groove player. Other bass players began to get nervous about this guy whenever musicians would casually remark that they had just left a session that Porky was on: "Oh man, what a sound", or "He read the 'black page' straight off." Small huddles would manage to quietly discuss Porky just as the more vulnerable bass players walked past. In desperation some of them would, in vain, even try to find Porky's phone number. But they would never succeed for the simple reason that Porky didn't exist. It was, in fact, a magnificent wind-up that lasted for over six months, and I have long suspected that it was the invention of the late and sadly missed drummer Graham Jarvis. It had eventually got so out of hand that the very mention of Porky's name would scare the shit out of some bass players.

There is an extension to the Porky Byford saga. Not so long ago, a drummer annoyed everyone by bragging about all of the famous names that he'd played with. Someone attempted to catch him out by asking casually if he'd ever played with the great Porky. "'Course I have," he replied confidently, and proceeded to explain in detail the gigs and sessions. What a twat! RIP Porky.

80 BARS

At the regular 2 p.m. Friday session which took place at CBS Whitfield Street Studios, MD Kenny Clayton was recording the music for a comedy programme on Channel 4 TV. The session was booked and organised by drummer Tom Nichol, and one of the musicians hired was guitarist Mitch Dalton. Mitch recalls: "I was called and told to bring everything, including acoustic guitar, twelve-string guitar, bouzouki, mandolin, and so on, as well as my usual gear. We were to do a pastiche of the show song 'Around the World in Eighty Days', which was re-titled 'Around the World in Eighty Bars'. Every four or eight bars there would be a different instrument, each representing a different country, and with only a two-bar gap in which to change over."

What Mitch didn't know was that he'd been hired specifically to be on this tune – he had nothing else to play on the session. As he checked through his part he noticed that a banjo was required, but he didn't have one with him. Why hadn't his wife told him to bring one? After all, she'd taken the phone call.

The session was about to start and, in a panic, Mitch ranted on the phone, blaming his innocent wife for not warning him, and organised a taxi to bring the banjo to the studio. What Mitch also didn't know was that the chart for the brass players looked like this:

'Around the World in Eighty Bars'

There then appeared a single line of music, on which was written:

80 BARS TACET

They had nothing to play at all. This line was then followed by a very bizarre instruction from Kenny: 'When I give the upbeat, hold your instrument as if about to play, then watch Mitch Dalton.'

The session was about to start. Mitch, realising the enormity and difficulty of the task ahead of him, yelled: "This is impossible, is anyone not playing?" Trumpeter Guy Barker owned up and volunteered to pass to him each of the instruments – mandolin, Spanish guitar, bouzouki, etc – in turn. Mitch whispered to him: "Keep an eye out for the banjo, it's coming by taxi."

Kenny counted in and the track started. It was very fast. In the confusion, Mitch wasn't afforded the luxury of checking out the parts in advance, and so he was sight-reading furiously, and doing very well under the circumstances. At the moment when the banjo was required it still hadn't arrived, and so Mitch, being a true professional and thinking he was being helpful in providing an overall picture for the run-through, leaned forward to the mic, announced "Banjo!" loudly and proceeded to vocally impersonate one: "Donk-dokka-donk-donk..." With a final flourish, the track was complete and over the fold-back, Kenny enthused: "We got there, Mitch, come and have a listen."

Mitch, bewildered and exhausted, gasped "Oh my God" as Tom walked in with a large glass of champagne. At this moment the banjo arrived and, to Mitch's horror, the grand wind-up became evident. He was not initially amused, and for many a session afterwards he would suffer the taunt: "Got your banjo, have you?"

Keith Grant and Pat Halling

Successful wind-ups take a lot of planning, such as one devised at Olympic Studios. Chief engineer Keith Grant and violinist/orchestra leader Pat Halling, both highly respected professionals, were working on an orchestral session with about 60 musicians, and there were mics everywhere on long boom stands. Whilst chatting in the control room before the session, Keith, a bear of a man with a rich sense of humour, showed Pat an old fiddle he had found and suggested a little game.

The session began. It was a well-known fact that Pat tended to query mic positions, and this occasion was no exception. He reached up with the tip of his bow, moved one of the overhead mics by a couple of inches, looked satisfied and sat down. Keith came back into the studio, noticed the altered mic position and, clearly annoyed at Pat's meddling, swung it to its original place. He returned, fuming, to the control room, followed by Pat, the two of them arguing all the way. Safely away from the orchestra, Pat carefully swapped his priceless violin for Keith's really cheap one. Pat returned to his seat, reached up and moved the mic again. There was almost an explosion as Keith finally snapped, stopped the session, burst from the control room again, and, as he made his way across the studio, shouted at Pat: "This is the last time!" He then grabbed Pat's violin (which everyone thought was his very expensive Guarnerius del Jesu), smashed it onto the floor, leaped on it, and then wrestled Pat to the ground. (Although Keith was a big man, Pat had studied judo and so was able to cope.) There was a huge gasp in the room, followed by groans of disbelief and then a silence, which was only broken when Pat and Keith, unable to keep the charade going any longer, both suddenly erupted into uncontrolled laughter. Needless to say, not everyone was amused, and unfortunately, because all of the musicians were still shaking (one poor violinist was in tears), no one could play for at least fifteen minutes.

SAUSAGE MYSTERY

One of Phil Palmer's funniest stories concerns the time spent on the road with Dire Straits as the back-up guitarist to Mark Knopfler, and a particular incident he calls the Straits' sausage mystery. "I lived Spinal Tap for a moment when, after several months' schlepping across the USA and suffering some of the worst catering in history, we finally crossed the border into Canada. Toronto was, I think on the face of it, not much different to look at, but it had one major bonus: a Marks & Spencer. On our arrival, about two hours before the show, there was a disturbingly wonderful 'pong' coming from the dressing room area. Upon investigation, two enormous silver containers with rollback lids were discovered, full of English sausages, mashed potatoes, fried onions and baked beans (Heinz). Alongside was Colman's English mustard and HP sauce, along with a few bottles of 1983 St Emillion. We all thought we'd died and gone to heaven, and proceeded to tuck in with great relish. Mark Knopfler and John Illsley, however, decided to wait until after the show to have theirs. Everyone was very controlled, and when we finally went on stage there were ten bangers, plenty of mash, onions and beans, and one bottle of St Emillion left.

"During the concert, the mystery occurred. After a fine show with two encores, Mark and John rushed back to the dressing room, drooling, to find three bangers and very little else – probably enough for one serving. Well, you can imagine. After the initial rage subsided, a major stewards' inquiry was organised and the crew and management were marched in one by one to be interrogated by the very hungry Knopfler and Illsley, still dressed in stage clothes, complete with headbands. Obviously, by this time the load-out is in full swing and tempers are getting frayed.

"I sat in the corner for one and a half hours, watching in disbelief as suggestions of docked wages, punches on the nose and the sack were offered to those who didn't come clean. 'Come on, you know whodunit – good guy, nasty bastard tactics. It was like *No Hiding Place* on a bad night."
Of course nobody owned up, and the missing seven bangers will always be a mystery, although the word is there was more than one culprit. The set-lists placed by the monitors the following night read:

"Money for Sausages"
"Sausages and Juliet"
"Sultans of Sausages"
"Private Sausages"
"Walk of Sausage", etc, etc

And for the first time in 24 hours, Mark and John smiled again.

Tim Renwick

Another joke was aimed at Tim Renwick, who heard news of a domestic crisis at home while he was in Italy on a European tour with Eric Clapton. "My wife and children had moved out of the family home because they discovered a thriving family of rats had been living underneath the floor. Imagine the horror! Eric's response was to instruct Lee Dickson, his roadie, to erase the first two letters of my guitar's name on the headstock. To this day it reads 'ratocaster'! What an absolute... stard!"

BERGERAC

The best wind-ups are, of course, those that are hardest to detect at the beginning. I was once a victim of a gentle one at BBC Lime Grove Studios on a session for an episode of the BBC TV series *Bergerac*. Ray Russell had written the music and was also playing guitar. Just before the session started I sat slowly leafing through the various cues (the chase scene, Jim's love interest, and so on), looking for the hard bits. Cue 17 looked especially difficult with lots of l6th-note patterns high up on fretless bass. I leaned over the screen to ask Ray about the tempo of the piece and he dismissed any problem: "Don't worry, it's quite slow."

We played the first couple of cues without a hitch. During a playback I stayed in my seat and began trying to play cue 17. Damn, it was difficult. Again I leaned over the screen to ask Ray for further help. "Don't worry, it's a nightclub scene, just you and congas," he said, unperturbed. And so it went on throughout the day as I increasingly felt like I was approaching a critical exam. I was quite apprehensive: I wanted to get it right.

At about 4.55 p.m., very near the end of the session, up came cue 17 – just me and congas. Everyone else had finished. Normally the other musicians would have been out of the building by now, but I noticed a sort of lingering, particularly by the cellists, who were taking far too long to put away their instruments. Up came the click... at a ridiculous tempo. The conga part was all over the place, and of course the bass part was an absolutely unplayable contortion. Thank you, Ray.

Ray Russell

I had my own little go at Ray on a session for composer Simon May at R.G. Jones Studio in Wimbledon, where I sneaked back early after a break and retuned Ray's guitar perfectly, from low E flat to high E flat, a semitone lower than normal tuning. The first chord of the next title was A major. During the run-through, Ray crashed in with a perfect A flat major, quickly moved up a semitone and spent the rest of the tune alternately staring in disbelief at the chart and his left hand.

Greg Walsh

An elaborate joke was played at Trident Studios, when engineer/producer Greg Walsh arrived some time ahead of the client. With the collusion of the rest of the staff he proceeded to rig the entire control room. Both the varispeed on the multi-track tape recorder and the master control room light dimmers were wired to controls on the mixing desk. The ancillary meter was fed by a 1kHz tone and its logo was expertly changed to read in PSI (pounds per square inch). They also installed a large polythene bag under the desk.

The session began and everything looked normal. After about an hour, the lights dimmed slightly and the tape machine slowed down just enough for it to be noticeable. Greg did a convincing impression of a worried man and tapped the meter: "The pressure isn't good. If it goes down to minus seven we'll have to get maintenance in." The client had never seen anything like this before.

As the session progressed, the state of the control room worsened until an apologetic Greg was forced to call for the maintenance engineer. A few minutes later, a man in a white coat appeared with a large water container, a funnel, a hosepipe, and a screwdriver. He proceeded to open a blank panel in the desk, inserted the hosepipe and poured in a gallon of water. Everyone watched but no one said a word. He closed the panel and before leaving uttered the advice: "Give it about half an hour to warm up." There was stunned silence. The client's mouth was open.

CLAIROL 500

If Greg Walsh arrived early for a session it was always advisable to be cautious. Prior to a vocal session at Audio International Studios, Greg spotted by chance a Clairol 500 hair dryer that someone had brought into maintenance for repair. With a little experimenting he discovered that a Neumann 84 microphone would slot just inside its casing, with the mic cable simply replacing the mains lead. During the soundcheck, Greg explained to the artist that the bright red object taped to the mic stand in front of him was in fact a new prototype, but since the vocal sound was so great anyway the session proceeded without a hitch. With meticulous professionalism, Greg wrote on the track sheet: "Vocals recorded with new Clairol 500."

The producer took the tapes to Nova Sound for mixing and vocal repairs. A while later Greg got a call from a bemused Nova engineer, who explained that the same artist, who quite naturally wished to be consistent, had insisted on using the same mic. Upon hearing the wonderful explanation, and not wishing to drop Greg in the shit, he discreetly popped out to nearby Oxford Street and bought a Clairol 500, which happened this time to be yellow. Again the vocal sound was superb. At the end of the session, the producer was heard to pronounce authoritatively: "It sounded great, but I think I prefer the sound of the red one."

On any mixdown session, everyone in the control room should have a clear idea of their aims and how they will achieve them. If a producer – or even occasionally the artist – was a real idiot the engineer could be persuaded to allocate a whole section of the mixing desk to him. It was known as the producer's panel or board, and on it he could play happily with all the faders and knobs, oblivious of the fact that they weren't connected to anything and did nothing, rather like a child's stick-on steering wheel.

Louis Austen

Louis Austen, the engineer at Kingsway Studios, would sometimes compound the fantasy by making elaborate and convincing rack-mounted panels with lots of knobs, switches and meters. They would have embossed names like "LUSTRAMIX" or "FABUTRON". When the producer asked what they did, the engineer would casually say, without raising an eyebrow, "Oh, they make mixing more difficult, and carry on pottering. Greg Walsh continued this tradition by mixing an album in "NEMESIS": Nominally Expanded Electronic Stereo Imaging System. It was amazing how many clients enjoyed the sound of a box with nothing in it. (See my DFA pedal).

Clem Cattini

During a session set-up at Decca studios, drummer Clem Cattini decided to have a little fun: he played his part with one hand whilst discretely screwing a sweet wrapper into a mic with the other hand. Engineers hate mics that make "frying" noises, and the guy instantly rushed into the studio to change it. All was then fine until Clem found the sweet wrapper again. It got worse. At that time there was a comedian by the name of Norman Collier whose brilliant act was to talk intermittently – but convincingly – as if there was a faulty mic cable. This was Clem's next inspiration: "There's...mthing...ong with this...crophone." The poor engineer thought he was going crazy.

Keith Grant

Chief engineer at Olympic Studios, Keith Grant, was aware of Clem's little games. The new digital samplers had just arrived and, as these could be triggered from any sound source, Keith was inspired to set up a small speaker inside Clem's bass-drum. Delightfully this meant that every time Clem (a.k.a. Thunderfoot) played his bass-drum he could hear someone shouting "ouch" from within.

Although Studio Two at Olympic was the smaller studio, it had a massive desk with room enough inside it for a small person. This gave Keith another idea: on one occasion he persuaded one of his engineers to climb inside holding a remote for the multi-track tape machine. When the session started he was able to casually demonstrate a tape machine that responded instantly to his voice commands – "stop", "rewind" – (whilst his friend obediently pushed the buttons from within the desk). Needless to say his client was mightily impressed.

Simon Chamberlain

The music for the TV series *Grafters* was being recorded at Air Edel Studios (formally Audio International) for composer Ray Russell. During a break, pianist Simon Chamberlain said to Rik Walton the engineer: "Can I have a little less bass in the cans, please?" I played a little for him to check levels. Simon: "It's no good, I can still hear it."

There is a corollary to this: sometime later on a Bill Tarmey session at Whitfield Street Studios I happened to make a couple of goofs on a run-through. Simon: "Can I have more of Mo's bass in the cans? – I can't believe what I've just heard."

John Williams/Herbie Flowers

On a recording session at EMI Abbey Road for his band Sky, classical guitarist John Williams was confused by the tonality at a certain bar – he didn't want to clash with the bass. He wandered over to where bassist Herbie Flowers was sitting, pointed at the music, and asked: "Bar 71, is that note there an E natural or an E flat?" Herbie looked up at him and said disarmingly: "Mind your own fucking business." They are still pals.

Forbes Henderson

Another classical guitarist, Forbes Henderson, describes a trip to Italy: "Mandolin is not my forte to say the least, but I learnt it to play in a Mozart opera, *Don Giovanni*. There's a famous aria for tenor with heavily featured mandolin solo with plucked-strings accompaniment. Quite a brown trousers moment!

"It was to be performed in an old monastery in Batignano, Tuscany. The gig was for three weeks so it was more of a holiday for me as my bit lasted less than two minutes! But because of delays on the train I arrived late. It was a hot day, and when I arrived I was not allowed to drink even a cold beer. In addition I became aware that the musicians had a cramped dressing room, whereas the singers did not.

"As a result of this cumulative frustration, on the last night I had this 'brilliant idea' to do it in the nude for a laugh, and (as the photo clearly shows) a real freshly plucked fig leaf (locally sourced from the garden) attached by gaffer tape was used to cover up the bits!

"The orchestra pit was a corridor above the main part of the monastery and the audience luckily could not see us, such that my entrance took the orchestra by surprise, but being true pros (amidst the suppressed giggles) they managed to get through the piece. I duly left the pit and, to my amazement, a lot of the lads thought this was a wicked idea and followed my example and took their kit off, including quite a few of the girls going topless!

"The opera producer – realising something was up – came upstairs and was horrified to see all these naked musicians (still playing away.) I will never forget his reaction as he visibly aged ten years!

"The following year they were doing a Kurt Weill opera, which included guitar and banjo. Needless to say, I didn't get the call."

Derek Wadsworth

I love all of these stories – in a way they explain how musicians see the world. But I think my favourite wind-up, for its simplicity and innocence, took place not too long ago at CTS Studio Three in Wembley. After the first run-through of the song, producer Derek Wadsworth spoke to me from the control room through the talkback: "Mo, you see that chord at bar 77? The E minor seven flat five?" Expecting a change or a new instruction I grabbed my pencil, scanned the part, found the bar, looked up and said: "Yes?" Derek replied: "It's nice, isn't it?"

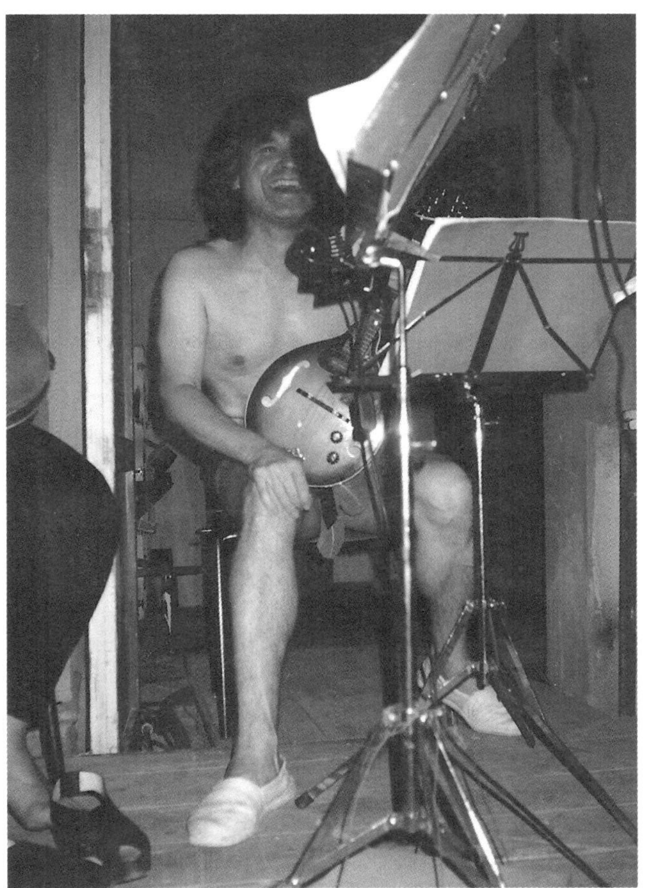

Forbes Henderson and the 'Fig-Leaf'

CHAPTER 15

MDs, PRODUCERS, AND FIXERS

MUSIC DIRECTORS

During the 1970s, some very fine French producers and MDs came to Britain to record. Their charts were exquisite, and some of the music was beautiful. Unfortunately I only remember the funny ones.

The French MD 1

For one project at Trident Studios I was booked to play bass, along with Ray Russell on guitar. The uninspiring music wasn't very good and, although I tried very hard to make it groove, nothing seemed to lift it from its plodding mediocrity. Halfway through one take, I noticed that I could sneak in the first few notes of 'The Sailor's Hornpipe' (diddle-om-pom-pom) and get away with it. I was trying to entertain myself for my own sanity, but I must add that the funky 16th note patterns did help the groove. Occasionally, Ray would notice one of my quotes and play a response to the line, or an echo. As we got bolder, more and more of the melody would be embedded in the riffs and phrases. I thought no more about this session, until I heard from percussionist Frank Ricotti, who had at a later time overdubbed on vibes. He had heard it, knew what was going on, and joined in. It had reached the point where one rhythm track had become almost entirely built up from bits of 'Hornpipe'. Eventually, the French MD had to notice, and said something like: "What is zis tune zat you are all playing?"

Joe Moretti and his trusty old Tele in the studio 1970

The French MD 2

A French arranger booked some sessions at Lansdowne Studios with Martin Kershaw on electric guitar and, in a booth, Joe Moretti on acoustic twelve-string. The MD explained to the band: "I come over 'ere for ze 'feel'. We cannot get zis in France." He then proceeded to completely miss the point by handing out parts with every single note written out. Joe Moretti recalls: "The crazy French MD had written the guitar parts in bass clef, but about six leger lines above the stave. We obviously couldn't read it, so we retired to the hostelry round the corner for about an hour while he recopied the parts." The guys returned, refreshed, and started to routine the song that was in front of them, but the MD became agitated and turned to Martin: "Zis is not ze right feel." Martin, being professional, tried out some pedals such as wah-wah: 'wakka-wakka...' The MD shouted: "*Non*!" Still trying to be helpful, Martin tried many other approaches and styles, but none of them met with the man's approval. It became evident that the French MD didn't know what he wanted.

Communication began to suffer and silliness crept in as the bass player had his part upside down while the drummer wore a bag over his head. The session was crumbling. After about half an hour, the Frenchman cried: "You're all wasting ma time! You're all *idiots.*" "Oh Joe," he sighed as he walked over to Joe in the booth. "I cannot get any sense out of zese fools. You are ze only sensible one in ze orchestra." As the MD opened the booth door, he screamed and staggered back four feet. Joe had, by this time, grown very bored in his isolation and involved himself in "alternative entertainment". His face, arms and guitar were completely covered in his entire collection of Green Shield stamps (thousands of pounds' worth of petrol), and only his eyes showed through. "Can I help you?" said Joe innocently. The MD grabbed his arrangements and fled back to Paris, never to return.

Martin Kershaw in the studio

The American MD

A team of session players rehearsed for what would become the cast album of a big West End show. The well-known American MD, under pressure of his own devising, started to panic and unnecessarily give this band of seasoned professionals a very hard time. Tension mounted further when he began addressing each member of the band, not by his or her name but by their instrument: "Harp, can you make it sound less plucked?" This was a question she had never been asked before. Her reply said everything "Well, I could bow it." And stopping the rehearsal in mid-flow, he snapped at Mitch Dalton: "Guitar, what's that *shit* you're playing?" Surprised, Mitch looked up at the MD, then down at his part, and back up at the MD. His response had an elegant simplicity: "It's *your* shit."

The English MD

Another MD story concerns guitarist Martin Kershaw. Harry Rabinowitz was conducting a large orchestra at CTS Studios in Wembley when Martin arrived late and proceeded to set up. With him was a stranger in a suit looking awkwardly out of place. During the session, the stranger sat on Martin's amp and Martin played his banjo for a while until a tacet appeared in the score. Martin was in the process of buying a house, and the stranger turned out to be Martin's lawyer, who quietly instructed: "Just sign here, and here, and here... and there." After eight bars, Martin resumed playing, but, clearly irritated, Harry called a halt to the session and enquired: "Martin, who is the man sitting on your amplifier?"

Martin: "He's my lawyer."

Harry: "And would you tell everyone assembled here what you have signed?"

Martin: "A mortgage. I've just bought a house."

Harry: "And how much was the house?"

Martin: "£21,000."

Harry: "Ladies and gentlemen... yet another Kershaw first. The first man to spend £21,000 in eight bars' tacet!"

Lateness, for some obscure reason, proved to be a frequent and insurmountable problem for Martin, much to the frustration of producers, fixers and colleagues. Adrian Kerridge recalled a jingle session at Lansdowne when Martin arrived late as usual, rushed down the stairs, set up and started playing – still only wearing his pyjamas. He said nothing, and neither did anyone else. At another jingle session, starting at 8 a.m., Martin was very late and arrived to find the fixer pacing up and down on the pavement outside the studio. He apologised, opened the boot of his car and discovered to his surprise and horror that he'd packed an amplifier and a fishing rod.

It should be noted that Martin's guitar playing and sight-reading skills were so efficient that his lack of punctuality rarely mattered. So much in demand was he that he is able to claim the world record for playing on the most sessions in one day: 6 a.m –7 a.m.: jingle at Advision; 7 a.m.–8 a.m.: jingle at Advision; 9 a.m.–12 a.m.: session at Pye; 1 p.m.–2 p.m.: jingle at Pye; 4 p.m.: fly to Belgium for session; 12 p.m.–1 a.m.: fly back for an overdub session at Abbey Road; 2 a.m.: play second set at Ronnie Scott's Jazz Club with John Dankworth.

PRODUCERS

The musicians reach the final tumultuous chords of a complicated ten-minute piece, which features many different time signatures and tempo changes. It took months to write, weeks to rehearse and hours to perfect in the studio. They stop, wait until the last chord dies to silence, look up and breathe deep sighs of relief as they remove their cans and mop their sweating brows. Through the foldback, the producer responds with great enthusiasm: "Alright lads, let's take one."

Or the producer, having been engrossed in a phone call for some time, suddenly becomes aware that he is required to make some kind of response.

"How's that, Bob?" said drummer Jason Bonham to producer Bob Ezrin.

"Oh, I'm sorry, were you playing then?" said Bob.

Joe Meek

One producer who certainly did know his onions was the brilliant pioneer Joe Meek, a man ahead of his time but who sadly died by his own hand in 1967. One day in 1963, thinking that it was a session, Russ Ballard played guitar for Joe at his studio in Holloway Road in Islington. Joe said: "Okay, what can you do?" Russ played "Trambone" and "Guitar Boogie", two instrumental hits of the day. "Okay, you're in," said Joe. Russ hadn't realised that he had actually been auditioning for one of Joe's regular studio bands, The Outlaws, but he passed on the opportunity and Ritchie Blackmore joined instead. One of the first singles to be graced by the future Deep Purple guitarist was the Meek production 'Just Like Eddie', by Heinz.

Eric Ford also worked for Joe Meek, playing with the likes of Clem Cattini and Big Jim Sullivan, especially on Joe's early recordings. He was responsible for that hectically strummed rhythm guitar that made 'Johnny Remember Me' by John Leyton such a standout track.

In John Repsch's celebrated book *The Legendary Joe Meek*, the backing is credited to The Outlaws. Eric remained adamant, however, that he was the guitarist concerned and added that he was present on most of John Leyton's recording sessions and also on many of his live dates, too. Eric also described Joe's studio as "a terrible mess", but commented that "although Joe was prone to temperamental outbursts he always treated me well."

George Martin

Arguably the world's most famous record producer, if only for his achievements with The Beatles, is George Martin, who was deservedly knighted in 1996. But even a man of his great wisdom was thrown into confusion when, in 1975, he produced Jeff Beck's powerfully adventurous, jazz-tinged album *Blow by Blow* at AIR Studios by London's Oxford Circus. Jeff was fastidious about over-dubs but never seemed to be happy with his solos.

A few days after a recording, when he'd had time to digest his own performance, he would telephone George and say "I think I could do a better one on this track", and they would return to AIR to try again. Jeff would play over and over until he was satisfied that he had performed his best. A couple of months went by and George received another phone call from Jeff: "I want to do this solo again." Bemused, George said: "I'm sorry, Jeff, but the record is in the shops!"

Brian Eno

As producers grew in stature throughout the 1970s, some like Brian Eno introduced unorthodox methods of gaining the best possible performances from their artists, sometimes through acts of subterfuge.

Frank Zappa

When Phil Palmer graduated to session work in the 1970s, he played on a session for the Indian violinist L. Shankar, produced by Frank Zappa. All of the musicians, including drummer Simon Phillips, sat in a circle on the first day, just clapping the complicated rhythms. Not a note was played until they knew all the patterns.

PRODUCER QUOTES

Not all producers are as cleverly motivated. It is a source of eternal mystery to me how some people not only reach the rank of producer but, having done so, keep working. It speaks volumes about the state of the record industry. Over the years, a number of entertaining pronouncements by notably less enlightened producers have been faithfully recorded and have become part of studio folklore. Here are a few of my favourites:

- Suggesting the need for a key change, a producer, speaking through the talkback, trawled through his vast knowledge of music theory and asked: "Can you take it down a crotchet?"
- I was playing on a jingle session at CBS Studios. The very jolly lady producer asked drummer Brett Morgan: "Have you brought those swishy things that drummers use?" It would have helped morale greatly if she could have learned the word "brush" before she'd arrived.
- Something was wrong with an arrangement. A decision was needed. All eyes turned to the producer, and he felt he had to make a meaningful suggestion: "It's either a trumpet or a drum."
- "Can I have more bass on the hi-hat?"
- A producer addressing a roomful of exhausted session players: "Very good, but I'd like one more just like that."
- I was on a French session where the plot was similar: "Zat was perfect. Let's do one more."
- Peter Van Hooke recalls that, on a French session, a well-known guitarist received the tragic news that his father had died. The producer, exhibiting zero tact, asked: "Could you just do one more take?"
- A producer spoke to double-bassist Pete McGurk, whose instrument was booming: "Could you slacken the strings off a bit?"

- Direct Injection (DI) is a process whereby an electric instrument is wired directly into the desk, without using an amplifier. A producer watched the engineer intently as he DI'd first the bass guitar and then the keyboards. He'd learned a new term. He had to use it. A while later, with experienced insight, he said: "The congas sound a bit thin. Can we DI them?"
- A producer couldn't make his mind up. He asked cellist Anthony Pleeth: "Can you take it up an octave?" Anthony: "Yes, how's this?" He played. There was a long pause while the producer considered the options. "No, can you take it up half an octave?"
- On a mixdown session, a producer gave the engineer his overview: "Can I have everything louder than everything else?"
- There's also a Jamaican version: "Maximum boost at all frequencies."
- To demonstrate that little had changed, even in the 1990s, a producer – while listening to a mix – offered the opinion: "I think it needs more MIDI." (MIDI is an abbreviation of Musical Instrument Digital Interface. It merely provides a stream of computer information.)
- Jingle writer and fine all-round musician Paul Hart told me of a session where he started a piece in a standard way by first laying down a click-track (i.e., an electronic metronomic pulse for timekeeping purposes). Gradually he overdubbed different instruments, such as bass, keyboards and percussion, until the content of the composition began to emerge. Much of this was done in the control room, so necessarily the click was still audible. At the back of the control room was a six-strong team of "clients" – people with media specs and clipboards – and not one idea between them. After about half an hour they went into a huddle, and a few seconds later the bravest one leaned forward, tapped Paul on the shoulder, and said: "Er, we don't like that ticking sound."
- There is an ironic corollary to this story, an event which occurred some years later at the same studio during a session for jingle writer Dave Arch. The client, sensing a subtle change in the sound, suddenly commented: "There's something missing." Dave, who was totally absorbed in the track-laying process but vaguely aware of the need for a simple explanation, replied: "We've taken the click out." The client, a little hurt, said: "Oh, we liked that."
- Legendary drummer Phil Seaman was booked to play on a session at Decca Studios, West Hampstead. Some time earlier producer Dick Rowe had learnt a new phrase – 'a bit more magic' – which he felt he must use, and between takes, pipe in hand, he leaned over to the talkback and made a request: "A bit more magic please, Phil." After this had happened a few times Phil could take it no longer and his intuitive response was to play a long blistering drum solo, a performance that was, perhaps, the best he'd ever played. But just in case his opinion was not yet made clear, he threw down his sticks, looked up at the control room, and topped this stunning display of virtuosity with his immortal challenging verbal addendum: "Abraca-fuckin-dabra!" I wish I'd been there.
- On another session Dick asked for "more arco (a term used for bowing on a string instrument) on the trombone".
- Another producer once foolishly asked Seaman: "Can you make a sound like a waterfall?" "Well, I could piss on my cymbals," Phil replied.
- A clueless American producer asked Peter Van Hooke: "Can you make that snare drum sound like a cowbell?" Pete, who always opted for simplicity, asked: "How about using a cowbell?"
- After the 20th take, the edgy, white-knuckled producer, head in hands, attempts to put the nervous young singer at ease: "Now relax, for Chrissake!"
- The producer gently breaks the news to the guitarist that, although his performance was quite remarkable, it was, perhaps, a tad inappropriate: "It was loud, confident... and wrong."
- It's true that nothing ever changes. Pointing to a Yamaha 02R digital console, a Jamaican client asked programmer Christian Henson what it was. Christian replied: "It's a mixing desk." The mist rose and the client said: "Oh I know one of dem – it's like a graphic equaliser but stronger."
- This is my all-time favourite. A producer sensed that a part wasn't quite right, and confronted the musician: "Can you make it... er..." He looked around, struggling for the word that will transform the performance. "Can you make it... er... *better?*"

FIXERS

From the late 1950s through to the late 1980s, the fixer – or, more correctly, the orchestral manager or contractor – wielded great power on the session scene. If a musician was on a fixer's books he worked; if not, he very simply didn't, although record producers increasingly began to book direct. Most fixers had been, or still were, working musicians themselves.

This was also a period when the session fixers (contractors) reigned supreme and you were supposed to be available at all times. If they called, your partner had to say that you were working so that they didn't realise you were actually out of town. Another problem was that, if you were away for a long period, other players would move in and, quite naturally, take over your studio gigs. It was a trade-off.

Ideally a fixer would have as wide a musical background as possible, but, as evidenced by some of the stories that follow, this clearly wasn't always the case, especially when the players were "electric" or rock 'n' roll, and the fixers were steeped in their "acoustic" or classical background.

One of the first casualties of the new-versus-old conflict was drummer Clem Cattini. On an orchestral session conducted by Harry Rabinowitz at Olympic Studio One, the engineer was setting up a foldback balance. Through the talkback, he asked Clem: "How are your cans?" (i.e., what are the various levels of the instruments like?). Clem's response was emotive, rather than technical, and based on the fact that the strings always seemed to lag behind the rhythm section. With a formidable irony, he replied, "Can I have the strings a bit earlier in my cans, please?" The room went quiet. Violinists stood up and stared to see who was in the drum booth. It was Clem's misfortune that the string section was comprised almost entirely of the main session fixers. His comment did not go down at all well, and he didn't work for about six months, such was the penalty for honesty.

Clem's outspoken nature reared its head again when he worked with bassist Les Hurdle at Philips Studios. Les: "A fixer of note pointed at me and asked Clem: 'Er, tell me, is this boy any good?' Clem replied – jokingly – with an elongated 'No'. I never heard from the fixer for two years, although he did call from time to time to ask me if I knew any new, bright, up-and-coming bass players!"

Fixers were never subtle. One player got a call one night but regrettably couldn't do the session. In kindness he suggested to the fixer a few names of other good players who were friends. The fixer said: "Oh, yes, I've tried everyone else!" On another occasion, a musician's wife answered a call for work but had to apologise and explain that her husband had just had a heart attack. The fixer's self-centred and stunningly insensitive response was: "Why does this *always* happen to *me?*"

The majority of the fixers were excellent at their job. Some, however, were confused by the rapidly changing musical styles, some manipulated the system, and others were just plain dim. Here are a few "fixing" highlights, the first from trumpeter and arranger, Ray Davies.

Davies: "One legendary fixer had also been one of the four violinists on the John Barry Seven Plus Four sessions. One night, after a Button Down Brass broadcast session at the BBC Paris Studios in Lower Regent Street, guitarist John McLaughlin told this fixer that he was soon leaving England to join Miles Davis in the USA. The fixer, who had a high-pitched and slightly whining voice, said: 'You silly boy, you could have done all my broadcast work.' He hadn't a clue who Miles Davis was, or what he meant." With a similar lack of vision, this same fixer would admonish Jimmy Page and John Paul Jones when they forsook sessions to form Led Zeppelin.

One musician had to make part of his journey to work across the Thames via the Woolwich Ferry; it was the quickest route. On one particular day, the ferry broke down and the guy was inevitably late for the session. He apologised profusely and tried to explain to the fixer, but the fixer's only response was to exclaim in his usual high voice: "How dare you come to my sessions by boat!"

In the early days it was absolutely unheard of to confront or disagree with a fixer, but, as one employee remembers, there was once a rare but almighty argument between one particularly notorious fixer and guitarist Richie Tattersall. It was a real slanging match, with Richie calling him names and aiming such gems as: "We don't need the likes of you... you talentless leech... we don't need you, you need us..." and so on. For the duration of this abuse the fixer remained silent, just puffing on his cigar. At the end of the tirade he took the cigar out of his mouth, turned, looked at the small crowd that had gathered and, with palms facing upwards and shoulders raised, said: "He must have independent means!"

In the 1960s, this same fixer became faintly aware of a new rhythm style from America called Tamla Motown. Desperate to keep up with the new trends, he asked one rhythm section player: "Are you any good at that 'Pamela Morton' music?"

At about the same time he'd heard the name Herb Alpert, but in his confusion he managed to ask a musician if he could play in the style of Alf Herbert! Dr Robert Moog had, by the late 1960s, begun to shape the future of pop music with his invention of a sophisticated electronic keyboard controller known as the Moog synthesiser. The fixer, in his unique way, once asked a keyboard player if he had "one of those new 'mood sympathisers'".

These confusions weren't just confined to musical styles or instruments. An American client once rang him with a simple request for a jazz-orientated guitarist. In a bout of lateral thinking, the fixer booked Dick Abell who, being of Indonesian descent and by trade a guitarist, must be an oriental jazz guitarist. Dick turned up at the session totally baffled. Confusion with name and instrument was also in evidence when bass player Tim Bell was booked by the fixer for a session that required a *timbale* player.

Dick Abell remembers how the fixer once tried to book baritone sax player Ronnie Ross. Unfortunately, Ronnie couldn't make it, so the fixer called other players to ask: "Can you play as rough as Ronnie Ross?"

And guitarist Ray Russell recalls fixer Charlie Katz booking him for a session, adding the request: "Don't forget to bring your 'gimmicks'!" Sensibly, Ray took his 'foot-pedals'.

However, the story that will immortalise our man in the fixer hall of fame concerns a recording session in 1970 for the jazz singer Jon Hendricks. His thought process dulled by decades of indifference and confusion, the fixer began to hire musicians such as Clem Cattini, he thinks, for Jimi Hendrix. On the day of the session, Clem was upset to hear the news of Jimi's death the previous evening, and assumed that the session would be cancelled. During a phone call, the fixer wondered why Clem wasn't at the studio. Clem: "But, Jimi Hendrix died last night." The fixer: "You'd better go along, someone's bound to turn up."

Mercifully, not all fixers were as appalling as this. One sweet story by guitarist Martin Kershaw concerns fixer Sid Margo, who had also been a violinist for John Barry's Plus Four. Looking impressive in his suit, and carrying a clipboard, Sid was organising a session at Chalk Farm Studios for a reggae band. While checking on some fine details, he asked one band member: "Are you on VAT?" The musician, interested, replied in a soft, slightly Caribbean accent: "No, man, but I'll try it if you've got some."

One fixer who has survived these changing times is the very excellent Isobel Griffiths who now books orchestral sessions almost exclusively, both for record – recent clients were Jeff Beck and Eric Clapton – and for film (her name appears on the credits of countless films during the last two decades). But there are very few electric instruments on these sessions any more, and on US film dates any rhythm tracks tend to be pre-recorded in LA.

How ironic: the first players in the eighties to be displaced by the samplers were the string players, the horns, the reeds, and the percussionists. Now they're the only ones being booked.

Herbie Flowers in a natural pose with his tuba

FIXER HUMOUR

- "Write your name and address on this piece of paper and throw it in the bin on the way out."
- "If the phone doesn't ring, that'll be me."
- "Bring your diary – and a rubber [eraser]."

(Incidentally, if there are not many dates in the book – or even none – the act of staring at the empty pages can induce "snow-blindness": "Hold on, I'll just get my diary, and some shades.")

Herbie Flowers

Around 1967, Herbie Flowers moved to a new house in Hillingdon, Middlesex. He knocked out the chimney breast from the roof right down to the lounge and, on a sequence of planks, took a wheelbarrow-load of cement to the loft. At just that moment, the phone rang and his wife called out: "A chap wants you for a session at Abbey Road straight away for Paul McCartney!" Excitedly, he left the barrow load of cement and took the call from fixer Laurie Gold, who said: "McCartney saw you in the Danny La Rue Club and liked your sound."

Herbie went straight to the session, still covered in cement, pausing only to buy an A–Z map on the way to find out where Abbey Road was. The session was for The Scaffold (featuring Mike McGear, Roger McGough, and John Gorman) and the song was 'Thank You Very Much' produced by Mike's brother Paul McCartney. Everyone was happy, and Herbie cites this as the session which – more than any other at the time – helped to raise his profile. Later that day, when he returned home, Herbie raced to the top of the house to discover that the cement had set solid in the wheelbarrow. Over 40 years later, perhaps the current residents of 237 Windsor Avenue, Hillingdon, will confirm whether it's still there?

(I think it's funny. This appeared in the original book and there have been no complaints)

At the start of his production career Gus Dudgeon asked around for musicians and someone recommended Herbie Flowers. Gus: "I thought with a name like that he must be good!" In June 1969, at Trident Studios, Gus produced "Space Oddity" for David Bowie, with Bowie himself on rhythm guitar, Rick Wakeman on piano, Terry Cox (from Pentangle) on drums, and Herbie on bass guitar (earning £7/10/-) (£7-50p). Around this time, Herbie, guitarist Alan Parker and drummer Barry Morgan played 75 per cent of their sessions as a rhythm "team". It was Barry (then owner of Morgan Studios) who suggested that they record some of the material they had written and arranged with Roger Cook and Roger Greenaway under the band name of Blue Mink featuring Cook and Madeleine Bell on vocals. In one long day in the late summer of 1969 they recorded and mixed four songs, including "Melting Pot", got a deal the next day, and achieved – to their surprise and pleasure – the first of several hits, which also included "Banner Man" and "Good Morning Freedom".

Herbie was reunited with David Bowie when the singer produced Lou Reed's album *Transformer* in 1972, on which Herbie played both double-bass and bass guitar. On the classic track "Walk on the Wild Side" it was Herbie's idea to play the main bass-line on double-bass, and then harmonise the top line in tenths (an octave plus a third) on bass-guitar. He received only the basic session fee of £72 for six sessions on the album. Overwhelmed by Herbie's immeasurable bass talents, Bowie hired him once again in December 1973 to work at Olympic Studios on his *Diamond Dogs* album, adding further weight to a CV which also included credits with Elton John, T-Rex, David Essex and, more recently, Joe Brown's daughter, singer/songwriter Sam Brown.

A few years later, when Herbie had become one of the UK's top session bassists, he went on holiday to Ibiza and entrusted his session diary to his mum, hoping that plenty of work would be in the book upon his return. He explained to her the role of session fixers and that several of them – Charlie, David, Laurie, and Harry – would be calling and leaving messages that might sound like shipping forecasts eg: EMI Two, ten to one, or Trident, seven 'til ten, or Pye at "Chinese dentist time" (i.e., 2.30). While he was away, Herbie remembered that it was his mum's birthday, and he greeted her from a call box. He also casually asked her about his diary, to which she excitedly informed him that on the day of his return he was booked for seven recording sessions: three in the morning, two in the afternoon and two in the evening. Unfortunately, in her enthusiasm she didn't realise that you could only do one session at a time, and of course these all overlapped! Poor Herbie – it subsequently cost him about £200 in phone calls to fix up deps.

Ray Russell

A similar near-tragedy happened to Ray Russell, who was phoned by session fixer George Hamer while enjoying a rare and well-earned night out with his wife – the babysitter took the message. When Ray and his wife returned, to his horror he found a crumpled piece or paper, on which was scrawled: "George phoned tomorrow. Bring two sticks." Ray spent the next hour ringing all the fixers and musicians trying to crack the code of this message. Eventually he got through to George; it transpired that the message should have read: "George Hamer phoned, session tomorrow, 10–1 CTS Wembley, bring your acoustics!"

Big Jim Sullivan

Guitarist Big Jim Sullivan began to enjoy session work, and in 1962 he received a call from a fixer to work on a film session at Elstree. Jim explained to him that he couldn't read dots, but rock 'n' roll was okay and he could also read from a chord chart. The fixer said: "No problem, it's just chords." Of course, there was a problem: the chords were written in dots, like bunches of grapes. Impossible to read! Alongside Jim were seasoned players, including Judd Procter and Ike Isaacs. Jim struggled, and after half an hour, through the talkback speakers came the voice of the MD, Stanley Black: "Would the third guitar pack up and go home." Jim was mortified and nearly gave up. He walked around the building and was in tears. Judd came to his rescue – he talked to him, advised and suggested which books to read. He also drove him home. Eight months later he did another similar session without a hitch and soon became one of the

John Paul Jones, Joe Moretti, and Big Jim Sullivan in the studio

The Krew Kats in the dressing room. Jim Sullivan recalls: "We all look so serious because we wanted to be serious musicians. The pose we are in is a copy of a Modern Jazz Quartet album cover: it was Brian Bennett's idea"

UK's busiest studio guitarists.

Many of Jim Sullivan's sessions were with Jimmy Page. The deal between them was that if the music was more country-orientated, Big Jim would do the solos; if more rock, Jimmy would. As a result of their awesome partnership, Big Jim and Little Jim did all the rock sessions at one time. Producer and engineer Gus Dudgeon says: "When recording at Olympic Studios, the secret of success was to book both Big Jim and Jimmy Page on guitar, and these sessions were known as 'Two Jimmy Sessions'. You had, in effect, a good housekeeping seal of approval. You never knew in advance which one of them would play lead.

Jim Sullivan played the incredible lead break on P.J. Proby's 'Hold Me': it was a one-take wonder; and Big Jim spent ages afterwards trying – but failing – to improve on it." Jim often played a Maton acoustic, with its custom-made neck fashioned by luthier Dick Knight. It was, in fact, Jim who played the choked-chord acoustic intro on The Small Faces' "Itchycoo Park".

Dick Abell

By a twist of fate, a BBC deputy director who knew Dick Abell out East phoned and asked him to form a band to play "funny music" – i.e., Chinese! Dick responded by forming a seven-piece of top sessioneers for the BBC Overseas Service to record at BBC Maida Vale Studios. One morning in 1962, he recorded three programmes and six tunes, and earned what was then the fortune of £19. More sessions followed, including live broadcasts of *Sing Along with Joe Henderson* from factories all over Britain before working with John Dankworth, Sammy Davis Jnr, Henry Mancini (*Return of the Pink Panther* film), and playing on TV shows including Benny Hill, Tommy Cooper and The Muppets. He remained the "first call" guitarist for Stanley Black film score sessions until Stanley died in 2002.

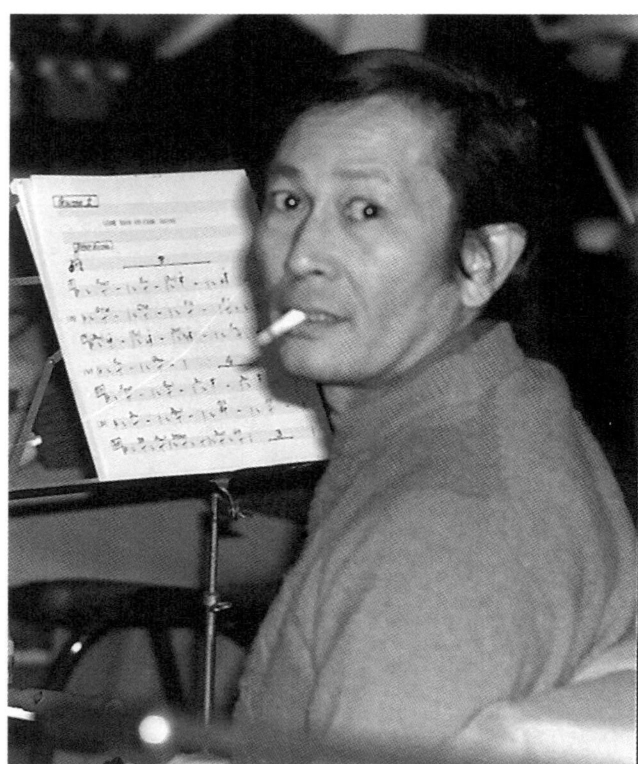

Dick Abell in the studio

Dick's blinding versatility is the envy of his colleagues. He is the only session musician in London who can sight-read for the Arabian instrument the *oud*, which he describes as sounding like a deep lute. His introduction to the instrument came via a call from an Arabic guy, possibly Iraqi, to perform on an album of Beatles' music! He gave Dick the *oud* and, not having too much of a clue at that point, Dick tuned it in fifths like a mandolin or violin. A while later, someone named John Leach showed him how to tune it properly. At the end of the sessions, the Arabic guy then gave the instrument to him (to put on his wall). Although it traditionally has gut strings and is played with an eagle's quill(!) Dick uses nylon strings and a pick – not least, one supposes, due to a shortage of eagle quills.

On rock sessions, Dick Abell would play rhythm on his Strat but never lead. If the part said "wild fills", he would defer to Judd Procter. To this day, if Judd meets Dick, he greets him with: "Done any wild fills lately?"

Alan Parker/Monty Python

Herbie Flowers' guitarist colleague in Blue Mink was Alan Parker. One of the funniest and most unusual engagements he ever played on was booked through fixer Ronnie Hazlehurst, who required Alan to play solo bouzouki on a session at the BBC TV Centre in White City. This was a strange request, but Ronnie was unable to enlighten Alan as to what the session entailed. Bemused, Alan arrived in the studio on the set of what looked like a shop counter. The director sent him to wardrobe for a pinstripe suit and then instructed him to "sit down on a chair and ad-lib on the bouzouki". He further stressed: "During the show, when I point to you, start playing, whatever you wish, but on no account pay any attention to the actors. It may be strange, but take no notice, just keep playing." Alan can be forgiven for his look of utter bewilderment when John Cleese and Michael Palin bowled in to perform, to the accompaniment of his solo bouzouki, what we now know as Monty Python's "Cheese Shop" sketch.

Greek

Bouzoukis were also featured on the soundtrack of the film *Shirley Valentine*, recorded in Abbey Road Studio Two. Playing them were Martin Kershaw, Mitch Dalton and Judd Procter, who were surrounded on the session by a large string section. The conductor was Harry Rabinowitz.

Bouzoukis are delicate instruments, fraught with danger. During a cue for a "Greek holiday scene" there was a mounting tuning problem. It grew so bad that Martin suddenly yelled: "For Chrissake, will somebody give me an Alpha?"

Phil Seaman

Jazz drummer Phil Seaman was one of the select few musicians able to play the difficult and complex pad of Bernstein's visionary West End theatre show *West Side Story* – when he was awake, that is. During a performance one evening he fell asleep, waking up with a sudden start during a tender love scene. Convinced that he had nearly missed a cue he swung round at his gong, making such an absurdly loud and exquisitely inappropriate noise that the audience nearby began laughing. Phil, never one to miss an opportunity, stood up, turned round, bowed, and announced: "Dinner is served."

Phil once played on a session with a big orchestra. His dog, who slept through most of the recording, was tied, as usual, to his hi-hat stand. In a break, a violinist across the other side of the studio opened a packet of sandwiches. The dog, woken by such a familiar and seductive rustling sound, assumed that the food was for him and tore off through all the instruments and microphones, pulling the hi-hats with him in the manner of a deranged husky.

John McLaughlin

After a spell with Herbie Goins and The Nightimers, John spent a couple years as a session guitarist, playing alongside such other guitar greats as Big Jim Sullivan, Joe Moretti, Ray Russell, Jimmy Page (to whom he gave lessons) and Vic Flick, who says: "John played acoustic guitar on a lot of sessions, even though his heart wasn't in it. At that time he had to earn money. In between takes he was always doodling, with those fantastic runs and arpeggios of his. That habit of John's used to bug some engineers, as they were forever having to open and close his mic. Perhaps they should have recorded John's doodlings and forgotten about the main track."

On one occasion at Olympic Sound Studios in 1967, a session was actually for Big Jim Sullivan himself. The piece was called "The Kone" and was in the daunting time signature of 21/8. While John played guitar, Jim played sitar and now feels that this particular piece may have contributed to John's later fascination with Indian music.

John's finest achievement from this period was his own 1969 *Extrapolation* album produced by Giorgio Gomelsky and featuring a line-up of John Surman on baritone sax, Tony Oxley on drums and bassist Brian Odgers. I had the privilege of watching the quartet rehearse in the downstairs bar at Ronnie Scott's. One track, 'Pete the Poet', was a tribute to Cream lyricist Pete Brown, who recalls an occasion when "John was playing with Hammond organ player Mike Carr, and a summer gig in Majorca was imminent. At that time John's personal life was unhappy and he hated most of the sessions he was playing." Attempting to cheer him up, Pete confessed his feelings: "You're the best jazz guitarist in Britain today." It was a well-timed, astute observation, for one week later, courtesy of a recommendation from British bassist Dave Holland, John took a call from Miles Davis in New York. His life was about to change. John says: "You couldn't find a happier person than me in New York. For a European jazz musician to find himself playing with Miles Davis, Tony Williams, playing Harlem... it's paradise. I was in heaven."

This photograph of John McLaughlin was taken on the 1967 session at Olympic for the recording of Big Jim Sullivan's project 'The Kone'. Jim's sitar is visible in the background. I showed this photo to guitarist Mike Jopp (of Affinity), who once worked at Ivor Mairants' shop in Rathbone Place. He said: "I sold him that guitar. It's a Gibson L4 with Charlie Christian pickups." Lyricist Pete Brown remembers: "John had a little DeArmond amplfier which was about a foot square – it was so 'live' you got a shock off the wood!"

John Paul Jones and Jimmy Page

In the early 1960s, John Paul Jones visited Archer Street in Soho, a location which was at the time the main focus for musicians looking for work. There he met Jet Harris, and this encounter led to an audition for Tony Meehan, which he passed. Recording and touring followed, and, as Jones says, "We even had John McLaughlin with us for a while on rhythm guitar – rhythm guitar!" He started recording – with Meehan as producer – at Decca's studios in West Hampstead. Much session work followed, and he soon found himself playing alongside future Led Zep cohort Jimmy Page.

Jimmy ultimately became one of the most sought-after studio session guitar players around, during which time he had a few lessons from John McLaughlin. Another guitarist, Vic Flick, became friendly with Jimmy during the sessions they did together. "Jimmy was quite busy on the session scene at the time, even though he couldn't read and didn't really want to. His inventiveness made him popular with arrangers who were looking to absorb any new sound or lick. Jimmy was kind enough to acknowledge at one time the help I gave him on recording dates, when I used to play for him the odd few written parts he had. He listened a couple of times then put them down. A great musician."

Jimmy Page entered the session scene in 1962, and on his first of many sessions with Big Jim Sullivan ("My Baby Left Me" by Dave Berry, recorded in late 1963) he played his black three-pickup Les Paul custom. Among Jimmy's many classic but uncredited performances were lead breaks on early Who records, the solos on "Baby Please Don't Go" by Them with Van Morrison, and the superb intro to Joe Cocker's 'With a Little Help from My Friends'. Tommy Eyre, who arranged and played Hammond organ on the track, recalls recording the song at Olympic Studio Two, and it was Joe Cocker's idea to play the song in 3/4 time. On day one, Steve Winwood was on guitar and Jim Capaldi was on drums, but Jim was unhappy with the feel. On the session the next day, Jimmy was on guitar and formed his intro idea, with B.J. Wilson on drums and Chris Stainton on bass to create the lead-up line.

In a break, Tommy started playing Bartok's "Mikrokosmos". Jimmy, enjoying it, responded: "I use that for guitar." They then went to the pub for a drink and a chat during which Jimmy advised Tommy to see the new film, *2001: A Space Odyssey* and told him of a new band he was forming to be called Led Zeppelin.

Jimmy, often with John Paul Jones, did countless sessions with artists such as Tom Jones, Frank Ifield, Dave Berry, and Petula Clark. On the day that they announced they were quitting sessions everyone thought they were crazy. Little did they realise what was to follow.

When Zep ended its monumental career after John Bonham's death in September 1980, Jimmy didn't play for a while, although he did jam with us (The Jeff Beck Group) on our end-of-world-tour gig at Hammersmith Odeon in 1981.

John Paul Jones and his Burns 'Split Sound' six-string bass

CHAPTER 16

LAUGHTER AND TEARS

THE GIGGLES

"Giggling is rarely a solitary occupation. It depends on mutual feedback; a painful attempt to suppress one's own snorts, tears, and whinnies conflicting with an unpleasant desire to see one's co-giggler reinfected." (George Melly)

Goodbye Yellow Brick Road

Flushed with the success of "Your Song" and his *Tumbleweed Connection* album, Elton John felt it appropriate to expand his band by one guitarist in February 1972, and chose ex-Magna Carta member Davey Johnstone for the role. Being an acoustic player, however, Davey was forced to learn electric guitar from scratch. But as hits like "Saturday Night's Alright for Fighting" and "Candle in the Wind" demonstrate, his progress was far from slow.

Davey recalls one particular horror to befall him during sessions in 1973 for the classic *Goodbye Yellow Brick Road* album in Kingston, Jamaica. He says: "In those days we had one roadie, Bob Stacey, a true giant in his field. The methods of shipping our equipment were basic, to say the least, and usually involved wrapping gaffer [duct] tape around the instruments cases and placing them on the conveyor belt with all the other passengers' luggage. Dodgy! Then, as a particular instrument was required, it would be unwrapped as necessary!

Davey Johnstone on banjo

"The studio, which should remain nameless, was set up for reggae recording and therefore not as well equipped as we were used to. We sensed trouble when the local engineer yelled to the tape operator: 'Carlton, get de macrapone.' Anyway, Gus Dudgeon and our producer and engineer Ken Scott hastily requested extra gear from a studio in Miami and we soldiered on. With abundant local ganja, our job became even more light-hearted and hilarious than usual.

"One day, Elton was in the middle of composing the song 'Social Disease', and I thought: 'Oh, banjo would be good on this,' and began unwrapping my banjo case. While doing this my attention was mostly directed to Elton, and didn't really notice the state of my poor banjo as I opened the case. Gripping the instrument by the neck, it seemed a lot lighter than usual, which was hardly surprising since the neck had been totally separated from the body of the banjo, probably by the throwing action of baggage handlers, leaving the neck of my banjo adorned simply with dreadlock-like broken strings!

"My reaction was one of open-mouthed surprise, which led Nigel Olsson to fall laughing into his drum kit and thence to Elton John rolling on the floor in pain. We laughed for about 15 minutes (aided in great part by the marijuana), and then Elton asked the immortal question: 'What kind of organ was it?' Of course, that started us off into another bout of laughter and we had to abandon the session for the day. You had to be there!"

Talk of the Town

In the late seventies Kim Goody, Annie Kavanagh, and Sharon Campbell (known to her friends as Karen Shambles, for obvious reasons) were often booked together on backing vocal sessions. Their voices blended perfectly, but there was occasionally a problem: as a team they were simply hopeless when it came to the giggles!

They were to be part of the band on the Marti Caine show for two weeks at the Talk of the Town (later the Hippodrome) at Leicester Square in London.

Kim explains: "The house was packed full – Marti was enormously popular then and very much loved. The show was in two halves: after the interval and in traditional style we three girls – Annie, Sharon, and me – would open the second half with our featured 'spot'. Marti had given us that old favourite 'Mr Bojangles'. Picture the scene: close harmonies, front of stage, all around one mic, big single spotlight, and a piano... you know, the sort of intimate atmosphere thing...

"Marti had been very keen about how we looked – and what we wore (she was herself a very glamorous artist) – and 'different but similar' was our brief. She was happy with our dresses but not our shoes (which had to be silver) and had given us a very generous 'shoe budget'.

"Annie and I spent all of our budget on some really nice silver shoes but Sharon, seeing a bit of profit in this, had purchased a second-hand pair of the biggest, ill-fitting, awful silver shoes we had ever seen. We had a few giggles over them but on that night as they (the shoes) came out on their first 'outing', a nightmare began – the kind which we all dread when it comes to live performances.

"The lights went down, the audience hushed, and the piano began the plaintive opening to 'Mr Bojangles'. Annie and I made our entrance as usual through the huge velvet curtains centre-stage, but Sharon fell over in her great big shoes and had somehow got caught up in the hem of the curtain.

"Annie & I were now alone at the mic, very much aware of a ridiculous amount of movement behind the curtains as Sharon tried to sort herself out. And with all this struggling noise going on behind us we began the most painful 'duet' version of 'Mr Bojangles'.

"For me, there was simply no hope of any sound coming out of my voice at all. I shook painfully inside with laughter (tears and all), and coupled with this was the awful feeling of fear and horror at just standing there shaking under the hot spotlight in front of that enormous packed house as the piano played on.

"For Annie, what a star! She gave it a go 'solo' with a sound that came out totally unrecognisable as her usual voice, and which was more like a strangled cat! I simply found this even funnier! Sharon did eventually join us (like an Eric Morecombe entrance) but that made it all the worse, and there was no hope we were ever going to get this together. Looking back it was the longest three minutes on stage I have ever experienced."

Shadow Birds

An attack of the giggles is invariably problematic on a recording session because, no matter what state you're in, once the red light is on you have to focus on the music for the duration of the piece.

On one occasion I was booked to play in the rhythm section of a small orchestra and record live tracks at Lansdowne Studios with Roger Whittaker. There was no room for mistakes. Time is money. When a lot of musicians are recording simultaneously at Lansdowne it's necessary – for reasons of separation – to place various sections of the orchestra in rooms dotted around the building. On this session, the strings and brass were in the main room, Roger and the backing vocalists were in a room overlooking the studio, while the rhythm section – including Ray Russell and Jeff Crampton on electric guitars, and me on bass guitar – set up in a hallway. (Our music stands were always being knocked over by anyone passing through.)

During the morning session I noticed that a light was shining through a screen in such a way that my hands and fingers could produce shadow animals on the opposite wall near to me. When Ray joined in, the fate of the day was sealed. Now, Roger is a fine singer and an expert whistler, but unfortunately the juxtaposition of Roger's whistle in our cans and my pathetic attempts to produce a convincing shadow bird on the wall during the song suggested a game that both guitarists felt the need to join in. Unwritten rules began to emerge, the best one being that during a one-bar tacet (i.e., four-beat break) one should create as many fairly exotic animated flying shadow creatures on the nearby wall as possible. At first we were careful, with just the faintest suggestion of an owl (it could have been a cat) during one of Roger's interludes. As the day wore on we became more daring, until kittiwakes and kestrels were nothing. The only requirement was that, after four beats, we should return impeccably to the downbeat of the next bar. We did. Thankfully, what didn't appear on tape were the suppressed convulsions, muffled shrieking, and the tears which soaked our charts. Sorry, Roger.

Scaffolding

Drummer Gary Husband recalls a soundcheck with the Syd Lawrence Orchestra: "We turn up at a venue and Syd walks on the stage. His expression is of disbelief at what he sees there, and he turns to the stage manager, demanding to know why there is scaffolding situated high on both sides of the stage. The poor guy explains nervously that the towers are necessary for structural security until the surveyors have finished checking for any possible building faults. Syd argues this for a good few minutes, but finally gives in. He's in such a bad mood that we don't see him until showtime. The band squeezes onstage, and after they play through the first number Syd gets on the mic – 'Good evening ladies and gentlemen,' he says, 'it's wonderful to be here. But before I go any further I feel I really must apologise for all the erections on stage!' There are loud guffaws from the band, but he has no idea why they are laughing. He turns around and says 'What?' The musicians are now helpless."

A Cappella

A singer was on tour with his band and a large orchestra. He had decided to start the song "Country Roads" a cappella, with just him and his three backing vocalists singing in a rich harmony. The intro was meticulously rehearsed: cue note from the piano for pitch, a downbeat from the conductor, and all of the vocalists would sing. Perfect.

One night the conductor observed that the singer had not seen his downbeat, and hastily cancelled the intro. Unfortunately one of the backing singers didn't notice the cut-off, and innocently proceeded to sing – with great conviction – the opening syllable: "cunt..." Any attempt by the conductor to resolve this moment and carry on was rendered futile simply because the rest of the band was on the floor, hysterical.

Hypnotherapy

There's now a name for it: performance anxiety. However, on one occasion, just before a big tour, I was feeling apprehensive. It was not stage-fright, I just felt a little "edgy". A friend advised me to see a hypnotherapist.

On the first visit I sat in a comfy chair. The therapist asked me to relax and then switched on an old wooden metronome standing next to me. Tick-tock, tick-tock. I pointed out that this was ridiculous because I heard this sound every day in my studio headphones – the click-track. We talked and I tried again to relax, but I could hear planes going overhead and distant dogs barking. I agreed to come back the following week.

The comfy chair again. Eyes shut. This time he asked me to relax by thinking about each part of the body in turn. We started with the forehead, eyebrows, cheeks, and jaw – I let them sag. The neck unstiffened. The shoulders dropped. The stomach felt less tense. Suddenly – in anticipation of the next downward stage – I started giggling: I realised that there was a huge fart sitting there, waiting to ambush the session. Had I relaxed fully I would have destroyed his chair.

I never went back, but I have since learnt how to relax by deep-breathing. It's less dangerous.

In Arm's Way

Alan Parker depped one night with The Phil Tate Band at the Hammersmith Palais. Phil had a false arm, but this didn't deter him from conducting: he would wedge the baton firmly in its grip and wave away. The place was crowded, as was usual on a Saturday night, and at one point Phil announced: "And now we'd like to feature Alan Parker on guitar, playing the latest hit from The Shadows, 'Atlantis'." As he did so, he swung his right arm with the intention of pointing at Alan but unfortunately... "It came flying out of his jacket and went skating across the dance floor. It was like the parting of the Red Sea as the whole of the audience frantically moved out of its way." The band members were helpless.

A MOMENTARY LAPSE OF PROFESSIONALISM

Parkinson

On *Parkinson*, the late night TV chat show, the resident band was led by MD and keyboard player Harry Stoneham, and included saxophonist Cliff Townshend (Pete's dad). At one time, the guitarist was Vic Flick. Before one show, Vic and the percussionist Jim Lawless had popped out for a drink, but Vic accidentally had one too many. During the show, while Michael Parkinson was chatting to the softly spoken James Stewart, Vic fell asleep. His Strat, with volume fully on, slid off his leg and fell to the ground. *Kerrang*! It was an impressive sound to all but Harry Stoneham. The outcome? Vic out, Dick Abell in. He did the show for the next eleven years using his Gibson 17SD.

"60 Years On"

Elton John's breakthrough album, often referred to as *The Black Album*, was notable for guitarist Colin Green's contributions. A different kind of hysteria to that of Davey's came into play when, in the spring of 1970, Colin was called to make some repairs to one performance at Trident Studios – after some serious imbibing. "On the track '60 Years On' the whole of the first chorus is just Elton's voice and my Spanish guitar. The song was recorded, everyone was pleased with Paul Buckmaster's arrangements, and we finished the session. As I did in those days, I went straight to The Ship, the pub on the corner, and demolished its entire stock of brandy. About an hour later, the engineer rushed into the pub and said 'We've got a noise on the guitar track; you'll have to do it again.'"

There was no guiding click-track or any indication of tempo on tape, only Elton's voice. By now Colin was very drunk and shaking with fear. Nervously, Colin warned the engineer, Robin Cable: "You'd better get this right – we've got one shot at it!" He says: "It seemed like an eternity but it was only 32 bars; I didn't know if it was right until the cellos came in. Luckily, we got it in the first take."

Bass Solo

Double-bass player Roy Babbington was often asked to take solos. All during the week leading up to a big show he tried out some showbiz moves inspired by Ted Heath's bassist, Johnny Hawksworth, whose own act featured comedy. It was all about giving the audience a show, and Roy's plan was simple: bass on its side, cue, foot on spike, bass up ready to play. It worked great at home. On the night there wasn't much space for the bass neck to rise up between the sax desk and the MD's music stand (bearing the name "Leslie Thorpe" and carrying his clarinet). The inevitable happened: foot on spike, neck up, crash into the MD's stand, clarinet flying, a collision with saxes, music fluttering, chaos, paper everywhere, people falling over each other... a classic moment

Blue Peter

I was always a fan of comedy records that were more like sketches with music, and those that spring to mind were by artists such as The Goons, Stan Freberg, and Spike Jones. It was with these artists as mentors that my friend – actor/writer Mike Walling – and I wrote and recorded "The Popadom Song", a fun piece that essentially concerned two losers arguing over an Indian menu. It was really an early form of rap, although we spoke the lyrics simply and realistically because neither of us could sing. We were known as The R.J. Wagsmith Band.

To our surprise, the song received a fair amount of airplay on BBC Radio 1, and would have been a minor hit but for the perfectly timed three-week strike at Polygram, our distributor. Not a single record reached the shops! A couple of TV appearances emerged from the mess, however, one of which was on the children's programme *Blue Peter.*

I assembled some friends to accompany us, namely Ray Russell on sitar, Nic France on tablas, Peter Van Hooke (dressed as an Australian, for reasons only he will know) on drums, Gary Taylor on bass, and Pete Arneson on Wurlitzer piano, while vocal backing was provided by the three presenters, Sarah Greene, Peter Duncan, and Simon Groome. We began camera rehearsals in the morning at BBC TV Centre, where Mike and I sat at a table, and my friends played their instruments nearby. Mike, being an actor, was cool but I was nervous and had to hide my lines in the menu in front of me.

At the end of the song we had scripted an argument about a Bombay duck, an Indian delicacy that resembles a sort of smelly burnt fish. Towards the end of this sketch I held up a little kipper – the nearest that the BBC props department could find – and was supposed to say in an absurd Wolverhampton accent: "Well, it's the funniest duck I've ever tasted." During the first recording, with five cameras around us, I managed to say: "Well, it's the funniest fuck I've ever had." I was *so* embarrassed, and slumped in a blushing heap on the table.

The Blue Peter badge

The technicians rewound the tape and played back the last few seconds over every monitor in the whole studio. Everyone just fell about, shrieking with laughter, although I don't think producer Biddy Baxter was too amused and I had to go for a quick run around the block to calm down.

We did a retake, which was fine for transmission later that afternoon. And I still got my *Blue Peter* badge.

VIGNETTES

Working as a session player for the last 40 years, I have been privy to many bizarre and hysterical sights and experiences. These are just a few.

- In the 1970s, seeing drummer Brian Bennett walking down a corridor at Abbey Road wearing just one cycle clip (which was to prevent his bass drum pedal from entering his flared trousers while he played.)
- The first *Little and Large* series from Thames TV's studios in Teddington: seeing the look of panic on MD Tony Hatch's face when he realised that Peter Van Hooke played a drum fill every time they had eye contact.

Sunday morning rehearsal at Thames Television: Peter Van Hooke in a state of maximum readiness for the first downbeat

- Pete coming to my rescue on one show. Unbeknownst to me, my "safety" power supply was in fact very unsafe; whilst I was checking it, my bass happened to touch the metal music stand: sparks flew and I was blown off my chair into an upright and exceedingly baffled position. My bass flew off into guitarist Ric Morcambe's lap. It was only when Pete noticed the state I was in and yelled "Fire!" that the band stopped playing. I was carried out and given a very large brandy.
- One Saturday afternoon at Trident Studios: noticing that, for the entire session, drummer Ronnie Verrall was looking to his right whereas his music stand was to his left. He later admitted that his passion for horse racing meant that he had secreted a small portable TV in the drum booth and an earpiece inside his headphones. He still didn't miss a beat.

- In the spring of 1977 I was booked to be part of Neil Innes' backing band for an appearance on *The Old Grey Whistle Test*, recorded at the BBC TV Theatre in Shepherd's Bush. On the same show were the freshly reformed Small Faces (minus Ronnie Lane). I have a fond memory of watching Steve Marriott, in an outrageously padded suit, wandering around selling "protection" to the cameramen during the rehearsals, and demanding, in an over-the-top cockney spiv accent, "Unless you pay me half a crown *right now*, this camera *might* catch fire."

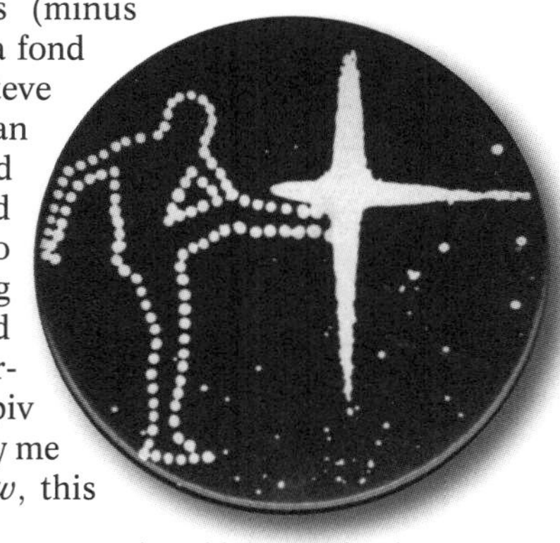

The Old Grey Whistle Test

- 1977: a week of French disco sessions at Trident. As soon as a track had finished, pianist Alan Hawkshaw launched into Gershwin's "Rhapsody in Blue", pausing only when the next track was about to start. In this fashion he played the whole piece during the week, albeit cut into several hundred short segments. He claims that he's still trying to learn it.
- A small orchestral session at Lansdowne: after making the same mistake ten times, drummer Tony Carr threw down his sticks, stormed out of the booth, shouting at the ceiling with arms outstretched: "Will you leave me alone?"
- A rhythm section and string quartet were in AIR Studio One. Guitarist Ray Russell was conducting for the first time. It's always a challenge for a rhythm player to conduct a string section, so when one of the pieces broke down, an animated discussion ensued. The leader, violinist Gavyn Wright, suddenly shouted across at Ray, tongue in cheek: "Look, any more of this and we'll start following you!"
- Well-built trumpet player Alan Downey arrived for a ten o'clock session at Audio International Studios, entered the control room, attempted in a mock fashion to look cool and, clearly holding his stomach in with great difficulty, enquired: "Hi guys, are there any women on this session?" "No," said the producer. "Thank God for that," said Alan, letting out his stomach with great relief.
- I once played bass on a session for MD Richard Hewson, a good arranger who cared for his music. All of the players were the best. Unfortunately, the song was really limp and, as is usual in such situations, we routined it over and over, with each player chipping in ideas and riffs to try to make the song happen. After about an hour, Richard crystallised all of our feelings when he suddenly flung down his pencil and said despairingly: "This is like trying to polish a turd!"
- A recording session was going horribly astray at Pebble Beach Studio in Worthing, and producer Peter Van Hooke desperately needed reassurance from his co-producer, John Altman, who was reading quietly. In frustration he yelled across the control room: "John, for Chrissake say something!" Altman, slumped in a chair, unruffled and without looking up from the cricket pages of his newspaper, replied: "I see that Surrey were all out for 183."
- 1977. We were booked for a day's recording sessions for Brigitte Bardot at Trident Studios. Almost every musician brought in his camera, claiming that it was to be repaired at the little shop opposite the studio in St Anne's Court, just off Wardour Street. Alas, Bardot never turned up.
- Affinity were booked to play on the new BBC2 TV programme *Colour Me Pop*, the predecessor of *Whistle Test*. Prior to our recording at the new TV Centre, a long-haired floor manager – holding a little tin – came over to us. It was his job to relax the artist before the show. In a gentle – almost secretive – voice he spoke to Grant, the drummer: "I've got a couple of small joints if you'd like them before the show."

We were naïve, and Grant, who had no idea why this guy should be offering us leftovers from his previous Sunday meal, replied: "Thank you, you're very kind, but we've eaten already".

It's strange to hear that we are now considered to have been a "psychedelic" band.

COMMUNICATION

Funeral March

British comedian Spike Milligan and jazz-man Ronnie Scott, a seemingly unlikely pairing, were good friends and used to attend the occasional classical concert together. Featured on one programme was a performance of Beethoven's "Funeral March". It dragged on and on and on. Finally Ronnie, unable to stand it anymore, whispered to Spike: "Christ, this bloke must have lived fucking miles from the cemetery."

Wine Glass

One night I had gone with some friends to the Durbar Indian restaurant in Notting Hill. During the meal I noticed that my hero Spike Milligan and his guest had sat down at the next table. I've always thought it impolite to speak to someone you admire, unless they speak first: you should respect their privacy.

Towards the end of the meal I began absent-mindedly rubbing my finger along the top of my wine-glass until it produced a high ringing tone. Suddenly Spike joined in, except that the pitch of his glass was a semi-tone lower. This was my chance. I looked at him and said, "Yours is lower than mine." Without missing a beat he replied, "That's because I'm *older* than you." Wonderful! I was in heaven. It was enough.

"Delilah"

Songwriter Barry Mason tells the story of when he once had to stop at a motorway café in Britain. In the gents' toilet he heard a guy whistling Tom Jones' recent hit "Delilah" whilst he was pissing. Unable to miss the opportunity Barry said to him: "I wrote that." To his surprise the guy replied: "No you didn't, Les Reed did." Trying to regain some semblance of composure Barry said: "Well *I* wrote the lyrics." But pedantic to the end, the guy responded: "I'm not whistling the lyrics."

Plymouth

During a party on a naval base in Plymouth, an extravagantly dressed woman marched up to the band and attempted to use her social position to demand a reduction in volume: "I'm the admiral's wife – can you keep it quiet?" The guitarist leaned over and whispered in her ear: "I won't tell a soul."

NYC

Glaswegian singer Frankie Miller and guitarist Ray Russell were recording in New York City. They arrived at their hotel and the cab driver, expecting a fat tip, said: "Have a nice day now, sir." Frankie walked up close to the guy, stabbed him in the chest with a forefinger, and, in the only accent that could possibly disturb a New Yorker, said: "Don't tell *me* what to do, pal."

Madison Square Gardens

Dougie Boyle, guitarist with Robert Plant's band, was about to play at Atlantic Records' 40th anniversary concert at Madison Square Gardens. It was his first ever experience of New York City. During a rehearsal he became desperate for a cigarette and, employing his best Essex dialect, innocently enquired of a local stage hand: "Can I bum a fag off you, man?" There was a short pause while the American crew member assessed this novel question. He then uttered the immortal observation: "You're new here, aren't you?"

Funky Banjo

Some time in 1999 guitarist Mitch Dalton was hired by a Japanese producer to play "funky" banjo for a Japanese artist at a small studio in Acton (West London). Mitch walked into the studio to be greeted by the producer, and also to be stunned by his stupendous collection of American vintage guitars and British retro amps.

"Wow! Are these all yours?" said Mitch. "Sure – I love these guitars and amps. I go to States all the time and buy them," said the producer, thrilled that another musician would recognise the significance of his display of historical instruments. Mitch couldn't resist playing as many of the Gibsons, Fenders, and Gretsches as he could. "Wow, these instruments are the best examples that I've ever seen!"

The producer humbly thanked him, but politely suggested that the session should start, and with extreme reluctance Mitch set up in the acoustic booth. The man from Japan walked in to adjust the mike position for the banjo ("like it matters", Mitch thought). "Wow! That banjo! Fantastic sound! What is it?" said the producer. "Oh, it's just a piece of Japanese rubbish," said Mitch as a throwaway. But even as he spoke, he began bashing his head against the music stand.

Mitch Dalton plays and endorses Ibanez banjos.

The Invitation

Malcolm Atkin – studio manager of Air Studios, Montserrat – recalls: "George Martin had the initial inspiration for a studio on this delightful Caribbean island, Dave Harries built it, and I designed and installed the desk.

"Government House called one day when everybody was out, and somehow I took the call. There was a request: 'Could the governor's wife bring up a couple of visiting dignitaries who were over from England for a tour of the studio?' Sure enough next day the official car turned up – complete with little flags, and motorbike outrider. Out stepped three little old ladies and, not having much to do, I gave them the full tour. We had a great time. At the end of my detailed enthusiastic explanation of how it all worked one of my audience – trying her hardest to keep up with me – asked: 'It all looks very complicated, but... erm... where do the records come out?' – What can you say?

"It got sillier after that because the next day the motorbike turned up again, this time with one of those beautiful gold-edged invites for me to go to the governor's Easter dinner party. This was an invite that all of the ex-pats on the island (including Dave Harries) were killing each other for."

The Tour

As general manager of EMI Abbey Road studios Ken Townsend was called upon to give guided tours of the building to important guests. Ken remembers one such occasion: "I was near the end of showing some very boring South Africans around and we had reached the penthouse cutting-room on the fourth floor. It had been a long afternoon, I was tired and, as I pointed to the door, I quite innocently said, 'And finally here is the cunthouse petting-room.'" The Reverend William Spooner would have been impressed.

Avant Garde

Drummer Rob Townsend recalls: "A few years ago The Blues Band were playing a big festival in Belgium. We were sitting in the dressing room when Lari, our roadie, came to tell me that the drum kit I was to use was in position if I would like to check it out. No time like the present, so off I went. When I got to the stage and looked out at the huge crowd I felt a little self-conscious about sitting alone on the drum riser tuning the kit, but then I noticed a keyboard player on stage making a racket setting up his gadgets and keyboards. Fair enough, so I climbed on the riser and started making a noise tuning the toms, positioning the cymbals, and crashing them to make sure they were right. After a while I noticed one of the stage-hands standing at my side. He rather sheepishly leaned over to me and enquired if I could stop tuning the kit until the keyboard player had finished his set. I later found out that he was a solo avant-garde keyboard player. One of the band commented afterwards that the audience probably thought I was part of the show!

"If"

Keith Grant was recording an album with Telly Savalas at Olympic Studio Two. Engineer David Hamilton-Smith recalls: "Savalas was trying to record the David Gates song "If". Towards the end there is a key change, which the artist found a little difficult – there was a bit of a 'car-crash'. They spoke to each other through the talkback:

Telly (optimistically): 'Hey Keith, did I make the key change?'

Keith (diplomatically): 'Some of it.'"

New York Town Hall

In 1972, The Maynard Ferguson Big Band was about to tour the United States, and its first gig was to be at New York Town Hall. Sitting in the first few rows of the auditorium were some of the finest musicians in the USA, but trombonist Derek Wadsworth, having spotted Duke Ellington, Don Ellis, and the brass section of the Chicago Symphony Orchestra, felt a little uneasy about playing jazz in such illustrious company. Some of the players in the band were English "hicks from the sticks", and just before they went on stage, bassist Dave Linane, from Eccles, enthusiastically shouted encouragement to Derek: "Come on, let's put this fooking town on the map!"

Fire

Sessions weren't always affected by manic laughter; some were downright hazardous. Being young and foolish, I used to smoke. On one session at Central Sound in Denmark Street, I had lit a cigarette out of boredom as I sat with headphones on, endlessly waiting. Suddenly, the red light summoned action. I rested my cigarette and book of matches on the music stand as we were counted in to start playing, eyes down. Equally suddenly, and very surprisingly,

Chris Rae, the human fire extinguisher, in the studio

guitarist Chris Rae threw down his guitar with a clang, rushed across the room and began hitting me on the head. I was too bewildered to object. We'd always been good mates, and I didn't think I'd played that badly. The reason for the assault? My hair was on fire! A piece of burning phosphor from the match had shot in the air and landed on my head, but the fully enclosed Beyer headphones prevented me from hearing the crackling. With industrious flair, Chris extinguished the flames and the session continued with an interesting smell in the air.

CONFUSION

Rehearsal

The musicians are ready with their pencils as the band leader outlines the changes he wants to make: "Okay guys, let's rehearse 'The Girl from Ipanema', key of F, two bars as is, a bar of 5/8, up a semitone for half a bar, a bar of 7/4, down a minor third for a bar and a half, then two bars of 'Moon River', three bars tacet..." All of the musicians are frantically scribbling on their parts, but the female vocalist, with mounting horror, interrupts: "I can't possibly do that!" Band leader: "Well, that's what you sang last night."

"Laura"

Arranger Kevin Townend recalls that singer Bobby Breen was going to be performing the pop standard "Laura" on a live radio broadcast. He rehearsed the song with the band during the afternoon and each time he came to the last line, he would sing: "That was Laura, but she's only a girl." The producer and studio manager gently and tactfully explained that the correct lyric was: "But she's only a dream." "Right, right... only a dream," said Bobby, taking this on board. By the time of the live broadcast, Bobby had become so confused by all these instructions that on reaching the final line, he ended up singing: "That was Laura, but she's only... a drool."

There's a similar story recalled by pianist Mike Moran where a singer became very confused while trying to shake hands with the ladies on the front row. In a bit of a flap he started the song "It's impossigivable..."

Sardines

Gary Kettel, one of the finest percussionists in London, was relaxing in the Green Room after a concert with The Nash Ensemble at The Queen Elizabeth Hall on the South Bank. An older woman approached him and asked: "What do *you* do?" Gary simply replied: "I play percussion". She seemed baffled; her life hadn't trained her to cope with such a concept, and she extended the question: "What I mean is, what do you *really* do?" Gary, having experienced this kind of stupidity before, felt the need to turn the conversation around, and asked: "Tell me, what does your husband do?" The woman proudly exclaimed: "Oh, he's in oil." Unable to miss this opportunity, Gary swiftly responded: "What is he, a fucking sardine?"

Alan's Dog

Countdown is a long-running TV show based on a word game.

It originated in France and was brought to Britain by Belgian Marcel Stellman, then the MD for Decca Records. The main theme and incidental cues were composed by Alan Hawshaw, and the original music sessions took place at Alan's home studio in Radlett.

At the end of the main 30-second cue (where a clock hand rotates) a tympani bend was required. Brian Bennett struggled in with his tymps, but as they would only reach the first landing of Alan's house, and his studio was on the top floor, there was a problem. Easily solved – extensions for microphones and headphones were set up, and the session started.

The main jingle ends with a keyboard riff "didut – didut – diddly-dit" followed by a typmani hit lowered in pitch by Brian releasing the pedal, thus making a 'doyng' sound. During the actual session Alan's dog – which had been sleeping quietly nearby during the setting-up – suddenly woke when he heard the loud "doyng" from the tymp, rushed over, and began noisily savaging Brian Bennett's leg. The tape exists. What a pity it's not played in full on the programme.

The Haircut

Jazz guitarist Martin Taylor relates: "For many years I had very long hair, and the week after having the lot chopped off I went on a solo UK tour. At the Norwich gig I popped in to The Vines for a quick beer on my way to the venue.

"The landlord spotted my guitar and said 'Ere, give us a song mate!' and added 'I'll pay you fifty quid.' I jokingly replied 'Add two more zeros to that fee and I may consider it.'

"Not recognising me with short hair, the landlord said 'Fuck me, who do you think you are, Martin Taylor?' It was all in good humour, and I never did let on who I was.

Another Haircut

Songwriter and current PRS Chairman Guy Fletcher recalls this event:

During a party for Music Business luminaries at Buckingham Palace (part of the royal celebrations for British Music Day) the Royal Family including the Queen, Prince Philip, Prince Edward and Sophie Wessex mingled informally with their 500 guests. A party of about ten of us including Eric Clapton and Brian May were standing in the central gallery when our little circle was joined by the Queen who approached Brian May (about 6ft 6ins with the hair) and said: "what do you do?" The group shifted uneasily in her imposing presence and Brian replied:

"I was the chap who played the 'National Anthem' on the roof of the palace for your Jubilee Party, Maam". Her Majesty (who's height allowed her only to have eye contact with Brian's lower chest) stepped back and laughed, saying very loudly "OH THAT WAS YOU!!!"

DREAMS

The Ukes

In 1985 The Ukulele Orchestra of Great Britain dreamed of filling the

Albert Hall with Ukuleles. On Tuesday 18th August 2009, at the BBC Proms, the Ukes attracted a sold-out audience, over six thousand people, with more than a thousand bringing their own ukuleles. During the concert David Suich held up his Uke, pointed at the hole, and made the wonderful connection: "Now we know how many holes it takes to fill the Albert Hall" Magic.

John Lennon would have been impressed.

The Pad

A long time ago I'd read that the Italian violinist Giuseppe Tartini, born in 1692, dreamt that he had handed his violin to the Devil who proceeded to play it with such a dazzling beauty that Tartini awoke in terror and amazement and hurriedly wrote down as much as possible of what he had heard. The sonata, the best music he had ever composed, later became known as "The Devil's Trill".

Many years later I read that Paul McCartney kept a notebook by his bedside in case he awoke with an idea. If this simple ploy worked for both Paul and Giuseppe then perhaps it might work for me. I was going through yet another creatively barren phase of my life and was desperate to try anything.

One night, as I surfaced from a deep sleep, I became aware of the most beautiful spiralling, cathedral-like harmonies that I had ever heard: shimmering voices merged with vast orchestras that seemed to extend as far as I could see. I suddenly remembered the pad that I'd left by the bed and managed, in my half-awake state, to excitedly scribble down as much as possible of the exquisite harmonic textures that I had just experienced. I fell into a happy and extremely relaxed sleep, content that I had preserved a moment of beauty. The following morning I awoke, and within seconds remembered the jottings of the night before. My pulse raced as I eagerly studied the scrawl I'd written on the pad: with amazement and a sinking depression I stared at "C, Am, Dm7, G7", a chord sequence that is one of the commonest turn-arounds in popular music. It is a source of endless frustration that I'll never know what it was I thought I'd heard.

Abu Dhabi

One morning I awoke dreaming of a poster for a concert in the United Arab Emirates. The featured artists were the Swedish group ABBA, ex-Manfred singer Mike d'Abo, experimental rock group Pere Ubu, American band the Doobie Brothers, Italian conductor Claudio Abbado, and UK comedy team the Bonzo Dog Doo-Dah Band.

The poster read:

ABU DHABI

ABBA D'ABO

UBU DOOBIE

ABBADO DOO DAH

(Okay, I cheated on the last line, but the rest really was a dream.)

POSTERS

Argent

One evening in the 1970s, keyboard player Rod Argent's eponymously named band, Argent, were headlining at a university gig, supported by Trevor Burton's new group, Balls, and the local college band, wittily called Bum.

The poster read:

ARGENT

with

TREVOR BURTON'S BALLS

and

BUM

PART FOUR: THE LATER YEARS

CHAPTER 17

ROAD TALES

EARLY DAYS

The words "tour manager" and "itinerary" had not been invented when rock 'n' roll bands first toured in Britain. There was no SatNav or GPS, there were no credit cards, and no motorways (until 1959 when the first national motorway – the M1 – was finally opened.) Before that it was all A-roads, and tours seemed to be planned by idiots with no concern for the distances required to be travelled.

In the fifties and sixties the really ambitious touring rock musicians – pioneers such as Brian Bennett, Colin Green, and Big Jim Sullivan – studied music theory by correspondence courses with The Berklee College of Music at what became known as "the University of the A1", or "British Rail School of Music" (BRSM). They were the smart ones.

Communication was nothing like it is now: there was no mobile phone, no texting, no email, no fax, and no international dialing; I remember that in France in 1969 it was still such a pain to have to shout into a crackly hotel phone with a carbon microphone – and in one's faltering O-level French – a phrase such as "Je voudrais téléphoner à Londres." On a good day the French telephone operator actually understood the request and would make a high-speed connection to London – sometime during the next five minutes. Possibly. As late as 1975, whilst on a ferry crossing the North Sea *en route* to Denmark, I had to book a call ahead: there was a three-hour queue for the ship-to-shore radio-telephone. What you did not say was: "Hi, honey, I'm on the boat."

An exhausted Clem Cattini waiting at Doncaster Station: a glimpse of life on tour with the Billy Fury band in 1958. Clem: "So this is showbiz!"

We had to entertain ourselves on long journeys: there were no iPods, no DVD players, and no videos. We read books, told stories, played endless word games, stared out of the window, attempted ludicrously complicated a cappella vocal harmonies, argued a lot, tried to keep warm, lit farts, or just simply slept. If all went well we even made it home.

A DAY IN THE LIFE

Although there may be many variations on this theme, what follows is a typical day in the life of a professional musician on the road in the seventies or eighties in, say, the USA. On occasions it may have been fun, but mostly it was just relentless hard work:

- wake-up call (assuming that the night porter has remembered)
- wake up
- shower
- try to remember where you are
- find glasses, wallet, room key, passport
- breakfast – pre-arranged in room/in restaurant; miss and regret
- check that you have not left anything drying in the bathroom
- assemble in the hotel lobby
- car to the airport
- hang around at the airport for (seemingly) ages

- buy rubbish at the airport shop selling pointless tat
- get confused by time-zone/eat second breakfast by mistake
- short flight/possibly coffee
- identify luggage on carousel
- car to the hotel
- at the hotel; brief check of room – is there a view? Where am I?
- throw into a corner any pointless promotional cardboard items
- make sure that the evening's stage clothes are in a reasonable state
- assemble in the hotel lobby
- car to the gig
- hang around for ages at the gig for a soundcheck which seems to be exclusively for the bass-drum
- car back to the hotel
- at the hotel – brief sleep/wash clothes/watch crap TV/write postcards
- assemble in the hotel lobby
- car back to the gig
- in the backstage dressing room pre-show, individual pre-concert rituals manifest themselves, such as pacing up and down, tapping on chairs and tables, staring, practising scales, or even playing ping-pong
- play concert/feel good
- in the dressing room post-show – in an exceedingly sweaty state try to cope with back-stage visitors and be amazed at how unbelievably stupid and ill-informed most of these people can be
- car to (one hopes) a quiet restaurant
- meal at a restaurant which is nowhere near the hotel – i.e., not convenient for the journey back
- expensive taxi back to the hotel
- at the hotel – initially in the lobby – unwind/drink/party/pass out/sleep
- drift upstairs
- wake-up call (assuming that the night porter has remembered)

This process is repeated every day – for several weeks. As I used to joke at the time: "Still, it's better than working!"

TOUR PHILOSOPHY

Strangely, it is possible to work alongside people in the studio for many years and yet not really know them at all. But after just one overnight gig, a hotel, or a long journey, something happens and the relationship changes. There is a bond.

On tour all sorts of alliances occur – whether it is through chess, computers, cars, film, food, architecture, museums, or even (for the very sad) golf (a method of ruining a perfectly good walk). There is a camaraderie, and people naturally split into twos and threes. Even the major British orchestras are roughly divided into the ravers and the non-ravers.

You could sometimes kid yourself that being on tour is a kind of holiday but even though you do sometimes get to see some exotic or strange places – destinations that you would not normally consider possible to visit – the total exhaustion you are experiencing tells you otherwise.

On the road you become part of a microcosm: a self-contained unit defending itself against the world. It's very powerful but, bizarrely, it is also possible to be alone on tour – even when surrounded by twenty people!

Touring should also be about experiencing different cultures, observing and enjoying local detail, and not trying to impose your own ideas and prejudices.

I loved playing old theatres in the States. At soundcheck I would look up at the dust, visible in the lights, and thrill to the idea that I was standing on the same spot where W.C. Fields, or the Marx Brothers, once reduced their audience to tears of laughter.

TOURING

1969: Affinity UK

When you are hopelessly lost in a strange town, now very late for the soundcheck/concert/interview/lecture, you might be tempted, in desperation, to ask for directions. There are only two possible outcomes to this request: the first person you ask won't have a clue what you're talking about but will appear to spend ages thoughtfully scrutinising the sky as if receiving exclusive information from a geo-stationary satellite. The more likely alternative is that your chosen victim knows the answer, but will be totally incomprehensible.

In Affinity's standard-issue grey Ford Transit we had been cruising some of the less interesting parts of Plymouth for over half an hour failing to find the Van Dike (sic) Club, our gig that night. In desperation we finally stopped to ask a pedestrian who, we foolishly imagined, looked like he might be able to help us. It would have been more useful to have asked a combine harvester. In his impenetrable Devonian accent he politely explained that we should look out for "the Staar Bingaall". We naturally assumed that this must be an Indian restaurant and, reassured, started scanning the streets for the Star of Bengal. After a while we found the club completely by accident and noticed, with amusement, that it stood next to the Star Bingo Hall.

1970 Affinity UK

A BBC TV film crew followed our Ford Transit on the A4 (there was no M4 in those days), filming the band on its journey from London to Bristol to play at a club called the Granary. Presenter Anne Nightingale came with us for the trip. My back was still very painful, so much so that when travelling, the only position that didn't hurt was kneeling. As a consequence – and as hundreds of miles of beautiful scenery flashed past – all I could see from the windowless back seat was a few rivets on the van's central partition, as they vibrated up and down, inches from my nose.

(I knew her as Anne)

We arrived in plenty of time, allowing Anne to interview each of us about life on the road whilst we set up and checked our gear. That evening – just before we went onstage – someone spotted a small backstage black and white television set, which was showing *Monty Python's Flying Circus*. We couldn't resist, and stopped to watch. Some time later we learned that all over the country gigs were regularly running half an hour late because of this amazing show. (This was well before the advent of VHS video recorders: if you missed your favourite programme – tough).

After the gig the camera was set up for an interview in the tiny backstage dressing room. Anne was interested to find out what motivated us to play, in spite of the hardships:

"What are you all in it for – I mean, if you're only earning £20 a week each it's not a fantastic living is it?" she asked.

"For the glamour," said Linda with joyful irony, whilst her hand gestured around the awful dingy room.

Grant and Mike rambled on about being paid for doing something you enjoy, but it wasn't convincing. It was 2 a.m.: time to drive the 150 miles back to London. The fifteen minute film was later broadcast on a show called *Search*.

1972: Michael D'Abo, USA tour

We spent a week at the Bitter End club in Greenwich Village, New York City, supporting John Prine, a friend of Bob Dylan. One afternoon I entered our dressing room and said a friendly "hi" to the denimed figure with the Ray-Bans slouching in the corner. As I began checking my stage clothes for the evening I must have lost my nonchalant look for just a brief moment when I suddenly realised that the cool figure only four feet away from me was Bob Dylan himself – Bob and I were alone in a room together! I had recently watched *Don't Look Back*, the powerful documentary of Dylan's UK tour made by D.A. Pennebaker, and felt vulnerable: what can you possibly say to the man who wrote *Blonde on Blonde!* I began to mentally compose the perfect introductory sentence, full of enticing subclauses, designed to let him know that I was okay really. But while this ludicrous inner construction was evolving to perfection he quietly left the room. This came to be known as "the day I didn't meet Bob Dylan", and since then I often haven't met quite a few famous people.

Some weeks later, on the same tour, we supported Lisa Minelli and her orchestra at the Garden State Arts Centre, a beautiful amphitheatre in New Jersey. By the third day I was bored and restless and in need of stimulation. I do like investigating theatres from all angles – it's like being a tourist; you'll probably never be there again – and during the show I began climbing up in the lighting rig only to discover, to my sudden surprise and horror, that I had reached an area directly above her backstage changing screens. I tried very hard not to look when, without warning, she rushed offstage, threw off her top, and exposed the Minelli tits. I froze and frantically began composing plausible explanations for my implausible location. Mercifully no one noticed my presence and Lisa continued her show, completely unaware of her reluctant voyeur.

1973: Joan Armatrading, Tour of Germany, Supporting José Feliciano

Apart from two longish flights the whole tour was by train. Within a couple of days we were exhausted, trying to catch what sleep we could in very stiff and uncomfortable seats. One night our train suddenly came to an abrupt halt at a station. Drummer Henry Spinetti, bleary-eyed but curious, cautiously lifted up the blind, stared out of the window, and was confronted by a very large sign displaying the name of this small German town: Worms. For anyone from Britain this image would be confusing enough. In his delirium Henry opened the window and began singing (to the tune of "Alfie"): "What's it all about, Germany?" It was a perfect moment, and our compartment soon shook with insane laughter and hysterical giggles.

Every night Joan, who was, at the time, terrified of talking to any large crowd, would boldly attempt to greet the audience in German, a language she had never studied in depth. Unfortunately the small amount of phonetic German she had learnt was imbued with a strong Birmingham accent and inflection – and with Caribbean overtones. During the simple greeting "Guten Abend, meine Damen und Herren. Er ist..." the unintentionally extreme, and also unexpected, rise and fall of the cadence of her innocent display of affection was a moment of true comedy that we all looked forward to.

When on tour it's hard enough anyway to keep track of which town you are in – blindness only compounds the problem. One night I was watching José Feliciano's show from the back of the theatre, and enjoying his flamboyant chat: he had that special kind of ease, of which only Americans are capable. Suddenly I heard him say: "Hey, it's great to be here in Hamburg." Immediately there was a clearly audible stage whisper from his tour manager in the wings: "Pssst, we're in Frankfurt!"

Stewart Copeland and Henry Spinetti struggle with life on the road

1973: Joan Armatrading, UK Tour

Prior to the UK tour we had met our new tour manager, Stewart Copeland, at his parents' home in St John's Wood, north west London. Whilst we waited for some business to be completed by his brother Miles Copeland – our promoter – he was keen to show us his drums in the basement. His playing reminded me of a demented Tony Williams.

One afternoon, as we left a motorway service station and began to merge with the northbound traffic, Stewart suddenly realised, with horror, that he'd left his briefcase on the roof of the car. We looked out of the back window and watched as a chaos of paper spread itself across all six lanes of the M1. Apart from that he was a great tour manager – but in the future he would be a much better drummer and film music composer!

1973: Magdalena Buznea, the Mermaid Theatre

Occasionally, musicians were pulled from the ranks of the studio world to play at one-off concerts. One such event took place in July 1973 at the Mermaid Theatre down by the River Thames, in London. Magdalena Buznea was a Romanian singer whose repertoire consisted almost entirely of the songs of legendary French singer Edith Piaf, and this was to be her showcase.

Gathering in the afternoon for a three-hour rehearsal was a keyboard player, a string quartet, Chris Karan (who had played drums with Dudley Moore) on percussion, Paul Keogh on guitars, and me on bass guitar. It became apparent that three hours was not enough. There were 20 songs to learn, which was normally not a problem, but each part was about ten pages long and covered in signs, repeats and codas. It was a ludicrous and impossible task – but the show had to go on.

During the show Magdalena sang beautifully, and between each song she told stories about the tortured life of Piaf. Whilst telling these stories, she chose to animate them by walking left and right, the full width of the stage. But since there was only one solitary unidirectional microphone on the stand at the centre, the bulk of her chat – as perceived by the audience – was mostly an incomprehensible mumble, punctuated by a sudden very loud – and context-free – couple of words each time she innocently strolled past the mic-stand.

Meanwhile, we had our own crises as we struggled to understand the parts and tried to prevent the pages from wobbling off the music stands. During one heart-wrenching, grief-stricken ballad I became hopelessly lost. A knitting pattern would have been more use to me at that moment. I noticed Paul staring intently at the music in front of him, playing a sustained tremolando on his guitar. "Ah, rescue," I thought. "Here's someone who knows what he's doing."

The song was very quiet and the theatre was silent. I somehow had to discreetly attract Paul's attention. I leaned towards him slightly and with my lips almost closed whispered to him through the left side of my mouth: "Psst! Hey, Paul! where are we?" His body didn't move; he kept playing, he kept staring ahead. But he did answer me, this time through the *right* side of his mouth, and in a slight Dublin accent he whispered: "Fuck knows."

To make matters worse, at this point Chris Karen

Paul Keogh in the studio

accidentally fell asleep, relaxed his grip, and let a drumstick fall to the floor. In that quiet space it was deafening.

I had invited a few friends to see the show, and we had planned to meet afterwards for a drink. Mercifully, whilst I was playing, I had been unaware of what was happening in the audience. My friends – who were English teachers, social workers, and landscape architects – could see what was happening onstage and had begun giggling – and with the giggling came the rocking. Unfortunately at the Mermaid the seats were joined together in rows, so that if one person rocked, ten people rocked. My friends were thrown out at the interval. It was embarrassing.

Ian Whitwham – who was in the audience – explained to us: "The tension between the seriousness of her songs and our stifled laughter was *too* much. It meant so much to her – all that European *chanteuse* tradition – the wounds of love. Adult stuff. And us lot making those stifled laughter noises. It wasn't fair. Her wandering past the mic did it for us. And your solemn faces: *faux*-rapt attention during her anecdotes."

Fancy at The Whisky A Go-Go on Sunset Strip in December 1974

"And then, the dropped drumstick. She was in mid flow and suddenly in the hushed silence of the vast room a drumstick skittered gently across the kit on to the floor – we could not choose but hear it. She ploughed on. We had to be ejected – or die laughing."

1974 James Griffin, UK Tour

Everybody remembers David Gates from the American group Bread. But another key member of that band was singer/guitarist/songwriter James Griffin. Along with pianist Pete Wingfield, guitarist Chris Rae, and drummer Jim Toomey, I was booked by fixer Johnny Watson to back the visiting American artist on a ten-day tour of the UK, supporting The Hollies.

It was a fun event and everyone got on really well. Halfway through the tour we travelled with The Hollies by train from Sheffield to Glasgow, but what James (a resident of LA) didn't realise was that during that journey we had crossed a border into another country.

The Scots – especially Glaswegians – are fiercely nationalistic, and are protective of their country. So it was rather unfortunate that at the start of the show at the Apollo our singer – who was also still jet-lagged – launched into his confident opening speech with the line: "Hey, it's really great to be here in England!" The noise from the audience that followed this statement resembled that made by a herd of unspecified large animals debating whether to stampede or not, with life-threatening overtones. I seem to remember that they didn't really calm down until The Hollies came on.

1974: Fancy, USA Tour

Fancy were a session band put together by producer Mike Hurst to capitalise on a top-ten hit the band had achieved in the USA. It featured Annie Kavanagh on vocals, Ray Fenwick on guitar, Les Binks on drums, and me on bass. Although the "hit" was a cover version of the Troggs' "Wild Thing" we had also recorded an excellent album of funky songs.

OPENING NIGHT

We wound our way to the West Coast and played five nights at the legendary Whisky A Go-Go club on Sunset Strip in Los Angeles.

I had brought with me an amusing tape that had been circulating in the London studios featuring Peter Cook and Dudley Moore in a drunken improvisation (this was released years later as *Derek and Clive*). Ray and I thought this could be a witty opening act for our show.

What we didn't know was that our producer Mike Hurst – who had flown over specially from England – had met actor Donald Pleasance in the bar at the Beverly Wilshire hotel and had invited him to our opening night. They sat in the gallery overlooking the tiny stage.

The show started with the unmistakable voices of Pete and Dud, except that this was different from their normal banter – this language was unusually strong: "Are you calling me a cunt? You fucking cunt." It was a cascade of filth – but very funny. Ray Fenwick and I were hysterical backstage. Meanwhile Pleasance, in shock, and slightly spooked by the extravagant costumes of the weird clientele turned to Mike – who was by now cowering with embarrassment – and asked: "Is this normal?"

GRITS

Late one night after a concert in Charlotte, North Carolina, we stumbled, pleasantly drunk, into the welcoming ambience of that uniquely American post-gig refuge, the diner, and sat on high stools at the counter. I fancied a large fry-up which, when it finally arrived, looked and smelled wonderful. Wonderful, that is, except for the strange creamy splodge on one side of the plate.

"What is this?" I asked pleasantly of the huge African-American lady behind the counter as I pointed to the item which, to my untutored eye, looked as if it hadn't quite died yet. "They's grits," she replied with casual authority in her local dialect.

To an Englishman from a small village in Staffordshire this response was culturally exhilarating and yet not terribly informative.

"What are 'grits'?" I asked, perhaps a little too loudly, genuinely needing a more sophisticated explanation.

"Grits is grits, honey," she stated in a tone of irritated and bored finality. Her reply would have suggested to any rational person that any further semantic discussion would be pointless. But in my befuddled, but strangely inquisitive, state I refused to be deflected from my line of enquiry.

"No, I mean what are they actually made of?"

The diner had now gone silent. I was being scrutinised by a clientele who were not used to strangers, especially strangers with long hair and strange accents who asked weird questions about the local dish. Mercifully my friends advised me to leave the place quickly and quietly before we were thrown out.

At the time it seemed such a simple question. And in case you're wondering – grits is ground, hulled corn that is boiled.

SILENCE

I'd had a very noisy, exhausting day's travelling. I needed peace and tranquillity, but as I entered the hotel lobby in Las Vegas the vast space was filled with the "wobbly" violins produced by an ancient 8-track cartridge. It was awful. I just wanted it to stop and – with no thought of any consequences – I rushed over to the desk and yelled: "Will you turn this fucking row off?" The poor girl just looked bewildered, even frightened: she had no idea who this person with an unusual accent was, or what he was talking about. It was no better in the lift up to the room, but here I had a weapon: a sharp upward jab with an umbrella to the loudspeakers in the ceiling can do a lot of damage. The silence was bliss.

My favourite picture of the tour: Fancy at Oshkosh Airport – on the way home. L-r: Les, Ray, Henry, Nick, Mo, Pete, Annie

KARMA

That night Ray, Nick the roadie, and I wound up at the bar of a smart nightclub where we noticed a pretty girl continually rejecting any poor guy who had simply asked her for a dance: it was the *way* she did it that was unpleasant and unnecessary. Now Nick happened to have a very large wristwatch – the kind that will tell you the phases of Jupiter's moons, or the local time in Gstad; it probably also kept working down to a depth of 100 metres. Ray and Nick slowly – but casually – moved over to the girl until they stood either side of her. She was just getting ready to repel all boarders when Ray politely spoke: "Excuse me, but have you just farted? It's just that my friend here has a fartometer (points to Nick's watch) and we're getting a very high reading in this area." The poor thing just crumbled. Nothing in her life had prepared her for this moment, and she fled the building. I was on the floor.

SURREALISM

After a show one night we all happened to drift to Ray's hotel room to unwind. We were in a good mood and the music and laughter slowly got louder and louder. It then occurred to us that the noise might be annoying guests in nearby rooms and, in an attempt at pre-empting any serious problems, Ray rang down to reception to complain about the noise... in his *own* room. I was impressed.

CHRISTMAS

Towards the end of the tour we checked in to a Holiday Inn somewhere in South Carolina. The plastic nativity scene set up near the entrance to the lobby gave us a clue that Christmas was approaching and, as so often is the case, the display was grotesque and tasteless. Instantly Ray Fenwick and I felt the need do a spot of re-arranging. Within minutes Mary was up a tree, the wise men were less wise, there was bestiality. What amazed us was that our reinterpretation was still there when we left the motel three days later. It speaks volumes.

PANIC

A touring band needs a constant supply of money to survive. This money is either part of the received gig money, or it is transferred from another source. The problems started as soon as we arrived at the motel in Memphis, Tennessee, and discovered that several gigs had been cancelled. It was a bit *Spinal Tap* (although I should point out that we were there first). Our mood sagged and any Elvis-related visits were out of the question. In desperation I telephoned our manager Mike Hurst at his home in England and tried to explain our predicament. He, of course, knew nothing of what had led to this problem and was very worried: "I don't own an oil-well, you know." We needed an immediate solution. It was simple: early in the morning climb out of the ground-floor window of the motel, get in the truck, and go! There are probably still "wanted" posters for us.

IN-FLIGHT CANS

Walkman-style headphones – which were not invented until the late eighties – are the ones that we use on most flights these days. But in the early seventies the in-flight audio was conveyed by acoustic tubes: what you placed in your ears was, in effect, a stethoscope. And it was great fun to see someone asleep, pull out the plug from his or her arm-rest, point the tube at your mouth and yell: "Fire!".

1975: Roger Glover, *The Butterfly Ball*

There was a noisy after-show party backstage at the Royal Albert Hall following Roger Glover's successful concert presentation of his musical based on Alan Aldridge's book *The Butterfly Ball*. When many rock musicians – and their wives or girlfriends – get together like this there is always a chance that the language might get a little bawdy. Deep Purple's Jon Lord – a deeply moral man – was seen to tower above the throng, admonishing the revellers: "Come on lads, keep the language down, there's cunt about."

Meanwhile none of us realised that the legendary actor Vincent Price – who was the narrator for the show – had been accidentally locked into the organ loft several floors above us. He nearly spent the entire night alone in the Albert Hall. How apt.

The concert had been filmed and we were all eager to see the finished result, although that would have to wait until six months later when we were invited to a private showing at a cinema in the King's Road. Everybody was there, but we were all in for a shock: the concert footage and the sound mix were both excellent, really capturing the atmosphere of the night. But intercut with the concert – at strangely random moments – were shots of very bad actors in very bad animal costumes running pointlessly around Hampstead Heath. The director was totally insane. He had completely missed the point. It was awful. Poor Roger was so embarrassed he just got up and walked out. I felt very sorry for him – all that effort. I hope that director never worked again.

The concert is available on DVD now. The sad mess is there for all to see.

1976: Véronique Sanson, the Paris Olympia

It was during rehearsals at the Paris Olympia for a series of concerts with singer and pianist Véronique Sanson (at that time Mrs Stephen Stills) that I encountered bassist John Gustafson in the doorway of the basement where he was rehearsing with the Ian Gillan Band. Mo: "Do you know where Ray [Fenwick] is?" Gus: "No thanks, man, I've just put one out." John is the master of the *non sequitur*, and could keep a conversation going for ages without it ever making any sense. If Groucho Marx could have heard him, he would have been very impressed.

On the fifth night of my two weeks with Véronique, I was backstage calmly having "the last piss" when I suddenly heard my cue – oh no! Because the little toilet had no light I couldn't see what I was doing and in a frantic desire to finish as quickly as possible I accidentally pissed down the outside of my trouser leg. I rushed round to the side of the

The Paris Olympia

stage and, hoping no one would notice, casually sauntered on and started playing purposefully at the start of the middle eight (as if that's what I did every night). So far, so good. However, Véro often invited celebrity guests backstage and it was then that I realised that I had just run past one of her special friends: I couldn't think of anything worse than knowing that Catherine Deneuve might be watching the still-expanding wet patch on my trousers.

A few days later a journalist friend invited drummer Simon Phillips and me round to his apartment for lunch. During the afternoon he placed an LP on his hi-fi and said: "I think you're going to like this", and a moment of magic ensued – the sounds were mesmerising. I asked who the artist was. "Jaco Pastorius," he replied. It was a life-changing moment.

1976: Cliff Richard Band, Tour of Russia

Whilst checking in at reception in the Leningrad hotel, the guys noticed to their surprise that they were being checked in – very unusually – by their first name, e.g., drummer Graham Jarvis would be "Mr Graham". When it came to keyboard player Cliff Hall there was pandemonium: "Ah, Mr Cliff please come this way", and Cliff (Hall, not Richard) was escorted up to the Yuri Gagarin Suite. What he saw was stunning: a vast set of rooms with four-poster beds, gold candelabra, a piano decorated by *trompe-l'oeuil*, a fridge full of all known vodkas, and beautiful artwork on the walls. This was not the room he had been expecting.

One by one Cliff telephoned the other members of the band to come and have a look at his "room". Uniformly the stunned response was: "Fuck me!"

Brian Bennett thought he should go and check if Cliff Richard was okay. He reported back that Cliff was happy with his room, although the door did bang into his bed when it was opened wide.

It was obvious: Cliff Hall's room became the post-gig party room. But there was a catch: you had to know the secret knock in order to gain entry. This secret knock would start as a very slow knock – about 60 b.p.m. – but which, over the next 30 seconds, would gradually speed up until it metamorphosed into a frenzied blur. It was hard to execute. The band had a great couple of weeks, and Cliff Richard never did find out about his missing suite.

(Recalled by Cliff Hall.)

1977: Cliff Richard Band, UK Tour

After a gig in Southport various members of the Cliff Richard band were relaxing, drinking, and playing word games in the lobby of the hotel. It was the drinks round of drummer Graham Jarvis: "Four large brandies, please," he asked of the night porter. Graham was unaware that they were drinking from his small, and rapidly dwindling, personal supply. "I'm sorry sir," the porter apologised "but from now on they're going to have to be singles". Graham instantly, and wittily, replied: "Alright, can I have eight single brandies, please?"

1977: Cliff Richard Band, European Tour

Normally, when there is a terrible sound emanating from the PA, the defence from the stage is: "It was all aright when it left me." There was a wonderful reversal of this statement when the guitar sound was terrible at a soundcheck in Antwerp. The front-of-house engineer, Colin Norfield, spoke through the stage monitors to the guitarist, Terry Britten, and admitted: "Well, it was alright when it left you."

For the tour Terry Britten had bought a shiny new fuzz-

On tour with Cliff Richard in Europe: The two drummers, Graham Jarvis and Clem Cattini, appointed themselves to be the official tour brown-noses, 'Grovel' and 'Cringe'. In this picture, taken at Munich airport, 'Cringe' has thrown down his leather jacket so that Cliff does not wet his shoes in a puddle that was approximately two inches across

The Cliff Richard Band at Knokke in Belgium 1977

box made by the US company Electro-Harmonix. It was called a Big Muff. Every night as Cliff danced in front of Terry during the guitar solos he could see this shiny box on the floor, and liked the look of it. Some days later we were in a dressing room listening to Cliff's ideas for his next album cover: he fancied the idea of this pedal superimposed on his own image – very funky. What he actually said to us was: "I'd like to see my face, with a Big Muff on it." It's hard to describe the speed at which everyone left the room, but the laws of physics came close to being flouted.

Whilst we were criss-crossing Europe I had noticed that the Cliff band and our heroes, the brilliant fusion band Weather Report, were playing the same gigs as us, and staying at the same hotels as us – only at different times. My fantasy that we might meet came true when we had a night off in Frankfurt, and managed to secure tickets to see them play. It was so exciting to see my new bass hero – Jaco Pastorius – playing live. The way he played was so original, and so emotional. Joe Zawinul and co finally played their big hit of the day, "Birdland", and it was stunning, as each section seemed to move into yet a higher gear. I couldn't believe how anyone could play at such intensity, and as the final tumultuous chord rang around the theatre everyone stood up to applaud ecstatically. Everyone that is, except for me. I was so overcome with what I had just experienced I became aware that my legs weren't working, and I couldn't move: I was immobilised by ecstasy. But a huge wave of emotion suddenly welled up within me, and I found myself recklessly out of control, shouting the word "cunt" very loudly. It was meant as a compliment. Terry Britten – who sat next to me – was hysterical.

1978: Cliff Richard Band, Australian Tour

We spent two nights in each of the major cities. Distances in Australia are vast, which meant that every journey had to be a flight, and this in turn meant that we saw none of the countryside. In an attempt to get a glimpse of the *real* Australia, pianist Graham Todd and I, plus two of the crew, rented a car and drove from Melbourne to Adelaide along the coast. It took fifteen hours but was worth it: the scenery was spectacular.

Two more crew members travelled further inland and – as so often happens in the bush – they accidentally drove into a kangaroo and stunned it. At first they felt very sorry for it but within a couple of minutes – being road crew – one guy lifted it up and put its arm around his neck whilst the other took photos. They suddenly had an idea: a silk Cliff Richard tour jacket was brought from the car, draped around the poor beast, and its arms were carefully inserted into the sleeves. The final indignity was to zip up the front. It looked wonderful, but at this point the unexpected happened: the kangaroo regained consciousness, didn't like hanging out with road crew, and hopped off into the bush, never to be seen again. I think it would probably have preferred an AC/DC tour jacket.

1980: *Only in America*, the Roundhouse.

This musical, showcasing the songs of Jerry Leiber and Mike Stoller, was a beautiful evocation of fifties American rock 'n' roll. Devised by Ned Sherrin, it ran for just three weeks. The 14-piece band featured Ray Russell and Mitch Dalton on guitars, Frank Ricotti and Maurice Pert on percussion, Simon Phillips on drums, and me on bass. It was the only musical I've ever performed in.

The band was tight and the songs were wonderful to play, but after a couple of days – for reasons unknown – the company built a box around the musicians, so that we could no longer see the actors and dancers. As a consequence everyone lost interest, we no longer felt involved, and boredom set in.

One night – whilst we were playing – I happened to stand close to Simon's hi-hat. This proximity suggested a plan to help us keep up our interest, and during one of the simpler pieces we played half of each other's instrument: my left hand fingered the notes on the bass as usual, but the strings were plucked by Simon's right hand. Simultaneously he played his snare drum with his left hand whilst I played his hi-hat with a stick in my right-hand. Got it? It looked ridiculous, but we didn't miss a beat, and no one noticed.

It had to happen – there was a break-in one night. The thieves found the band area, and amongst their trawl was my beloved HH Combo 2x12 amplifier that I'd used on every session. Unbelievably they didn't notice my two Fender basses sitting in flight-cases nearby. Phew.

1980: Jeff Beck Band, Tour of the USA

The *There and Back* tour began on the West Coast. One evening, I was hanging around in the dressing room with Jeff, drummer Simon Phillips, and keyboard player Tony Hymas just before going on stage somewhere in California. Each of us had a pre-gig preparation ritual: Simon was beating the hell out of a towel resting on an armrest with a complex stream of paradiddles, Tony sat and scowled, I paced up and down, and Jeff began to doodle on a guitar plugged into a little practice amp. Although I had my back to him as he played, the sounds were familiar: an insane mixture of Chet Atkins-type thumb and finger picking, bursts of Bo Diddley rhythms, heavy metal power chords and sudden shimmering cascades of rapid scales and arpeggios. I was fully expecting Jeff to be cradling his beloved old Stratocaster, but when I turned around I was surprised to see him playing some terrible old guitar that he'd found in a cupboard. It's all in the fingers.

On a short internal flight from San Diego to Santa Barbara, California, the pilot of our hired seven-seater began experimenting with one of the two engines, and kept stopping it. As we neared the airport fuel began leaking and the engine caught fire, with bright orange flames pouring out of the back of the wing. Normally, when a plane lands, its descent feels like an uneventful glide – this was more of a "plummet" and, having banged loudly onto the runway, the plane stopped very quickly. The first guy out was the pilot, even though he had to run past everyone else to reach the main door at the back of the plane. Sitting nearest the door was Jeff's manager, Ernest Chapman, who helped everybody else off the plane before he exited himself. I had to ask him later why he did this – his answer was simple: "Because I'm the oldest." What a gent.

It was the start of the East Coast tour. We were all waiting at Heathrow Airport for a flight to Miami, Florida – all, that is, except Jeff, and we missed the flight. But he did finally appear – carrying a big box of Heinz baked beans (he was vegetarian) – and with sump-oil still on his hands. You probably know that Jeff's true passion is hot-rods, especially Chevys. We eventually made the gig at Fort Lauderdale (after being awake for 25 hours, and having travelled via Chicago, with a 5-hour stopover), but we still love him.

1980: Jeff Beck Band, Tour of Japan

The band – Simon Phillips, Tony Hymas, Jeff, and I – were about to go onstage at Yokohama. The normally attentive Japanese road crew suddenly became agitated and huddled around a backstage television. With a mixture of sadness and disbelief they told us that John Lennon had just been shot dead outside his apartment in New York. Stunned, we walked onstage and started playing, knowing that the 10,000 people in the auditorium knew nothing of this and couldn't possibly be aware of the strange emotions we were experiencing. It certainly affected how we played.

JEFF BECK (G)
ジェフ・ベック
SIMON PHILLIPS (Ds)
サイモン・フィリップス
MO FOSTER (B)
モー・フォスター
TONY HYMAS (Key)
トニー・ハイマス

1981: The Secret Policeman's Other Ball, Theatre Royal Drury Lane

This was Amnesty International's big bash – an incredible cast of the finest actors, comedians, and musicians. Simon Phillips and I had the call because Jeff Beck had agreed to take part. As is the nature of these shows there is never a chance of a proper rehearsal, or even a soundcheck – you just get on and do it.

We were allocated a dressing room backstage up several flights of stone steps. This was handy because we could – at least – talk through the arrangement of any tune we were about to play, and having done the homework we could then relax a little. In the few minutes before we were due to go onstage I began chatting in the doorway to a friendly guy with "twinkly" eyes – I had no idea who he was. Suddenly a voice yelled up the echoey stairway: You're on!" I apologised to my new friend that I now had to go and play, struggled down the stairs with my bass, and walked onto the stage. Billy Connolly was doing his act in front of the closed curtains as I set up next to Simon on a riser at the back. Jeff plugged his Fender Telecaster into an amp in front of me but then I suddenly noticed that the guy I'd been talking to in the dressing room was plugging *his* Fender Stratocaster into an amp on the other side of the stage. I leaned across to guitarist John Etheridge – who was nearby – and asked, in confusion: "Who is that?" His incredulous reply was "Eric Clapton." Oh, shit! I was so embarrassed. But the music was fantastic.

It got worse: a year later I played a concert with Phil Collins at Hammersmith Odeon. After a show there tends to be a migration to the backstage bar, which is accessed via a narrow corridor. On this particular night I was blocking the way slightly as I chatted to my actor friend Mike Walling: people were squashing past. Suddenly – out of the gloom – this bright-faced person appeared, who said: "Nice show, Mo." I was a bit distracted, and answered with a perfunctory kind of thank you. He said: "It's Eric." We shook hands, but my continuing lack of recognition motivated him to add: "Clapton." Not again! I apologised profusely to both him and his friend Patti. I felt such a twat.

Mike loved this story. In telling it, his version was modified to the point where I had said to Eric Clapton: "And you are?" Sorry, Eric.

1981: Barry Humphries, The Last Night of the Poms

The Albert Hall was the natural venue for this concert, which featured The London Symphony Orchestra under the baton of Carl Davis, along with Dame Edna Everidge and Australian cultural attaché Sir Les Patterson, who were under the control of Barry Humphries. Ray Russell and I were temporarily under the control of the LSO.

The music was inspired by Prokofiev's *Peter and the Wolf* – in this case *Peter and the Shark* – and instead of the established motifs such as the Cat and the Duck, Humphries had created unique characters such as the Duck-Billed Platypus, the Dingo, and the Kookaburra.

At one point during the evening the principal bassoonist of the LSO, Martin Gatt, stood up and began to play his solo: the plangent theme for the Duck-Billed Platypus. Down at the front of the orchestra Sir Les, who was smiling insanely

The Secret Policeman's Other Ball. L-r: Jeff Beck, Eric Clapton, Mo Foster

and enjoying the music, and who had already sprayed the first violins while talking with a mouthful of what was supposed to be whiskey (but was really ginger beer), suddenly vented a resonant belch that filled the Albert Hall.

The bassoon has a double reed, and the embouchure required is incredibly difficult to control at the best of times. As Sir Les' formidable belch continued to reverberate around the room for several seconds Martin, who was desperate to laugh at this wonderful incongruity, struggled to keep playing until it became impossible for his lips to maintain their grip on the double reed any longer: his shoulders shook and his whole body convulsed with a release of pent-up energy such that any chance of completing the motif was relinquished. It didn't matter. The whole auditorium was already shaking with laughter.

1982: Phil Collins, Rehearsal

Prior to the tour we rehearsed on the soundstage at Shepperton Film Studios. For the first week it was just the basic rhythm section of Phil on vocals and drums, Chester Thompson on drums, Peter Robinson on keyboards, Daryl Stuermer on guitar, and me on bass. On the second week the Earth, Wind & Fire horn section: Don Myrnick on alto sax, Louis Satterfield on trombone, and trumpeters Rhamlee Michael Davis and Michael Harris, arrived from the USA and brought their own special talents.

And on the third week the complicated lighting rigs were incorporated into the show. It was a fascinating – and absolutely professional – process.

Phil Collins Band: the first week of rehearsals at Shepperton Studios, 1982

1982/83: Phil Collins USA tour

One night as we drove back from a concert in Buffalo we noticed that there was a jazz club in our hotel, and that musicians were invited to play. After weeks of playing the same tunes the same way every night this was just the release we needed. Keyboard player Peter Robinson and I jammed with guitarist Daryl Stuermer, drummer Chester Thompson, and the two trumpeters Rhamlee Michael Davis and Michael Harris (from the Earth, Wind & Fire horn section.) We played "Freedom Jazz Dance" for over an hour. It was exhilarating, and led to a massive new respect for each other – we could all play! The vibe in the band was definitely enhanced after that evening.

The following morning I got up early and drove across the Canadian border to see Niagra Falls. Everything was covered in spray that had frozen white – it was quite magical. I was the only person there. I drove back and the customs man asked: "How long have you been in Canada?" "Oh, about 45 minutes."

Prior to the recording of the live show from Perkins Palace, Pasadena in California I wandered around the back of the theatre to the Airstream trailer that contained the mobile studio. It was a joy to discover that the recording was being made by Bob Margouleff, who was one half of the team Margouleff and Cecil that had pioneered the Moog synthesizer sounds that featured so heavily on Stevie Wonder's albums from the early seventies. That night it was also a joy to meet fellow bass player Leland Sklar, who outranks me in the beard department.

The Phenix Horns (sic) – the Earth, Wind & Fire horn section – had a penchant for carrot juice. They had their own industrial juicer – in its own flight case – on the road with us. Every night you would be getting ready for the show when from the next room you would suddenly hear "voooooooo" – the sound of this huge juicer disgorging gallons of the precious fluid. In time we got used to it.

Washington DC: fifty concerts later, the last show of the tour. This moment has a tradition – it's roadies' fun night. The show would normally start with the basic five-piece rhythm section playing the opening song in a subdued half-light. At the end there would be a fade to black whilst the horns – two trumpets, trombone, and tenor sax – walked on to be ready, each of them poised before a large Sennheiser microphone. There would be a count-in from drummer Chester Thompson, the stage would be bathed in brilliant white light, and the second song would start. But not on this night. I first became aware that all was not right when I saw the horns doubled up with laughter on the floor. The reason? The crew had been to the local market during the afternoon and bought four of the largest carrots they could find. These had been cut to shape, inserted carefully into the mic stands, and cables attached – very convincing in the dark.

The crew had also managed to find time to "doctor" the set-lists propped up on our monitors:

For example: "I Don't Care Anymore" had become "I Don't Have Hair Anymore", "The Roof Is Leaking" had become "The Roof's Fucked", and – I'm afraid – "Coming in the Air Tonight" had become "Coming in Her Hair Tonight".

It *was* the last night of an exhausting, but very happy, tour. Check out YouTube: http://www.youtube.com /watch?v=93aTLDQRMYo

At a later gig Tom Tom 84 – the American horn arranger of the charts for Phil's first and second albums – was denied access to the backstage area. He was asked for his "pass". Incredulous and insulted, this very flamboyant, beautifully dressed man said: "Pass? – I *am* the pass."

1983: Gil Evans – the British Orchestra

Miles Davis, never one to over-praise, unequivocally called Canadian composer/arranger Gil Evans "the world's greatest musician". I had been a fan of Gil's music for years so I was very thrilled to get a call, inviting me to tour with the Gil Evans British Orchestra. The band consisted mainly of luminaries from the UK jazz scene, including John Marshall, Stan Sulzman, Ray Russell, John Surman, and Henry Lowther.

Rehearsals began at the Nomis Complex in Shepherd's Bush. Gil, then 73, was a self-effacing, free-spirited, quietly spoken man who nevertheless commanded great respect and authority. At one point he discussed with the brass section a particularly difficult dissonant chord, giving them this helpful advice: "This is the note I've written for you. If you don't like it, play another note." This approach was a revelation.

Although the music was wonderful and liberating to play, the running of the tour itself was placed in the hands of idiots. Three weeks before the tour I had informed them that I needed a large 300-watt Ampeg SVT amplifier set up ready at every show – not an unreasonable request. But to my mounting dismay at every show the amplifier was always the wrong one, and always under-powered. A moment of drama ensued when – after a particularly freezing bus journey from Bradford to Birmingham – I arrived onstage to find that they had ordered an amplifier for me the size of a cornflakes packet. "I didn't order a fucking flute amplifier," I shouted at the promoter, who had never seen me behave like this before. It got worse: "I didn't have the time," was his tragic excuse.

After the tour, and through a mutual interest in British history, Ray took Gil for a drive to see the White Horse carved into the chalk at the Vale of Pewsey. It's a magical place and Gil was enchanted. On the way home they popped into an Indian restaurant for a relaxing meal. Ray seized this moment to ask his mentor about the voicing of a particular exotic chord that featured in *Sketches of Spain*, the iconic album on which Gil had collaborated with Miles Davis. Gil was very happy to help and wrote a stave and a few notes on a paper napkin. Ray was ecstatic: he now had the Holy Grail of harmony – the "knowledge" – in his grasp, or rather he did until the waiter unceremoniously screwed up the napkin and took it away with the dirty plates.

The Gil Evans Orchestra at the Royal Festival Hall 1983

1983: RMS and Gil Evans, The Montreux Jazz Festival

Our session-band RMS (Ray Russell, Mo Foster, and Simon Phillips) was offered the chance to play at the Montreux Jazz Festival later in July. There was one condition: we had to have a guest performer. We tried a variety of artists we had worked with, such as Phil Collins and Van Morrison, but their own near future had already been mapped out.

In the unlikely setting of St George's Hall in Bradford, Ray and I happened to be standing at the bar having a pint with Gil Evans, and we thought the impossible: would he be interested?

"Would you like to guest with our band, RMS, at the Montreux Jazz Festival in July?"

"Sure, I'd love to" he said quietly, and without hesitation.

It was that easy.

Ray, Mo, Simon, and the horns – trumpeter Henry Lowther, saxophonist Ronnie Asprey, and trombonist

Malcolm Griffiths – flew in from London, trumpeter/keyboard player Mark Isham flew in from San Francisco, and Gil flew in from New York. Montreux looked beautiful. The musicians converged on a small room in the basement of the Casino for a mere half-hour rehearsal. It was hot: about 33°C. What passed for a soundcheck was chaotic: the French monitor crew were hopeless.

That evening, inspired by the beautiful music of Herbie Hancock's VSOP, who had preceded us, we went onstage at midnight and played a wide-ranging collection of titles, running the gamut from Hendrix to Gershwin. Everyone had a ball. Everyone, that is, except for me: during parts of the show I couldn't see my hands because of a blinding orange light – set in the stage directly underneath me – which made it very hard to play fretless bass guitar. In addition my stage-monitor – my lifeline to the rest of the band – contained just Simon's gong drum. I was forced to play the whole gig using all of my senses except hearing and sight. It was hard work. But as the final chord of "Gone" died away, there was huge applause, and Gil shook his clasped hands above his head – boxer-like – his now familiar gesture: we got there!

Later – even though it was now 2.30 a.m. – the night air was still pleasantly warm as everyone sat outside on the terrace of the hotel. Relaxing with some wine, we watched the moon slowly descend behind the mountains on the other side of the lake. Nobody spoke. We felt exhilarated. This was a gig to remember.

1984: Jeff Beck, Rehearsal

There was rumour of a possible new tour with Jeff. Tony Hymas was available, but Simon Phillips was on the road with Stanley Clarke. Not knowing what to expect, I turned up for rehearsal to discover – to my surprise and pleasure – Tony Williams sitting behind the drums. Tony Williams! I'd been a fan of his playing since his tenure with Miles Davis in the sixties. I *adored* his playing.

In between playing the songs he said little, but sat quietly at his kit reading a large book called *Understanding Wall Street*. I decided to play it cool, imagining that I would have time to get to know him on the road. In the event there was no tour, and now – sadly – I'll never get to know him. He was such an inspiration.

In the evening Jeff and I went to the Electric Cinema in

Portobello Road for the UK opening of *Spinal Tap*. Christopher Guest's brilliant portrayal of guitarist Nigel Tufnell had Jeff on the floor.

1985: Dusty Springfield, Live At The Hippodrome

To get the call to be part of an orchestra backing Dusty for a one-off TV show is a rare treat: she's a very special artist. Unfortunately there was a dress code of full tuxedo and bow tie, an outfit I no longer owned. No problem – I called BBC wardrobe and gave them my measurements. On the day I arrived in plenty of time for the afternoon rehearsal, and checked out the dressing room where my outfit would be waiting for me. I tried on the shirt – it was comfy, the jacket was a perfect fit, the trousers – aaaaargh! If I wore them with the waist in the usual place, the crotch sat just above my knees – these were clown's trousers, and it was too late to change them. My solution was to hitch them up to the correct crotch height with braces. Unfortunately this now meant that the trouser waist was just a few inches below my neck, but after some experimentation I discovered that if I kept the jacket closed the problem wasn't too visible. Throughout the show Dusty was completely unaware of the potential sartorial catastrophe standing just behind her.

1991: The London Symphony Orchestra, the Barbican.

It was one of the most exhilarating experiences: hearing the incredible racket an orchestra makes on the inside, the sound of all the instruments close up, the clicks, the scrapes, the rattles. It was also one of the most terrifying: trying to sight-read a long and complicated Leonard Bernstein piece – where every bar seemed to be in a different time-signature – under the watchful eye of conductor Michael Tilson Thomas.

I sat – and felt very small – between eight double-basses and nine percussionists. When I got hopelessly lost at rehearsal the principal tuba player – Patrick Harrild – helped me out with discreet cues from his spare hand (letter A, letter B, etc). He was a nice man.

I felt very privileged to be part of the band since this kind of experience is denied to most rock musicians. Playing on orchestral sessions and concerts has allowed me the luxury to learn about – and later write for – instruments outside the rhythm section, such as the oboe, tuba, trumpet, and flute.

CONDUCTORS

Because my musical background is so different from that of the classical players, I have always had a problem with trying to interpret the gestures of the conductor. To me the visual downbeat represents the beat "1".

But this is not the case orchestrally, in that this gesture is merely the start of a note, which will express itself a fraction of a second later. Rhythm-section players have to learn how to cope with this disparity, and it can be a frightening experience trying to judge where to place a note. Percussionist Alasdair Malloy says: "The conductor's role has been described as 'taking a jelly for a walk on an extending lead'."

1991: The Royal Variety Show, Victoria Palace Theatre

There is a very old joke, which goes: 'Why are musicians like mushrooms?'

Answer: 'Because they put you in the dark and throw a lot of shit at you'.

Whilst the Royals and their VIP guests sat on plush, comfy chairs many feet above us the whole orchestra was squashed into the dark and dusty space underneath the stage of the Victoria Palace Theatre. The catering outside was excellent (although embarrassing because of bewildered local tramps watching us in awe from each end of the street) but the nearest useable toilet – for the whole orchestra – was in the pub across the road from the theatre.

The running order of the show was complicated – with 55 separate pieces of music – such that during rehearsal there was only enough time for one full run-through. During the show itself a medley from the successful musical *Cats*, featuring members of the original cast, was slotted into a tribute to impresario Cameron Mackintosh. There was almost no time between songs and pianist Ronnie Price had already started playing the intro to "Memories", a 12/8 arpeggio in the key of B flat, whilst I was still juggling with a wobbly pile of music that was threatening to cascade to the floor. In my haste to join in I didn't notice that a rogue piece of music had accidentally covered the key signature, subliminally telling me that this tune was in the key of C, a key with no flats. A consequence of this was that the first note I played was a bold B natural – a spectacularly inappropriate choice. Conductor John Cameron ducked below his podium as if avoiding a missile, I was given "looks" by the strings, and poor Elaine Paige – a true professional – coped admirably. The only giveaway was her face which, I discovered later, twitched imperceptibly.

I was so embarrassed by my seeming lack of professionalism that I asked if I could "repair" the note on the multi-track, but I was informed that the whole show had been recorded "direct to stereo". My goof, regrettably, can now be enjoyed by all for posterity.

2005: The Tradewinds, Sixties Night

For fun, my school band – The Tradewinds – decided to reform for a one-off concert at our old haunt the Jubilee Hall in the centre of Brewood. It sold out (all 250 tickets), and raised £1,000 for Amnesty International. We also made a CD of the evening which raised a further £800 for Cancer Research.

Prior to the event a long period of cajoling had been required, guitars had to be prised out of wardrobes,

The Tradewinds' reunion

techniques had to be rediscovered. It may have been fun, but it was very hard work. We met on the day before the show, and within minutes old friendships were rekindled: the humour was intact. It seemed appropriate to learn the school song, "Forty Years On". We did, but played it as an instrumental in the style of "Apache"!

On the night, the actual reunion was wonderful, allowing us to meet friends – and even some teachers – we hadn't seen since the sixties.

At late notice the excellent drummer Ian Thomas helped us out and played beautifully.

Everybody went home very happy.

And what has happened to the chaps forty years on?

- Roger Swaab became an architect.
- David Left became an advisor to the government on agricultural policy.
- Peter Watkins became an accountant and continued to play in bands. Sadly he died in 2009.
- Patrick Davies became a language teacher and translator, and continues to play in bands.
- Peter Gallen is a textile salesman in Canada.
- Rick Hallchurch is an electronic aviation engineer, and continues to play in bands.
- Mo Foster studied to be a physicist, but became a session musician.

BACKLINE INFORMATION RE JEFF BECK TOUR

When we first got together in the States I hadn't done a road gig of this intensity for some time. The last big amp that I'd used live was an Ampeg SVT – which is pretty loud anyway – so it made sense to hire one.

But at the opening show in Portland, Oregon I discovered that I couldn't hear it at all – it was like a tiny transistor radio in the distance. Even two SVTs were hopeless, because Simon – who is a loud player anyway – had his kit on a rostrum underneath which was a row of 15in monitors kicking out the bass and snare drums. All I could hear was this tremendous, but very loud drum thing. Plus I had Jeff's guitar screaming at me from the side-fills.

I realised that I was going to have to upgrade my equipment. We happened to be near a town called Eugene, Oregon and I met some guys there from Advanced Audio Design who helped out by building a rig for me over a weekend. It featured two BGW power amps (of around 750 watts output each), which are normally used for PA work. Then I had three pre-amps built in as well for the three bass guitars I was using.

With onstage bass amps my experience had been that either the sound is clear for you (on stage) and nobody else hears it, or it's long-throw and everybody else hears it but you can't. So we had a compromise in the end. I had a row of four JBL 12in speakers at the top, then two 15in JBLs to handle the mids, and then two folded horns (like cinema speakers) at the bottom with Gauss or Altec, all with crossovers. I definitely became aware of my clothing being moved as I went near it: my trousers flapped in the breeze. So maybe there was a draught when I played, but at last I could hear myself.

At the end of the UK tour we played at the Hammersmith Odeon. It was an emotional night, the band played beautifully, and Jimmy Page joined us onstage for an encore. Magic. Afterwards, an English-teacher friend of mine – Ian Whitwham – tried to describe the sound of the show: "It was very powerful, but it was the first time that I have ever experienced bass in my neck."

I used that rig two years later on the Phil Collins tour, but I'm now back to 60 Watts. It's less stressful.

The Wind Machine

Virtuoso guitarist Jeff Beck decides on a quick string change during the end of tour gig at Hammersmith Odeon, London, in 1981

CHAPTER 18

STUDIO TALES

1972: Jimmy Helms, "Gonna Make You an Offer"

The upper circle of a disused cinema in Clapham High Street was the unlikely location of Majestic Studios, where this song was recorded. The track was produced by composer John Worth (who had written all of Adam Faith's early hits). The rhythm section (guitarist Joe Moretti, pianist Mike Moran, drummer Barry de Souza, percussionist Frank Ricotti, and me on bass) very quickly found the feel for this delightful soul ballad, which reached no 8 in the UK charts. During the next few months we played on many more tracks for Jimmy. Unfortunately he had a very strange manager who insisted that a bodyguard should be present on all sessions, and the earlier relaxed atmosphere began to dissipate: it's very hard trying to be creative when there is a motionless hulk wearing shades sitting in the corner staring at you. But Jimmy survived – he's a lovely man, and a stunning singer.

1973: John Kongos, Tapestry Studio

Drummer Henry Spinetti and I were asked by South African singer John Kongos (who had recently had a couple of hit singles) to help him sort out his new 24-track studio in his basement in Mortlake near Barnes. Producer/engineer Gus Dudgeon was organising the technical side and lining up the tape machines. The session went on and on into the night (there were a lot of problems) and – with some inevitability – I fell asleep on the studio floor. Through the sleepy haze I suddenly became aware that I was needed and, although reluctant to wake up, I made an attempt to sound as if I'd been ready all along. What I managed to say was: "Oh well, it's all go from the word up."

1974: The Interview

Job interviews are always difficult. The young Chris Dibble (inevitably immortalised as Officer Dibble) can be forgiven for being baffled when he applied for an engineering position at Lansdowne Studios. At his second interview the owner, Dennis Preston, unexpectedly asked: "Do you fuck women, and do you drink?" Chris, somewhat thrown by this unorthodox set of questions, replied: "Well, yes". Dennis was satisfied: "I will recommend you to Mr Kerridge!"

Many years later Chris became senior engineer and manager of Lansdowne studios. And, since you ask, yes, he still does.

1976: *Evita*

Song: "Don't Cry For Me, Argentina"
Location: Henry Wood Hall in South London
Orchestra: The London Philharmonic
Conductor: Anthony Bowles
Rhythm Section: Mo Foster: bass guitar
Ray Russell: guitar
Simon Phillips: drums
Joe Moretti: guitar
David Snell: harp

Henry Wood Hall may have been a beautiful location for a recording session but the rhythm section was having a terrible time. Whilst the orchestra was spread out in its usual formation, radiating from the conductor, we were tucked away in a corner behind screens to prevent any sound leakage. As a result the orchestral players couldn't

A moment of deliberation: Andrew Lloyd Webber and Anthony Bowles at Henry Wood Hall 1976

hear us. Meanwhile, although we were wearing cans and could just about hear each other, we couldn't hear the orchestra at all.

In theory we should all have been synchronised by the man at the centre, the conductor. At that time, however, none of the rhythm players were really aware of the orchestral interpretation of conducting and during a tea break, while the can balance was being improved, we had a meeting with the various section leaders. The outcome was a deal – they would arrive earlier and we would arrive later on the beat. It seemed to work.

Meanwhile, in the control room, composer Andrew Lloyd Webber had become a gibbering wreck and was threatening to throw the tapes into the River Thames. Supervising engineer David Hamilton-Smith remembered the event: "I wondered why it sounded so fucking awful, the drums sounded like Phil Spector, and the eighty-piece orchestra sounded like a string quartet!"

David went into the hall and discovered that the engineer had put twenty-five microphones around Simon's impressively huge drum kit (but he played mostly cymbals) leaving about three mics for the entire LPO. He quickly, and simply, redistributed the mics and finally got a workable can balance together. At a later session Julie Covington sang her part beautifully and the record eventually reached number one in the charts.

I was surprised recently to hear my own semi-improvised line (it had originally been mostly a chord part), now played by Steve Pearce, appearing on the 1996 film version – until I discovered that it had been transcribed from the original record, written down and was used in the West End show.

Evita overdub sessions

I later overdubbed on several tracks of the original *Evita* album in the control room of Olympic Studios. Engineer David Hamilton-Smith reminded me that, at the end of all the sessions, Tim Rice got out his cheque book and asked me how much I would charge. We were all in a good mood and I said: "Let's see, there were those many sessions, there were overdubs, doubling, porterage... let's just call it a million pounds." Without flinching, and keeping in the spirit of silliness, Tim actually began writing out the cheque! He reluctantly stopped when Andrew Lloyd-Webber had the horrors, made lots of mumbling noises about accountants, and said something like: "I really don't think you should be doing that." To my horror Andrew then came over and ripped it up. I was *that* close! It would have looked good in a frame.

1977: Van Morrison/Dr John, Hilversum TV studios

Peter Van Hooke, Mick Ronson, Mac Rebennack (Dr John), and I were booked to play a one-hour TV show from the national studios in Hilversum, Holland. On the day before we flew out, there was a three-hour rehearsal in London during which we tried to learn the basic structures of about eighty songs! As he sang Van sat motionless in a large armchair whilst I watched Mac's left hand very carefully. Needless to say during the show itself it was very hard to remember some of the songs that we were now playing live for the first time, until I noticed that Van was giving me hand signals behind his back. It was the "Nashville" system whereby the number of fingers pointing up tells you the chord. For anyone who watched it, now you know why I spent a large part of show watching Van's bum.

1979: Judie Tzuke, Air Studios, "Stay With Me Till Dawn"

The excellent producer John Punter had assembled a fine bunch of players for Judie's first album, *Welcome To The Cruise*. For the haunting track "Stay With Me Till Dawn" I needed to tune down to "low D" (there were no 5-strings then) and ran the bass through an MXR Flanger pedal. John also added "phasing" to Peter Van Hooke's cymbals. As the last note faded away, he rode the bass fader up to expose the noisy "swishing" of my pedal – it sounded like a seashore. Paul Buckmaster added his beautiful strings on a later session.

1979: Dennis Waterman, "I Could Be So Good for You"

Making an album was a career move for the well-loved TV actor. For this session at Audio International Studios producer Chris Neil booked Gerard Kenny on piano, Graham Jarvis on drums, and me on bass. Arranger David

Cullen wrote some simple chord charts for us. The track was a little "ploddy" at first, but as I had recently been listening to the bass playing of both Louis Johnson and Larry Graham I hit on the idea of playing a "slap" part on my Kramer 650B bass (the one with an aluminium neck), and the track sprang to life. Some time later the producers of the TV show *Minder* thought that this tune would be good for an opening title – over 30 years later it still is.

1980: Jeff Beck, EMI Abbey Road Studios

On the recommendation of drummer Simon Phillips and keyboard player Tony Hymas, I got the call to play on some tracks for what would become Jeff Beck's next album, *There and Back*. (John Paul Jones and Rick Laird had been on the shortlist to replace the departing Stanley Clarke – I was in good company).

I just remember that the material was incredible: Simon and Tony – both of whom were formidable musicians – had made some amazing demos, and I was aware that I'd have to work hard to contribute the right parts. For one track – "Space Boogie" – I approached the session with both excitement and fear. I had to overdub my part while standing in the control room of the legendary Abbey Road Studio Two. As far as I can remember Jeff had not yet played on the track. Tony had written out a guide part which covered several sheets of manuscript paper, Sellotaped together, balancing precariously on three music stands, all of which monopolised half of the control-room. With the time signature changing from 4/4 to 6/4 to 7/4, I necessarily had to play the piece in sections.

I played my Fender Precision direct into the desk, and played standing in the room, listening to the large monitors, which was a great way to feel the depth of the bass and also the power of Simon's incessant double bass drum patterns. When the final note of the whole piece had decayed to silence, Simon and Tony, who'd sat impassively and maintained blank expressions all day, reached under their chairs, brought out score-cards, and awarded me 4.5 and 5.3. Bastards!

Later that year – on tour in the USA – this tune would occasionally present a problem when the echo return from the back of the room of Simon's amplified snare drum was not in time. I would look up at him just to confirm where "1" was, and he would give me a reassuring nod. Until, that is, he began to give me a nod that was not on "1", but on "3" – the bastard was having fun and checking me out, as if I needed something *else* to worry about!

1980: Alan David/Bruce Welch, Air Montserrat

In July a whole rhythm section – drummer Barry Morgan, pianist Mike Moran, guitarists Paul Keogh and Ricky Hitchcock, percussionist Frank Ricotti, and me on bass – flew from London for two weeks' work at George Martin's Air Studios on the delightful Caribbean island of Montserrat: it really was paradise. Alan David was the artist, and Bruce Welch – of The Shadows – was the producer. It was a great team.

On the plane over I sat next to Geoff Emerick, the legendary Abbey Road engineer who had worked with The Beatles. Later in the studio I watched him at work, where he was setting up to record a Fender Rhodes electric piano. He walked around, moving his head up and down, left to right, until he found the perfect spot for the mic: the exact x,y,z co-ordinates. In the control room was the most realistic Fender Rhodes sound I'd ever heard – with no need for equalization eq! at all.

During a 'swim break' at Air Montserrat

If you looked out of the control-room window you could see the very inviting swimming pool – perfect for a quick dip whilst one of the musicians repaired a minor mistake. One morning it was my turn to make the goofs: I had no idea why, but I kept accidentally playing the wrong string – but with great conviction. Mike Moran gave the affliction a name – "Foster fourths" – and every time I made this simple mistake it gave the other guys a chance to have a quick "swim break" whilst I played the part again. During the afternoon session all was fine until about 4 o'clock when it happened again. I didn't know if anyone else had noticed, but I looked up from my part and caught the eye of Frank Ricotti, who kept playing his congas whilst simultaneously performing a very exaggerated breast-stroke gesture. Bastard.

The studio wasn't far from the sea, and there was rumour of a boat with an engine. We took an afternoon off to try water-skiing – it was to be my first time. Unfortunately the boat was tiny, and the engine could have powered a model aeroplane. Nevertheless, some of the guys did have a couple of successful runs. But when it came to my turn, Mike, Frank, Malcolm Atkin (the studio manager), and Bosun (the studio Alsatian), had all climbed aboard – I hadn't a hope of getting up on the skis. There is a photograph of my head ploughing through the water with a fine wake behind it. I commented afterwards: "I didn't realise that there were so many ways in which the sea could enter the human body."

(Malcolm remembers: "That bloody boat. It did the same thing to Paul McCartney! By that time, the thing had had enough of running on lawnmower fuel and decided to die half way round the bay with Paul in tow. I have a snapshot memory of him shaking his fist at me as he was descending into the water.")

1981: BBC Cardiff for Radio 3 Broadcast.

I was booked to play with the BBC Welsh Symphony Orchestra for a Radio 3 broadcast. It seemed like a good idea at the time and I never could resist a challenge. Guitarist Ray Russell and I travelled from London to Cardiff together on the very early train to be ready for a 10 a.m. start: we were professionals and were the first musicians to arrive. We set up our gear at the back of the orchestra, hiding behind mountains of percussion, but just before 10 o'clock the alarming news was sprung on us that we were to be the featured soloists; we watched with horror as our chairs and amplifiers were repositioned at the front of the orchestra, on either side of the conductor's podium. We had just a few minutes to quickly examine the music and discovered to our dismay that it was virtually incomprehensible. Ray shot me one of his special expressions of doom; although unvoiced it said: "This is a terrible mistake. We really shouldn't be here."

The long piece was modern, pretentious, and worse, not very interesting: even the orchestra hated it. In addition the first violins were certainly not impressed by a bass-guitar amplifier sitting only a couple of feet away from where they sat; during the rehearsals there was an audible sigh of despair whenever I made the slightest mistake. Eventually this mass exhalation from the strings, which sounded like an old steam train about to leave Paddington, became cumulatively daunting to the point where my hands became bathed in the sweat of fear. This was unfortunate since at one point I was required to bend a high G up to a high A very slowly, a technique that, although it requires strength and accuracy, is not normally a problem.

I watched the conductor carefully and listened to the orchestra intently, trying to fit this phrase accurately to the contours of the music. At the extremity of the "bend", with the top string now pushed over half an inch across the neck, my now very moist fingers suddenly slipped off the string, shot sideways and embedded themselves under the remaining three strings with a cartoon-like "*doyingg*" sound. Nearby even more steam escaped as I sat there pathetically, impaled on my own instrument.

On the late afternoon train journey back to London, Ray and I were in shock: we said little but spent the entire journey in the bar.

1982: Frida, Polar Studios, *Something's Going On*

One of the funniest sights I have ever seen occurred late one night at the bar of the Grand Hotel in Stockholm. Along with guitarist Daryl Stuermer and pianist Peter Robinson, I had been booked to record an album at Polar Studios with Annifrid Lyngstad, perhaps better known to most people as Frida, of the Swedish group ABBA. Genesis drummer and vocalist Phil Collins, who was at that time a rising solo artist, was to be the producer. We had never met before and on the first evening Phil and I adjourned to the bar for a drink and a chat. At the back of the hotel was a small television theatre and from its doors suddenly emerged Lonnie Donegan, the star guest that evening.

Instantly Lonnie and Phil, upon recognising each other, struck up an animated conversation. I just sat and listened. A hotel guest nearby suddenly noticed that he was sitting very close to two of his idols and couldn't resist coming over to introduce himself. These kinds of moments are not normally a problem, but this guy was seriously boring and just wouldn't shut up. His infuriating interruptions became so annoying after a while that Lonnie, without taking his eyes off Phil, slowly reached out his right hand and, simply using his thumb and forefinger, clamped the hapless guy's lips shut: it was an emphatic gesture. The idiot just sat there, baffled, his face tumescing, mute except for a distant mumbling sound, while Phil and Lonnie had a moment's peace. I nearly fell off my stool. It was a wonderful image, and a delightful start to an album that was great fun to make. Frida was a lovely person.

Whilst we were in Stockholm, the US band Earth, Wind & Fire happened to pass through town on part of their world tour. Phil made contact, and invited the horn section over to Polar to play on the album. And that – with the later addition of Genesis drummer Chester Thompson – is how the Phil Collins band (The Fabulous Jacuzzis) came together.

(With Affinity in the seventies we travelled everywhere in Sweden in a grey Ford Transit. I vowed that if I should ever return to this country it would be in style. On this trip I flew first class on SAS, we were booked into the Grand Hotel opposite the Palace, and every day we travelled to ABBA's Polar studio in a grey Ford Transit!)

1982: Ringo Starr, *Old Wave*

I played bass on an album for Ringo Starr. It was produced by Eagles guitarist Joe Walsh at Ringo's home studio, Startling, in Ascot. This was the studio where, some years earlier, John Lennon had recorded "Imagine". Gary Brooker and Chris Stainton, who played various keyboards, completed the rhythm section. The sessions were friendly and relaxed.

During the first week of recording I attempted to become friends with Ringo's ever-present pet Alsatian. Unfortunately the dog was an animal of unpredictable affections and was, perhaps, confused by the necessity of being both guard-dog and pet.

On the first day of the second week I arrived about an hour early. It was a sunny day and, as I needed to do some warm-up exercises on my bass, I went for a stroll in the grounds of Tinnenhurst Park: it's a lovely feeling to play scales in the fresh air.

When I was about 100 metres from the house I happened to turn and noticed that Ringo's wife Barbara – along with her daughter and the dog – had appeared on the grass slope just outside the house. I waved hello to them, at which point the dog started running towards me. I had genuinely thought that the animal and I had become friends, and it took a while for me to realise that the drooling mass of teeth that was rapidly approaching, in fact belonged to a psychopath.

As it launched its whole body at me I turned with difficulty, the bass swinging round. Fearing mutilation, I raised my hands in the air whilst frantically yelling to the dog's owner, who was still on the grass bank, "Will you call this fucking thing off!" This was not how you normally addressed the wife – an ex-Bond girl – of the artist you are working for. Four incisors made intimate contact with my bum, and I still have the shirt – which features four neat holes. Ringo and Barbara were very apologetic and the session was held up while I was taken to the local hospital for a tetanus jab.

Ringo and I are still pals and I still enjoy playing the album.

1986: David Palmer *Genesis* (orchestral)

On an orchestral session at CBS Whitfield Street Studios drummer Brett Morgan (Barry's son) and I had special problems – we had headphones and a click, whilst the rest of the orchestra only had a conductor (the violins would obstinately put their cans on their knees). I was supposed to play unison lines with the trombones and cellos. There was such a time delay between the sections it was a recipe for disaster, and I felt very uneasy.

During a tea break the principal trumpeter of the LSO, Maurice Murphy – the man you have heard on every *Star Wars* film soundtrack, and who had recognised the problem – comforted me with a sweeping look at the strings: "This lot, they swing like an elephant's bollocks!"

1988: Solo album, *Bel Assis*

Clutching a box containing a 2-inch, 24-track master tape, I took the early flight from London to Dublin on this bright Sunday morning. Guitarist Gary Moore had been booked to play on a couple of my tracks at Windmill Lane Studios. He played beautifully and, within three hours, it was all over and time for a swift pint of Guinness.

On the flight home I carefully placed the tape box in the overhead rack, but as I sat down I became plagued by worries: is the tape safe where it is? (there were no back-up copies), and do jet engines have large magnets in them?

A guy arrived to take the seat next to mine and casually placed his bag in the overhead rack, next to my tape box. Suddenly paranoia set in. Absurd, and irrational, thoughts began to flood my mind: perhaps this guy is a magnet salesman, and his case is full of samples? I suppose it was daft, but during that flight I even began to hate him for ruining my tape.

I managed to play the tapes the next day at Eastcote, Chaz Jankel's studio in Notting Hill. They were fine – panic over.

1988: Ian Carr, *Old Heartland*

Ian had written a suite for trumpet and orchestra. As requested I took along my fretless bass and set up ready for overdubbing in the massive control room of Studio One at Abbey Road. My little Roland Cube-60 amplifier looked a bit silly all alone in the cavernous main room. To my surprise I then noticed that there was no music written out, but Ian gave me this simple Zen-like instruction: "Think 'swamp', and it's in G." So I did.

1990: *Sky Star Search*

If you have read my Introduction to this book you will realise that if I had not sat next to Vic Flick on this weird TV programme this book might never have existed. It was another magnificent convergence.

I played in the band behind the curtain (guitar, drums, bass, keyboards, trumpet, and sax) for two further series of this eccentric talent show. It was financially rewarding, but exhausting work: we played from 8 a.m. until 8 p.m. every Saturday and Sunday for months – 24 hours of television each weekend. Each of the five shows per day featured seven acts, which meant that by Sunday night we had played for seventy acts! I would come home with my eyes crossed, desperate for a glass of whiskey.

MD Brian Gascoigne remembers: "The producer of the show, Jim Brown, a dour Scot, was funnier than any of the comics who came on the show. After the first week the band realised that I was pissing myself with laughter all the time and they couldn't understand why. The reason was that I could hear the gallery (control room) in my cans, and having discovered this, the whole band asked if they could have the gallery in their cans. So from then on a comic would come on: 'a funny thing happened to me...' followed by no laugh at all. There would then be a pause in his act and suddenly the whole band would piss themselves laughing because Jim Brown had cracked a much funnier joke than anything the comic was doing. His treatment of singers was even worse."

(There would inevitably be long gaps in the show where we would not be required to play. I used this time to write out the charts for my next solo album, which was to be called *Southern Reunion*. It was hard, though, because I was always on call, and had to continuously wear one side of the headphones so that I was ready instantly for any instructions).

1990: José Carreras, Air Studios

I was playing on an album for José Carreras, produced by George Martin, at Air Studios on Oxford Circus. I happened to walk past him in the narrow corridor that connects the studio with the control room. I don't know what possessed me, but I couldn't resist saying to him: "You must be one of the two Spanish firemen – Hose A and Hose B." He looked at me with confusion and embarrassment, and hadn't a clue what I was talking about. Fair enough. It may have been spontaneous, but it was a stupid thing to say. Sorry.

1992: Toshi (of X)

(A momentary lapse of professionalism.)

A friend of mine calls it "ghetto mentality": the strangely redundant need to eat or drink everything that's made available – especially when it's free. The danger zones are parties, especially record company receptions, backstage events after concerts, and long flights.

I flew to Japan with drummer Simon Phillips to play some sessions for Japanese artist Toshi with producer Akira Inoue. Although Simon is younger than me, on this flight he was smarter than me and settled down to sleep with an eye mask and a blanket.

Slightly confused by the non-setting of the sun throughout the entire flight (which took us over Siberia), exhausted from watching every film on board, and pleasantly pissed from an excess of champagne, my willpower crumbled to zero. Half an hour before touching down at Narita airport the stewardess politely asked: "Would you like an ice-cream?" (An ice cream was the last thing I needed). I heard a pathetic voice (mine) say "Oh, alright then."

We were met by charming people who took us straight to a restaurant for a delightful meal where (naturally) we ate with chopsticks. This would not normally have been a problem, but because of the state I was in the food sprayed everywhere and within seconds I had acquired the pitiful aura of a grandad with bits of his last meal all down his cardigan. I was, after all, the bass guitar ambassador for England.

Sound Inn Studios in Tokyo were state-of-the-art, the sessions were fine, and everyone was happy.

1995: George Harrison, EMI Abbey Road Studios

Peter Van Hooke had a great idea for a TV music programme to be called *Live from Abbey Road*. It would feature artists and bands playing live, but it would have no presenter and no audience. He organised a full video crew and hired some of the best musicians in town. Studio Two had never looked better. I had already done a little interviewing for my book, *Seventeen Watts?*, and had interviewed bassists Marcus Miller and Tony Levin for *Making Music*. So Pete asked me to come down to help out on the pilot episode.

It was strange being on the other side of the camera – especially as some of the interviewees were my friends. The director, Gary Dyson, gave me helpful advice – such as "Don't giggle!" – and we initially chatted to guys from the studio: MD Martin Benge, producer Alan Parsons, and chief engineer Peter Vince, who showed us round the entire building.

Later, it was the turn of the musicians: Rod Argent, Paul Carrack, Clem Cattini, Katy Kissoon, Robbie McIntosh, Andy Newmark, Tessa Niles, Tim Renwick, Bruce Welch, and Keith Wilkinson, all of whom chatted amiably.

On the following day I'd just got back from a morning recording session when Peter Van Hooke rang, breathless. He'd just found out that the three surviving Beatles, plus George Martin, were working on a project – which was to be called *Anthology* – in the control room of Studio Two at Abbey Road. (George later recalled that 'it was like looking into an old scrapbook'). Pete asked me if I could go round immediately with a film crew and interview them for the programme about their very first impressions of the studio. Oh yes? Predictably it proved to be impossible to reach them internally. The crew and I slumped in the canteen, fully prepared to drink lots of tea, and waited.

After about an hour, and to my great surprise and pleasure, Ringo Starr came in. "'Allo, Mo. Are you still playing that fretless bass?" boomed the voice of *Thomas The Tank Engine* (I'd worked on Ringo's solo album some years earlier). I bowled over and gave my pitch, at which point the others arrived, and I found myself drinking tea and chatting to Ringo, George, Paul, and George Martin. They eventually returned to the studio, suggesting that there was no problem, and that we should come in and set up in about twenty minutes. This was far too easy!

Neil Aspinall, who was , in effect, the fifth Beatle, and who had been listening from the next table, then came over and politely explained to me that, since the three Beatles were shortly to announce to the world that they were together again, what I proposed to do would be impossible. In panic my hasty response to this depressing news was: "Well, two of them will do!" Aspinall smiled, went away, and came back with the news that George Harrison – who sadly died in 2001 – was happy to be interviewed. It's good to persevere.

I was now in such a state that a run around the block was needed but within a few seconds I became aware of a breathless sound man running after me, yelling: "He's waiting for you!" And so it came to be that for George's first interview in 25 years in that legendary building I arrived in a state of shock, soaked in sweat, out of breath, and without a single question planned. But George was very sweet and helped me out – he even answered questions that I hadn't even asked!

Sadly the pilot was never transmitted but what follows is a transcript of our interview. George is leaning over a Hammond organ. I'm sitting on a stool, facing him.

MF: Hello George.

GH: Hi Mo.

MF: Welcome to Studio Two.

GH: Thank you.

MF: What brings you here at this time?

GH: Well, at this point we're going through all the old music from the very beginning – the very first thing we ever did. Long before we came to Abbey Road we recorded "That'll Be the Day" in a studio in Liverpool – it was just a place you go in and go straight onto disk – and we paid for it ourselves. And we are compiling an album which could be around six CDs, three doubles. It's going from A to Z (or zee if you show this in America) to go along with the TV programme of the anthology of The Beatles.

MF: So, is this resurrecting the actual old records themselves?

GH: It is. We are trying to put on more or less something from every period, and all the stuff that's never been heard before. And in cases like now what we've done is we've sifted through the early tapes, but a lot of them were done in mono. The only tapes remaining are the actual masters: all the out-takes were thrown away, long before people thought we were any good (smiles). And now we're up to the four-track tapes which started with "This Boy" and "I Wanna Hold Your Hand". Then we're up to "Can't Buy Me Love", which was February 1964. The thing about those is that they've got all the out-takes on them. So what we are trying to do is compile all the songs that people know from "Love Me Do" to the end of Abbey Road. If any of those songs are included, which many of them will be, they'll be a completely different take, or a different version, to the one that's normally available.

MF: With embarrassments and all, or not?

GH: Yeah, well I mean we keep hearing funny little bits between the takes. You know there's just a bit there (looks up at the control room) where "Can't Buy Me Love" breaks down and John just says: "I dropped me plectrum." You know, (pause) it's *so* funny. So we'll probably compile a segment just of all those little bits, y'know the nonsense stuff.

MF: And of all the studios you could have chosen to listen back to it you came to Abbey Road?

GH: Yeah, there was an obvious reason for that and that's because the tapes are locked in a security vault in Abbey Road. And it makes sense to listen to them here than go carting them all around the city. It's a great room. The very first session we did here, which was before Ringo was in the band, was in June 1962. We set up right here (points to far end of studio), where the end of that piano is, and we recorded "Love Me Do" with Pete Best. Now that's the version we're using on here because when we came back – I think in October of that year – we'd got Ringo in the band, but George Martin didn't know about Ringo and he hired a session drummer. The famous story is that he put out the single without Ringo playing on it. And then on all the versions that came out after that – like on the album – Ringo is playing. So now we're going to put out the version with Pete Best on it because it never did come out.

MF: What do you remember about first coming into this building, or this room?

GH: Well it was pretty awesome coming into the building as a whole because it was only the second time we'd been in a proper recording studio. In those days there were only a few record companies anyway – Decca, and Pye, and EMI, I think. We did an audition in Decca Studio which is also going to be on the anthology. Those Decca tapes – we got turned down and they hired Brian Poole and The Tremoloes instead. That's the famous story – somebody said to Brian Epstein: "Guitar groups are on the way out, Mr Epstein." And that was probably the biggest error in music history. So coming in was pretty awesome, but George Martin kinda made things as easy as possible for us. I just remember that I had a black eye and we took a photograph there (points to corner) with all the guitars stacked up. It must have been the second trip back because we'd just got Ringo in and I got the black eye because people were shouting to get Ringo out: "Ringo never, Pete Best forever." And also we did so many takes of "Love Me Do". In those days we never had light-gauge strings and I used to have to cope with really high action and very heavy gauge strings – and after take 20 it was pretty hard on the fingers.

MF: And what are you doing now? You mentioned earlier that there was a tape with John singing – can you tell me about that?

GH: Well, we're gonna go through from the very first sessions right through till the end of our career – actually I mean the end of The Beatles' career. But earlier this year and February last year – that's 1994 – we recorded two new songs. They were songs that John had written. One of them was called "Free as a Bird" and it was just on cassette with him playing the piano and singing the song. "Free as a Bird" wasn't complete. He never had written or finished writing the bridge section to it. Paul and I wrote the lyrics to the middle part and we routined the song and actually changed a chord or two here and there – more or less the stuff you'd do anyway with each other in the earlier days. And we put down a track – made a totally new record – and put John back into it, his voice singing. And we've just done that again with another song called "Real Love". So there are two brand new songs which are complete Beatles. We did consider doing something with just the three of us, but this way its better cause then it is the four of us: it's the complete Beatles. (At this point the control room door at the top of the stairs swings open and we hear John Lennon singing "You Can't Do That". George looks up to the door and points and smiles.) There he is – Mr Lennon.

MF: (laughing) Timing! That's lovely. Are you pleased with it? Are you happy?

GH: Yeah – it's great. I mean the thing that's most pleasing is that we're all friendly again. We had some turbulent years in the meantime but it is fun to have your old friends back again.

MF: Great. Thank you.

There is a wonderful PS to this story: Pete had sensibly kept out of the way during the actual interview, but a while later I met him on the stairs and told him the good news. He was so excited that he rushed back down towards the canteen, to encounter George, Paul and Ringo just coming out again. I'll never forget the look on Peter Van Hooke's face when, in the excitement and thrill of this surprise moment, he attempted to introduce himself to them: "Hello, I'm..." and promptly forgot his *own* name.

1996: Library Album, CTS Wembley, Classical Guitar

I had been commissioned to compose some music in the style of a Vivaldi guitar concerto. I hired Mitch Dalton who brought along his beautiful Takamine nylon-strung guitar. One of the pieces was a little demanding when played "finger-style", and Mitch asked if I would mind if he used a "pick" (not exactly authentic) although he hadn't brought one. There were four studios at CTS – unbelievably in not one of them could we find a pick. Our engineer solved the problem by cutting one out of his phone card with a pair of scissors. It worked – you'd never know. And I don't think that Vivaldi minded too much.

1999: Solo album, *Time to Think*

I recorded my solo album *Time to Think* in St Michael's Church, Oxford. It was to be recorded as complete performances, with no overdubs. On the first day guitarist Ray Russell and I arrived early to set up our gear. Half an hour later pianist Simon Chamberlain and vibraphone player Frank Ricotti entered the empty church and, as they did so, the latch of the old wooden door made a "clank", which reverberated hauntingly around the building. Intrigued by this sound, and feeling the need to test the acoustics still further, these fine musicians employed that most basic of techniques – they farted. Of course I was appalled.

On day two – during a break from recording – Simon innocently blew his nose and, in the process, accidentally generated a long constant note. Frank, amused by this sound, immediately checked its pitch and was overjoyed to discover that the note was 'A' concert pitch. Simon wittily replied: "Oh, I must have 'A' fever then!"

Some time later – as producer of the album – I spent a long time going through every performance that was recorded, looking for suitable edit points. The music was entirely acoustic and at the end of any particular "take" it was important that every musician – being so exposed – should remain totally silent until the reverb trail of the church had decayed. On one take – at the end of a ballad – I heard this whispered threat: "If that stinks, you're dead." I still don't know who said it – or to whom.

However, I can think of no greater joy than recording with friends who just happen to be the finest players in town: it was overpowering to experience my written notes being transformed into music of great honesty, integrity, and passion. This wonderful and exhilarating couple of days was also the best laugh I had had in ages.

2006: Cliff Richard, EMI Abbey Road Studios

EMI Abbey Road Studio Two was booked for an all-day session. Cliff Richard wished to re-visit his song "Move It" – but with a more Joe Bonamassa swampy groove – and had hired the same room that had originally been used for his legendary 1958 hit (48 years earlier!). The musicians – Brian Bennett on drums and me on bass – assembled at twelve noon, but guitarist Brian May was inexplicably missing. He eventually arrived about an hour later, looking a little tired around the eyes. We wondered what had been the problem. Eventually he owned up, and explained: "I'm sorry guys, I've been up all night proofreading a book I've just co-written with Patrick Moore on the history of the universe." There was a profound silence. That excuse for being late will simply *never* be beaten. And I'm now the proud owner of a signed copy of his book.

In the control room of Abbey Road Studio 2 for the re-recording of "Move It". L-r: Brian May, Cliff Richard, Brian Bennett, Mo Foster

(The nearest I can get was in 1995: on my way to a session for composers Guy Fletcher and Doug Flett in Wokingham, I accidentally discovered that I could do a pretty good impersonation of the French horn part from the theme of *Star Trek: The Next Generation* – it's quite sophisticated. Unfortunately I made this discovery on a roundabout and, by the time I had exited, I was totally lost. That was my excuse.)

2006: Martha Wainwright, EMI Abbey Road Studios

For a while I worked as both archivist and occasional interviewer for Peter Van Hooke's Channel 4 TV programme *Live from Abbey Road*. For one programme I was asked at fifteen minutes' notice (just enough time to consult Wikipedia in the production office) to interview Martha Wainwright, who was guesting with Snow Patrol. I had to squeeze past loads of people in order to reach her and I remember impatiently pushing this older woman out of the way. I found out later that she was the well-respected folk singer Kate McGarrigle – Wainwright's mum. Sadly she died in 2010 – before I could apologise. Sorry, Kate.

2006: Bakithi Kumalo, EMI Abbey Road Studios

Just before one show I got to speak to various members of Paul Simon's touring band (including my hero, Steve Gadd). South African-born bass player Bakithi Kumalo, a native of Soweto township outside Johannesburg, was – at first – a little reluctant to talk (he naturally spoke Xhosa and felt that his English was not good enough – he was wrong). After learning that I, too, was a bass player, he came nearer and told me some stories about his early days: "We had one Fender bass between about ten players. But if one player held on to it for too long we eventually found a way to get it back: we would offer him some chocolate, but this was no ordinary chocolate – it was the kind that makes you want to go to the bathroom between five and fifteen minutes later!" We talked about the influences that led to his style: "European music is dependent on harmony, whereas with African music it's about the rhythm, and the life that you lead – not the notes." It was, for me, a wonderful insight.

THE ARCHIVE MUSEUM

I also did some research in EMI's massive archive in Hayes, Middlesex. There is a stunning collection there that's not open to the public: the Archive Museum, a room filled with antique Edison and Berliner players, original Beatle costumes, early tape recorders, ancient microphones, etc.

EMI Archive Museum at Hayes

It is the kind of place where you walk through the door and you are rendered speechless. It was heaven.

2008: *Jean de Florette*, British Grove

I had composed the main theme for a new musical based on the book *Jean de Florette*. Playing to a guide, Mitch Dalton played acoustic guitar – beautifully – at RAK Studio Two. Ray Russell helped me to arrange the strings, influenced by Frank Mendoza and Aaron Copeland. He also agreed to be at the session to lend a helpful ear. Kevin Townend copied the parts, and had agreed to conduct the orchestra. With the help of engineer Wes Maebe I organised the session for the strings – Isobel Griffiths' finest – at Mark Knopfler's own studio, British Grove in Chiswick. It is simply the most beautiful studio I have ever seen.

The session was due to start at 2 p.m. I arrived at 1 p.m., just to settle in. Ray and Kevin arrived at 1.30 p.m., which was fine. I knew Ray had been away and assumed that he had got back the day before. We hadn't had time to chat – there was lots to do. The strings played superbly and the track was completed within two hours. It was time to relax and, expecting a simple answer, I asked Ray how his flight was. Looking a little sheepish, and a little reluctant to answer, he confessed: "Well, I woke up this morning in Copenhagen." (Sounds like a blues.) He later recalled the 24 hours that led up to the session:

"There were two dates in my diary in the same month, which were three days apart. One was a meeting in Copenhagen with a publisher, the other was a studio date to supervise an arrangement of a piece of music composed by Mo. There would clearly be no problem.

"When I arrived in Denmark I discovered that the publishers had moved the day of the meeting. I didn't want to worry Mo, and I couldn't cancel the meeting, so I had to buy a full-price fare home. But the earliest flight would still only give me 45 minutes' grace before the start of the session. I was quietly panicking.

"After this meeting the publisher took me and two other people to dinner. I got back to the hotel around 1 a.m. but during the night I developed some sort of food poisoning and spent most of it balancing on porcelain. I made a contingency plan. I arranged with Kevin Townend – the copyist and conductor – for him to meet me at Heathrow (originally Gatwick, what was I thinking?) and drive us straight to the session with all the parts and the score. I had to leave at 7 a.m. to get the flight.

"The morning light came and I was not well. The cab was late and I had to run for the flight (dangerous) which of course was at Gate 45. Eventually I saw the view of the English Channel and a calm came over me. On arriving on time, my blood pressure had almost returned to normal when I was tapped on the shoulder by a customs official who started asking me silly questions. It was only when I told him I was about to poo myself that he let me go. Dear friend Kevin was waiting for me and we made it to the studio.

"Mo asked me how I was, totally unaware of any of this saga. If you can panic in retrospect, this had now been achieved by Mo. May I take this opportunity to publicly apologise!"

CODA

The technology that has developed over the last thirty years has given musicians the ability to record the perfect performance, and it is the responsibility of the record producer and the artist to decide to what extent and in which manner that technology will be used. There have been many changes. Some bands have returned to the practice of playing together live in the studio in order to capture the "feel", sometimes even without a tempo-guiding click-track. Now there's a novelty! It has also become acceptable for all of the musicians in these bands to play on their own records: at one time it would have been quicker and more economical to use "ghosting" session musicians. The best overall performances can now be achieved by sophisticated editing between takes.

Reflecting on the technological advances between the days of "Apache" and the modern digital world, Bruce Welch says: "Now we have anything up to 48-track [and more], the 'red light syndrome' has gone. In the 1950s and 1960s, when it was initially mono, the music was spontaneous and exciting – even if there was the odd wrong note." The pressure involved when the red light goes on does still exist, but it tends to be limited to the film world, where a large orchestra is involved. Whilst a multi-track machine may be used to facilitate a later mixdown, the performance, along with any goofs, is recorded in one pass: everyone is depending on your expertise, and it's a case of "eyes down" – you *cannot* get it wrong.

At one time, session work embraced many areas: pop/rock, film, radio broadcast, TV, jingles, and touring. This list has now narrowed. Except for a few talented players there is now very little work in the pop/rock area: bands are mostly self-contained, and many solo singers perform to tracks built up by a single musician, sometimes recorded in a bedroom using highly sophisticated, but affordable equipment. The once specialist roles have now blurred, and it is now commonplace for one person to be the composer, artist, musician, producer, engineer, and even the record company and publisher. The internet has blurred these roles even further.

Whilst film work is returning to British musicians and studios – as their rates are becoming more competitive on the international market – there is almost no broadcast work for the freelance musician. This is in stark contrast to earlier years, when musicians could survive on broadcasts alone, never going near a recording studio. Jingles involving session players also began to reduce in number as budgets decreased and the use of samplers proliferated.

Compared to its more glorious past, the stature of TV light entertainment music has sadly dwindled. There was a time when every variety show would feature a large orchestra playing live, which was good for both player and audience alike (it was wonderful to watch musicians playing – we don't see this now). Budgetary restrictions have reduced this to the point where the largest orchestra on a TV show now has only about twelve musicians. And it's cheaper to pre-record: the world now accepts miming as the norm. Where is the tension, the spontaneity, the danger?

Whilst some of the more illustrious players chose to spend all of their time on the road as sidemen to top international artists, one of the greatest migrations from the studio has been to the West End theatre pit orchestras, where the standard of playing is the highest it has ever been. Musicians take themselves seriously these days. It's an era of mobile phones, and checking answering machines and diary services for the next job.

At the peak of session work (1970s to 1990s) there were 92 studios in London. But as a result of collapsing record company budgets, and the rise of the digital Mac-based home studio, there are now sadly only 5 major studios remaining. Who knows how long they will survive? There has already been a scare with EMI threatening to sell Abbey Road, which would be an artistic catastrophe. The legendary Olympic Studios in Barnes has already been sold. The Townhouse, Lansdowne, Whitfield Street, CTS, Pye, Phonogram, Advision, Decca, and many more have all gone.

APRS (The Association of Professional Recording Services) member Dave Harries passionately stated: "Temples of creation are closing down and turning into blocks of flats." Dave built Air Studios at Oxford Circus in London, Air Montserrat in the Caribbean, and British Grove in Chiswick, London. He has a right to be annoyed.

More optimistically, music itself has now matured to the point where the once-warring camps of electronic and acoustic have merged into a happy blend, and wise producers have returned to a way of thinking which necessitates the hiring of seasoned players. It's a sensible way forward.

In the market-place there is the rise of the mp3 format, a platform which, whilst convenient, can be sonically unrewarding – it's a bit like listening to Radio Luxembourg, but without the magic; in the past this quality would have been considered unfit for release, and only of use for demos – a bit like the function of the audio cassette. It is possible that some of the iPod generation have never even seen a record player.

There is also a rise in internet file-sharing, coupled with the expectation that music is in some way "free". How can it be? Are plumbers free? Are cornflakes free? The composers, the publishers, the collection agencies, and the performers are at last attempting to set up more sensible arrangements to collect royalties via the internet.

For many bands – both young and old – there is a return to live playing. Their revenue is now made not only by ticket sales, but by selling CDs and T-shirts at gigs, and also by online sales from their own websites.

Whereas a band once consisted of guitar, bass, drums, and vocals, in the future the line-up will be guitar, bass, drums, vocals, and webmaster.

The internet has been enabling: it has allowed many of us to return – in effect – to a cottage industry.

A CHRONOLOGY OF STUDIO DEVELOPMENT IN BRITAIN

Until the end of the eighties most recordings were made to tape

PERIOD	MULTI-TRACK CAPABILITY	RECORDING OBSERVATIONS
1950s	• Mono • Stereo	• Recognition of the guitar in the studio. Small band, or orchestra, all playing together, mostly for broadcast • Rise of the session scene
1960s	• 4-track • 8-track	• Playing together, or sometimes rhythm section first • Overdub strings/brass/and vocals
1970s	• 16-track • 24-track	• There is more flexibility, and there is more separation; i.e., it is now possible to record each instrument on its own track • The "click-track" starts to dominate recording, especially for disco • Many studios started to incorporate the Eastlake Studio design, a concept where the acoustics would – essentially – be the same in any room in the world. • Great idea but it was uninspiring to play in. You needed headphones to hear each other • From the late 1970s, the "social" side of day-to-day rhythm sessions, i.e., many people gathering to play together, slowly dwindles • There are over 90 studios in London • Album work moves out of London because of the rise of the residential studios – the Manor, Chipping Norton, AIR Montserrat, etc
1980s	• 24-track • 32-track digital • 48-track digital • Fairlight CMI • NED Synclavier	• There is more use of ambience in the room, especially for drums • It starts to get very clinical. There is less tension to get a take right first time, i.e., we can drop in a part later • Stand-alone MIDI sequencers, such as the Roland MC500, appear • Drum machines such as the Linn, Simmons, and Roland appear • Rhythmic time becomes very strict and inflexible • Samplers such as the Emulator begin to replace many other instruments

1990s	• Analogue • Digital • ADAT (8-track digital) • Computer • Hard disk with sequenced parts • Software with plug-ins • Magneto-optical storage • Proliferation of new dedicated formats such as Radar Digital improving with 24-bit 96kHz/192kHz challenging the sound quality of analogue	• Unusual to have the rhythm section together: often it's artist/producer/engineer and perhaps one player • Players record one by one along with sequenced parts • There is the facility for great control, but sometimes too much • Some people lose their way – there are too many options • Very few major studios remain in central London • Proliferation of small "project" studios with ADAT and/or hard-disk recording running on Cubase • Every bedroom is now a "studio" • Collapse of the original session scene as it was. It is the end of an era. The fun has gone
2000s	• Pro Tools running on Mac X becomes the industry standard for recording • Logic Audio running on Mac X becomes the industry standard for composing	• The cost of building a small studio plummets • Many one-time studio players now have their own studio, which is where the bulk of TV and library work takes place • Apart from some lead vocals and guitars, most instruments are sample-based • Amp-modelling – no need for amplifiers • With the advent of Pro-Tools most major studios are now "tapeless" • Only 5 studios remain in Central London • It is now commonplace that some smaller studios own only one microphone

POSTSCRIPT

In just over 50 years, the guitar has risen from relative obscurity to a point where life would now seem strange without it. The first instruments to dominate rock 'n' roll were the piano and tenor saxophone, but it was not long before the guitar and, a little later, the bass guitar caught up. Both reigned supreme until the 1980s, at which point the first decent synthesisers were emerging and both computers and sampling began to take the strain out of playing. Unfortunately, they also took the soul out of the music.

Since the 1990s we have seen a backlash: the guitar has returned with a vengeance in both its raucous electric, and its more gentle, acoustic versions. Quite simply, the guitar is sexy; the synthesiser is not. (I always felt that synth players on TV looked like they were doing the ironing.)

Largely due to interest in the Clevinger bass – and other electric upright instruments – the double-bass has also made a comeback and is now widely used on film sessions, and in the orchestra pits of West End shows. This interest has been mirrored by the welcome emergence of the acoustic bass guitar, a vital tool on MTV's popular *Unplugged* show.

A bizarre contemporary phenomenon is the worship of all things "retro". Many of today's bands base their music and visual image on styles that were current 30 years ago – a concept that would have been inconceivable when I first started playing. It is as if we are now victims of strange, style-driven loops with the various instruments all jostling for position. (Similarly, I'm hoping that my trousers will be back in fashion some day soon.)

Fads may come and go but the guitar is here to stay. It is the perfect accompaniment to the human voice. It is more portable than the piano, relatively inexpensive, and readily adaptable to almost any musical style. The novice guitarist of today has one distinct advantage over his predecessor 50 years ago, namely that the guitar he buys brand new will be essentially playable and the chord of F is at least theoretically possible.

Musicians are indebted to the current generation of luthiers who have made quantum leaps in design. We salute these guitar builders, both amateur and professional, for their tireless experimentation. Modern guitars are beautiful.

It was great fun to be around at a time when nobody knew anything, but, in a different way, it is probably just as much fun now. There's so much more music to play.

BIBLIOGRAPHY

Books

The Story of The Shadows, Mike Read

Rock and Roll I Gave You the Best Years of My Life, Bruce Welch

The Complete Rock Family Trees, Pete Frame

The Ultimate Guitar Book, Tony Bacon and Paul Day

The Fender Stratocaster, A.R. Duchossoir

The Guinness Book of Hit Singles, Paul Gambaccini, Jo Rice and Tim Rice

The Guinness Book of Rock Stars, Dafydd Rees, Luke Crampton and Barry Lazell

The Legendary Joe Meek, John Repsch

Good Vibrations – A History of Record Production, Mark Cunningham

The Guitarist Book of Guitar Players, Cliff Douse

The Top Twenty Book, Tony Jasper

My Fifty Fretting Years, Ivor Mairants

Rum, Bum and Concertina, George Melly

Funny Old World – John Henry Rostill, Rob Bradford

Abbey Road, Peter Vince, Allan Rouse and Brian Southall

The Vox Story, David Peterson and Dick Denney

Making Music, George Martin

Groups Galore, David Rees and Brian Coombs

The Who: Maximum R&B, Richard Barnes

The Steve Winwood Story, Chris Welch

Citizen Welles, Frank Brady

The Complete Beatles Chronicle, Mark Lewisohn

Oxford Companion to Music, Percy A. Scholes

Let's Go Down the Cavern, Spencer Leigh

Jazz Man, John Fordham

Jazz at Ronnie Scott's, Kitty Grime

The Story of Ronnie Scott's, John Fordham

Lyttleton's Britain, Iain Pattinson

Stories of Great Music, John Horton

Encyclopedia of Hits of the 1960s, Dave McAleer

Magazines

Bassist

Beat Instrumental

Brewood Grammar School Magazine

The Darlings of Wapping Wharf Launderette

Guitar (1973)

Guitarist

Making Music

Melody Maker

Mojo

Musician

New Scientist

Pipeline

Practical Householder

Practical Wireless

Prom Night, The Ukulele Orchestra of Great Britain *Prom Night* (DVD booklet notes)

Q

Radio Times

Record Collector

Sound International

That Classic Twang, Duane Eddy (CD Booklet notes)

The Mix

Total Guitar

Victory Review

PHOTO CREDITS

Apple Corps Ltd
Ralph Baker
John Beecher collection
Brian Bennett
James Cumpsty
Dick Denney
Bobby Elliot
EMI Archive Trust
Jean Ford collection
Kay Foster
Mo Foster archive
Richard Galbraith
Brian Goode
Brian Gregg
Harry Hammond
Handle
Jet Harris archive
Mike Hawker
Dave Hawley
John Hellier
Forbes Henderson
Clive Hicks archive
John Huckridge
Christina Jansen
Leslie Kierney
David Kossoff
Geoff Leonard
London Transport Museum
Chas McDevitt collection
Tom McGuinness archive
Tony Meehan archive
Steve Phillips
Bill Price
Ronnie Price
Punch Magazine Cartoon Library
Noel Redding
Redferns Picture Library
Rex Features
Dave Richmond
Jim Sullivan
Johan van der Levin
Bernard Watkins
Bert Weedon
Laurie Winwood Collection
Bob Young

THE CAST

Dick Abell

Guitar, Clarinet, Sax, Double Bass, Oud
Sessions, The Parkinson TV Show.
Dick grew up in Jakarta

John Altman

Saxophone, Piano, Arranger, Conductor, MD
Van Morrison, Bjork, Monty Python, The Rutles, The Secret Policeman's Other Ball

Rod Argent

Piano, Organ, Vocals, Composer, Producer, Arranger
The Zombies, Argent
Sessions inc. John Dankworth, Cleo Laine, Colin Blunstone, Gary Moore, and Andrew Lloyd Webber
Productions (with Peter Van Hooke) Tanita Tikaram , Joshua Kadison, Nanci Griffith, Soraya.

Joan Armatrading MBE

Guitar, Piano
Singer/Songwriter
Joan – who was born in Saint Kitts, West Indies – gained her BA Honours in history from the Open University in 2000

Tony Ashton

Piano, Organ, Vocalist, Composer, Producer, Artist
The Remo Four, Ashton, Gardner, and Dyke, Family, Paice, Ashton, Lord
Sessions for Jerry Lee Lewis, George Harrison, Eric Clapton, Paul McCartney, Eddie Hardin, and Roger Glover's *Butterfly Ball*.
Roger: "He was an original, he invented many things, he had a wicked and wonderful sense of humour, he wrote some great songs, he had the kindest thoughts, and was one of the gentlest men I have ever met."

Brian Auger

Hammond Organ, Piano, Composer
Julie Driscoll, Rod Stewart, Jim Mullen, The Trinity, The Steampacket
A formidable player – a huge inspiration

Roy Babbington

Double Bass, Guitar, Bass Guitar
Sessions, Nucleus, Soft Machine, the BBC Big Band, The Stan Tracy Big Band.

Russ Ballard

Guitar, Keyboards, Vocals, Songwriter
The Roulettes, Unit 4 + 2, Argent

Martin Barre

Guitar, Bouzouki, Mandolin, Flute, Saxophone
Jethro Tull

Bruce Baxter

Guitar, Producer, Arranger
The Terry Young Five, The Bruce Baxter Orchestra

Jeff Beck

Guitar, Electric Sitar
The Deltones, The Tridents, the Yardbirds with Jimmy Page, the Jeff Beck Group with Rod Stewart and Ron Wood.
Jeff is now playing better – and more beautifully – than ever.

Brian Bennett OBE

Drums, Percussion, Composer, Producer, MD
Vince Taylor and The Playboys, Marty Wilde's Wildcats, The Krew Kats, The Shadows, The Brian Bennett Orchestra, Sessions, Survivors.
For TV: *The Ruth Rendell Mysteries*, *New Tricks*, *Murder in Mind*, *Great Natural Wonders Of The World*, *Nomads of the Wind*, *The Harpist*

Les Bennetts
Guitar
Les Hobeaux, Lonnie Donegan, The Shadows
Les was in at the birth of Skiffle

Ritchie Blackmore
Guitar
The Outlaws, Deep Purple, Rainbow

Andy Brentnall
Vocalist, Guitar
The Baskervilles

Dougie Boyle
Guitar, Composer
Caravan, Robert Plant, Nigel Kennedy

Joe Brown
Guitar, Ukulele
Sessions, Joe Brown and The Bruvvers

Richard Brunton
Guitar, Composer
The Epidemics, Sattva featuring Sappho Korner, Sessions: Pete Sinfield, Greg Lake, Gerry Rafferty

Hugh Burns
Guitar, Banjo, Mandolin, Producer, Arranger, Composer
Sessions, inc. Gerry Rafferty, Jack Bruce, Joan Armatrading, George Michael, Scott Walker, The Pet Shop Boys

Jim Burns
Guitar, Hawaiian guitar
Felix Mendelson's Hawaiian Serenaders
He began designing and building guitars helped initially by Ike Issacs, and eventually Hank Marvin.
Jim has been described as the British Leo Fender.

Ronnie Caryl
Guitar, Vocals, Composer
Flaming Youth, musicals *Elvis* and *Good Rockin' Tonight.*
Ronnie attended the Corona Stage School with Phil Collins

Clem Cattini
Drums, Percussion
Johnny Kidd And The Pirates ('Shakin' All Over'), The Tornados ('Telstar'), Tom Jones ('It's Not Unusual'), Cliff Richard ('Devil Woman'), Top Of The Pops Orchestra, toured with the Cliff Richard Band.
During his long session career Clem played on 42 No.1 singles.

Phil Chen
Bass Guitar
Seassions inc. Bob Marley, Jimmy Cliff, Jimmy James & The Vagabonds, Jeff Beck's *Blow By Blow,* the George Martin-produced classic which remains the only instrumental record in history to sell 3,000,000 copies.
Phil was born in Jamaica.

Simon Chamberlain
Piano, Orchestrator, Composer
Sessions inc. George Fenton

Eric Clapton CBE
Guitar
The Roosters with Tom McGuinness, The Yardbirds, John Mayall's Bluesbreakers, Cream with Jack Bruce and Ginger Baker, Blind Faith with Stevie Winwood and Ginger Baker, Derek & The Dominos.

Frank Clarke
Double Bass
Sessions inc. 'Move It' by Cliff Richard and 'Your Song' by Elton John.

Clem Clempson
Guitar, Mandolin
Bakerloo, Jon Hiseman's Colosseum, Humble Pie (with Steve Marriott), Jack Bruce & Friends (with David Sancious and Billy Cobham). Sessions.

BJ Cole
Pedal Steel Guitar, Composer, Producer
Sessions, Hank Wangford Band, Cochise, Emily Burridge, Lush Life (with Roger Beaujolais and Simon Thorpe).
Under BJ's guidance the Pedal Steel produces music of great beauty.

Billy Connolly CBE
Banjo, Guitar, Autoharp, Comedian
The Humblebums (with Gerry Rafferty)

Phil Collins LVO
Drums, Vocals, Songwriter, Producer, Actor
Genesis, Brand X, Flaming Youth, Eric Clapton.

Jeff Crampton
Guitar
TV and Tours: Rick Wakeman, Cilla Black, Val Doonican, Dusty Springfield, Tommy Cooper, Dana, Roger Whittaker, Elaine Page, Bert Weedon, Faith Brown, Max Bygraves, Lulu, Christopher Cross, Norman Wisdom, and more.

Jim Cregan
Guitar
Stud, Family, Rod Stewart Band

Ray Cooper

Percussion, Drums, Actor
Elton John, Bill Wyman, Eric Clapton, George Harrison, Blue Mink, The Rolling Stones, Ringo Starr, Eric Clapton, Pink Floyd, Mark Knopfler.
Producer for Hand Made Films.
It's a joy to watch Ray playing tambourine.

Tony Crombie

Drummer, Pianist, Bandleader, Composer
Ronnie Scott, Johnny Dankworth Victor Feldman.
In 1956, Crombie set up a rock and roll band he called The Rockets which at one point included future Shadows bassist Jet Harris.
He later worked with organists Alan Haven and Mike Carr.

Mike d'Abo

Piano, Singer/Songwriter, Broadcaster
Band of Angels, Manfred Mann, *Jesus Christ Superstar*, D'Abo/Smith (with Mike Smith), The Manfreds

Mitch Dalton

Guitar, Banjo
Countless Sessions
Once depped for Barney Kessel.

Bryan Daly

Guitar, Composer
6.5 Special , Sessions (John Dankworth & Cleo Laine, Burt Bacharach, Barbra Streisand, Tom Jones)
Bryan wrote the theme song for the children's TV programme *Postman Pat*

Patrick Davies

Drums
The Peasants, The Tradewinds

Dick Denney – inventor of the VOX AC30 amplifier

Guitar, Hawaiian Steel Guitar
The Skyriders dance band

Paul Day (aka the 'Guitar Guru')

Guitar, Author: *The Ultimate Guitar Book* (with Tony Bacon)
The Downtowns.

Lonnie Donegan MBE

Guitar, Banjo
Ken Colyer's Jazzmen, The Chris Barber Band
His record –'Rock Island Line' – sparked the nationwide skiffle craze

Shirley Douglas

Bass Guitar, Vocalist
The Chas McDevitt Skiffle Group

Gus Dudgeon

Engineer, Producer
The Zombies, Elton John, David Bowie

Duane Eddy

Guitar, Danelectro 6-String Bass, Banjo
At the end of the 50s this American guitar soloist – who grew up in Phoenix, Arizona – was a major influence on British players

John Entwistle

Bass Guitar, French Horn, Piano
The Detours. The Who

John Etheridge

Guitar
Darryl Way's Wolf, Soft Machine, Stephane Grappelli, Nigel Kennedy, Andy Summers, John Williams

Gil Evans

Piano, Arranger, Composer
Notably collaborated with Miles Davis on *Sketches From Spain*
Gil was born in Canada

Andy Fairweather-Low

Guitar, Singer/Songwriter
Amen Corner, Fairweather
George Harrison, Roger Waters, Eric Clapton, Gary Brooker, Bill Wyman

Ray Fenwick

The Spencer Davis Group, Fancy, Ian Gillan, Force Field

Vic Flick

Guitar
Bob Cort skiffle group, The John Barry Seven, Sessions
Vic played one of the most memorable guitar riffs in history – the 'James Bond' theme

Herbie Flowers

Bass Guitar, Double Bass, Tuba
Sessions, Blue Mink, Sky
Most famous riff: 'Walk On The Wild Side'.

Eric Ford

Guitar
The George Evans Band sessions

Andy Fraser

Bass Guitar, Piano
John Mayall's Bluesbreakers, Free

Peter Gallen

Vocalist
The Tradewinds

Mel Galley

Guitar
The Staccatos, Trapeze (with Glenn Hughes), Whitesnake (with Colin Hodgkinson)

Brian Gascoigne (brother of Bamber)

Keyboards, Percussion, Orchestrator, MD
Sessions with John Williams, Scott Walker, and Stomu Yamash'ta.
Films include *Gosford Park*, *Harry Potter and the Goblet of Fire*

David Gilmour

Guitarist, Vocalist, Producer
Jokers Wild, The Pink Floyd

Roger Glover

Bass Guitar, Piano, Producer, Songwriter
The Madisons, The Lightnings, Episode Six, Deep Purple (with Ian Gillan) and later played in Rainbow (with Ritchie Blackmore). He wrote the music for *Butterfly Ball*

Kim Goody

Vocalist, Songwriter, Actress
Hair, *Only In America*, Sessions

Graham Gouldman

Guitar, Bass Guitar, Autoharp, Vocalist, Songwriter
The High Spots, The Crevattes, The Planets, The Whirlwinds, Hotlegs, 10cc (with Eric Stewart, Lol Creme, and Kevin Godley), Wax (with Andrew Gold).
Wrote hits for Herman's Hermits ('No Milk Today'), The Yardbirds ('For Your Love'), The Hollies ('Bus Stop')

Mick Grabham

Guitar
Johnny Duncan and The Bluegrass Boys, Cochise with BJ Cole, Procol Harum, and many sessions.
A longtime hoarder of amps, record players and radios, Mick's collection of Watkins Dominators, Selmer Little Giants, and Elpicos are featured throughout this book. I asked him if he had a Dansette record player – he said: "what colour?"

Keith Grant

Engineer, Producer
Keith helped to develop both the desks and the acoustics for Olympic Studios in Barnes, and worked with The Small Faces, The Jimi Hendrix Experience, Traffic, Procol Harum ('A Whiter Shade of Pale'), as well as countless orchestral dates.

Colin Green

Guitar, Composer, Conductor, Arranger, Teacher
Colin Green's Beat Boys, Billy Fury, Georgie Fame and The Blue Flames.
Sessions include Elton John, Diana Ross, Paul Simon, Tom Jones, Kiri te Kawana, Gene Vincent, Jose Carreras, the Royal Philharmonic Orchestra and Bjork!

Mick Green

Guitar, Teacher
Johnny Kidd And The Pirates, Billy J Kramer And The Dakotas, Cliff Bennett & The Rebel Rousers, Van Morrison.
Mick influenced both Pete Townshend and Wilko Johnson

Brian Gregg

Double Bass, Bass Guitar
Les Hobeaux (with Les Bennetts on guitar), Terry Dene, Tommy Steele, Johnny Kidd And The Pirates (with Clem Cattini), and replaced Heinz Burt in The Tornados.

John Gustafson

Bass Guitar, Vocals
Cass And The Casanovas, The Big Three, The Merseybeats, *Jesus Christ Superstar*, *Butterfly Ball*, Roxy Music, Quatermass, The Ian Gillan Band, The Pirates.

Cliff Hall

Piano, Composer
Lonnie Donegan, Richard Harris, Cliff Richard, The Shadows, Jet Harris
Sessions: Buddy Greco, The Bay City Rollers, Top Of The Pops Orchestra. Has the onstage persona of Harpo Marx.

Richard Hallchurch

Piano, Organ, Guitar, Lap-Steel Guitar
The Peasants, The Tradewinds, Walker's Walkers, Biffo, Boxer, The Strollers

Jet Harris MBE

Bass Guitar, Guitar, 6-String Bass, Double Bass, Vocals, Composer
Tony Crombie's Rockets, Wally Whyton's group, The Vipers, The Kalin Twins, The Drifters, The Shadows.
Jet was possibly the first bass-guitarist in Britain.

George Harrison

Guitar, Vocals, Bass, Keyboards, Ukulele, Mandolin, Sitar, Tambura, Sarod, Swarmandal, Singer/Songwriter, Producer, Film Producer
The Quarrymen, The Beatles, The Traveling Wilburys
George's company (Hand Made Films) helped to finance Monty Python's film *The Life Of Brian*

Alan Hawkshaw

Piano, Hammond Organ, Composer, Producer
Emile Ford and The Checkmates, The Shadows, Sessions
Composed TV themes for *Channel 4 News*, *Countdown*, *Grange Hill*, *The Dave Allen Show*

Forbes Henderson

Guitar, Charango, Mandolin
Incantation, Soloist

Clive Hicks

Guitar
The Squadronaires, Betty Smith Quintet, Don Dang and the Frantic Five.
Sessions inc. *Jesus Christ Superstar,* Elton John
Live work with Henry Mancini, Sasha Distel, Stephane Grapelli

Tony Hicks

Guitar, Banjo, Vocals
Les Skifflettes, The Dolphins, The Hollies

Phil Hilborne

Guitar, Producer/Engineer, Teacher, Author, Journalist
Phil, a specialist in high-octane rock soloing, is also known for his informative column inches in magazines such as *Guitar Techniques,* for which he is music editor.

Colin Hodgkinson

Bass Guitar, Vocals
Eric Delaney's Showband, Back Door (with Ronnie Aspery and Tony Hicks), Alexis Korner, Jan Hammer, Whitesnake, Mick Jagger, Brian Auger, Chris Farlowe, The Spencer Davis Group, The British Blues Quintet

Allan Holdsworth

Guitar, Synthaxe
'Igginbottom, Tempest (with Jon Hiseman), Soft Machine, The New Tony Williams Lifetime, Jean-Luc Ponty, UK, Bill Bruford, IOU, Level 42, Soloist.
In the 1980s he found a new voice with the Synthaxe guitar synthesiser and continues to be a highly influential musician.

Bernie Holland

Guitar
Bluesology, Georgie Fame And The Blue Flames, Van Morrison, Joan Armatrading, Leo Sayer, and has jammed with Jimi Hendrix and Frank Zappa.
As a songwriter his work has included penning the beautiful 'Diamond Dust' featured on Jeff Beck's *Blow By Blow* album.

Hugh Hopper

Bass Guitar, Composer
The Wilde Flowers (with Kevin Ayers, Robert Wyatt, Dave and Richard Sinclair, Richard Coughlan and Pye Hastings). Pete Frame has described the band as the 'cornerstone of the Canterbury scene' - one which spawned Caravan and Soft Machine (with Robert Wyatt and Mike Ratledge),
Later played with Stomu Yamashta's East Wind, Isotope, Gilgamesh, The Carla Bley Band.

Steve Howe

Guitar
The Syndicats – on the side of the band's Dormobile was the sign "The Chuck Berry Appreciation Society" since they featured 14 Berry covers in their set. The In-Crowd, Tomorrow, Bodast, Yes, Asia (with John Wetton, Carl Palmer, Geoff Downes), Anderson Bruford Wakeman Howe

Linda Hoyle

Singer/Songwriter, Author
Affinity, Solo album (*Pieces of Me*)

Les Hurdle

Bass Guitar, Trumpet
Studied classical trumpet at Reading University when only eleven and found himself playing bass on sessions during the 1960s. Les became one of the most prolific disco bass players in the late 1970s, when that musical form was at the height of its popularity.

Mike Hurst

Guitar, Vocals, Record Producer
The Method (with Albert Lee and Tony Ashton), The Springfields (with Dusty Springfield), Sundance (with Mary Hopkin and Michael Albuquerque)
Productions include Cat Stevens ('Matthew And Son'), PP Arnold ('The First Cut Is The Deepest'), Manfred Mann ('Mighty Quinn'), Fancy ('Wild Thing').

Ike Isaacs

Guitar
The Leslie Douglas Bomber Command Band, Cyril Stapleton's BBC Show Band, The Ted Heath Band, Stephane Grappelli, Diz Disley's Hot Club of London. Sessions.
Ike was born in Rangoon, Burma

Davey Johnstone

Guitar, Banjo, Vocals, Mandolin, Dulcimer, Sitar, MD
Magna Carta, Bernie Taupin, Elton John

Alan Jones

Bass Guitar
Tom Jones, The Shadows, Dave Clark/Cliff Richard musical *Time*,
Sessions

John Paul Jones

Bass Guitar, Organ, Mandolin, Arranger
Tony Meehan Combo, Led Zeppelin, Paul McCartney, Brian Eno, Diamanda Galas
Arranged for Herman's Hermits ('A Kind of Hush', 'No Milk Today') Donovan ('Mellow Yellow', 'Hurdy Gurdy Man'), Lulu ('The Boat That I Row', 'To Sir With Love'), Jeff Beck ('Hi-Ho Silver Lining', 'Love Is Blue', 'Beck's Bolero').

Mike Jopp

Guitar
Replaced Jeff Beck in The Tridents, Affinity, Mike D'Abo

Laurence Juber

Guitar
Wings, Sessions

Paul Keogh

Guitar
Sessions
Paul was born in Dublin

Martin Kershaw

Guitar, Banjo, Bouzouki, Composer
TV sessions include The Jackson Five, Gladys Knight, Johnny Cash, Mel Torme, Diana Ross, Linda Ronstadt, and Blondie.
Tours include the Tom Jones Band and The James Last Orchestra. Martin has the distinction of being banjo-playing Gonzo in The Muppets!

Mark King

Vocals, bass guitar, drums
Level 42, is perhaps the best-known 'slapper' in the UK, although he began his music career as a drummer – a discipline halted because, he says, "I was too punctual! I also wanted to be a boxer, but I didn't have a speech impediment. That ruled me out."

Mark Knopfler OBE

Guitar, Vocals, Songwriter, Producer, Film Score Composer
Dire Straits, The Notting Hillbillies
Mark has built British Grove Studios in Chiswick. It was his passion: "it is the most beautiful studio I have ever seen" Mo

Paul Kossoff

Guitarist
Black Cat Bones (with Simon Kirke), Free (with Paul Rodgers, Andy Fraser, and Simon Kirke), Back Street Crawler.
The members of Free contributed to one of the true all-time rock classics: 'All Right Now'.

Denny Laine

Guitar, Singer/Songwriter,
Denny Laine And The Diplomats, The Moody Blues, Trevor Burton and Balls, Wings.
Denny co-wrote with Paul the two-and-a-half-million-selling 'Mull Of Kintyre', the biggest-selling British single of all time until Band Aid's Christmas fund raiser in 1984. Earlier number one 'Go Now'

Jim Lea,

Bass Guitar, Violin
The 'N-Betweens (with Noddy Holder), a swift name change to Ambrose Slade, and then Slade. Even today, one of the great Holder/Lea compositions, 'Cum On Feel The Noize', is a staple live encore for Britain's top contemporary band Oasis.
Jim is currently studying psychology.

Albert Lee

Guitar, Piano, Mandolin
Chris Farlowe and The Thunderbirds, Head, Hands & Feet, Hogans Heroes, The Everly Brothers, The Crickets, Eric Clapton, Jerry Lee Lewis, Joe Cocker, Emmylou Harris, Eric Clapton, Bill Wyman's Rhythm Kings
Famous for his country and rock fusion style of guitar playing, there are few major artists who have not benefited from Albert's touch.

David Left

Vocals
The Tradewinds

Adrian Legg

Guitar, Oboe, Composer, Author
Soloist, Instrument research and development.
Readers of *Guitar Player* voted Adrian the 'best acoustic fingerstyle' player four years in a row (1993–1996)

John Lennon

Guitar, Piano, Harmonica, Mellotron, 6-String Bass, Singer/Songwriter
The Quarry Men, The Beatles, Plastic Ono Band
How many rhythm guitarists have an airport named after them?

Julian Littman

Guitar, Piano, Singer/Songwriter, MD, Actor, Acrobat
Sessions and live work with Gerry Rafferty, Pete Townshend, Julian Lennon, Joe Brown, Joe Cocker, Gary Moore and John Entwistle.
Most recently, he played the character of Brother Juan Duarte opposite Madonna in the film version of *Evita*.

Brian 'Licorice' Locking

Tea-Chest Bass, Double Bass, Bass Guitar, Harmonica, Clarinet
Vince Taylor and The Playboys, Marty Wilde's Wildcats, The Krew Kats, The Shadows

Jerry Lordan

Piano, Guitar, Ukulele, Vocals, Composer, Comedian
Almost every guitarist in this book was inspired to play after hearing his composition 'Apache' as played by The Shadows in 1960
Jerry also provided songs for Petula Clark, Cleo Laine, Matt Monro, Cilla Black, Cliff Richard, Shane Fentone, Jet Harris and Tony Meehan, Johhny Halliday, Ricky Valance

Phil Manzanera

Guitar, Singer/Songwriter, Vocals, Producer
Roxy Music, 801 (with Simon Phillips and Brian Eno), Dave Gilmour
Sessions, Tours

Steve Marriot

Guitar, Singer/Songwriter, Piano, Harmonica, Drums, Record Producer, Child Actor
The Small Faces (with Ronnie Lane, Kenney Jones, Jimmy Winston – later replaced by Ian McLagan), Humble Pie (with Peter Frampton).
Worked with Bill Wyman, PP Arnold, Joe Brown, Alexis Korner, Traffic, Donovan, Jim Capaldi.
Steve tragically died in a house fire in April 1991

Bernie Marsden

Guitar, Vocals
Glenn Cornick's Wild Turkey, UFO, Cozy Powell's Hammer, Babe Ruth, Paice, Ashton & Lord, Whitesnake, Alaska, The Company of Snakes, The Moody/Marsden Band

Barry Martin (aka Snail's Pace Slim)

Guitar, Vocals
The Kursaal Flyers, The Hamsters
For a while Barry ran Making Waves Records

Hank B Marvin

Guitar, Banjo, Piano, Vocals, Composer, Producer
Riverside Skiffle Group, Crescent City Skiffle Group, The Railroaders, The Vipers Skiffle Group, The Five Chesternuts, The Drifters, The Shadows.
Hank needs no introduction, having already introduced himself! The Shadows, the Strat, the sound, the walk, the enormous influence over more than one generation of guitarists... enough said.

Brian May CBE

Guitar, Vocals, Banjo, Bass, Piano, Songwriter, Arranger, Producer, Author.
Nineteen Eighty-Four (with Tim Staffell), Smile (with Tim Staffell and Roger Taylor), Queen, The Brian May Band
May earned a PhD in astrophysics in 2007 and is currently the Chancellor of Liverpool John Moores University

Paul McCartney MBE

Bass Guitar, Guitar, Piano, Drums, Ukulele, Mandolin, Singer/Songwriter, Producer
The Quarrymen, The Silver Beetles, The Beatles, Wings
Bass legend and a versatile guitarist and pianist to boot, he weathered the storm of The Beatles' break-up and continues to enjoy one of the most successful solo careers ever known in pop music.
In 1996 Paul co-founded the Liverpool Institute for the Performing Arts (LIPA)

Brendan McCormack

Classical Guitar, Lute, Teacher, Comedian
He studied classic guitar with Emilio Pujol and jazz guitar with both Barney Kessel and George Benson. He also played renaissance lute, and became a highly respected teacher, arranger and raconteur. As a Skiffle and Merseybeat pioneer, he worked with many of Liverpool's leading poets, including Roger McGough and Adrian Henri. Brendan played sessions for BBC TV and Granada, and featured as a soloist with The London Philharmonic Orchestra for 'Cavatina'. Brendan was the founding Director of the International Guitar Festival of Great Britain based in Liverpool.

Chas McDevitt

Guitar, Banjo
The Crane River Jazz Band, Chas McDevitt Skiffle Group (hit 'Freight Train' featuring Nancy Whiskey on vocals).
A prime figure behind the skiffle movement, Chas soon founded his Freight Train club in London.

Tom McGuinness

Guitar
The Roosters (with Eric Clapton), Casey Jones & The Engineers, Manfred Mann, McGuinness Flint, Stonebridge McGuinness, The Blues Band (with Paul Jones), The Manfreds (with Paul Jones and Mike d'Abo)

John McLaughlin

Guitar
Georgie Fame And The Blue Flames, The Graham Bond Quartet. Sessions with Miles Davis. In the 1970s, he formed the highly influential Mahavishnu Orchestra with Billy Cobham and Jan Hammer.

Tony Meehan

Drums
Traditional Irish Music, The London Youth Orchestra, The Vipers Skiffle Group, The Shadows, Jet Harris and Tony Meehan, The Tony Meehan Combo (with Joe Moretti, John Paul Jones ,and John McLaughlin!)
Tony first began playing rock 'n' roll at the legendary 2Is club when he was only fifteen. A year later he joined The Shadows but at the height of their success – and whilst still a teenager – he quit the band for a career as a record producer for Decca.
He would be part of the first group of young rock & rollers in England to achieve recognition for their skills as *musicians.*

Mickey Moody

Guitar, Vocals, Mandolin, Author
Wildflowers, The RoadRunners (with Paul Rodgers), Snafu, Juicy Lucy, The Frankie Miller Band, Whitesnake, Moody/Marsden Band.

Gary Moore

Guitar
Skid Row (with Phil Lynott) Thin Lizzy (with Phil Lynott), Colosseum II (with Jon Hiseman), BBM (with Jack Bruce and Ginger Baker).
Gary was born in Belfast

Mike Moran

Piano, Film Composer, Arranger, MD
Ian Gillan Band, Sessions

Joe Moretti

Guitar, Arranger
Vince Taylor, Nero and The Gladiators, Johhny Kidd (intro to 'Shakin' All Over')
Countless Sessions.

Barry Morgan

Drums, Percussion
Johnny Scott Quintet, Blue Mink, Countless Sessions inc. Elton John ('Your Song').
Mike Moran: "If you arrived at a session and saw Barry's kit set up, you knew that the next few hours would be fun, and no problem."
Jeff Wayne: "Barry's infectious laugh could change the seriousness of a recording session into the most lighthearted moment."

Jim Mullen

Guitar
The Average White Band, Morrissey-Mullen, Brian Auger, Kokomo,
Mose Allison, Hamish Stuart, Claire Martin, Mike Carr, Jimmy Witherspoon, and Georgie Fame.

Alan Murphy

Guitar
Go West, Level 42, Sessions (Kate Bush)

Lynton Naiff

Piano, Hammond Organ, Arranger
The US Jazz Trio, Affinity, Ice
Created the UMI MIDI sequencer (as used by Vince Clark).

John Morton 'Nick' Nicholas

Double Bass
The US Jazz Trio
Brian Odgers aka 'Badger'
Double Bass, Bass Guitar
Van Morrison, Georgie Fame
Sessions John McLaughlin, Elton John, Jim Webb, PJ Proby and Charlie Watts

Jimmy Page OBE

Guitar, Composer, Producer
Neil Christian And The Crusaders, Carter-Lewis And The Southerners, The Yardbirds, The New Yardbirds, Led Zeppelin
Sessions inc. 'Diamonds' (Jet Harris and Tony Meehan), 'Tobacco Road' (The Nashville Teens), 'Baby Please Don't Go' (Van Morrison & Them), 'The Crying Game' (Dave Berry). 'As Tears Go By' (Marianne Faithfull).

Pino Palladino

Bass Guitar, Guitar
Jools Holland, Gary Numan, Paul Young, John Mayer Trio, The Who.
Sessions inc. Peter Gabriel, Joan Armatrading.

Phil Palmer

Guitar, Vocals
Mark Knopfler, Joan Armatrading, Eric Clapton, George Michael, and Tina Turner. Own band Spin 1ne 2wo (with Paul Carrack, Steve Ferrone, Rupert Hine, and Tony Levin).
His uncles are Ray and Dave Davies of The Kinks.

Rick Parfitt OBE

Guitar, Singer/Songwriter
The Highlights, Status Quo

Alan Parker

Guitar, Composer, Orchestrator, Producer
The Johnny Howard Band, Blue Mink, BBC TV Top Of The Pops Orchestra, backing artists such as Duane Eddy, Sonny And Cher, Stevie Wonder, and Elton John. Sessions (inc.'Rebel Rebel' for David Bowie 'No Regrets' for The Walker Brothers, 'Hurdy Gurdy Man' for Donovan)

Dave Pegg

Bass Guitar, Double Bass, Guitar, Mandolin
Ian Campbell Folk Group, Fairport Convention, Jethro Tull.
Sessions inc.Nick Drake, John Martyn, Sandy Denny, Richard Thompson, Ralph McTell.
Dave organises the Annual August Cropredy Festival.

Simon Phillips

Drums, Percussion, Producer/Engineer
(Father) Sid Phillips Dixieland Band, Jesus Christ Superstar, Chopyn (with Ann Odelle and Ray Russell), Jack Bruce Band (with Tony Hymas and Hugh Burns), Jeff Beck (with Tony Hymas and Mo Foster), RMS (with Mo Foster and Ray Russell), Protocol (with Ray Russell and Anthony Jackson).
Worked with The Who, Big Country, Toto, Steve Lukather, Judas Priest, Whitesnake, Michael Schenker (with Mo Foster), Brian Eno, Duncan Browne, Toyah, Mike Oldfield, Jon Anderson, Trevor Rabin, Gary Moore, 10cc, Mick Jagger, Ph.D., Mike Rutherford, Phil Manzanera, John Wetton, Asia, Stanley Clarke, Nik Kershaw, Gordon Giltrap.
His playing still amazes me.

Judd Procter

Guitar
Began freelancing as a guitarist in the mid 1950s. In 1955 he joined The Ray Ellington Quartet and his wages, mainly from broadcasts, rose to £50 per week which was then a fortune. With Ellington, he played on every *Goon Show,* and later diversified into mainstream session work.

Andy Pyle

Bass Guitar
Records and Tours by Blodwyn Pig, Savoy Brown, Juicy Lucy, Alvin Lee, The Kinks, Rod Stewart, Sutherland Brothers, Wishbone Ash, Otis Rush, Buddy Guy, Pops Staples, Albert Collins, Albert King, Jimmie Rogers, George Harrison, Mick Jagger, Ron Wood, Charlie Watts, BB King and Gary Moore.

Chris Rae

Guitar
Sessions inc Carl Douglas ('Kung Fu Fighting'), The Bay City Rollers, Tina Charles.
Live work with Luciano Pavarotti, Shirley Bassey, and was 'in the pit' for the Dave Clark/Cliff Richard musical *Time.* He also played with actor/singer David Soul, but was sacked in 1995 for "not reading his mind".

Gerry Rafferty

Guitar, Piano, Singer/Songwriter
The Humblebums (with Billy Connolly), Stealers Wheel (with Joe Egan).
After some experimentation with different chord progressions using the drop-D tuning, Gerry wrote a song called 'Baker Street'. It launched Gerry's enormously successful solo career and continues to be regarded as one of the true 1970s pop classics.

Chris Rea

Guitar, Singer/Songwriter
Sessions with Hank Marvin, Catherine Howe
His song 'Fool (If You Think It's Over)' was covered by Elkie Brooks.

Mike Read

Guitar, Radio DJ, Author, TV presenter

Noel Redding

Guitar, Bass Guitar, Vocals
The Strangers, The Lonely Ones, The Burnettes (as they used Burns guitars), The Loving Kind, The Jimi Hendrix Experience, Fat Mattress.
An audition for Eric Burdon And The New Animals as a guitarist led to the enviable position of bass player with The Jimi Hendrix Experience in 1966.

Tim Renwick

Guitar, Recorder, Mandolin, Bass Guitar
The Spanish Gentlemen, Wages of Sin, Junior's Eyes, The Hype, Quiver, and Lazy Racer.
Sessions inc. Alan Parsons, the Sutherland Brothers, Al Stewart, Elton John, Procol Harum, David Bowie, Gary Brooker, Roger Waters, Eric Clapton, David Byron, Richard Wright, Sally Oldfield.
Tours with Mike Oldfield, Pink Floyd, Mike And The Mechanics.

Dave Richmond

Bass Guitar, Double Bass
The Mann-Hugg Blues Brothers, Manfred Mann. The John Barry Seven,
The Bert Kaempfert Orchestra. Sessions inc. TV series *The Last Of The Summer Wine*

Frank Ricotti

Vibraphone, Percussion, Composer
National Youth Jazz Orchestra, Neil Ardley, Graham Collier, Mike Gibbs, Stan Tracey, Gordon Beck, Paragonne (with Chris Laurence and John Taylor.
Sessions with Freddie Mercury, The Pet Shop Boys, Clannad, Elkie Brooks, Rick Wakeman, Tina Turner, Mark Knopfler, Gerry Rafferty.

Jim Rodford

Bass Guitar, Tea-Chest bass
The Black Cats Skiffle Group, The Bluetones, The Mike Cotton Sound, Argent, The Kinks, The Swinging Blue Jeans. Sessions with artists as diverse as Lonnie Donegan, Barbara Dickson, The John Slaughter Blues Band, Bobby Graham's Jazz Experience, Mike Berry And The Outlaws, and Mick Abrahams.

Francis Rossi OBE

Guitar, Singer/Songwriter
The Scorpions, The Spectres, Traffic Jam, Status Quo. The band invented heads-down British boogie.

John Rostill

Bass Guitar, Singer/Songwriter
Zoot Money, The Interns, The Terry Young Five, Tom Jones, The Shadows, Sessions

Ray Russell

Guitar, Ukulele, Composer, Arranger, Producer
John Barry Seven, Georgie Fame & The Blue Flames, Rock Workshop, Nucleus, Smith & d'Abo, Chopyn, Gil Evans: The British Orchestra, RMS (with Mo Foster and Simon Phillips), Protocol (with Simon Phillips and Anthony Jackson). Sessions.
TV work includes *A Touch of Frost*, *Bergerac*, *Dangerfield*, *Stay Lucky*, and *Grafter*s.

Mike Rutherford

Guitar, Bass Guitar, Vocals, Songwriter
Mike And The Mechanics, Genesis

Ernie Shear

Guitar
Sessions, especially 'Move It' by Cliff Richard And The Drifters. This song was possibly the first, and certainly the most famous, British rock track of its day. The landmark descending fourths intro was played by Ernie.

Phil Seaman

Drums
Played mostly with big-bands inc. Joe Harriott, Tubby Hayes, Stan Tracey, Ronnie Scott, Dick Morrissey, Harold McNair, Don Rendell, Victor Feldman. Later he worked with Alexis Korner, Georgie Fame, and Ginger Baker's Air Force. A legend.

Grant Serpell

Drums, Percussion, Vocals
The Baskervilles, The US Jazz Trio, Ice, Affinity, Mike D'Abo , Sailor

Barry de Souza

Drums, Percussion
Shawn Phillips, Curved Air, Quatermass, Smith & d'Abo
Sessions: Herbie Flowers, Jeff Wayne, Lou Reed
Barry was great fun on the road: he could start a conversation between two strangers merely by tapping them both on the shoulder.

Chris Spedding

Guitar, Vocals, Piano, Violin, Bass Guitar
The Battered Ornaments (with Pete Brown), Roxy Music, Mike Gibbs, The Jack Bruce Band.
Sessions (inc. Gilbert O'Sullivan, Donovan, John Cale, Lulu, David Essex, The Wombles)

Henry Spinetti

Drums, Percussion
Scrugg, The Herd
Sessions: Joan Armatrading, Mike d'Abo, Jimmy Helms, Eric Clapton, Bob Dylan, George Harrison, Alexis Korner
Henry, who was born in South Wales, played on Gerry Rafferty's single, "Baker Street", and also played in the 2002 memorial concert for George Harrison, "The Concert For George"

'Big' Jim Sullivan

Guitar, Sitar, Composer, Producer
Marty Wilde's Wildcats, Krew-Kats
Tom Jones, James Last Orchestra, Olivia Newton-John.
Countless Sessions inc. TV shows *Oh, Boy!*, *Top of the Pops*, and *Ready Steady Go!*

Andy Summers

Guitar, Bass, Vocals, Composer, Producer, Author, Photographer
Zoot Money's Big Roll Band, Dantalian's Chariot, Eric Burdon and The Animals, John Etheridge, The Police
Sessions: Kevin Ayers, Kevin Coyne

Roger Swaab

Guitar, Vocals
The Peasants, The Tradewinds

Martin Taylor

Guitar
Ike Isaacs, Stephane Grappelli, Chet Atkins, Bill Wyman's Rhythm Kings.
"He is one of the most awesome solo guitar players in the history of the instrument. He's unbelievable" — Pat Metheny

Danny Thompson

Double Bass, Tea-Chest bass, Songwriter, producer
Tubby Hayes Band, Phil Seaman, Ronnie Scott, Pentangle, Alexis Korner's Blues Incorporated, and was a member of the resident band on *The 5-O'Clock Club* TV show (with Alexis Korner and Terry Cox.
His pride and joy is his French upright bass, a Gand made in 1860. Her name is Victoria.

Richard Thompson

Guitar, Composer
Fairport Convention, Linda Thompson

Kevin Townend

Guitar, Arranger, Orchestrator

Pete Townshend

Guitar, Vocals, Keyboards, Songwriter/Composer, Banjo, Mandolin
The Confederates, The Detours, The High Numbers, The Who, *Tommy, Quadrophenia*

Rob Townsend

Drums
Family, Medicine Head , Duane Eddy, The Blues Band, The Manfreds, Sessions (inc. Peter Skellern, George Melly and Bill Wyman)

Peter Van Hooke

Drums, Percussion, Record Producer (inc. Tanita Tikaram), TV Producer (*Live From Abbey Road*)
Van Morrison, Mike and the Mechanics, Sessions

Derek Wadsworth

Trombone, Composer, Arranger
Composed the music for the TV series *Space 1999*.
Arranged for Nina Simone, Kate Bush, Dusty Springfield, Shirley Bassey, Alan Price, Georgie Fame, Cat Stevens, Rod Stewart.
Sessions (inc. George Harrison, Diana Ross, Tom Jones, Charles Aznavour, Randy Crawford, Dionne Warwick)

Terry Walsh

Guitar
Sessions (inc Frank Sinatra, Bing Crosby, Fred Astaire, Henry Mancini, and The Tommy Dorsey Band). For many years he played in the band on *The Sooty Show.* Terry says it paid for the education of his sons, producers Greg Walsh and Pete Walsh!

Peter Watkins

Guitar, Vocals
The Peasants, The Tradewinds, Academy, Accolade, Mirage, Boxer, Luv Bug. Pete was also manager of cult retro artist Ronnie Rampant (in the same way that Barry Humphries manages Dame Edna Everage).

Bert Weedon OBE

Guitar, Soloist, Author
Sessions (inc Django Reinhardt, Frank Sinatra, Nat 'King' Cole, The Glenn Miller Band). He wrote the greatest-selling guitar tutor book of all-time: *Play In A Day.*

Bruce Welch OBE

Guitar, Vocals, Songwriter, Producer, Author
The Railroaders, The Five Chesternuts, The Drifters, The Shadows.
Bruce's rhythm guitar style inspired a nation of players.

John Wetton

Bass Guitar, Vocals
Family, King Crimson, Roxy Music, UK, Asia (with Steve Howe)

Geoff Whitehorn

Guitar, Singer/Songwriter
If, Crawler, Roger Chapman's Shortlist, Procol Harum, Elkie Brooks

John Williams

Classical Guitar
Soloist, Sky
Collaborations include: John Etheridge, Richard Harvey, Julian Bream, Itzhak Perlman, Andre Previn, John Dankworth, Daniel Barenboim.
John can be regarded as a foremost ambassador of the guitar.

Pete Willsher

Guitar, Pedal Steel Guitar
Houston Wells and The Marksmen, Sessions (inc. Johnny Cash and Jim Reeves). He later studied Hawaiian guitar, and worked with luthier Jim Burns on instrument design.

Steve Winwood

Guitar, Organ, Vocals, Drums, Mandolin, Composer, Producer
The Spencer Davis Group, Traffic, Blind Faith

Ron Wood

Guitar, Bass Guitar, Artist
The Birds, Creation, The Jeff Beck Group, The Faces, The Rolling Stones

INDEX